PRE-COLUMBIAN ARCHITECTURE IN MESOAMERICA

SITES ILLUSTRATED IN THIS VOLUME

● *Chapter 4: Pre-Olmec and Olmec Architecture*
1. Chalcatzingo
2. La Blanca
3. La Venta
4. Paso de la Amada
5. San Lorenzo
6. Teopantecuanitlan

● *Chapter 5: The Central Altiplano*
7. Cacaxtla
8. Calixtlahuaca
9. Cholula
10. Cuicuilco
11. Malinalco
12. Mount Tlaloc
13. Tenayuca
14. Tenochtitlán
15. Teotihuacán
16. Tepoztlan
17. Tula
18. Xochicalco

● *Chapter 6: Western Mexico*
19. El Arenal
20. El Opeño
21. Los Guachimontones
22. Los Toriles
23. Plazuelas
24. Tzintzuntzan

● *Chapter 7: Northern Mexico*
25. Balcón de Montezuma
26. Cerro de Trincheras
27. Cueva de la Olla
28. Cueva Grande
29. El Cerrito
30. Huapoca
31. La Quemada
32. Paquimé
33. Ranas
34. Toluquilla

● *Chapter 8: Central Veracruz*
35. Cerro de las Mesas
36. Cotaxtla
37. El Pital
38. El Tajín
39. El Zapotal
40. La Joya
41. Las Higueras
42. Paxil
43. Quiahuiztlán
44. Vega de la Peña
45. Yohualichan
46. Zempoala

● *Chapter 9: The Huastec Region*
47. Cacahuatenco
48. Castillo de Teayo
49. Celaya
50. Las Flores
51. Pitahaya
52. Rancho la Rosa
53. Rancho San Diego
54. Sierra de la Palma
55. Tamohi
56. Tamtoc
57. Tancol
58. Tetzacual
59. Vega de Otates
60. Vinasco

● *Chapter 10: Oaxaca*
61. Dainzú
62. Lambityeco
63. Mitla
64. Monte Albán
65. San José Mogote
66. Suchilquitongo
67. Yagul

● *Chapter 11: The Maya Region*
68. Bonampak
69. Calakmul
70. Chichén Itzá
71. Copán
72. Dzibanché
73. Dzibilchaltún
74. Edzná
75. Ek Balam
76. El Mirador
77. Hochob
78. Iximché
79. Kabah
80. Labná
81. Mayapán
82. Palenque
83. Piedras Negras
84. Tikal
85. Toniná
86. Tulum
87. Uaxactún
88. Uxmal
89. Yaxchilán

Claudia Brittenham, Annick Daneels, Jesús Galindo Trejo, Rebecca B. González Lauck,

Verónica Hernández Díaz, Mary Ellen Miller, Gustavo A. Ramírez Castilla,

Antonio Toca Fernández, María Teresa Uriarte, Erik Velásquez García, and Ilán Vit Suzan

PRE-COLUMBIAN ARCHITECTURE IN MESOAMERICA

Edited by María Teresa Uriarte

Translated from the Spanish by Tanya Huntington

ABBEVILLE PRESS PUBLISHERS

New York   London

Front cover: El Castillo, Chichén Itzá, Yucatán (see plate 14)
Back cover: Sculptured facade, Ek Balam, Yucatán (see plate 76)

For the English-language edition
Editor: David Fabricant
Copy editor: Ashley Benning
Production editor: Briana Green
Production manager: Louise Kurtz
Typography and composition: Julia Sedykh
Jacket design: Misha Beletsky

The map on page 2 was designed by Citlali Coronel and Rodrigo Fernández.

First published in the United States of America in 2010 by Abbeville Press,
137 Varick Street, New York, NY 10013

First published in Italy and Mexico in 2010 by Editoriale Jaca Book S.p.A., via
Frua 11, 20146 Milano, and the Instituto Nacional de Antropología e Historia,
Córdoba 45, col. Roma, C.P. 06700, México, D.F.

First edition
10 9 8 7 6 5 4 3 2 1

Library of Congress Cataloging-in-Publication Data
Pre-Columbian architecture in Mesoamerica / edited by María Teresa Uriarte ;
with contributions by Claudia Brittenham . . . [et al.]. — 1st ed.
    p. cm.
 Includes bibliographical references and index.
 ISBN 978-0-7892-1045-6 (hardcover : alk. paper) 1. Indian architecture—
Mexico. 2. Indian architecture—Central America.
3. Mexico—Antiquities. 4. Central America—Antiquities. I. Uriarte, María
Teresa. II. Brittenham, Claudia.
 F1219.3.A6P74 2010
 972'.01—dc22
                            2010021086

For bulk and premium sales and for text adoption procedures, write to Customer
Service Manager, Abbeville Press, 137 Varick Street, New York, NY 10013, or
call 1-800-Artbook.

Visit Abbeville Press online at www.abbeville.com.

CONTENTS

PREFACE

MARÍA TERESA URIARTE

Publishing a book has a lot in common with gardening. First you plant the seed of an idea, and then you work to make it sprout and grow. At last, the mature plant bears fruit when the reader holds the finished product in his or her hands.

So it was with this volume. The authors discussed their ideas at length, in numerous meetings. From the outset, we knew we wanted a new and different plant, one that did not repeat what had already been said about Pre-Columbian architecture. We agreed that this architecture should be considered in terms of its artistic values, and explored from an interdisciplinary perspective: architecture, urban studies, and art history would form the axis around which the contributions of archaeology, linguistics, and even astronomy would revolve. This approach was suggested in part by Beatriz de la Fuente, who in the course of preparing a previous volume on Pre-Columbian sculpture had realized the need for a study of Mesoamerican architecture that viewed it as art.

Our book's theoretical groundwork is presented in the first three chapters. In chapter one, Antonio Toca and I discuss what we consider to be the aesthetic qualities of architecture; in chapter two, we investigate the meanings that emerge from architecture's relation to people, its surroundings, and the cosmos; and in chapter three, we analyze Mesoamerican construction techniques. Jesús Galindo uses his expertise as an astronomer to illuminate ancient buildings' connections to celestial objects and the calendar, which reveal the Mesoamerican preoccupation with the measurement of time.

While the following chapters, which survey individual regions, are more conventionally organized, we still attempt to offer the reader novel analyses and hypotheses that permit different ways of looking at buildings. We explore the fundamental structural elements that Mesoamerican cultures, from the Olmecs to the Aztecs, used to create harmonious architectural environments of which people were an integral part.

In the innovative final chapter, Erik Velásquez presents his research on language and writing and their relationship to architecture.

This book is an invitation for the reader to learn about people who were different from him or her, but also similar, and to visit the places where they lived and went about their daily business. These were men and women like anybody else, and nobody else, typical yet also unique in their customs and beliefs, their myths and rituals, which they made into a tangible reality through their buildings and urban spaces.

It is an invitation to envision, and envision oneself in, ancient cities that can be as close or as distant as we choose. The authors have brought together words and images that will take the receptive reader on a journey beyond our contemporary time and space.

Thank you for coming along.

A NOTE ON THE TEXT

Illustration references

Plate numbers in parentheses—for example, (plate 1)—refer to the color photographs that appear alongside the text.

Figure numbers in parentheses—for example, (figure 1)—refer to the black-and-white images in the section "Maps and Drawings," which begins on page 289.

Chronology

Mesoamerican history is conventionally divided into the following periods.

	Approximate dates
Initial Formative *or* Archaic	1900–1500 BC
Early Formative *or* Early Preclassic	1500–900 BC
Mid-Formative *or* Mid-Preclassic	900–400 BC
Late Formative *or* Late Preclassic	400 BC–AD 200
Early Classic	AD 200–600
Late Classic *or* Epiclassic	AD 600–900
Early Postclassic	AD 900–1200
Late Postclassic	AD 1200–1521

PRE-COLUMBIAN ARCHITECTURE IN MESOAMERICA

I
ARCHITECTURE AS ART

MARÍA TERESA URIARTE AND ANTONIO TOCA FERNÁNDEZ

There is no doubt that architecture can be studied from multiple perspectives, and that in addition to providing shelter, buildings have always had political, social, and religious significance. However, they can also be examined for their aesthetic value (plate 1).

In the eighteenth century, the philosopher Alexander Gottlieb Baumgarten defined aesthetics as the "science of sensitive knowing," where sensitive knowing was the faculty, distinct from reason, of intuitively synthesizing sense perceptions into a coherent whole.[1] One important way we human beings exercise our aesthetic capacities is by identifying harmonious patterns in nature; throughout the centuries, we have sought ways of reproducing these patterns in our built environment. Of course, many other factors can influence the design of sacred, residential, or public spaces, and the ideology that configures a community's perception and way of thinking also determines its conceptualization of urban space and the form and function of its buildings. For example, the initial demarcation of a space for habitation has a long tradition in Mesoamerican history. This demarcation established the first boundary between the domesticated and the savage, between *civitas* and all that is foreign.

The values that we take into consideration in assessing the artistic works of human beings—proportion, harmony, rhythm, composition, and symmetry—are evident in Mesoamerican architecture from a very early time. But how did they first emerge?

In order to understand the evolution of architecture, scholars once turned to the Roman architect Marcus Vitruvius, who, in his treatise of the first century BC, explained the origins of his discipline through mythological narratives. Among these myths is that of the creation of the orders of classical architecture, based on examples of the Hellenistic period in Greece. Until the nineteenth century, this theory influenced practically all authors who wrote about European architecture, as well as—starting in the sixteenth century—Mesoamerican architecture.

The Vitruvian tradition made it difficult to explain the development of architecture in cultures that were not heir to Greece and Rome; it has certainly led to serious mistakes and injustices in the appreciation of Mesoamerican architecture. Only the scientific advances of the 1800s allowed another theory of the origins of architecture—one not founded in myth—to emerge.

In his book *The Four Elements of Architecture* (1851),[2] which was based on detailed research in the ethnological literature, the German architect Gottfried Semper proposed that the oldest

1. The Hall of the Columns, Mitla, Oaxaca, Late Postclassic. The facade of this building, with its geometric mosaics and intricate play of volumes, is an excellent example of harmony and symmetry in Mesoamerican art.

buildings of various cultures all had four original elements in common. The first and most important was the central hearth. Then came the earthen platform or terrace; the roof, supported over the platform by columns; and the wall, which initially took the form of a woven divider. He saw each of these four elements as the product of an early craft: for the construction of the hearth, ceramics and, later, metalworking were used; for the earthen platform, masonry and processes employing water; for the roof and its columns, carpentry; and for the wall, weaving. Semper believed that these crafts had evolved in the direction of increasing technical complexity, which corresponded to the hardness of their materials: weaving, which used elastic materials, and ceramics, which used soft ones, came first; then carpentry, with its more solid materials; and finally masonry, with its hard ones.

Semper's theory certainly contributes to a better understanding of Mesoamerican architecture, since it relates each of its components to the techniques and materials employed. It is unfortunate, then, that his work was read only in Germany and Austria, and, after an English translation was published, in Great Britain and the United States. It is still little known, and little applied, elsewhere.

PROPORTION, RHYTHM, COMPOSITION, AND SYMMETRY

Architectural proportion is usually derived from an established pattern related to man's stature. In Mesoamerica, too, the unit of measure is based on the dimensions of a human being. While this theme, which seems fundamental, has not been studied in depth, some articles do touch on it. In a paper published in 2001,[3] John E. Clark states that the early cities of La Venta, Chiapa de Corzo, Monte Albán, and possibly Kaminaljuyú each have a "special compound on a 1:4 scale," and that there is a basic north-south axis of orientation, as well as a perpendicular east-west axis (figure 3). All of the cities examined by Clark are two times longer than they are wide, and are based on the "indigenous arm span," which, according to him, is about 5 feet (1.5 meters). The arm length or *yaguén* unit, measuring from 10¼ to 10⅝ inches (26 to 27 centimeters), is used in Oaxaca even today, and can be found in several monuments.[4]

Whenever symmetry is mentioned, it is generally assumed to be bilateral. In the case of architecture, this supposition has been imposed by Western culture. In fact, the peoples of the world have employed many other symmetries besides this very simple one. The artists of ancient Egypt had already discovered and applied—albeit intuitively—many of the three-dimensional symmetries and practically all of the two-dimensional ones in their paintings, objects, and bas-reliefs. As a system of ornamentation, symmetry is found in practically all cultures, above all in ceramics, paintings, sculpture, and textiles. The very word for "pattern" in Spanish, *greca*, originally referred to an example of two-dimensional symmetry, namely the key pattern, or meander, that was widely used in classical Greek art. However, the application of symmetry to architecture has been little analyzed, even though there are noteworthy examples which prove that beneath apparently superficial variations of form lies the inevitable logic of geometry.

The close observation of nature, together with notable advances in their understanding of geometry, allowed Mesoamerican artists to discover the infinite variety offered by the 17 types

2. Great mask of Chaak on Temple 22, Copán, Honduras, AD 771. Masks like this one were sometimes used to decorate the facades of Maya buildings, which display various types of symmetry.

of two-dimensional symmetry, as well as some of the 230 three-dimensional ones (figures 1, 2).[5] In addition to axial or bilateral symmetry, they used spatial symmetry to achieve an enormous variety of artistic solutions over the course of two thousand years, ranging from the simplest to the most refined applications of reflection, translation, and extension. In order to understand these uses of symmetry, especially the spatial ones, it is necessary to look at temples and other structures in terms of their volumes, rather than their facades or sections; though valuable, the extensive research on the profiles of Mesoamerican buildings can obscure the fact that they were designed not in two dimensions, but three. That masks were placed on the corners of Maya temples (plate 2) is further proof that these buildings were conceived of as volumes. Having realized this, we can better comprehend the evolution, with its inevitable breaks and transformations, of the solutions—such as the pyramidal foundation, the platform, the *talud-tablero* style, and the cornice—that we find in Mesoamerican architecture across different regions. We might also gain a further appreciation of the amazing variety of these structures if we photographed their corners, since this would reveal numerous examples of a diagonal symmetry applied with great creativity.

In Mesoamerica, as in other places around the world, there were canons that defined the size, function, proportions, and orientation of structures. Local models of architectural construction and ornamentation were established in the different areas of the region. For instance,

3. (*left*) Substructure of Building 2, Calakmul, Campeche, c. 400 BC. This structure, from the earliest phase of the site, has a stairway flanked by masks of human faces with Olmecoid features.

4. (*below*) Building E-VII-Sub, Uaxactún, Guatemala, 353–317 BC. This early building exhibits four stairways flanked by great masks. (Reconstruction by Tatiana Proskouriakoff, 1946.)

5. (*opposite*) The Temple of the Feathered Serpent, at the Ciudadela, Teotihuacán, State of México, AD 150–200. On this building, heads of the feathered serpent alternate harmoniously with masks of an unidentified deity.

beginning in the Classic period, the sunken patio, the antechamber supported by two columns, and the double molding were diagnostic of Oaxacan architecture. The western part of Mesoamerica, on the other hand, was characterized by circular structures that reflect a desire for harmony with the cosmos. These architectural models also evolved over time: the colossal heads that are typical of Olmec culture may have been transformed in the Maya region into great masks affixed to facades, as is the case in a substructure at Calakmul discovered by Ramón Carrasco (plate 3). In this building of around 400 BC, the great masks that later would usually represent a solar deity have features that can be considered Olmecoid—a phenomenon that can also be observed at Becán. In the ongoing debate over the relationship between the Olmecs and the Maya, from a stylistic point of view it is evident that there is a correlation between the facial characteristics considered to be Olmec and those of the aforementioned great masks: almond-shaped eyes, lips turned down at the corners, and the general aspect of a human feline. These magnificent masks, which seem more like spiritual entities than representations of a specific individual, became a distinctive feature of Maya architecture, typically placed on either side of a stairway. They can be seen even at early sites like Cerros, El Mirador, or Uaxactún (plate 4).

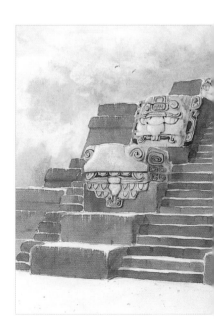

Harmony and rhythm make their presence known from the first centuries of our era, one of the most obvious examples being the Temple of the Feathered Serpent, or of Tlaloc and Quetzalcóatl, at Teotihuacán (plate 5). On this pyramidal foundation, we see heads of a fantastical serpent alternating gracefully with great masks of a being that wears spectacles or discs over its eyes and has therefore been referred to as Tlaloc (plates 6, 7). Other regions and eras also yield evidence of this quest for harmony and rhythm. We have already noted that at certain Maya sites of the Formative period, such as Uaxactún, we find stairways flanked by great masks. Quite independent of their purpose, these elements—carefully placed in relation to the mass of the building—display a harmonious repetition in their arrangement.[6]

It is in the monumental sites of the Olmec period, from around 1500 BC, that we begin to find the characteristic elements of Mesoamerican architecture and urbanism that would continue to present themselves in other regions and eras. One such element was the pyramidal foundation, which, in different proportions or with slight variations, would be used for nearly all public buildings. In fact, the nearly three-thousand-year history of architecture in Mesoamerica may be summed up as the evolution of the platform—the principal building mass—from a simple terrace of earth and stone to a delicate tiered pyramid with sharp or rounded

6. (*below*) The Temple of the Feathered Serpent, Teotihuacán. Detail of a head of the feathered serpent.

7. (*opposite*) The Temple of the Feathered Serpent, Teotihuacán. Detail of one of the masks, which have been interpreted as heads of the rain god Tlaloc, or as headdresses placed atop the body of the feathered serpent.

corners and, on its summit, a small building with a cornice and roofcomb. Some of these structures also incorporated slope-and-panel, or *talud-tablero*, facades with polychromed sculpture and painting (plate 8). Different cultures and eras were characterized by themes and variations on this basic course of development, ranging from a powerful massiveness in earlier times to a sophisticated dematerialization in three-dimensional planes and projections later on; however, throughout this long process of transformation, builders always relied on the careful management of symmetries.

The pyramid may have had antecedents in earthen constructions, such as at La Venta, but it is certainly a constant form in Mesoamerica. It has been suggested that the pyramid is a replica of the mountain and its counterpart, the cave, thus joining opposing elements and, at the same time, alluding to the origins of the Mesoamerican cultures—in both cases, referring us back to the Olmecs. The caves of Juxtlahuaca and Oxtotitlán in Guerrero are an example of the sacred nature conferred upon subterranean enclosures. On the other hand, the builders of the aforementioned pyramid of La Venta and others that exist in the same zone—which are described by Rebecca González Lauck, Annick Daneels, and Gustavo Ramírez in their texts—used earth to shape their mountains of origin, in accordance with a myth that would survive until the arrival of the Spaniards.

Another common architectural form, the stele-building complex, existed among the Olmecs from the Mid-Formative period onward. However, at La Venta, the altars or stelae are sculptural objects, aligned with each other so as to create a ritual space. This is demonstrated by Offering 4 from this site, representing a group of men congregated in a space bordered

8. Detail of the slope-and-panel (*talud-tablero*) construction of the Temple of the Feathered Serpent, Teotihuacán. This style of building was traditionally identified with Teotihuacán, but is now thought to have originated in the Valley of Puebla.

9. Offering 4 from La Venta, Tabasco, Mid-Formative. A group of people gather in a ritual space marked by carved basalt stones. This offering re-creates, even if on a small scale, a symbolic moment important to the community.

by great basalt slabs (plate 9). This scene, which re-creates a moment of celebration in miniature—its components are no taller than 10 inches (25 centimeters)—marks the beginning of a tradition of scale models that would endure for a long time and in different regions, for example in western Mexico and among the Nahua.

In most Mesoamerican cities, public life revolved around the open space of the plaza. It is believed that plazas were ritual spaces, and that temples were placed atop the structures that surrounded them. Some buildings, it is thought, were intended for astronomical observation and calendar-related activities (plate 11), such as the structure in front of the Pyramid of the Moon at Teotihuacán, the one at El Tajín known as Xicalcoliuhqui, or El Caracol at Chichén Itzá, to mention three sites from different eras. The so-called E Groups of the Maya also had a similar function from an early time. On occasion, plazas were connected by avenues built for this purpose, such as the Avenue of the Dead at Teotihuacán, which was perhaps an ideal space for processions. The same can be said of the so-called *sacbes* in the Maya zone, which sometimes connected one city to another, or one part of a city to another, or simply acted as roadways within the city itself.

All city plans have a specific orientation that links them both to the cosmos and to their natural setting. The clearest example of this is Teotihuacán, the great metropolis of the Classic era, which was not only oriented astronomically, as Jesús Galindo demonstrates in chapter 2, but also carefully positioned with respect to its immediate surroundings, Cerro Gordo and Cerro Patlachique. Like other Mesoamerican centers, Teotihuacán has a module of construction. Its planning commenced at the beginning of the Christian era, when the Pyramid of the Sun was erected over a cave that may have had astronomical associations.

Teotihuacán exemplifies the problems we face when we study Mesoamerican architecture and urbanism. For example, it is believed that the diagnostic element of Teotihuacano construction is the so-called *talud-tablero* or slope-and-panel (figure 4); however, we now know that the origin of this style may go further back than the emergence of Teotihuacán, to the Valley of Puebla. The so-called residential compounds of Teotihuacán also present a challenge to our understanding (plate 10). Perhaps conceived as habitations, these compounds resemble buildings found in other parts of Mesoamerica, such as the so-called palaces of the Maya. However, they are so abundant in Teotihuacán that López Luján has suggested that they were used not only by the governing elites, but by the general population as well.[7] In general, the difficulty of determining the true purpose of ancient buildings is compounded by the inadequacy of the techniques that were employed until recently in archaeological research: excavations were not carried out properly, and the context in which artifacts were found was not recorded.[8]

10. View of one of the so-called residential compounds at Teotihuacán, AD 200–450. These structures were used as housing, perhaps by groups specializing in a particular activity.

During the Epiclassic period—or, among the Maya, the Late Classic period—an era of eclecticism and great mobility in Mesoamerica, we encounter structures that amalgamate the styles of different regions and even past eras. We must also take into account that Teotihuacán had already been abandoned at this point for ideological, social, or environmental reasons. Its disappearance from the role of metropolis that it had played for over 500 years, and the absence of the kind of leadership it had provided, led to widespread chaos, which is reflected in Mesoamerican art, and architecture as well. For instance, while some cities had been walled as early as the Formative period, this practice became more common in the Epiclassic.

THE CITY AS CONCEPT

The building of sacred spaces has a long history among Mesoamerican peoples. We would therefore like to address the conceptualization of the city as a mythic space and, at the same time, the interaction between the idealized concept of a space and its actual construction.

In Mesoamerican cultures, the different words for, and visual representations of, buildings vary considerably. The same is true of the idea of the city; we seem to encounter the same sorts of synonyms that we ourselves have for the word "city," which refer not only to cities of dif-

11. Building A, El Tajín, Veracruz, AD 600–900. This structure was likely associated with the calendar and the beginning of time. The part of the entryway above the lintel recalls the shape of a ballcourt.

ferent sizes (e.g., metropolis, town, village), but also to the same city conceived of in different ways (e.g., capital, populace, settlement).

We know that among the Nahua, the word *altepetl* alludes to the Mountain of Sustenance, an idyllic entity that contained seeds and water. This word became a synonym for city, but as Joyce Marcus has demonstrated, its broader meaning includes not only the territory, but the ruler as well. It is also the root of related vocabulary such as "*altepetlianca*, subject or district of the city; *altepenayotl*, main city that is the head of the kingdom; *altepetenametica*, city closed off by a wall; or *altepetequipanoliztli*, public work or public office."[9]

At Teotihuacán there are representations of the Maya glyph that alludes to the city, *puh*, which literally means "place of reeds," as does the Nahua name for the ideal city, *Tollan* (plate 12). Both *altepetl* and *puh* represent an idyllic concept of the city, comparable, it is said, to the heavenly Jerusalem.

We also find at Teotihuacán depictions of buildings containing seeds, which lead us to believe that the city was a sacred mountain: "their water, their hill," "hand and foot of the people."[10] Aztlán, the place of origin in the Aztec migration myth, takes on the character of an ideal entity as well, of the cave as beginning, and then the city as foundation.

Just as Plato places in his world of ideas the concepts of objects that exist in everyday life, cities and buildings—like human beings—have their spiritual equivalents in the Mesoamerican world of ideas. The city and its structures passed through different stages of existence as intellectual entities before being converted into built realities. And in the same way as a man could be represented by the creature that was believed to be his co-essence, a city or building could be depicted artistically in a form that was based on its spiritual essence rather than its actual physical appearance. Along these lines, Erik Velásquez observes that the spaces represented in Maya vase paintings do not correspond with actual physical locales, at least not those known among the Maya.

A building or city was always planned in accordance with a predetermined sacred geometry, as well as with its topographic, geographic, and cosmological setting, and was always based on the dimensions of the human body. The calendar, too, was reflected in the design of certain Maya buildings of the Formative period, particulary the E Groups, which are so called after Group E at Uaxactún, described by Frans Blom in 1924. This type of architectural complex, which displays characteristics typical of the lowlands in the final stages of the Mid-Formative period, is also found in the Eb and Tzec phases of Tikal, and at El Mirador, Balakbal, and Naachtun, among other sites. The E Groups generally consist of a large structure on the west side of a plaza, facing a row of three smaller structures on the east side.[11]

The western buildings of the E Groups, with their square plans and four staircases, created a model that was repeated at various sites in the Maya zone over a long period of time, as at Copán, at Dzibilchaltún (plate 13), and in the Castillo of Chichén Itzá (plate 14), which was copied at Mayapán (plate 15). However, this same configuration can also be found at Teotihuacán, in Structure 1B¹ of the Ciudadela, as well as the building in front of the Pyramid of the Moon (plate 16), as Rubén Cabrera has indicated.[12]

Seen from above, these buildings have the shape of a cosmogram, with the four cardinal directions marked by their stairways, and the center point by the temple at their peak. If we also take into account the diagonal axes defined by their four corners, we see that the plan

12. (*opposite above*) An example of the *puh* glyph from Acanceh, Yucatán. The Maya used this glyph, which meant "reed," to refer to Teotihuacán; thus it was evidently an antecedent of the Nahua name *Tollan*, "place of reeds," which referred to the prototypical city.

13. (*left*) House of the Seven Dolls, Dzibilchaltún, Yucatán, c. AD 700. This building is aligned with the equinoxes, and hence is also associated with the calendar.

14. (*above*) El Castillo, Chichén Itzá, Yucatán, AD 900–1200, with its square plan and four stairways.

15. (*left*) Mayapán, Yucatán. There is a notable resemblance between the architecture of this Postclassic city and that of Chichén Itzá.

16. (*below*) Calendrical structure in the Plaza of the Moon, Teotihuacán, AD 200–450.

17. Folio 1 of the Codex Fejérváry-Mayer, before 1521. As Rubén Cabrera has pointed out, there is a direct relationship between the way space is configured in this drawing and the calendrical structure found at the foot of the Pyramid of the Moon in Teotihuacán.

of these structures resembles the design on folio 1 of the Codex Fejérváry-Mayer (plate 17), which merges the cosmogram with the ritual calendar. We therefore accept Blom's suggestion that these buildings are linked to astronomy, and hence the calendar, even when they are not aligned with the solstices or equinoxes; indeed, there are other solar alignments that are just as signficant, as Jesús Galindo shows in chapter 2.

Another interesting quality of Mesoamerican cities is that they were continually "abandoned." There has been all sorts of speculation as to whether this was due to environmental catastrophe, wars of conquest, or religion. However, perhaps we should begin by asking ourselves why some sources of the sixteenth century, such as the Aztec Pilgrimage Strip, show groups leaving Aztlán with a serene demeanor, under a divine mandate from Huitzilopochtli or Itzpapalotl, while the texts and illustrations compiled by Father Sahagún show people crying as they leave the city they founded. In one way or another, migrations were a constant in the Mesoamerican world. We know, for example, that Copán underwent a radical renovation following the arrival of the Teotihuacanos and the installation of Yax' K'uk Mo' as the founder of the local dynasty. Later on, perhaps during the era of Teotihuacán's collapse, Copán experienced another abandonment of artistic forms and systems of construction, after which a different kind of urban planning emerged.

MIGRATIONS, PILGRIMAGES, AND PROCESSIONS

In most cultures around the world, migrations eventually came to be commemorated as starting dates, marking the beginning of an era that the community regarded as its own. Thus the Jews date their birth as a chosen people to their exodus from Egypt. Likewise, the Muslim calendar begins in the year of the Hegira, Mohammad's journey from Mecca to Medina. This event is commemorated by the Hajj, the pilgrimage to Mecca that is one of the five pillars of Islam.

There are many other examples of pilgrimages and processions that are re-creations of migrations. We believe that in most Mesoamerican cities, there were spaces for such re-creations, which were also commemorations of the beginning of time. The appearance of the buildings and their positioning around the plaza contributed to the theatricality of the rites. In fact, Joyce Marcus and Kent Flannery have proposed that the tunnels found in some cities of Oaxaca, such as Montenegro, San José Mogote, and Monte Albán, were used by members of the elite to move from one place to another without being seen.[13] Perhaps these secret passages allowed them to "magically" appear and disappear during ritual celebrations.

We need only look at the depictions of community celebrations that survive in mural paintings and ceramics to understand how important these events were to Pre-Columbian peoples. In fact, they justified the very existence of plazas. The sacred space within the temple that sat atop a pyramidal foundation was so limited that only a handful of initiates could participate in the rituals that were held there. In contrast, other public spaces allowed the community to participate en masse in celebrations such as the ones held before and after the ballgame. Consider Copán, where numerous spectators can be accommodated around the plaza, or Pechal, Campeche, which offers the best example of what is, according to some authors, an amphitheater (figure 5).[14]

SIMILARITIES AND DIFFERENCES AMONG CULTURES AROUND THE WORLD

For some decades now, the study of comparative religion has allowed us to identify similarities and differences among human cultures through the centuries. James George Frazer, Mircea Eliade, Carl Gustav Jung, Claude Leví-Strauss, and many other scholars have devoted innumerable studies to the common aspects of the rituals that have developed out of human responses to natural phenomena. Among the most frequently encountered themes are the association of the sun with the ruling classes; the connection of the feminine to the moon, water, and earth; and of course what Eliade called the *coincidentia oppositorum*. These shared beliefs were certainly not alien to the peoples of Mesoamerica, and indeed many of them were represented in various ways through their architecture.

Solar priesthoods and their connection to the governing elite are manifested through architecture in Egypt, India, and Mesoamerica alike. Just as the Inca were the children of the sun, the Aztecs followed the sun god Huitzilopochtli as their tutelary deity; according to their creation story, they were the people of the "fifth sun," their own era having been preceded by those of four other suns. In both its mythological associations and its real-life manifestation, the sun was an important presence in Mesoamerican architecture. There is abundant evi-

18. The water lily, or *ninfea*, a flower with solar associations.

dence of this, some of it well-known—like the arrival of the plumed serpent to the Castillo of Chichén Itzá, or the use of certain caves as solar observatories—and some of it more surprising, such as the phenomenon that may be observed in the so-called Quetzalpapalotl Palace at Teotihuacán, where on set dates the sun projects the shadow of the building's battlements onto the patterns of the mural painting on the opposite wall. Solar allegories are in fact very common in the paintings of Teotihuacán, particularly in the image of the water lily, which emerges from the water and opens its petals at dawn, and then closes them and submerges itself again at dusk—like the sun (plate 18).

We believe that it is absolutely natural that certain similarities have presented themselves among the cultures of the world, as responses to the day-to-day existence of man, transposed onto the cosmos and his immediate geographic surroundings. It is natural, too, that buildings reflect these similarities, which are proof of a shared humanity that has been present all across the globe and throughout history. We could delve deeper into any of these themes, but for now we leave that task to the curious reader.

THE INFLUENCE OF MESOAMERICAN ARCHITECTURE ON THE MODERN ERA
Antonio Toca Fernández

The influence of Mesoamerican buildings on modern ones was based on the initial explorations that gradually brought to light the achievements of the Pre-Columbian civilizations. The amazement and fascination that many Europeans felt toward the Mesoamerican cultures are reflected in the chronicles of Alexander von Humboldt and a number of other travelers. Over the course of the nineteenth century, these explorers complemented their written observations with drawings and plans of buildings from the Altiplano and the Maya zone. At first, they analyzed these materials with criteria borrowed from the civilizations of Europe, the Middle East, or Asia; Mesoamerican architecture was thus explained as a bizarre case or, at best, a strange one. But we need only look back at the nineteenth-century World's Fairs, where the pavilions of many countries featured ridiculous pastiches of their own ancient architecture, to see how mistaken the early interpretations of "exotic" cultures frequently were.

One early example of the influence of recently discovered Mesoamerican architecture was the proposal that New York's Statue of Liberty (1865–75) be placed on a terraced pyramid; this is illustrated in a drawing by the statue's sculptor, Fréderic Auguste Bartholdi. In Mexico, even though a museum dedicated to the archaeology and history of the young nation was opened in 1825, the vast majority of people were either unaware of the Pre-Columbian past or, without comprehending it, looked down on it. This lack of understanding was confirmed by the Mexican Pavilion built by the engineer-architect Antonio de Anza and the archaeologist Antonio Peñafiel for the 1889 Exposition Universelle in Paris, which was a caricature of Mesoamerican architecture (plates 19, 20).

The explanation for this ignorance is simple; it is that the education of American architects was powerfully influenced by the European academies, especially the École des Beaux-Arts in Paris, which many of them in fact attended. This education left them with no point of reference but the classical orders illustrated in their textbooks. When the influence of the

19, 20. Lithographs of the
Mexican Pavilion at the
1889 Exposition Univer-
selle in Paris.

academies was threatened by the emergence of new materials and construction techniques, which were quickly incorporated into bridges and industrial buildings, architects generally resisted these changes and took refuge in eclecticism, borrowing elements from the styles of different cultures in an attempt to update their buildings. It was the engineers, who were more inclined to take advantage of modern technology, who created the most important structures of the nineteenth century. The "monkey styles," as eclectic buildings were sometimes called, remain as proof of the architects' inability to take advantage of the diverse riches of the cultures whose forms they copied poorly. An extreme case of ignorance was the Mexican Pavilion at the 1886 New Orleans Fair, built in a Moorish style (plate 21).

This eclectic approach can be seen in the many buildings, in Mexico and elsewhere, whose designers attempted, with very weak results, to incorporate elements of Mesoamerican architecture. However, there were some architects who succeeded in reinterpreting Pre-Columbian styles with a high degree of quality, among them Frank Lloyd Wright. A Mesoamerican influence appears in his A. D. German Warehouse (1915), and continues in the highly refined homes he built in Los Angeles, including the Barnsdall Compound (1920) and the "textile block" houses, such as the extraordinary Millard House, "La Miniatura" (1924). Wright did not simply mimic the forms and decorative motifs of Mesoamerican architecture, but studied the most significant Pre-Columbian structures in detail, so that he could employ their symmetries and proportions in new and creative ways.

In Mexico, the influence of Mesoamerican architecture has manifested itself in both sculpture and architecture since the late nineteenth century. For example, the Monument to

22. Monument to Cuauhtémoc, Mexico City, 1867. In an effort to recover the Pre-Columbian past, a statue of the last Aztec emperor was placed on an eclectic pedestal that portrays idealized historical imagery.

Cuauhtémoc (1887) (plate 22) features Pre-Columbian elements on its base. However, it was not until the twentieth century that the gradual integration of Pre-Columbian elements into modern architecture reached its culmination. In the initial phase of the Palacio de Bellas Artes (1905–10), the Italian architect Adamo Boari included—timidly—some masks with Pre-Columbian themes (plate 23); while these sculptures are of a high quality, it is evident that they are interpretations by European artists of a past they never knew. Some early modernist buildings in Mexico City also included sculptural elements inspired by Pre-Columbian art, such as the facade of the Health and Hygiene Building (1926), or the bas-relief of the rain god Tlaloc on the central fire station (1927). Another very interesting example was the Mexican Pavilion at the Ibero-American Expo at Seville in 1929, designed by the architect Manuel Amabilis. This building, laid out in an X shape, had an interior that was clearly influenced by European

23. Mask of a jaguar warrior, in an idealized European style, decorating an entrance of the Palacio de Bellas Artes, Mexico City, 1905.

24. The Park of the Americas in Mérida, Yucatán, 1925–45, designed by Manuel Amabilis, incorporates elements of Maya architecture.

rationalism. However, its facade included a reference to the decorative elements of Maya architecture, namely two columns with a serpent base at the front entrance. In Mérida, the Casa del Pueblo, the *Diario de Yucatán* building, and the Park of the Americas (plate 24) (1925–45) also display a Maya influence. Back in Mexico City, we may note again the Palacio de Bellas Artes (1935), whose interior featured great masks of the gods Chaak and Tlaloc, and ornaments that blended Pre-Columbian and art deco motifs; Diego Rivera's Anahuacalli Museum (plate 25); and the Monument to La Raza (1940). Soon afterward, the frontons (jai alai courts), the stadium (with bas-reliefs by Rivera), and the main library (plate 26), covered with its well-known murals in multicolored stones (1952), were built in University City. Ornaments, paintings, and sculptures of Pre-Columbian inspiration were included in some of the hospitals, residential compounds, and theaters of the Mexican Social Security Institute (IMSS), such

as the National Medical Center or the Cuauhtémoc and Independence housing units. At the National Museum of Anthropology (1964), certain decorative elements were incorporated as well. But it has been the architect Agustín Hernández who has most successfully updated Mesoamerican architecture in his works: the school of the Ballet Folklórico (1965); the Taller de Arquitectura (1973); the IMSS Ob-Gyn Hospital (1973); the Military College (1976), whose interior and exterior spaces are built on an impressive monumental scale; and the Calakmul corporate center (1994). Other recent buildings that display a Pre-Columbian influence are the University of Mayab in Mérida (1982) and the Mormon Temple in Mexico City, which literally copies a Maya temple (1983).

Finally, a curious fact worth mentioning is that two well-known science fiction movies, *Blade Runner* and *Total Recall*, use the interior of Wright's Ennis House, and the interior and exterior of Hernández's Military College, as scenery of the future; this is a strange coincidence, given that both works hark back to Mesoamerican forms.

25. (*above*) Anahuacalli Museum, Mexico City, 1942–57, designed by Diego Rivera to house his collection of Pre-Columbian artifacts.

26. (*opposite*) Main Library, University City, Mexico City, 1952. This building is covered with murals in colored stones by Juan O'Gorman.

2
THE HIDDEN MEANINGS OF ARCHITECTURE

MARÍA TERESA URIARTE AND ANTONIO TOCA FERNÁNDEZ

For visitors to an archaeological site in the Maya region, Oaxaca, or the Mexican Altiplano, the underlying significance of the ancient buildings is not always obvious. They may not understand, for example, that these were not fortuitous constructions, built at random, but rather carefully planned structures that had religious, military, or political meanings for the community that flourished at the site centuries ago. The first travelers to see the pyramids at Palenque could scarcely imagine that beneath the Temple of the Inscriptions was buried K'inich Janaab' Pakal I, apparently the ruler of the site from AD 615 to 683 (plate 28).

Likewise, few visitors to Teotihuacán know that the Pyramid of the Sun is associated with the solstices and equinoxes in such a way as to create four significant periods of sixty-five days each within the solar year,[1] or that it was built over an ancient cave that might have served as an astronomical observatory (plate 27). In fact, Doris Heyden proposes that this cave, in which

27. (*opposite*) The Pyramid of the Sun, Teotihuacán, State of México, AD 1–200. Of the thousands of visitors who come here annually, few know that this monumental structure was built over an ancient cave that may have served as an astronomical observatory.

28. (*right*) The Temple of the Inscriptions, Palenque, Chiapas, dedicated AD 690. Before 1949, few travelers to Palenque were aware that beneath this structure was the tomb of the K'inich Janaab' Pakal I, who ruled from AD 615 to 683.

there was probably a spring, determined the location of the other structures around it, and thus came to be considered an *axis mundi*. She also finds evidence of geomancy in the interrelation of the heavens, the mountains immediately surrounding the site, and the combination of cave and spring. This example faithfully reflects the Mesoamerican worldview: the four cardinal directions are indicated by the apparent path of the sun across the heavenly vault, and the point at their center is the cave beneath Teotihuacán's most spectacular building—which is also one of the most emblematic in Mesoamerican architecture.[2]

The existence of this cave was unknown for centuries. Its discovery has allowed us to gain a partial understanding of the city's deepest meaning, of its conceptualization with respect to its geographic surroundings, the stars, and the cave itself. This is an example of how, as we learn more about Pre-Columbian settlements, we can integrate discourses that were previously not accessible to us in a coherent form. The Pre-Columbian worldview that we have been familiar with is the one written and handed down in the chronicles of the conquerors and their indigenous informers. This has now been complemented by the deciphered writings of the Maya, which have told us more about some of the beliefs that were held in common in different areas and in different periods of Mesoamerican civilization. In particular, they have clarified the conception of the universe that Alfredo López Austin considers to be the nucleus of all Mesoamerican religions. Although this cosmography varies in some of its details from culture to culture, its fundamental aspects remain constant: the world is divided latitudinally and longitudinally by five points (the four cardinal directions and a central point), and into thirteen upper and nine lower regions. This results in a diagram with seven points of reference—the five cardinal points plus the ascending and descending levels—that is reflected in numerous works of Mesoamerican art, including buildings and cities.

Interdisciplinary studies, involving the collaboration of archaeologists, art historians, architects, and astronomers, have also shed new light on the significance of certain buildings. Nevertheless, some messages will remain undecipherable because we do not understand the language and writing of all the cultures that flourished in this territory.

MYTHOLOGY AND WORLDVIEW

Each Mesoamerican community was united and identified by a knowledge of time's passage, of the calendar, and of the beginning of its own era. These themes were also manifested in architecture.

The Mesoamerican peoples believed that they originated in a cave that had several special attributes: it was a source of birth and sustenance, a point of access to the underworld and the territory of their ancestors, a place of sacrifices, and the site where clouds were created. By virtue of the last two qualities, it was associated with earth and rain deities.

The cave was also the counterpart of the mountain. Numerous Mesoamerican buildings were constructed over caves or were somehow linked to them; thus their pyramidal foundations became a metaphor for the mountain, and the city itself an allegorical landscape of caves and mountains. We often forget that the pyramid was the base on top of which the temple was placed. The temple was a sacred chamber, access to which was restricted to a few distinguished members of the priesthood or the nobility, frequently incarnated in a single person who acted as both ruler and high priest.

In Mesoamerica, the cave is a place of origin, a primordial site of creation. From Chicomostoc, or the Seven Caves, began the journey of the tribes who would later found Tenochtitlán. The start of their pilgrimage was also the start of their era. In this way, the cave/mountain was connected with the idea of beginnings, and the pyramid came to be used as an instrument for marking time—not only through its association with solar or stellar events and thereby with the calendar, but also because rulers left the imprints of their reigns on it.

Here we should emphasize that buildings served as symbols of power in Mesoamerica, though we need not linger over this point. It should be evident that the rulers of imposing cities like Teotihuacán, Tikal, or Calakmul used architecture in this way, just as the emperors of Rome or Byzantium did in their day, and Hitler, Stalin, and Mussolini did in ours. These leaders believed that their new buildings would be historical landmarks, monuments of their regimes. Linked to this idea is a theme that we consider to be of prime importance, and which we find reflected first in painting, and later in architecture.

URBANISM, ARCHITECTURE, AND THE HUMAN BODY

In Oxtotitlán, Guerrero—an Olmec site associated with the cave—there is an image of a figure dressed as a bird, perhaps an eagle, and sitting on a throne similar to those found at La Venta, such as the so-called Altar 4. The man-bird takes on the role of the center of the universe, an *axis mundi* capable of joining together the different regions that compose the Pre-Columbian cosmogram. He is seated over the jaws of a feline, perhaps a jaguar, the supreme symbol of the underworld. If we compare the images at La Venta and Oxtotitlán, we observe that over the altars—now better known as thrones—the figure emerges from what appears to be the snout of the feline and, at the same time, a cave. This association between the mouth of the feline and the entrance to a cave is not an isolated one. We see it as well in Monument 9 of Chalcatzingo (plate 29).

In Mesoamerica, the cave is also a gateway to the aqueous and telluric regions of the underworld. In its interior were found warring opposites, the burning lava and the water that flows from the spring. On various occasions, the sacred struggle that these elements waged in the bowels of Mother Earth spilled over into the Mesoamerican landscape: volcanic eruptions, and the clouds of steam that emerge from the volcano's mouth, are living reminders of what the peoples of the region have experienced through the centuries.

In the painting at Oxtotitlán, the bird-man joins the celestial and telluric regions through his body, leading us to conclude that he is a ruler. Thus at this early date, around 1000 BC, we already find that the human figure can also be a metaphor for the axis of the world. There are numerous examples of this theme in Pre-Columbian sculpture and painting, and also of course in the emblematic buildings that have the same function. For example, on the central Altiplano, the Pyramid of Cuicuilco was, like the Pyramid of the Sun at Teotihuacán, built over a cave and acted as a link between the telluric and aboveground regions. At Cuicuilco, this symbolic function was established between 1000 and 800 BC.

There is another important theme in architecture about which relatively little has been written. We have commented elsewhere that the human form serves as a reference and measure for architecture. But a specific motif that emerges, like our previous one, in the Olmec era is that of the human figure as a support. Thus in Monument 2 at Potrero Nuevo we see two figures

whose raised arms support what has been interpreted as a throne (plate 30). On the front of this throne appear what could be eyes. Their meaning is hard to decipher, although images of the Bacabs, beings who carry or support the universe, do exist in the Maya tradition.

It is interesting that after this example of the Formative period, we do not encounter any further instances of the human support in the Early or Middle Classic period. In the Post-classic, however, it is found in two cities that were certainly united by iconography, even if we do not know whether they shared royal bonds: Chichén Itzá and Tula. In the Maya city, examples of the human support abound (plate 31), but it is the so-called Atlantes or Warriors of Tula that present the clearest example of this motif.

These warriors supported on their heads the roof of Pyramid B, also known as Tlahuiz-calpantecuhtli (plate 33). They must have belonged to a very special military order, not only because they alternate with columns in the form of the plumed serpent, but also because they

29. (*above*) This bas-relief at Chalcatzingo, Morelos, known as El Rey (The King), represents a figure seated in a space that has been identified as a cave, from which emerge volutes representing clouds. In-terestingly, Chalcatzingo is aligned with the volcano Popocatépetl, which is still active and emits clouds of vapor and ash. Mid-Formative.

30. (*below*) Monument 2 at Potrero Nuevo, Veracruz. Human figures supporting thrones or other structures are common in the Epi-classic and Late Classic, but this Olmec example is unique.

wear butterfly breastplates. We do not know the meaning of this ornament, which appears in other Mesoamerican sculptures, such as the bas-reliefs of the Lower Temple of the Jaguars at Chichén Itzá (plate 34) and at some Aztec sites. The human figure also supports buildings at Chichén Itzá and other sites in the Maya region, such as Kabah, but in the guise of a bas-relief carved on a pillar (plate 32), whereas at Tula, the figure of the warrior itself serves as a column. This is a unique case in Mesoamerica, given that figural columns usually took the form of the body of the plumed serpent, as at Chichén Itzá, in the Temple of the Warriors (plate 35) and the Upper Temple of the Jaguars over the ballcourt (plate 36).

ORIENTATION AND THE CALENDAR

Orientation played a fundamental role in the geomancy of the Mesoamerican peoples. We have already mentioned the intervals of sixty-five days that must pass in order for us to observe sunup or sundown from four different vantage points at Teotihuacán. Now let us address the antiquity of these astronomical observations and their relationship with architecture.

31. (*below left*) Atlas from Chichén Itzá, Yucatán, AD 900–1200. This relief, which retains traces of its original polychromy, is an example of the use of the human figure as a support.

32. (*below right*) Another atlas from Chichén Itzá, AD 900–1200.

The ballgame holds multiple meanings for indigenous cultures even in our own day, since it continues to be played in various forms across the Republic of Mexico. One meaning of this ubiquitous game, relevant to the present discussion, is illuminated by the site of Teopante-cuanitlan, located to the east of the Mezcala River in the state of Guerrero, and inhabited from 1400 BC; its earliest buildings date to around 1200 BC.[3] Here we may confirm, for the first time, that a relationship exists between the ballgame and the concept of the founding of a city, or the inception of an era.

At Teopantecuanitlan, there is a symbolic ballcourt in one of the structures with a sunken patio. It cannot be a real court, because its measurements would make it impossible to play the game, but it does function as a solar marker. On the solstices and equinoxes, the shadows of four sculptures located along the perimeter wall of the sunken patio are projected into the center of this allegorical terrain. These sculptures have the shape of a thick inverted T and bear the anthropomorphic faces of supernatural beings, perhaps related to corn (plate 37).

Not only this allegorical ballcourt, but all the ballcourts we encounter elsewhere—whether real ones, as that of Xochicalco (plate 38), or those represented on page 16v of the *Historia tolteca chichimeca* (plate 39) and in the Tepantitla mural paintings at Teotihuacán (plate 40)—are associated with the establishment of a city and with the beginning of time ordered by the calendar.

COLOR IN ARCHITECTURE

When we visit a Pre-Columbian site, it is difficult for us to imagine that all the buildings were once painted. But in fact they were covered in bold colors like solid red and adorned with equally polychromed carvings, creating a spectacle that merged sculpture, painting, and architecture, which we usually think of as distinct media (plate 41). We can get some idea of how other buildings must have looked from the facades at Balamku and Calakmul in southern Campeche, which were discovered relatively recently, and whose polychromy and stuccoed masks have consequently been preserved. Also indispensable to visualizing this effect of colored stone are the drawings left by earlier visitors to certain sites. For example, we know that the little atlantes at Chichén Itzá were fully polychromed thanks to the drawings of Adela Breton, and the colors of various monuments at Tula can be appreciated from those of Désiré Charnay.

37. (*below*) On the equinoxes, this monolith casts a shadow onto the center of a symbolic ballcourt at Teopantecuanitlan, Guerrero, 1000–800 BC.

38. (*opposite top*) At the Epiclassic site of Xochicalco, Morelos, the ballcourt also indicates the equinox.

39. (*opposite bottom left*) Page 16v of the *Historia tolteca chichimeca*, 16th century. This illustration shows a clear relationship between the founding of a city and the ballgame that sets time in motion. The upper register is filled with sugarcane or reeds, called *tules*; the word *tollan*, or "place of *tules*," also meant "city."

40. (*opposite bottom right*) This mural in the Tepantitla compound at Teotihuacán depicts different forms of the ballgame in various settings, such as the *altepetl*, or mountain of origin, seen in this detail. Classic period.

Mural paintings in the interiors of building or tombs also formed an integral whole with architecture and sculpture, whether freestanding or affixed, as we can see in Oaxaca (plate 42). The Temple of the Feathered Serpent at the Ciudadela in Teotihuacán must have had a very different visual impact on the people who saw it with all its colors intact than it does on those who see it today without its "skin." We might say that envisioning the former state based on the latter is like trying to picture a person's face by looking at a bare skull.

ENVIRONMENT AND SETTLEMENT PATTERNS

In addition to following a grid layout, as at Teotihuacán or Tenochtitlán, the planning of Mesoamerican cities was affected by many other factors, political, economic, social, topographic, geographic, and cosmological. For example, at Copán and Monte Albán, topographic elevations were exploited in the construction of major buildings, in order to lend the structures extra height. The effect of regional geographic differences on architecture can be seen, among

41. Great mask flanking a staircase at Kohunlich, Quintana Roo, c. 400 BC.

42. Mural on the west
wall of the funerary
chamber of Tomb 5,
Suchilquitongo, Oaxaca,
AD 700–900.

other places, in the Huastec area and the northern zone near Balcón de Montezuma, where
structural forms change radically. And of course the necessity of obtaining the foods required
by the human diet also influenced the location of Mesoamerican cities.

One framework for understanding Mesoamerican sites is provided by Donald Thompson,
who proposes that natural or man-made environments can be "read" in terms of categories
that make up a sort of "grammar."[4] The basic spatial categories he identifies are "domain,"
"center," and "path," and to these he adds concepts like "edge" and "transition." He clarifies
that these ideas are of course not mutually exclusive, giving the example of a highway or street,
which is both a pathway and a limit; likewise, he suggests that rivers like the Amazon or the

Thames are both pathways and frontiers. A bridge is at once a gateway and a reference point of transition, just as a plaza can also be a path.

In Mesoamerica, these categories are at times very clear, as in the case of the Avenue of the Dead in Teotihuacán, which is a road, a plaza, perhaps a ballcourt at several points along its length, and a path that conceptually joins two geographic reference points: the Patlachique and Gordo hills. Undoubtedly this architectural complex forms a sacred geography that was of great importance to the city's residents. If we add to Thompson's categories the relationship to the cosmos established by astronomical orientations, we may ask ourselves whether the San Juan River, which crosses this path perpendicularly, also played a role in the settlement of the city.

It is feasible to identify one or several centers in Mesoamerican cities, as Joyce Marcus has demonstrated. However, there are some types of structures whose function and place in the city's hierarchy we have been unable to clarify. In this category are the so-called "palaces" or "residential compounds," which must have been spaces occupied by the elites in order to control the trade in sumptuary goods, thus establishing a separation from the rural residential zones that have left little or no trace on the great cities that existed in this vast territory.

ASTRONOMY, CALENDARS, AND COSMOGRAPHY
Jesús Galindo Trejo

Ever since man first came to Mesoamerica, he has had to satisfy his intellectual and material needs in order to survive in an unknown and at times hostile environment. When Pre-Columbian man decided whether to settle at a site and raise his dwelling there, he considered not only practical concerns such as accessibility, provisions, and protection, but also his symbolic environment, which was based on the notion of the world that he derived from his constant observation of nature. This fact may be especially appreciated in the great architectural structures and even the layout of Mesoamerican cities.

From this observation of nature, including the heavens, he established some basic guidelines for the spatial organization of his environment. Great hills, springs, and certain other places took on a sacred meaning. The heavens introduced order to this landscape in a spectacular fashion: the movement of the stars across the firmament unequivocally marked the fundamental directions on the surface of the earth. The coincidence of the solar disc with the sacred elements of the landscape permitted the generation of a spatial pattern for the measurement of time. The Mesoamerican calendar system was indispensable to the inner workings of society, attaining the highest importance in Pre-Columbian thought. It was held to be a gift from the gods to man ensuring the correct functioning of the universe, and everything related to it was deemed sacred.

According to Mesoamerican reasoning, the universe possessed an ordered configuration that emphasized the concepts of levels and preferential directions within man's surroundings, with him at the center. There were three distinct zones where both men and deities could reside: the heavens, the earth, and the underworld. The heavens were divided into thirteen levels, and the underworld into nine. The world was a large, flat, rectangular surface, often represented as a great crocodile.[5]

The Mesoamerican calendar system consisted of two counts that advanced simultaneously: one, known as *xiuhpohualli*, was a solar cycle of 365 days, organized into 18 periods of 20 days plus 5 days to complete the year; the other, called *tonalpohualli*, was of a religious nature and had a duration of only 260 days, organized into 20 periods of 13 days. These counts began at the same time but quickly fell out of sync, and it was necessary to wait precisely 52 periods of 365 days, or 73 periods of 260 days, for them to coincide again. Thus the basic equation of the Mesoamerican calendar was: $52 \times 365 = 73 \times 260$. When the counts coincided, great ceremonies were performed to celebrate the cycle.[6]

As we shall see, Mesoamerican man masterfully embedded in his architectural works a great deal of the ideology related to his worldview and his system of measuring time. Often, Mesoamerican architects would choose one of the numbers significant in the cosmological and calendrical context (9, 13, 18, 20, 52, etc.) to determine the number of steps, moldings, battlements, or columns in a structure, or the number of tiers in a pyramid.

The first buildings of the Formative era already display careful planning in their layout and orientation. One notable example is the Circular Pyramid at Cuicuilco, in the southern Valley of Mexico (plate 43). Built around 600 BC, this structure possesses four circular tiers and two entrances aligned east-west (plate 44). Toward the east, the axis of symmetry of this building points to the top of an isolated hill, which is almost hemispherical: Cerro Papayo. Twice a year at dawn, on March 23 and September 20, the solar disc emerges exactly at this point on the horizon (plate 45). These dates, which are two days different from those of the equinoxes, are related to a balanced division of the year. If we count the days that pass between the solstices and divide this quantity in half, we obtain precisely the two dates indicated by the Cuicuilco Pyramid.[7] It is a kind of temporal equinox, instead of the traditional spatial one that basically marks the date on which the sun rises at the midpoint of the horizon, between the solstitial extremes.

Around the beginning of the Christian era, Cuicuilco was annihilated by a great eruption of the nearby Xitle volcano. It is thought that the city's population emigrated to the north as a result of this cataclysm, where they probably founded Teotihuacán, the City of the Gods. In terms of extent and population, this city was one of the greatest in all of Mesoamerica. The urban layout of Teotihuacán possesses two main axes, the so-called Avenue of the Dead, aligned north-south, and a perpendicular one that coincides with the orientation of the city's greatest structure: the Pyramid of the Sun (plate 47). All buildings in the city are parallel or perpendicular to these axes, producing a highly uniform layout (plate 46). However, this urban grid is not aligned with the cardinal directions. The axis of symmetry of the Pyramid of the Sun, and hence the city's layout, is deviated by 15.5 degrees. Thus this impressive pyramid, and the city itself, points toward the sunset on two dates without any astronomical relevance whatsoever: April 29 and August 13 (plate 48). Yet if an observer were to position himself on top of the pyramid for an entire year and watch all the sunsets, the importance of these dates would become clear to him. Starting from the first alignment of the year, on April 29, fifty-two days would have to go by for the solar disc to reach its extreme position on the horizon on the day of the summer solstice. Another fifty-two days would have to pass in order to reach August 13, the second solar alignment of the pyramid. After that date, sunset after sunset, the solar disc would gradually move south along the horizon until it reached its extreme position on the

43. (*top*) The Circular Pyramid at Cuicuilco, Distrito
Federal, c. 600 BC, is one
of the earliest buildings in
the Valley of Mexico.

44. (*bottom left*) The
Circular Pyramid with
the Popocatépetl volcano
and Cerro Teuhtli visible
beyond. In Mesoamerica,
geographic features such
as these served as reference
points for observers of
the sky.

45. (*bottom right*) Sunrise
observed from the Circular
Pyramid on March 23. The
solar disc rises above Cerro
Papayo.

winter solstice. Then the sun would slowly return, day by day, until sunset number 260 coincided with April 29 of the following year. That is to say, the dates of alignment indicate the
division of the year in a 104/260 ratio. It is worthwhile to point out that the axis of symmetry of
the pyramid as it extends toward the east determines a solar alignment at dawn on February 12
and October 29.[8] These dates divide the solar year in the same ratio, using the winter solstice
as the pivot for counting the days.

All the efforts of Teotihuacán's architects were directed toward manifesting the importance
of the numbers that define this sacred system of time measurement. The sun provides only
a spectacular setting for announcing the arrival of these dates. The people of Teotihuacán
adopted this orientation in order to give their material works a symbolic value of the utmost
importance, in harmony with the principles of the calendar.

46. (*top left*) Teotihuacán, the City of the Gods, was one of the largest cities in Mesoamerica between AD 100 and 700. Its plan has two perpendicular axes, one marked by the Avenue of the Dead (seen here from the Pyramid of the Moon), and the other by the axis of symmetry of the Pyramid of the Sun (to the left in the middle distance).

47. (*top right*) The Late-Formative Pyramid of the Sun, Teotihuacán's largest, represents the desire of its builders to imbue their entire city with a symbolic and religious value.

48. (*bottom*) Sunset observed from atop the Pyramid of the Sun on April 29. The solar disc is aligned with the pyramid's axis of symmetry.

This particular solar orientation was widespread across all of Mesoamerica. There are numerous examples: the Pyramid of the Five Floors at Edzná (plate 49),[9] House E of the Palace at Palenque,[10] the Great Temple of Tula (plate 50),[11] Structure A at El Consuelo, Tamuín,[12] the Upper Temple of the Jaguars at the ballcourt (plate 52) and the main window of the Caracol observatory at Chichén Itzá (plate 51),[13] as well as the residential compound of Tomb 105 at Monte Albán.[14] The zenith observatory at Xochicalco was designed in such a way that the extreme dates of the incidence of solar rays in its interior are the same as those of the solar alignment of the Pyramid of the Sun at Teotihuacán.[15] The date August 13 is particularly important. According to epigraphic studies, the Maya long count, a calendar variation from the Classic era, begins its computation from this date in the year 3114 BC.

One example of another group of architectural orientations based on the Mesoamerican conception of time is found in Tenochtitlán, the Aztec capital. The Templo Mayor was one of the grandest pyramids when the Spaniards arrived, and its orientation coincides with the main axis of the layout of both the Pre-Columbian and the colonial city. The double sanctuary at its summit, dedicated to Huitzilopochtli and Tlaloc, aligned with the sunset on April 9 and September 2 (plates 53, 54). Once again, these dates have no astronomical significance, but are enormously important for the calendar.

Starting from the first alignment of the year, April 9, exactly seventy-three days must pass for the solar disc to touch the horizon at its extreme position on the day of the summer solstice. After another seventy-three days, the sun returns to reach the second alignment of the year on September 2. On subsequent days, the solar disc gradually moves farther along the southern part of the horizon, reaching its extreme position on the winter solstice. Returning

49. (*top*) The sanctuary atop the Pyramid of the Five Floors at Edzná, Campeche, AD 600–800, has the same solar alignments as the Pyramid of the Sun at Teotihuacán.

50. (*bottom*) The Great Temple at Tula, c. AD 1000, the city that was a symbol of wisdom in the final centuries of Pre-Columbian history. This pyramid also has the same solar alignments as Teotihuacán's Pyramid of the Sun.

51. (*top*) The observatory at Chichén Itzá known as El Caracol, AD 800–1000. Various elements of this building are aligned with astronomical events. The main window points toward the sunset on the same days as Teotihuacán's Pyramid of the Sun.

52. (*bottom*) The Upper Temple of the Jaguars at the ballcourt in Chichén Itzá, AD 900–1200, is another building that shares the solar alignments of Teotihuacán's Pyramid of the Sun. The murals in the temple's interior clearly allude to the sun and the plumed serpent, which are very important to the Mesoamerican calendar.

slowly to the north, the solar disc will complete its course on April 9 of the following year. From September 2 to this last date, 3 × 73 days will have passed. It is obvious that the number 73—the number of *tonalpohualli* cycles necessary to complete fifty-two *xiuhpohualli*—forms an exceptional part of this scheme.

Here as well, the Templo Mayor also aligns with the sunrise on two dates that have the same relationship with regard to the winter solstice: March 4 and October 9. In this case, the effect is very showy. On either of these days of alignment, we can observe how the solar disc touches and peels away from the horizon, framed by the buildings, lampposts, and sidewalks of the streets that run along the temple's axis of symmetry. The heart of Mexico's capital city still beats to the rhythm of the Mesoamerican calendar, like a great cosmic clock that keeps ticking even though its designers have ceased to exist.[16] Other architectural structures that were aligned to these dates can be found across Mesoamerica: the Pyramid of the Niches at El Tajín

(plates 55, 56),[17] the Great Sun Mask in the eastern patio of Copán (plate 57),[18] the substructure of Building 38 at Dzibilchaltún,[19] the archway (CA-9a) entering the Ah Canul group at Oxkintok,[20] the Room of the Frescoes at Mayapán.[21] In this last place, the sun's rays obliquely illuminate a polychromed mural with solar iconography on the aforementioned dates. This family of solar orientations has the property of permitting the calibration of an important period of observation of the planet Venus. That the synodic period of Venus lasts 584 days was recorded by the Maya in the Dresden Codex; this information may be obtained by tracking a succession of eight sunsets on the dates provided by this set, given that $8 \times 73 = 584$.

A third group of orientations can be identified, particularly in the Zapotec territory of Oaxaca. The so-called Jeweled Building at Monte Albán, with the *talud-tablero* architecture

53. (*top*) The Templo Mayor of Tenochtitlán, AD 1325–1521, defined the orientation of the urban grid of the Aztec capital, and of modern Mexico City as well. Tlaloc, the rain god, and Huitzilopochtli, a war god with solar attributes, were worshipped in the double sanctuary at its summit.

54. (*bottom*) The sunset observed from the Templo Mayor on April 9. The solar disc is aligned with the double sanctuary on top of the pyramid.

55. (top) View from atop the Pyramid of the Niches, AD 800–1000, toward the Plaza of the Stream, El Tajín, Vera-cruz. The petroglyph in the foreground is thought to be a board for playing *patolli*, a game involving various calendar numbers.

56. (bottom) The Pyramid of the Niches is associated with the calendar not only by its 365 niches, but also by the solar alignments that it shares with Tenoch-titlán's Templo Mayor.

typical of Teotihuacán, is aligned with the sunrise on February 25 and October 17 (plate 58).[22] According to an ethnohistorical source of the sixteenth century, the Zapotecs divided the ritual year of 260 days into four sections of 65 days each, naming these periods after Cocijo, the rain god.[23] February 25 and October 17 fall precisely one Cocijo before and after the winter solstice. On these dates, in the northern room of the Arroyo compound at Mitla, the angled rays of the sun illuminate a mural depicting a solar disc framed by two buildings and held up by two figures in the sky.[24] The two dates that fall one Cocijo before and after the sum-mer solstice, namely April 17 and August 25, mark the first and last entrance of the sun's rays into the zenith chamber of Building P at Monte Albán (plate 59).[25] Because the first and last dates of these pairs are precisely 52 days apart, they represent a balanced embedding of the

ritual year within the solar count. A highly suggestive piece of information comes from certain documents in Zapotec related to time counts and associated festivals, confiscated in the Sierra Zapoteca by the Spanish Inquisition in the seventeenth century. According to these documents, among the Zapotecs the new year began on February 25.[26]

It is important to point out that in order for the division of the solar year described here to be valid on both the western and the eastern horizons, the site of the building in question must have practically uniform horizon lines in both directions. This obviously implies that the designers of these structures exercised special care in choosing their locations, taking nearby mountains into account.

Beyond a doubt, the Zapotecs used the heavens to establish the urban plan of Monte Albán. One indication may be found in Stele 18, located on a small platform in the northeastern sector of the city (plate 60). Measuring over 16 feet (5 meters) in height and bearing several still-undeciphered glyphs, the stele is positioned so as to indicate, with great precision, celestial north, which today nearly coincides with Polaris in Ursa Minor (plate 61).[27]

Cholula enjoyed one of the longest periods of continuous occupation of any Mesoamerican settlement. In the Formative era, construction began there on what would become the world's largest pyramid in terms of volume, consisting of several superimposed structures that basically maintained the same orientation (plate 62).

In this case, the pyramid formed the nucleus of the city, whose plan survives only in its colonial form. However, this probably coincides with that of the Pre-Columbian era, as is the

57. (*above*) The Great Sun Mask in the eastern patio at Copán, Honduras, AD 400–800. The sun god, with his characteristic large eyes and single tooth, is flanked by two great glyphs of Venus. The calendrical significance of this mask is indicated by its alignment with the rising sun 73 days before and after the summer solstice, and the Venus glyphs suggest the connection between the number 73 and the synodic period of that planet.

58. (*above*) The Jeweled Building at Monte Albán, Oaxaca, c. AD 500. Due to its *talud-tablero* architectural style and other archaeological indications, it is thought that this structure might have been built by Teotihuacanos. However, its solar alignments are associated with the 65-day periods into which the Zapotecs divided the ritual year.

59. (*right*) The main plaza at Monte Albán. The plan of Building J, c. 200 BC, in the foreground, recalls the glyph for "year." Its axis of symmetry points east toward Building P, where a zenith observation chamber is found. The first and last dates on which the sun's rays enter this chamber fall 65 days before and after the summer solstice.

case in several cities reoccupied by the Spanish conquerors. The pyramid is oriented toward the sunset on the summer solstice, and the streets of the present-day city extend in the same direction. Due to the selfsame characteristics of the sun's movement, the rear part of the pyramid is aligned with the sunrise on the winter solstice.[28] This solstitial orientation allows the pyramid to be used as an enormous sundial: on the days of the aforementioned alignments, for the few brief minutes when the solar disc is on the horizon, the ancient structure indicates with its pointed shadow where the sun will be six months later.

The murals inside Structure 1 at Bonampak provide an excellent example of the skill of the Maya in representing the heavens (plate 63). In the upper part of the main room, four heavenly bodies were apparently depicted within small squares containing the star glyph. Above, along the entire length of the vault, we find a painting of the Sky Monster, which some researchers have identified with the Milky Way. The Maya painters left a date in one of their murals: August 6, AD 792, which marked the inferior conjunction of Venus. It happens that on that same day, one could see how the Milky Way aligned with the building's axis of symmetry: just before dawn, it unfolded along the facade of the structure. Thus the Sky Monster was

60. (*opposite left*) Stele 18 at Monte Albán, 100 BC–AD 300. Located in the northeastern part of the city, this stele is precisely oriented toward celestial north.

61. (*opposite right*) A long exposure of Stele 18 at night, showing the heavens revolving around Polaris, the North Star.

62. (*below*) The Great Pyramid (c. 200 BC–AD 1521) of Cholula, Puebla, Late Formative–Postclassic, is the largest in the world in terms of volume. The front of the pyramid is aligned with the sunset on the summer solstice, and its rear with the sunrise on the winter solstice.

63. (*right*) Drawing of the murals in the main room of Structure 1 at Bonampak, Chiapas, AD 792, showing the celestial objects that were depicted in the upper register: the Pleiades, Mars, the red star Aldebaran and the constellation of Orion.

oriented in the same direction as the Milky Way, which supports the proposed association. In these moments, there were visible above the eastern horizon a group of four celestial objects that may be identified with the paintings in the building's main room: the Pleiades, Mars, the red star Aldebaran, and the constellation of Orion.[29]

This brief tour of some Mesoamerican sites shows how the observers of the Pre-Columbian skies established a particular pattern of architectural alignments that was in keeping with the characteristics of their calendar system. Certainly it is still not possible to definitively establish all the details of this pattern, given that archaeoastronomical research has not yet penetrated all regions of Mesoamerica. However, based on the studies carried out thus far, it can be stated that the Mesoamericans mastered a subtle way of ordering space by systematically selecting time intervals and fixing them in the orientation of their main buildings (plates 64–68). In this manner, they placed their architectural works in harmony with the divine precepts that governed the universe.

64. (*above*) View of Tikal, Guatemala, showing Temple 2 in the foregound and Temple 1 in the background. The sight line between the upper sanctuaries of these eighth-century pyramids points toward the sunrise 65 days before and after the summer solstice.

65. (*opposite top*) A night view of the Pyramid of the Niches at El Tajín.

66. (*opposite bottom*) The Platform of Venus at Chichén Itzá, AD 900–1200, provides evidence that the Maya understood the synchrony of the movement of the sun and Venus. A stele found in this structure clearly indicates that 8 solar years of 365 days are equivalent to 5 synodic periods of Venus of 584 days.

67. (*top*) Night view of El Caracol at Chichén Itzá.

68. (*bottom*) Night view of the Pyramid of Quetzal-cóatl, Xochicalco, Morelos, c. AD 680, another building with astronomical orientations.

3

ARCHITECTURAL FUNCTION AND TECHNIQUE

MARÍA TERESA URIARTE AND ANTONIO TOCA FERNÁNDEZ

The primary function of architecture is to provide shelter for human beings. In addition, every culture imprints its own character and ideology first on its buildings, and then on the organization of the urban space that surrounds them.

The earliest Mesoamerican structures were made of earth, as is evident on the Gulf Coast and in the Huastec region. It has been proposed that these were re-creations of the mountain, which played an important symbolic role as the mythic place of origin, and which is seen, together with its counterpart the cave, in many Pre-Columbian buildings.

At Cuicuilco we find a circular pyramidal foundation that, despite its early date, was built in stone, and which has in its base a hollow recalling the cave. There were also circular structures of this kind in the west, as we shall see in chapter 6. The circular platform has been associated with the worship of Ehécatl-Quetzalcóatl, a tradition that reached the Altiplano from the Huastec region during the Postclassic. But as the example of Cuicuilco demonstrates, this type of structure long predates that era, and the cult of that deity.

REGULATOR LINES

Mesoamerican architecture, like that of other cultures, was constructed with the aid of design schemes, units of measurement, instruments, and geometric knowledge that are lost to us, except insofar as they can be deduced from the remains of the structures themselves. This deductive task is neither easy nor certain, since it demands that analyses be backed by hard facts and not suppositions or subjective theories. There have been many attempts to explain the complexities of these cultures using arguments that, although attractive, do not seem to be backed by any concrete evidence.

Some of the most important Mesoamerican cities were decisively structured by their alignments and design schemes, which established a geometric order that is still little understood and, for that reason, has sometimes been deemed nonexistent. However, on the scale of both the city and the individual building, certain measurements, proportions, and geometric relationships have been encountered that do not seem to be due to chance.

The first attempts to identify such patterns and relationships in the plans and sections of Mesoamerican buildings were made by the architect Manuel Amábilis, based on the proposals of Cook, Hambidge, and Macody Lund regarding regulator lines and the golden section (figures 6–8). The nature of Amábilis's work is clearly illustrated by the following passage, in which he describes how he applied Macody Lund's analyses of Gothic architecture to the building at Chichén Itzá known as La Iglesia:

> We decided to perform on the transverse section of this building a test of Macody Lund's regulator lines, having chosen this system due to the 72° angle (the interior angles of a pentagon) formed by the plane of the vaults and the floors. . . . We found that the elevation of this building is integrally and precisely determined *ad pentagonum*. In consequence, the plan of this building should also be determined by the same procedure in order for us to deduce a definite intent rather than a simple coincidence without importance. . . . We have applied the *ad pentagonum* regulator lines to all of the plan drawings of ruins that we have obtained, not only the ones that we have made, but also those carried out by the architects Ignacio Marquina and Federico Mariscal. . . .
>
> In this architecture, as in the Gothic, Egyptian, etc., there were no orders, but rather a system of regulator lines that, establishing a perfect architectural unity, allowed architects to manifest their personal factors; impressing upon their works different modulations and different proportions in keeping with certain traditional canons related to the building's purpose.[1]

Amábilis's study, honored in 1930 by the Real Academia de Bellas Artes de San Fernando in Madrid, illustrates with drawings and photographs his conviction that he had discovered a system based on geometry and arithmetic that governed the construction of Pre-Columbian buildings and cities, particularly among the Maya. His conclusions may seem surprising at times, because—given the technical limitations of that era—these buildings were designed with drawings or, with greater difficulty, simply by means of tools on the ground itself.

Significantly, in the case of classical Greek architecture, for which we also lacked evidence about the design and construction process, a recent discovery at the Temple of Apollo at Didyma (begun in 313 BC) shows that the outlines of various architectural elements were engraved into the stone of the structure itself as it was built. Because the temple is unfinished, it was possible to ascertain that the plan of the columns and the walls was drawn on the platform, and that once the walls were built, the vertical section of the columns was drawn on them. The lines on the platform were later covered by the bases of the columns and the walls, while those on the walls were meant to be effaced when the walls were polished.[2]

There seems to be sufficient evidence that many other cultures developed systems of design and proportion that they applied to their buildings, sculptures, portable objects, and paintings. However, these systems are still largely unknown to us, and we do not even know if any diagrams or texts exist that explain them. A valuable document of the fifteenth century reveals that in Europe, the basic principles of designing the section and plan of a building were a secret that was jealously guarded by the masons' lodges, and which most people were forbidden to know: "No worker, nor master, nor head master, nor journeyman may teach anyone, whatever his name, who does not belong to our guild and has never worked as a mason, how to erect a building from its plan."[3]

69. (*below*) The House of the Governor, Uxmal, Yucatán, early 10th century AD. The Maya frequently used the false, or corbelled, vault, in which courses of stone are gradually laid closer together as they ascend, until the angle is closed.

70. (*opposite*) The House of the Governor, Uxmal. The upper part of the facade is angled slightly outward in order to achieve a more harmonious optical effect.

Given that today, many people find it difficult to draw a pentagon or an octagon with a ruler and compass, we can only imagine how esoteric this knowledge must have been in past cultures. We must also recall how recently it was that our system of numerals was standardized: it was not until the fifteenth century that Roman numerals were exchanged for the Arabic ones now in use, and the decimal system only came into widespread use between 1586 and 1614 in Europe, and somewhat later in its colonies.

Following the work of Hambidge and Macody Lund, other well-documented studies have been published that apply systems of geometric relations and proportions to the sections and plans of numerous buildings, with very significant results.[4] Unfortunately, these studies have focused on structures in Europe; it is vital, therefore, that we continue and expand this kind of work in Mesoamerica, where it has already yielded valuable findings.

BUILDING IN STONE, WOOD, AND STUCCO

We have seen that the earthen platform was one of the four primordial elements of architecture identified by Gottfried Semper, and that in Mesoamerica, as in other cultures—such as those of Egypt or India—the foundation or platform remained a fundamental architectural form.

The construction of platforms, due to their volume, was a long process that demanded an enormous quantity of material resources and labor; it took thousands of people to gather, transport, and position the stones and the materials used to join them. Even a cursory analysis reveals, for example, the tremendous efforts that were necessary in order to shape, stabilize, and cover the faces of the Pyramid of the Sun at Teotihuacán. The great cost of building a

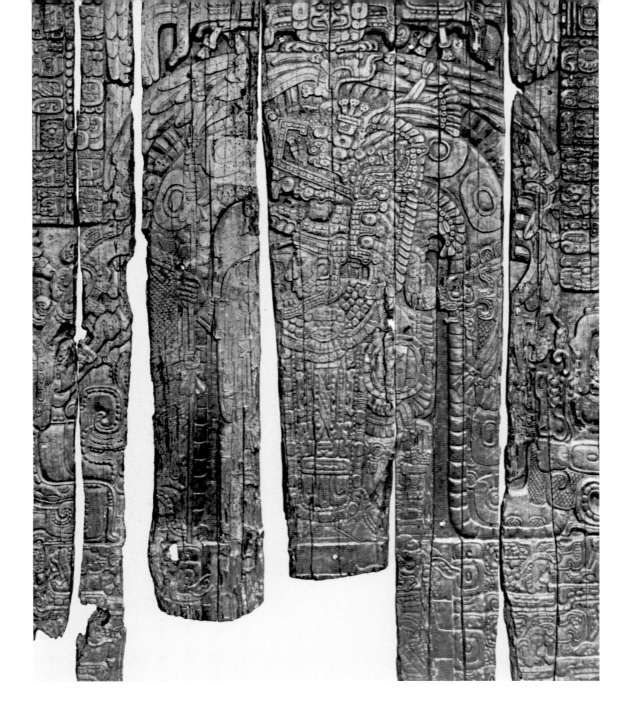

pyramid led to the development of some ingenious solutions. Many pyramids were the result of successive accumulations on top of an original pyramid, which acted as a core; the pyramid at Cholula, Puebla, offers one of the best examples of this kind of construction in stages. And we have already mentioned how topographic elevations were used to lend pyramids extra height, as at Copán.

Studies of the evolution of pyramid faces in Mesoamerican architecture have revealed the extraordinary creativity with which these surfaces were manipulated in order to achieve special meanings and effects. These studies have also shed light on the technical problems that Pre-Columbian builders had to solve in order to first stabilize the slopes of their platforms, and then build the angled facing walls, or *taludes*, using thin stones that acted as wedges. The most difficult detail was obviously the construction of the vertical panels, or *tableros*, which were made to project from the mass of the platform by means of stone cantilevers known as *ixtapaltetes*.

In Mesoamerica, as in classical Greece, the limitations imposed by building materials—specifically, stone—prevented the development of the techniques and tools necessary for the

71. Lintel from Temple 4, Tikal, Guatemala, 8th century AD. The lintels from Tikal are among the few wooden architectural elements that have survived at Mesoamerican archaeological sites. The carving on this lintel shows the ruler Yax Kin Caan Chac sitting on his throne, surrounded by an immense plumed serpent with two heads. From one of these heads emerges a deity, whose T-shaped tooth may indicate that it is solar. A bird of prey is posed on the upper part of the serpent's body.

construction of stone arches and vaults. The Maya did use the so-called false, or corbelled, vault (plate 69), but this did not permit them to build interior spaces as large as those found in European structures.

It has often been asserted that interiors were not actually important in Mesoamerican architecture, which was instead characterized by grand exterior spaces. It should be clarified, though, that due to the region's benign climate, buildings intended for habitation did not have to be very substantial. With the exception of the kind of residential compounds built at Teotihuacán or Tenochtitlán, domestic architecture was constructed of perishable materials—adobe, wood, and palm roofs—and thus has almost disappeared from Mesoamerican cities with the passage of time. However, the few examples of Mesoamerican woodworking that have survived, such as the lintels of Temples 1, 3, and 4 at Tikal (plate 71), are outstanding, and we can infer that there were other pieces of a similar quality that did not withstand the climate.

Buildings constructed of stone, using the techniques of masonry, have naturally been preserved in better condition. The facades of stone buildings were designed to consolidate the vertical faces of the walls, and to open the spaces of the doorways. This latter task was accomplished with wood or stone lintels that were strong enough to bear the weight that rested on them. Mesoamerican architects achieved a great refinement in their solutions to the problem of the vertical facade; in certain cases, such as in the exterior panels of the Hall of the Columns at Mitla or the eastern building of the Nunnery quad at Uxmal, they even inclined the upper section of the facade slightly outward, probably to achieve a more harmonious optical effect (plate 70), just as the builders of the Parthenon created a subtle *entasis* in the columns of that structure.

In order to protect them from the elements, the facades of buildings, as well as the faces of platforms, were covered with a plaster made of lime and sand, which was used to create stuccoes of a superior quality. Later, these would be augmented with sculptures, colors, or mural paintings, in accordance with the importance and religious significance of the structure.

ARCHITECTURAL FORMS

We have already discussed the significance of pyramidal foundations in Mesoamerica, and the methods by which they were constructed. Now we would like to mention some of the other architectural forms and spaces that were built in the region.

In Oaxaca, as in the west, tombs were enormously significant compared to other types of structures. The tombs constructed beneath residential areas in Oaxaca came to have an importance equal to, or greater than, that of the buildings over them, not to mention the treasures that accompanied the dead on their journey into the next world—like those found in Tomb 7 at Monte Albán.

Probably the most spectacular tomb found to date in Mesoamerica is that of K'inich Janaab' Pakal I, both because it is located beneath the great Temple of the Inscriptions, and because of the quality of the funerary chamber and cache. Other remarkable tombs in the Maya region, such as at Copán and Tikal, attest to the fact that burials of the ruling class were carried out with notable dedication in Mesoamerica.

72. (*top*) The Avenue of the Dead, Teotihuacán, State of México, segments of which may have served as a ballcourt. Constructed AD 1–150.

73. (*bottom*) The Upper Temple of the Jaguars, Chichén Itzá, Yucatán, AD 900–1200. The serpent-shaped columns found in certain Mesoamerican structures, of which these are perhaps the most spectacular examples, demonstrate the facility with which the form of the snake was adapted to different media.

The ballcourt was another architectural form to which much care was devoted. Probably the most complete study of the locations, typology, and construction of ballcourts is that of Eric Taladoire.[5] From his work we learn that the majority of these structures have an I shape that may be closed or open at the ends. Sometimes only one end is closed, as in the small ballcourt at Copán, which is open on its southern face and features spectacular macaw heads that emerge from bodies depicted in bas-relief on the walls of the structure. The ballcourt at Chichén Itzá, which is closed on its northern end, is the largest in Mesoamerica. Its sloping panels are completely covered by bas-reliefs that allude to the celebration of the game, while on its southeast part is perched the Upper Temple of the Jaguars, a grandstand of sorts that displays the two most spectacular serpent columns in the Maya zone (plate 73). Xochicalco's ballcourt, on the other hand, has a clear astronomical and calendrical connotation, like that at Teopantecuanitlan, which we have already discussed. The site from which the ballcourt is most notably absent is probably Teotihuacán, where the ballgame may instead have been played in sections of the Avenue of the Dead (plate 72).

74. Bas-relief on the wall of a ballcourt at El Tajín, Veracruz, AD 600–900. This scene shows the celebration of a ceremony in the ballcourt, following the ritual of the game itself.

The ballgame's meaningful and enduring presence in Mesoamerican history[6] is underlined by its representations in art, whether in bas-relief on the walls of the court itself, as at El Tajín (plate 74); in paintings, as at Las Higueras (plate 75); or in codices, as on Folio 22 of the Codex Borgia.

As we have written, residential architecture is little known, since the use of perishable materials condemned most of it to disappearance. However, it is worthwhile to mention once again the residential compounds of Teotihuacán, which, due to both their extent and their design, are noteworthy examples of the interaction between covered spaces and patios. At the city's La Ventilla compound, we can see small streets with canals, and the houses of people who were surely of modest social rank.

75. (*left*) Fragmentary painting from Las Higueras, Veracruz, AD 600–900. Several different variants of the ballgame are depicted in Mesoamerican mural paintings; here the players hold sticks.

76. (*above*) Ek Balam, Yucatán, AD 300–900. These statues, whose significance is unknown to us, represent one of the most spectacular examples of a sculptural group as an integral part of the facade of a Pre-Columbian building.

Leafing through the pages of this book, the reader will come to appreciate the wide variety of structures found in the Pre-Columbian architecture of Mesoamerica, from modest circular earthworks to the formidable pyramids of Teotihuacán or Tikal. The religious, astronomical, and calendrical associations of these structures attest to the spiritual wealth of the Mesoamerican peoples. Meanwhile, the magnificent residential compounds, adorned with paintings and sculptures, and the noble tombs with their rich offerings give us another approach to understanding the cities of this region, which were, as Bernal Díaz del Castillo would say, "worthy of the books of Amadis."

If this architectural abundance seems amazing to us now, it would be even more so if all the buildings had retained their rich polychromy and sculptured facades, as certain structures at

Ek Balam, Balamku, or Chicanna have (plate 76). The authors of the chapter on Maya architecture mention that in the Río Bec, Chenes, and Puuc areas, entryways are adorned by the monstrous jaws of an imaginary being. Mercedes de la Garza has suggested that these acted as portals to another reality, linked to initiatory ceremonies; the priest or ruler was devoured by, or expelled from, the jaws of the monster in what she considers to have been a true rite of passage.[7]

The use of color unites the architecture of the different cultures of Mesoamerica. The cardinal points of the Mesoamerican cosmogram were assigned specific colors, which vary from source to source. Among the Maya, north and east corresponded to red; west was white; south was black and yellow; and the center, the most important point, was the precious *yax*, turquoise. Among the Nahua, west was white; east, red; south, blue; north, black; and the center, green.[8]

To date there has been no systematic study of the use of color in Pre-Columbian architecture. However, based on the traces of pigment found on certain structures, reconstructions have been made that allow us to picture how these urban complexes must have looked to inhabitants and visitors; their colors would have functioned as tools of persuasion, sending a direct message of power and supremacy.

Finally, we would like to mention fictional architecture, that is, artistic representations of spaces both quotidian and imaginary. An immense range of buildings, and even whole cities, are depicted in codices, mural paintings, and models, such as those of western Mexico; these images illustrate the existence of architecture as a concept. As for the verbal descriptions of architecture that survive in Maya and Nahua texts, these are examined by Erik Velásquez García in chapter 12.

4

PRE-OLMEC AND OLMEC ARCHITECTURE

REBECCA B. GONZÁLEZ LAUCK

INTRODUCTION

Pre-Olmec and Olmec cultural elements are encountered in the Formative or Preclassic period, which spans more than two millennia and is divided into four sub-periods: the Initial Formative (1900–1500 BC), Early Formative (1500–900 BC), Mid-Formative (900–400 BC), and Late Formative (400 BC–AD 100).[1] The pre-Olmec era falls mostly in the Initial Formative, and the Olmec era in the Early and Mid-Formative.

Olmec cultural manifestations are characterized by their artistic style. The monumental sculptural works in this style are concentrated in southern Veracruz and western Tabasco, on the coastal plains of the Gulf of Mexico (figure 9). The same style and its variations in different media—portable sculptures in clay and stone, as well as paintings and ceramic vases—may also be found throughout a great deal of ancient Mesoamerica. Although the causes and nature of this vast diffusion are not yet entirely clear to us, the archaeological evidence points toward contact between the elites of the different societies that made up the Pre-Columbian world at this time.

This diffusion left a large quantity of remains in the Olmec style, which provide an account of an era of great cultural dynamism and constitute the main evidence that the Olmec culture was deeply rooted in much of Mesoamerica. Just as this culture influenced the other societies of its era, it also adopted ideas foreign to the Gulf Coast, which are reflected in its material culture. The importance of Olmec culture is that it established certain patterns that long endured in Mesoamerican history.

PRE-OLMEC ARCHITECTURE

Some of the earliest traces of pre-Olmec architecture have been found in the vicinity of Mazatán, on the coastal plains of Chiapas, around the Paso de la Amada site. In its earliest phase (1900–1700 BC), this site measured 25 acres (10 hectares), and over the following centuries (1700–1500 BC) it grew to 350 acres (140 hectares), including a civic-ceremonial area of nearly 100 acres (40 hectares). Other settlements on a smaller scale emerged in the surrounding area, more or less at the same distance from the main site.[2]

Among the architectural remains we find a ballcourt built of packed earth measuring 260 feet (80 meters) long.[3] Another impressive building is Structure 4, measuring 72 feet (22 meters) long and 33 feet (10 meters) wide with a dirt floor and an ovaloid layout (plate 77). It features recessed porticoes on both sides of the central section, as well as low, wide wall foundations over which walls of wattle and daub were erected. Numerous postholes point to the existence of an enormous roof made of a perishable material, such as palm fronds. Inside were found hearths for the preparation of food, as well as traces of the process of making obsidian tools. This platform has been interpreted as an elite residence, and as a center of public ceremonies.[4]

In San José Mogote, Oaxaca (plate 78), around 1650–1400 BC, houses for commoners and other buildings, perhaps with ceremonial functions, have been found. The former had a rectangular layout of roughly 13 by 20 feet (4 by 6 meters), with walls constructed of wattle and daub, supporting a roof of some perishable material; burials were discovered in their patios. The second kind of building was constructed over a small earthen platform of a similar size but with lime plaster on the walls and floors. These structures lack any traces of domestic occupation, but they do have a standardized orientation of 8 degrees west of north, as well as a cavity in the central part of the floor that apparently held lime and was used in rituals involving tobacco. They have been interpreted as "houses for men."[5]

77. (*opposite*) Structure 4, Paso de la Amada, Chiapas, c. 1400 BC.

78. (*right*) Public building at San José Mogote, Oaxaca, 1500–1200 BC.

79. (*below*) The Red Palace, San Lorenzo, Veracruz, 1400–1200 BC.

OLMEC ARCHITECTURE

THE GULF COAST

Olmec architecture presents different regional and temporal manifestations. For the Early Formative, most of our information comes from the San Lorenzo site and the surrounding area (figure 11). The main section of this site was constructed on a butte that juts out over the coastal plain, around which we find a network of settlements that vary in size and shape. From 1750 to 1400 BC, San Lorenzo had an area of 50 acres (20 hectares), and there were more than 100 settlements in its immediate vicinity. Between 1400 and 1000 BC, the site grew to an estimated extent of 1,200 acres (500 hectares), with more than twice as many settlements around it as in the previous period.[6]

All across the top of the San Lorenzo butte, which has an area of 131 acres (53 hectares), architecture dating back to the Mid-Formative can be seen on the surface. However, archaeological excavations have brought to light various structures that apparently belong to the Early Formative. An outstanding example is the building called the Red Palace, whose walls and floors of packed earth were covered in red sand dyed with hematite. The fragments of bentonite and limestone found in the ruins were perhaps used as part of the building material for the walls. The roof of this building seems to have been held up by at least one enormous basalt column 13 feet (4 meters) tall, while the stairs were finished with stones carved into an L shape. The building was associated with a sinuous canal for water distribution, also carved in stone (plate 79).

Another elite residence excavated on the butte has an oval layout; it measured nearly 40 by 30 feet (12 by 9 meters), with twenty holes for the posts that held up a roof made of a perishable material. This residence and others like it present packed-earth floors, covered with gravel or paved with blocks of bentonite.

The houses inhabited by common people are generally found along the lower terraces of the butte. They were similar to the dwellings that can still be seen in the region, with packed-earth floors, wattle-and-daub walls, and wooden posts supporting palm-frond roofs.[7]

The Pre-Columbian city at La Venta, Tabasco is the characteristic example of the Olmec architecture of the Gulf Coast and, in particular, of the Mid-Formative period. Its structures were built primarily of earth; stone was used sparingly, since it had to be imported. It is estimated that the original size of the site was about 500 acres (200 hectares), although only a little more than half of it has been preserved.

The positioning of the buildings shows a degree of planning and organization unknown in earlier times. Although the site's architectural history is long, going back at least to 1200 BC, the existing surface remains are from 600 to 400 BC.

Packed-earth platforms were constructed in parallel rows along north-south axes, forming avenues and plazas of sorts. Outstanding architectural groups include the ceremonial precinct (Complex A), the main pyramidal foundation (Complex C), and the enormous Stirling Acropolis.

Complex A, the smallest architectural compound at the site, covers about 5 acres (2 hectares). It consists of two groups of buildings organized around two small plazas or patios. The north patio was bordered by a barrier made of basalt columns, which restricted access. Most of its nine buildings were constructed from deposits of clays and sands of various colors; in some cases, their foundations were bordered by rectangular blocks of basalt and serpentine. Two of the buildings, as well as the wall supporting the fence of basalt columns, were made of adobe

80. (left) Mosaic from Complex A, La Venta, Tabasco, 900–400 BC. Composed of large blocks of serpentine and measuring 15 ft. 2 in. by 15 ft. 5 in. (4.63 by 4.70 m), this geometric design may represent a cosmogram.

81. (*above*) Structure C-1, La Venta: the Great Pyramid, 900–400 BC.

blocks. Inside some buildings were deposited "tombs" of different materials, such as basalt columns or slabs of limestone (plates 82–85).

Five massive offerings were found in the ceremonial precinct, consisting of enormous deposits of serpentine blocks (figure 12). Two of these form platforms 6.5 feet (2 meters) tall, on top of which were laid mosaics in an abstract pattern initially described as a "jaguar mask" (plate 80). These mosaics were covered with thick layers of clay, over which adobe mounds surrounded by basalt columns were constructed.[8]

Directly to the north of Complex A is Complex C, the main pyramidal foundation of this ancient Olmec city (plate 81). The pyramid, which is more than 100 feet (30 meters) tall and rests on a platform over 10 feet (3 meters) high, was made of a sandy packed clay held in place by buried slabs of limestone that act as internal buttresses. It presents a main entrance on its

82–85. Monument 7, or Tomb A, from La Venta, 900–400 BC. This structure, also called the House of the Jaguar, measures 6 ft. (1.8 m) high and 13 ft. (4 m) wide, and is constructed of 44 basalt columns. Inside were found figurines and furnishings covered with powdered cinnabar, which was often used in funerary offerings.

south face and a series of indentations near its corners. Six gravestones have been found at its foot, symmetrically positioned at either side of the main entrance.[9]

The Stirling "Acropolis" is a platform more than 1,000 feet (300 meters) long and 23 feet (7 meters) high, on which we find a series of rectangular and oval buildings, in addition to a series of channels for water distribution made of carved stone.[10]

The remains of houses have been found in and around the urban area of La Venta. The simplest ones present a packed-earth floor with a thin layer of sand and holes for the posts that held up the roof. Some show remains of wattle and daub around their perimeter, which suggests that their walls were constructed with this technique. Other, more elaborate houses had floors of fine, compacted gravel up to a yard in height.

Olmec sculpture has also been found at other sites on the Gulf Coast, like Laguna de los Cerros and Tres Zapotes, both in Veracruz. However, we have little information about the architecture from that era at these sites, since it has been covered by later phases of construction.

GUERRERO AND MORELOS

There are three sites in the states of Guerrero and Morelos that can be considered part of the Olmec sphere due to the sculptural remains they have yielded, all dating to around the Mid-Formative. Teopantecuanitlan, Guerrero (plate 86), is a site of nearly 400 acres that offers a singular example of an Olmec ceremonial precinct. In its first phase of construction, from

86. (*left*) Plaza with a monolith, Teopantecuanitlan, Guerrero, 1000–800 BC.

87. (*right*) Ceremonial precinct, Teopantecuanitlan, Guerrero, 1000–800 BC. Visible here are the two small parallel platforms that may form a ballcourt.

1400 to 900 BC, it was made of earth and measured about 320 square feet (30 square meters). From this phase four small stairways have been recovered, measuring from 6½ to 13 feet (2 to 4 meters) wide; they are symmetrically arranged around the four sides of the precinct and associated with a corridor. One of them has a balustrade bearing a stylized representation of a face. In the second phase of construction, around 800 BC, blocks of travertine were used to form a kind of sunken patio 62 feet (19 meters) long by 46 feet (14 meters) wide. Two of its walls were crowned by symmetrically arranged pairs of sculptures with an inverted T shape, carved with bas-reliefs representing the torsos and faces of supernatural beings. Within the precinct are two small parallel platforms made of round stones that have been interpreted as a ballcourt (plate 87).

This site also presents structures used for water distribution: two different systems of canals and a dam. Other rectangular platforms, including Structure 3, have facades decorated with patterns of horizontal, vertical, and inclined stone blocks—known as "points and bars"—which create niches of sorts. In addition, there is a ballcourt that dates back to 600 BC.

At the site of Zazacatla, on the outskirts of the city of Cuernavaca, Morelos, a wall almost 165 feet (50 meters) long was recently discovered. Its facade is similar to that of Structure 3 at Teopantecuanitlan, with small niches. Inside these niches were found two small sculptures in the Olmec style of the Gulf Coast, as well as two other stones that retained their natural form. Because this site has been severely damaged by highway construction, the true extent and form of its Mid-Formative architecture are still unclear.

88. View of Chalcatzingo, Morelos, 900–400 BC.

The site of Chalcatzingo, Morelos (plate 88), has been known to us for over half a century, mainly due to the bas-reliefs in the Olmec style carved into the side of the hill known as La Cantera or Chalcatzingo. Like other sites mentioned here, Chalcatzingo had a long cultural history that began around 1400 BC. Its contact with Olmec culture is limited to the period between 800 and 450 BC, when it reached an extent of 106 acres (43 hectares).[11] The site's terrain was modified to form a series of terraces on which platforms and sculptures were placed (figure 10). It has been postulated that the construction of the terraces on the lower slopes of the hill began in the Early Formative.

On one of these lower terraces, number 25, a small sunken patio was found with walls measuring 3 feet (1 meter) high and 14½ feet (4.4 meters) long by 4½ feet (1.4 meters) wide. The design of these walls is similar to the "point and bar" pattern of the two previous sites. Here, however, the central section is interrupted by a long bench of sorts, slightly raised, that is constructed of great blocks of stone, on which was carved an image in bas-relief that has been interpreted as the upper part of the face of a supernatural being. This architectural element has been described as an "altar" (plate 89).[12]

Both public and residential buildings have been identified at Chalcatzingo. The most representative of the former category is Structure 4 on Terrace 1, measuring 16 feet (5 meters) high, 230 feet (70 meters) long, and 100 feet (30 meters) wide. This earthen building underwent various phases of construction. Two high-ranking individuals were buried inside, and it appears that more than one sculpture was also associated with this structure. Meanwhile, at least one residential building was found on each terrace. These houses, which measure 680 square

89. The stool or "altar" at Chalcatzingo, 900–400 BC.

feet (63 square meters) on average, present rows of round stones over which walls of wattle and daub and adobe were erected. In some cases, evidence has been found of a white kaolin finish on the insides of the walls. Since these structures were much larger than contemporary houses in other regions, archaeologists believe that they were also used to store food and as domestic workshops for stone tools.[13]

CENTRAL MEXICO

On the central Altiplano, various sites occupied during the Early Formative period have been recorded and excavated. These sites are not Olmec per se, but they share certain themes and symbols in their portable objects. Tlatilco is perhaps the most famous site, due to the large quantity of objects that were looted from it. Numerous graves were found there, apparently associated with homes that display deposits shaped like truncated cones, the remains of garbage dumps or food caches. At Coapexco, the Pre-Columbian settlement covered 109 acres (44 hectares) and basically consisted of small houses made of wattle and daub.[14] In contrast with other regions of Mesoamerica, there was no great differentiation in domestic architecture, and no structures have been recorded that might be considered public or ceremonial.

CHIAPAS AND GUATEMALA

Around the Mid-Formative in Chiapas and Guatemala, we can see a reflection of the architectural changes that were taking place along the Gulf Coast, specifically at La Venta. This goes hand-in-hand with the presence of Olmec-style sculpture. The site of La Blanca, Guatemala,

90. The pyramid at La Blanca, Guatemala, 900–400 BC, after its partial destruction.

located almost on the border with Mexico on the coastal plain, has a pyramidal earthen structure similar in dimensions to that of La Venta. Although it was severely altered three decades ago, it is estimated that its original height was 80 feet (25 meters) and its base measured 390 by 460 feet (120 by 140 meters) (plate 90). Other platforms, between 6½ and 20 feet (2 and 6 meters) high, are scattered around the same site; these may also be considered public structures. They are usually associated with platforms of smaller dimensions that might have had a residential function, thus creating distinct groups of habitations, each with its own public building.[15]

Other Mid-Formative sites, like Finca Acapulco, Chiapas, present a fairly organized pattern in their monumental architecture, with pyramidal foundations and large platforms creating grand plazas (figure 13). Not long afterward, monumental architecture emerged in places like Chalchuapa, El Salvador, and Takalik Abaj, Guatemala, taking the form of terraced terrain, pyramidal foundations, or large platforms.

FINAL COMMENTS

During the more than one thousand years encompassed by the Early and Mid-Formative periods, Mesoamerican architecture underwent great changes. Fundamentally, villages of various sizes, whose houses did not display any major architectural differentiation, grew into regional centers or cities with public architecture. Such sites manifested a greater or lesser degree of planning, and attained larger dimensions than in previous eras. These architectural changes reflect the political, social, and economic developments that took place in the heterogeneous societies that flourished throughout ancient Mesoamerica at this time. Olmec architecture and other contemporary styles exemplify the cultural diversity of the age.

5

THE CENTRAL ALTIPLANO

MARÍA TERESA URIARTE AND ILÁN VIT SUZAN

In these pages, we will discuss nearly three thousand years of history and the passage of many ethnic groups through a broad territory, not to mention an influential system of construction and the legacy of a place that has survived marginalization, pollution, and the horror of becoming a twentieth-century megalopolis.

GEOGRAPHY AND SETTLEMENT PATTERNS

The geography of Mesoamerica has been a determining factor in the cultural development of its peoples. Almost from the time when small bands prowled the areas that could provide them with food, to the emergence and development of the great urban centers, the uneven distribution of natural resources has required a great interdependence between the groups inhabiting different regions of Mesoamerica.

Few parts of Mesoamerica are completely self-sufficient; most possess only a handful of resources, which by themselves do not provide a sufficient diet. If we consider that more than half of the current Republic of Mexico has an arid or semiarid climate and that a considerable portion of its surface area is occupied by a vast mountain chain, we realize that Mesoamerica possessed only a few areas suitable for the development of human groups.[1]

The Valley of Mexico and the Central Valley of what is now the state of Oaxaca are two of the areas most favorable to the development of urbanism in Mesoamerica. To these we might add the coastal plains of the Gulf of Mexico, as well as a smaller part of those found along the Pacific Ocean in the far south. The rest of the country may, for practical purposes, be divided into two major regions: an arid one in the north, and one blanketed by various kinds of tropical forests in the south.

The importance of the first two areas we have mentioned corresponds to their extent, strategic location, and variety of natural resources. The Valley of Mexico measures slightly more than 2,700 square miles (7,000 square kilometers), of which one-seventh was covered by salt and freshwater lakes, surrounded by mountains with coniferous forests (figure 15). The Central Valley of Oaxaca covers just over 770 square miles (2,000 square kilometers), a little more than one-fourth the area of the Valley of Mexico.[2] However, despite these favorable environmental conditions, changes in settlement patterns did take place from time to time.

For example, the population of the southeastern part of the Valley of Mexico decreased after Cuicuilco was buried by the eruption of the Xitle volcano, which substantially affected the entire surrounding area. From then on, most of the region's inhabitants were located in its northeastern part, around Teotihuacán and other neighboring zones such as Ecatepec, which was perhaps dedicated to salt production.

The interdependence of the different civilizations of Mesoamerica led to the emergence of a homogeneous religious tradition, which was strengthened by the fact that these cultures all shared the same basic diet: a combination of corn, beans, squash, and chili peppers, complemented with any animal protein that was available. Their interdependence also generated a series of contact routes connecting different regions. Thus we find evidence of continuous occupation not only in the best zones, like the Valley of Mexico, but also along these contact routes, such as the one that joined the Valley of Mexico and the Central Valley of Oaxaca via the valleys of Puebla-Tlaxcala and Tehuacán, following the basins of the Atoyac, Tetzoyocan, Cacaloapan, and Valsequillo rivers. Along this route we find archaeological sites of all eras, from those of the Archaic, such as the caves of Coxcatlán; to those of the Formative and the Classic, such as Cholula and Totimehuacán; those of the Epiclassic, when Cacaxtla would become one of the most important sites; and finally those of the Postclassic, such as Tecamachalco and México-Tenochtitlán itself.

THE DEVELOPMENT OF URBANISM
ON THE CENTRAL ALTIPLANO

Human groups have been present on the central plateau, or Altiplano, of Mexico for 20,000 years. They probably retained a certain mobility in areas where different natural resources were concentrated, such as the northern shore of what was once Lake Chalco in the Valley of Mexico, or the Caulapan region in the state of Puebla.[3]

One of the most ancient ceramic complexes of Mesoamerica—that of the Tlalpan phase in the vicinity of where Cuicuilco would later develop—dates back to 2100 BC.[4] Generally, the discovery and use of ceramics accompany the gradual transformation of migrating groups into agricultural societies. From the time this process began on the central plateau, certain groups attained a standard of urban development whose influence extended beyond the borders of the region. This was due, above all, to the way in which they exploited the geographic characteristics of this area, which enjoyed a strategic location within the complex territory that we call Mesoamerica, as well as an excellent supply of natural resources that could support large human populations.

The major urban centers that developed in the Valley of Mexico after 100 BC all had estimated populations greater than 20,000, displayed highly developed social hierarchies, and engaged in artisanal production, commerce, and tax collection. In addition to enjoying environmental conditions that were highly favorable for the establishment of large communities— a lake basin with abundant edible flora and fauna—these great cities were surrounded by areas of arable land with irrigation systems that allowed for two harvests per year, using improved varieties of corn. However, some of them did not derive their subsistence entirely from agriculture, but also relied on other activities, such as trade. This was established by Sanders and Santley in their essay "A Tale of Three Cities," which describes conditions in Teotihuacán,

Tula, and Tenochtitlán. These authors use the amount of energy consumed and produced in cultivating corn to estimate the population of these sites, as well as the surface area needed to maintain a set number of individuals.[5]

According to George Cogwill, the population of Teotihuacán may have reached 60,000 in the Tzacualli phase that took place around AD 100, or perhaps even in the preceding Patlachique phase. This was an era of social instability in the Valley of Mexico, but after Teotihuacán consolidated its hegemony, a stage of active construction began in the city. According to different authors, the population doubled or tripled from this date to AD 600. This increase was reflected in an improved system of commercialization and trade in Teotihuacán's main products, obsidian and thin orange-colored ceramics; because the arable land around the urban core could not have maintained such a large population, even with improved varieties of corn and irrigated fields, more manufactured products had to be exchanged for food. According to Spence, the remains of obsidian workshops indicate that there were other zones of controlled artifact production, mostly located in the so-called residential compounds. It can be established from the archaeological data that distinct occupations were practiced in the workshops near the Pyramid of the Moon, as well as those in the Great Complex.[6]

One of the fundamental characteristics of Mesoamerican architecture is that buildings rarely remained unaltered from their earliest stages, but were frequently renovated in response to the accession of a new ruler, a conquest, or the calendar cycle. There are generally two reasons for building over an existing structure: first, the ease of reusing the same infrastructure; and second, that certain sites are important in and of themselves, and lend their importance to the buildings erected over them. This is true of Jerusalem, a single location of extraordinary importance for the world's three major monotheistic religions. The same phenomenon can also be observed on the Altiplano, thanks to recent research projects at the Pyramid of the Moon in Teotihuacán and the Great Pyramid of Cholula, as well as the excavations at the Templo Mayor in México-Tenochtitlán.

CUICUILCO AND TEOTIHUACÁN

María Teresa Uriarte

Around 1500 BC, the earliest permanent settlements were established on the banks of the lake system in the Valley of Mexico, located more than 7,900 feet (2,400 meters) above sea level. This lake system, which offered abundant fish and game, would witness the development of the region's first urban centers. The oldest of these, built on a strategically positioned and resource-rich site, was Cuicuilco.

It has been determined from ceramics that Cuicuilco was founded by 1000 BC (in the Mid-Formative era) and that it was continuously occupied until around AD 215. According to various authors, the population was then displaced to the north following an eruption of the Xitle volcano. This was not the only incident of its kind in the Valley of Mexico: previously, another eruption, of the Popocatépetl volcano, had apparently affected an area of about 1,150 square miles (3,000 square kilometers).[7]

Thanks to archaeological excavations, we have been able to reconstruct, in a fragmented fashion, the settlement pattern of Cuicuilco over time. Some of the city's early phases have been discovered, and it is believed that between 200 BC and AD 100 it came to have a popula-

tion of around 20,000 inhabitants.[8] Its geographic position undeniably provided it with certain advantages that allowed for this remarkable growth.

Like Pompeii, Cuicuilco conceals its past beneath tons of lava. Moreover, the rapid growth of Mexico City has literally devoured the remains of this ancient settlement. Only a few visible foundations remain, of which the most important is the Circular Pyramid (plate 91). It has been respected better than the others, even though it is stranded between the Periférico beltway, the Avenida de los Insurgentes, the Olympic Village, and more recently, the Cuicuilco Plaza shopping center. While we have only scanty evidence of its original state, it has been established that the Circular Pyramid is aligned in an east-west direction, and that other temples in this area also have significant alignments, as Jesús Galindo demonstrates in his essay.

In this context, I would like to refer to the work of the architects Romel Rosas and Héctor Vega, who have identified certain geometric relationships, as well as references to geography and astronomy, in the monuments of Cuicuilco, Xihuingo, Teotihuacán, Tula, Tenochtitlán, and some other centers of the Altiplano, such as Xochicalco, Cholula, and Malinalco. Their study stresses the importance that calendrical events had for the peoples of Pre-Columbian Mexico. For example, they note that from the vantage point of such structures as the Circular Pyramid of Cuicuilco, the Pyramid of Quetzalcóatl at Xochicalco, or the Templo Mayor of México-Tenochtitlán, the rising sun was aligned with Popocatépetl on the winter solstice.[9]

91. The Circular Pyramid of Cuicuilco in the Distrito Federal, c. 600 BC, is one of the most ancient pyramidal foundations in Mesoamerica. Similarly shaped structures are found elsewhere on the Altiplano: the circular Epiclassic pyramid at Tula known as El Corral, another at Calixtlahuaca that resembles El Corral, and the semicircular rock-carved temple at Malinalco.

It is clear that cultural factors of this kind were taken into account in the establishment of the population centers of the Valley of Mexico and other parts of Mesoamerica. We have already explained that the city, according to the evidence available to us, was preceded by a concept: first it was imagined, and then it was built. Let us take as examples Cuicuilco and Teotihuacán, which from 200 BC to AD 150 had similar estimated populations—around 20,000 people—meaning that there were two major population centers in the Valley of Mexico, one in the south and one in the north. In both these cities, as in other Mesoamerican centers, the pyramidal foundations reveal strong astronomical, geographic, and topographic relationships. Underneath the pyramid, an allegory of the mountain, we find the cave. Thus, opposites are joined: the celestial and the terrestrial.

Now, we know that the Pyramids of the Sun (plates 92, 96) and the Moon (plates 93, 94) were built nearly simultaneously at Teotihuacán, followed a few years later by the Ciudadela, with the Temple of the Feathered Serpent at its core (plate 95). In all three cases, the calendar is present. I am certain that the ballgame, associated with the beginning of time and the construction of important pyramids, was played at Teotihuacán as well.

The excavations carried out by Rubén Cabrera, Saburo Sugiyama, and Leonardo López Luján at the Pyramid of the Moon revealed six stages of construction between AD 100 and 600 (figure 14). The first small building, located where the projecting front platform of the

92. View of the great Classic city of Teotihuacán in the State of México. In the foreground is the Plaza of the Moon, from which extends the Avenue of the Dead. The Pyramid of the Sun is visible at the left.

93. (top) The Pyramid of the Moon at Teotihuacán, AD 100–600, framed by Cerro Gordo.

94. (bottom) Another view of the Pyramid of the Moon, whose various phases of construction have been clarified by recent excavations.

pyramid is now, dates to the Tzacualli phase, AD 100, and is thus Teotihuacán's most ancient monumental structure. It is skewed slightly toward the west, leading the excavators to assume that it predates the site's urban grid, which would be strictly oriented 15°30' east of north. Building 2 belongs to the first half of the second century. Building 3, built about fifty years later, was completely destroyed. It was in this phase that the projecting platform was added to the pyramid's facade.[10] Each phase of construction was accompanied by propitiatory sacrifices, most of them of young foreigners. The excavators conclude that they were probably high-ranking, and perhaps prisoners of war.[11] In Burial 6, which corresponds to the final stage, there were also numerous skeletons of different animals. Thus the pyramid tells us a story of repeated constructions superimposed on the same site over the course of 500 years, both because the place was important in and of itself, and because burials and offerings belonging to high-ranking individuals were to be found there.

Teotihuacán presents us with an interesting coincidence of forms. The structure in front of the Pyramid of the Moon is unique in Mesoamerica: it has a perfectly square base, with sides about 65 feet (20 meters) long, and a single entrance facing west. Inside are ten altars positioned at the five cardinal points (the center and the four directions). In 1975, Otto Schondube noted that the plan of this building resembles the diagram on Folio 1 of the Codex Fejérváry-Mayer, which relates the 260-day ritual calendar to the cosmogram. In addition, Rubén Cabrera has pointed out the similarity between the plan of this building and the designs painted in Structure 1B' of the Ciudadela (plate 97). Here I would reemphasize the importance of the calendar, and of beliefs concerning the renewal of time, in the construction of buildings.

95. (*right*) The Ciudadela of Teotihuacán, with the Temple of the Feathered Serpent at its center. Late Formative.

96. (*overleaf*) The Pyramid of the Sun, Teotihuacán. Late Formative.

97. (*opposite top*) Mural in Structure 1B' of the Ciudadela, Teotihuacán. These designs, painted around AD 200, resemble the plan of the square structure in front of the Pyramid of the Moon, as well as a diagram found in the Codex Fejérváry-Mayer.

98. (*opposite bottom*) Tepantitla, one of the so-called residential compounds of Teotihuacán, which probably served as living quarters for groups dedicated to particular activities. The murals at Tepantitla represent various forms of the ballgame and are associated with name *puh*, *tollan*, or *tula*—the place of reeds, that is, the city. This suggests that the compound was inhabited by ballplayers, who were perhaps even priest-emissaries from different parts of Mesoamerica. Classic.

99. (*above*) Tetitla, another residential compound at Teotihuacán. Classic.

RESIDENTIAL COMPOUNDS AND PAINTINGS OF ARCHITECTURE AT TEOTIHUACÁN

Certain architectural forms are considered to be characteristic of Teotihuacán, such as the well-known *talud-tablero*, or slope-and-panel, system, or the so-called residential compounds. Despite the many excavations carried out in the city, the function of these latter structures has still not been definitely established. However, it is generally accepted that they were elite residences dedicated to specific activities; I believe that the Tepantitla compound, for example, was connected to the practice of the ballgame (plate 98). The residential compounds share some common traits, such as porticoed patios surrounded by rooms, and roofs supported by square-based pillars that are sometimes decorated with bas-reliefs. In the larger patios, we sometimes find an altar, as in the Tetitla (plate 99) or Atetelco compounds. The roofs display an open rectangle at the center, which seemingly had two purposes: to illuminate the interior, and to allow rainfall to accumulate in small pools that may have acted as a kind of impluvium, as in Tepantitla. The reflection of the sunlight or moonlight on the paintings that covered the surrounding chambers must have produced dramatic effects. On the flat rooftops around the

100. (*opposite top*) The Quetzalpapalotl Palace, or Palace of the Quetzal-butterfly, a residential compound at Teotihuacán, exhibits such characteristic features as a porticoed patio with carved pillars and battlements on the roof. The battlements, which are carved with the Teotihuacano year symbol (a trapezoid and ray), are placed so that their shadows align with the compound's mural paintings on significant dates. Classic.

101. (*opposite bottom*) The Teotihuacano Temple, Tikal, Guatemala. The bas-reliefs on this building display the "goggles" associated with the widely worshipped deity whom the Aztecs called Tlaloc. This is a notable instance of the conservation of visual resources: with just two circles, the building is made to personify the god of rain and time. Classic.

patio were placed battlements of various shapes that were sometimes used to make astronomical observations, as in the so-called Quetzalpapalotl Palace (plate 100).

Here I would like to identify some connections between mural painting and architecture that can help us to better understand the art of Teotihuacán. Starting from the knowledge that painting re-creates a time and space different than those experienced by the spectator, let us analyze some of the varied depictions of architecture that appear in Teotihuacán's murals. Representations of buildings appear, for example, in the paintings in Portico 14 of Tetitla, or those housed at the Museo de Murales Teotihuacanos Beatriz de la Fuente, which came from the Temple of the Feathered Snails in Portico 11 of Tetitla. In the latter murals, we see the image of a man dressed as a feline heading toward a temple (plate 102). This temple is covered with jaguar spots and crowned with feathers, making it a replica of the figure who reverently approaches it.

We encounter a related phenomenon in the Temple of Agriculture, whose murals may, I believe, be interpreted as anthropomorphic representations of a building. This will not seem strange to us if we recall how the "goggles" of Tlaloc adorn a vase from Copán or the Teotihuacano Temple itself at Tikal (plate 101). In fact, it seems to me that buildings were believed to possess the same kind of spiritual essence as the majority of the other animate and inanimate beings that populated the world. The mountain, the cave, the wind, the cloud: these were not merely objects of animistic worship, but shared in a vital respiration that united all beings, living or not.

This leads us to the topic of architectural images that are difficult to understand because they employ visual conventions different from our own. Pre-Columbian art often represents

what could not be seen in reality, like a simultaneous angle of vision showing the hidden side of things. Take for example the North Portico at Atetelco (plate 104). In this mural, which depicts a figure standing on a terraced platform, we see a *talud* that would not be visible to us if we were physically inside the space of the painting. By inverting the masks on this facade, the painter signals that he is representing the image from the other side.

Finally, let us consider how we might imagine the three-dimensional space of reality based on the images painted on the walls of Teotihuacán. According to Eduardo Matos, there was a moat surrounding the Pyramid of the Sun that, during the rainy season, collected the large quantity of water that slid down the pyramid's immense slopes.[12] This calls to mind the image

103. Mural in Portico 2 of the Tepantitla compound at Teotihuacán. Usually described as a representation of Tlalocan, a supernatural realm, this mural may also be seen as an allegorical depiction of the Pyramid of the Sun and the celebration of the ballgame in the Avenue of the Dead. Classic.

of the mountain that holds water within itself and is at the same time a fountain of life, whose waters flow forth and gather into channels. And in the murals of Tepantitla, we do in fact see a mountain from which water springs, flowing into channels and into an aquatic border at the sides and top of the image (plate 103); near this mountain are depicted some ballplayers. It is possible, then, that this mural represents the Pyramid of the Sun in the guise of the watery mountain, and the celebration of the ballgame—which set time in motion, as many documents of the sixteenth century attest—in the Avenue of the Dead to its west.

This interaction between painting and architecture does not merely represent the fusion of forms of expression that we normally think of as separate, but presents us with a construction of reality in which buildings exist both as physical entities and as symbols: the pyramid as a structural form, and as the mountain of sustenance.

THE ABANDONMENT OF TEOTIHUACÁN AND ITS REPERCUSSIONS IN MESOAMERICA

What took place in this city for it to be "abandoned"? There has been talk of invasion, disease, climate change, and social revolt—in other words, a series of explanations that seem logical from our own perspective. However, we must take into account that the Mesoamerican worldview included certain religious principles that do not factor into our own understanding of events. The so-called Pilgrimage Strip or Codex Boturini includes a scene that, for this reason, may elude our comprehension: Huitzilopochtli tells the people that they must set forth from Aztlán, and they weep, because once again they are leaving a home behind. We would propose that Teotihuacán was abandoned due to ideological factors that we may come to understand better in the future, and which affected not only this site in the Altiplano, but also the Maya zone. We must recall that the individuals sacrificed and buried in the Pyramid of the Moon were of foreign origin, and that the interaction between central Mexico and the Maya zone had been constant from ancient times. During the Classic period, this relationship seems to have been consolidated through the establishment of Teotihuacano dynasties in leading Maya cities. These connections, previously denied, prove that new answers must be sought for the unresolved questions about Mesoamerica in the sixth century.

No one doubts any longer the economic, political, social, and ideological importance that Teotihuacán had in Mesoamerica. That the deities we call Quetzalcóatl, the plumed serpent; Tlaloc, associated with rain and water; and Huehuetéotl, associated with fire, were worshipped across Mesoamerica seems to indicate religious bonds that spanned space and time. These three gods are related to lineage, and therein lies perhaps their lasting importance through the centuries, whenever some power attempted to claim Teotihuacán's past as its own.

The period following the abandonment of Teotihuacán is known in the central Altiplano as the Epiclassic. As we might imagine, it was a time of change and migration in which symbols and beliefs were adopted and adapted from various places. Eventually, other centers of regional significance appeared in the Valley of Mexico, such as Xochicalco, Cholula, and Cacaxtla.

104. Mural in the North Portico of the White Patio, Atetelco compound, Teotihuacán. Classic.

XOCHICALCO

According to Silvia Garza, Xochicalco (plates 105, 106) was founded on a hill around AD 650 by people whose advanced knowledge enabled them to choose a suitable location for a city that they had planned in advance.[13] They excavated or filled in the slopes of the hill to create great terraces that, finished and stuccoed, gave the impression of a gigantic pyramidal foundation from a distance.

Xochicalco is the clearest example of an Epiclassic city, surrounded by walls and incorporating major defensive systems within the settlement itself, namely ditches, barricades, stairways, and narrow doorways that restrict access to the different levels of the site. Avenues connect the city center to the hills of La Malinche, La Bodega, and Jumil.

The city is made up of complexes of patios surrounded by buildings. On the main plaza, in the highest part of the city, was built its most emblematic building, the Pyramid of Quet-

105, 106. (*left*) Aerial views of Xochicalco, a fortified Epiclassic site in the Valley of Cuernavaca, Morelos.

107. (*below*) The ballcourt at Xochicalco.

108, 109. (*above and overleaf*) The Pyramid of Quetzalcóatl at Xochicalco, c. AD 680, whose *tablero* is crowned by a small inverted *talud*. The split snails that appear on the serpent's body are a symbol of Quetzalcóatl.

zalcóatl (plates 108–12). We have already seen that this mythical being originated in the Ciudadela of Teotihuacán, where its body stretches across the *tableros* of the pyramid in bas-relief, with heads of the serpent and another supernatural being projecting from it in alternation, while the smaller *taludes* depict the head and body of the serpent in bas-relief. At Xochicalco, the undulations of the serpent in bas-relief create niches for different figures, and its body displays split snails, one of the symbols of Quetzalcóatl. The Ciudadela was linked to the calendar by the large number of burials found there, and calendrical associations are also apparent in the pyramid at Xochicalco, where we see numerous glyphs connected with years or days, as well as a hand pulling a cord attached to the 11 Monkey glyph. The importance of the concept of time is also implicit in the chronological distance between these two structures: centuries after the Ciudadela was built, the image of the plumed serpent was recalled at Xochicalco.

This city, like the ancient metropolis that preceded it, possesses buildings with clear astronomical orientations. These include the ballcourt, where the sun shines through the stone ring on the vernal equinox (plate 107); the famous observatory cave, whose main purpose was clearly to observe the passage of celestial bodies on certain dates; and the Pyramid of Quetzalcóatl itself.

The architecture of Xochicalco, like that of other Epiclassic cities, is eclectic. In Structure A, we find stairways protected by wide balustrades in the Oaxacan manner. Inverted *taludes* similar to those of the Maya zone were also used, as can be seen in the Pyramid of Quetzalcóatl. In this structure, the body of the serpent occupies a wide inward-sloping *talud*, while other reliefs are located on a protruding *tablero* crowned with a small inverted *talud* that acts as a cornice. We see the same arrangement in the Puuc district of the Maya zone, albeit with different proportions; there the *tablero* is a narrow band uniting the *taludes* above and below. The Pyramid of Quetzalcóatl has a stairway on its western side with balustrades formed by the rattles of the serpent; this stairway, like those of other buildings at the site, occupies about half the facade. Seen in elevation, the facade of this building is divided into three sections, the

110, 111. (*opposite*) Details
of bas-reliefs on the
Pyramid of Quetzalcóatl
at Xochicalco, showing
what might be glyphs,
perhaps toponyms.

112. (*above*) Another
detail of the Pyramid of
Quetzalcóatl at Xochi-
calco. Although this figure
has Maya features, he
wears a caiman or croco-
dile headdress similar
to those of the so-called
"sowing priests" and other
personages from Teoti-
huacán.

first consisting of the wide *talud* and the other two, of about equal height, being formed by the *tablero* and the third tier of the pyramid. Other noteworthy architectural features of Xochicalco include the use of pillars instead of columns, and the presence of a sweat lodge next to the ballcourt (plate 113). This type of structure was associated with the ballgame here and in other parts of Mesoamerica.

CHOLULA

The city of Cholula, which went through different phases of occupation, was located in a very fertile valley watered by the Atoyac River and its tributaries. Of all the archaeological sites in Mexico, this one is perhaps the most difficult to understand as an ancient urban center. Because its enormous mountain-pyramid is covered by vegetation and crowned with a Christian church, the so-called Plaza of the Altars does not appear to be integrated with it, but simply seems like an open space next to a hill (plate 114). If we tour the inside of the pyramid, the result is even less comprehensible, because the exploratory tunnels excavated by different

archaeologists over the years do not provide us with any external reference points; we cannot find our bearings in relation to the great foundation. And if we look at the arrangement of the buildings around the open space of the plaza, we understand even less, because the exposed ruins belong to different periods of occupation and stop when they reach the mountain; we come away only with the impression of a series of walls on different planes surrounding a small square.

But the site does provide a very eloquent image of the Conquest: the Christian church superimposed on the pyramidal foundation; the Tlalchihualtépetl, the hill made by hand, which for the indigenous people was a bridge to the divine, finished off with the temple of the new gods, whom they had to worship after being conquered.

The Great Pyramid's first phase of construction, around AD 100, corresponds to the so-called La Olla Building.[14] According to two archaeologists who worked at this site, Gabriela Uruñuela and Patricia Plunket, this structure had a short life, because it was covered by the Chapulines (Grasshoppers) Building, which displays fantastical, semiflayed beings with heads that look like human skulls, ants, or grasshoppers (plate 115). These authors have discovered at least eight stages of construction in all (figures 17–19), which is three more than were reported by Ignacio Marquina. It is difficult to reconcile these two accounts of the pyramid's history, not only because of the complexity of the excavations, but also because the authors use incon-

113. (above) The *temazcale*, or sweat lodge, at Xochicalco. Sweat lodges, which are generally associated with ballcourts, may have been used for rites of purification before or after a game. Epiclassic.

114. (*above*) View of
the Great Pyramid at
Cholula, Puebla, with
the Plaza of the Altars in
the foreground. Late
Formative–Postclassic.

115. (*below*) Detail of the
Chapulines (Grasshop-
pers) Building, the sec-
ond phase of the Great
Pyramid at Cholula.

sistent nomenclature. For example, Marquina refers to the successive structures sometimes by numbers and sometimes by letters, and in the more recent publication it is equally difficult to understand which building stage the authors are referring to, much less glean a detailed description of any one of them. Moreover, the numbering of the stages changed with the discovery of the La Olla Building, which then became Structure 1, whereas for Marquina the first building was Los Chapulines.

The difficulty of understanding the stages of the Great Pyramid's construction is further compounded by the fact that this structure, which we now think of as one whole, gradually swallowed entire complexes of plazas, buildings, altars, and stairways as it grew. Structure 2, or Los Chapulines, was made up of seven tiers and eventually reached a height of 56 feet (17 meters) (figures 20–22). This complex structure presents some unique characteristics, such as an adobe core. Uruñuela and Plunket believe that it is an allegory of Popocatépetl, which erupted around that time; they hypothesize that populations displaced from settlements near the volcano took refuge at Cholula.

If the chronology established by these archaeologists and by Marquina is correct, Los Chapulines is more or less contemporary with the Temple of the Feathered Serpent at Teotihuacán. The *talud-tablero* systems of these two buildings are similar, though the *tableros* of Los Chapulines are distinguished by a double molding. At Cholula the supernatural beings

on the facade were painted, and at Teotihuacán they were sculpted, but the visual solution is the same: the head is seen from the front, while the body is extended to one side. It is difficult to establish the total number of images painted in this manner at Cholula and record their dimensions and characteristics, because much of the structure is still covered by the next phase of construction. But once the entire building is known and its original appearance reconstructed, perhaps we will be able to tell whether it had any calendrical associations, as the structures at Teotihuacán and Xochicalco did.

The same *talud-tablero* profile with the double molding was used, almost without variation, in the next three phases of construction. The third pyramid measured 620 feet (190 meters) on each side and had nine tiers totaling 112 feet (34 meters) in height. Stairways and other features were added all around the structure. Some phases of the pyramid had mural paintings that are very well known today, such as the so-called Bebedores (Drinkers) (plate 117), which belongs to the same time period as other murals found in Cholula. The final phase of the pyramid covered all the previous ones.

In general, the architecture of Cholula is distinguished by a unique and characteristic treatment of facades. These typically include stairways, *tableros* with a double molding, and wide *taludes* with a 45° slope and geometrically patterned moldings, as in Building 3, which is located on the Plaza of the Altars and displays evidence of different structures belonging to the same phase (plate 116).

On the southern side of the Great Pyramid were found four residences that follow a pattern common to other sites, that of chambers constructed around a patio with an altar in the middle. Cholula has also yielded other, less important residential compounds that display a different pattern, in which the patio is located to one side of the structure.

The city experienced another volcanic eruption between AD 700 and 800,[15] which triggered significant changes. Moreover, the Olmec-Xicalancas arrived around AD 800, followed some time later by the Toltec-Chichimecas, who would bring about a major increase in Cholula's population and elevate its commercial and economic status, to which the chronicles of the Spanish conquerors bear witness.

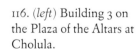

116. (*left*) Building 3 on the Plaza of the Altars at Cholula.

117. (*above*) The Mural of Los Bebedores (The Drinkers) at Cholula. The top register depicts participants in a ritual who drink what might be *pulque*, a beverage of fermented agave, and the bottom register is occupied by alternating knots and rhombuses.

118. (*top right*) Mural at Cacaxtla, Tlaxcala, AD 650–680, showing a battle between jaguar and bird warriors. The defeated bird warriors are realistically depicted as captive, wounded, or dead.

119. (*bottom right*) A stairway at Cacaxtla, AD 650–850.

CACAXTLA

Located in the Puebla-Tlaxcala Valley, the site of Cacaxtla was occupied for a long time, but did not undergo intense building activity until the period between AD 650 and 850. In those years, the local environment was very different than it is today. Because the water table was higher, there were permanent lagoons that have since dried up, such as that of El Rosario, and the land around the site was excellently suited for cultivation. A fortified redoubt located on a butte that shows signs of human modification, Cacaxtla was well protected by natural cliffs and man-made ditches. In their general form, its buildings are not too different from others found in Mexico, with porticoed patios, roofs supported by pillars, and stairs connecting one structure to another (plate 119). What distinguishes Cacaxtla is rather its mural paintings (plate 118) and a wealth of decorative solutions that combine architectural ornaments from other sites—such as lattices, moldings, recesses, different textures, columns, and pillars—as well as a fusion of painting, polychromed relief sculpture, and architecture that we can only imagine today. Archaeologists have recovered numerous pieces of what seems to have been a polychromed bas-relief with flowers and corncobs, although we do not know its architectural context. While Cacaxtla is best known for its paintings, few other sites have combined color and three-dimensional forms so creatively.

TULA

This site, located in what is now the state of Hidalgo, was given the name Tula, or Tollan, which literally means "place of reeds" and is a metaphor of gathering many together, and hence of the city. We know that there were several sites with this same name: Tollan Cholollan, Tollan Teotihuacán, Tollan Tenochtitlán, and Tollan Xicocotitlán, which is the one that retained this appellation and which we will now discuss. There is still an ongoing debate about the suggestion, made by Bishop Francisco Blancarte in the early twentieth century, that the Tula mentioned in sixteenth-century sources is Teotihuacán.

Tula is the sister city of Chichén Itzá, although we can no longer claim to be certain about why their artistic styles are so clearly related. It was long believed that the fierce Itzás, originating in the central Altiplano, had brutally conquered the peaceful, civilized Maya and imposed on them the customs of human sacrifice and war. However, the archaeological evidence has put an end to the traditional perception of the Maya as "noble savages" and the inhabitants of the central plateau as their barbaric opposites, and we are once more left in doubt as to the exact nature of the relationship between these two poles of Mesoamerican culture. Indeed, we have had to abandon many other paradigms of Mesoamerican history that were based on Europeanizing preconceptions, such as Laurette Séjourné's claim that Teotihuacán was a "paradise of Queztalcóatl" where there was no human sacrifice and the people were not warlike.

120. Pyramid B, Tula, Hidalgo, AD 900–1200. In front of this structure, which was dedicated to Tlahuizcalpantecuhtli, or Venus as the morning star, we see the remnants of pillars that once held up the roof of a portico.

The various debates about Tula are further complicated by the question of its relationship with northern Mesoamerica and the probable northern origin of the figure known as the Chacmool, which is associated both with this period and with Tula. In fact, a number of other cultural traits, such as the presence of circular buildings, link Tula to northern Mexico and the Huastec region, and the city's geographic location provides it with access to La Quemada and other Chalchihuite sites in the north, and to Huastec sites like Tamohi, Tamtoc, and Tancol on the Gulf Coast. Marie-Areti Hers, who has thoroughly studied these cultural connections, has demonstrated that the notion of the savage Chichimecs has no basis in the archaeological reality of the sites excavated in northern Mesoamerica.

Like other cities that flourished in the Epiclassic, Tula had a long history of occupation but did not become important until after the abandonment of Teotihuacán. The earliest developments properly attributable to the so-called Toltec Tula belong to the period AD 650–750/800, which corresponds to the Prado phase of ceramics localized in the part of the site known as Tula Chico.[17] (Prado wares belong to the broader Coyotlatelco ceramic complex, which is also found at Teotihuacán in this era.) The first settlements around Tula in this period were located mostly in high places, perhaps for defensive purposes.

At one such site, known as La Mesa, there were found circular buildings and elevated rectangular structures with pillared porticoes. Guadalupe Mastache and Robert Cobean remark

121. The Burned Palace at Tula, AD 900–1200. The roofs of its porticoes and three contiguous chambers were supported alternately by columns and pillars.

that these types of structure differ conceptually from those of Teotihuacán, because they are not group lodgings built around patios, while Verónica Hernández notes that their walls are made with stone slabs, recalling the western style. According to these authors, both the circular and the rectangular structures are domestic in nature, and may be considered antecedents of the system of construction that would be used in Tula at the city's peak in AD 900 to 1150, a period known as the Tollan phase.

Because Tula, like other Pre-Columbian cities in Mexico, has been partially obliterated by the encroachment of modern settlements, it is impossible to obtain a complete plan of the site. However, we can see that the city underwent three distinct phases of settlement, the transitions between them being clearly marked by a change in the orientation of the buildings. For example, Tula Chico seems to have been sacked and burned between 800 and 850, after which a new ceremonial precinct, known as Tula Grande, was constructed and the urban layout modified. We are uncertain as to the causes of this change.

Mastache and Cobean have identified certain similarities between the plans of Tula Grande

122. Atop Pyramid B at Tula, AD 900–1200, we find the well-known Warriors or Atlantes, as well as other columns in the form of the plumed serpent.

and Teotihuacán. Both cities had a smaller pyramidal foundation facing south and a larger one facing west (figures 16, 23). Furthermore, Ballcourt 2 at Tula Grande has a north-south orientation, as does the Avenue of the Dead at Teotihuacán. (In the earlier ceremonial precinct at Tula Chico, the ballcourt had apparently occupied a corresponding position.)

Tula's better-known pyramid is the smaller, south-facing one, which is known as Pyramid B, or Tlahuizcalpantecuhtli (plate 120). On the uppermost of its five tiers are found the remains of the human-shaped columns known as the Warriors or Atlantes, which alternate with columns in the form of the plumed serpent (plate 122). The figurated column, one of the most novel and expressive architectural solutions to emerge from this time period, is employed at Tula with a mastery not encountered elsewhere, even at its sister city in the Maya zone, Chichén Itzá. In the porticoes and chambers of the so-called Burned Palace, on the other hand, we encounter a combination of pillars and columns (plate 121; figure 24). This inclusion of different kinds of supports in the same structure is a noteworthy contribution of Toltec architecture, as are the use of decorated benches and the fusion of sculpture, bas-relief, and painting.

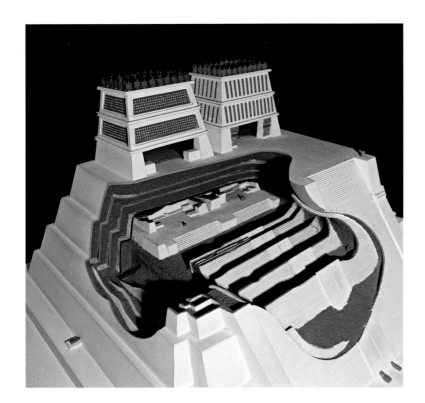

AZTEC-MEXICA ARCHITECTURE

The chronicles of the Conquest record the great amazement that the Spaniards felt when they arrived at the capital of the vast territory dominated by the Aztecs. Bernal Díaz del Castillo compares the monumental buildings and wide avenues of Tenochtitlán to the tales of fantastical cities in the book of Amadis, a popular chivalric romance, and Cortés himself, in his *Cartas de Relación*, says that the houses of the Iztapalapa district were as large and well constructed as those of Spain.

Díaz del Castillo tells us of the view from the Templo Mayor, and also about the three causeways that connected the island city to the mainland, the aqueducts that supplied it with fresh water, and the canoes that brought provisions to the city from all over the valley. These were precisely the supply lines that the conquerors would sever when they laid siege to the city, leaving it defenseless.

At the time of the Spaniards' arrival, Tenochtitlán was the center of a far-reaching network of economic, political, and social dominion and exchange (plate 131). The city had emerged as the leading force in the Valley of Mexico after numerous wars, which had resulted in the subjugation of the neighboring lords and the formation of the so-called Triple Alliance with Tacuba and Texcoco. This laid the groundwork for the expansion of Aztec power throughout much of Mesoamerica, a power that was consolidated by the collection of tributes from conquered communities. However, the Aztecs did not truly unify the territory they acquired, but instead controlled the subject populations by force. In the end, this would be the seed of their empire's destruction.

While Tenochtitlán was naturally preceded by a centuries-long tradition of urbanism and architecture, it was at the same time a new foundation. According to the Aztecs, their tutelary deity Huitzilopochtli had guided their pilgrimage from Aztlán or Chicomostoc to the site where the new city was to be built. A passage from Fray Diego Durán's account of the city's

123. (*left*) Model of the Templo Mayor of Tenochtitlán, AD 1325–1521, showing its successive stages of construction, as well as the two sanctuaries at its peak, one dedicated to Tlaloc and the other to Huitzilopochtli.

124. (*right*) The Templo Mayor, Tenochtitlán.

founding will illustrate the richness of the Aztecs' messianic conception of this event:

When the Aztecs heard what Cuauhtlequetzqui had said, they humbled themselves before their deity. They gave thanks to the Lord of All Created Things, of Day and Night, Wind and Fire. Then, dividing into different groups, they went into the swamp, searching among the reeds and rushes. Thus they found again the spring they had seen the day before. But the water on that day had been clear and transparent, and it now flowed out in two streams, one red like blood, the other so blue and thick that it filled the people with awe. Having seen these mysterious things [where the red and blue waters flowed as one], the Aztecs continued to seek [the omen of] the eagle whose presence had been foretold. Wandering from one place to another, they soon discovered the prickly pear cactus. On it stood the eagle with his wings stretched out toward the rays of the sun, basking in their warmth and the freshness of the morning. In his talons he held a bird with very fine feathers, precious and shining. When the people saw the eagle they humbled themselves, making reverences as if the bird were a divine thing. The eagle, seeing them, also humbled himself, bowing his head low in their direction. When the Aztecs observed the actions of the eagle, they realized they had come to the end of their journey, so they began to weep and dance about with joy and contentment.[18]

Like other cities founded in accordance with higher precepts, Mexico City was established on a large island among swamps surrounded by beds of bulrushes or reeds: Tollan Tenochtitlán. The initial size of this island was increased by an ingenious system of water and land management: the *chinampas*, which were created by heaping earth on a frame staked out in the water. These artificial gardens were anchored by the trees planted at their corners, whose roots grew down into the lake bed. However, the instability of the city's swampy ground has always caused its residents serious problems: several stages of the Templo Mayor were constructed in order to repair damage to the previous stage caused by settling. Building a city

125. (*left*) Sculpture of an undulating serpent over 20 ft. (18 m) long, located on the southern edge of the platform that supported the Templo Mayor. Period IVb (c. 1470).

126. (*right*) Stairway accessing the Precinct of the Eagle Warriors, to the north of the Templo Mayor. Period IV (c. 1500).

under these circumstances also required a great deal of hydraulic engineering, in order to contain the waters of the lake with dikes, maintain irrigation channels, and construct streets and avenues on the swampy terrain. Before the Aztecs, no one had attempted such an enterprise in the hydrological basin of the Valley of Mexico.

Because the ancient Tenochca capital was buried by colonial Mexico City, our knowledge of its urban plan is based on documentary sources and archaeological excavations. We do know that the Pre-Columbian city was divided into four main neighborhoods or *calpulli*: Cuepopan, Moyotla, Zoquiapan, and Atzacoalco.[19] Each of these had a tutelary deity, a school, and one-story homes, those of two stories being reserved for the ruling class and located in the center of the city. The four-part division of the city was nothing new in Mesoamerica, being based on the ancient division of the cosmos into four quadrants, which is amply documented by the sixteenth-century chroniclers. The Maya believed that the quadrants of the cosmos were supported by the Atlas-like *bacabes*, while on pages 27 and 28 of the Codex Borgia, the quadrants are represented by four Tlalocs. Another Tlaloc occupies the fifth point of the cosmogram, the center, which in the case of Tenochtitlán was defined by the Templo Mayor.

Aztec architecture owed a great deal to the traditions of Teotihuacán and Tula; serpents adorned the balustrades of stairways, as at Teotihuacán, and benches were covered with polychromed bas-reliefs, as at Tula. Aztec temples, like those of other Mesoamerican cultures, were placed atop pyramidal foundations constructed around a plaza. Here, as elsewhere, the pyramid was an allegory of the mountain and its counterpart the cave, the place of origin. The immediate reference was to Chicomostoc, the Place of the Seven Caves, from whence the Aztec migration began, but this was blended with many other concepts borrowed from the diverse peoples that made up the Aztec empire.

Dual temples were common, and according to Pasztory, Chichimecan in origin. The best-

127. (*below*) The Post-classic settlement of Tenayuca, which was occupied by the Toltecs of Tula, has now been almost entirely absorbed by the outskirts of Mexico City. Its pyramid displays a great double stairway, divided by a double balustrade.

128. (*opposite*) Mount Tlaloc, Tlaxcala. The path between these parallel drystone walls, now tumbled over, led to a sanctuary of the rain god that was one of the most important sites in the sacred geography of the Aztecs. Fray Diego Durán describes an annual procession to this mountaintop, which is located near the volcanoes Ixtachihuatl and Popocatépetl. Late Post-classic.

known example, whose antecedent may have been the double pyramid at nearby Tenayuca (plate 127), is the Templo Mayor: a double stairway ascended its pyramidal foundation, which was crowned by two sanctuaries, one dedicated to Tlaloc, and the other to Huitzilopochtli (plates 123–26, 134). Thanks to the excavations coordinated by Eduardo Matos, all seven phases of construction of the Templo Mayor have been revealed; in its first phase, the pyramid was constructed of perishable materials, as were other early buildings at Tenochtitlán.[20] Matos and his colleague Leonardo López Luján believe that the tomb of the ruler Ahuizotl (r. 1486–1502) may be located beneath a spectacular monolith of an earth goddess that was

129. (*right*) Malinalco, a ceremonial center in the State of México, was partly carved from the living rock of a mountainside shortly after AD 1500. Its Temple of the Eagles and Jaguars may have been a site of initiation for warriors.

132. (*below left*) View of El Tepozteco, a mountain near the site of Tepoztlán, Morelos, which was conquered by the Aztecs. A temple dedicated to the deities of *pulque*, a beverage of fermented agave, was built on the mountain, perhaps at the command of the Aztec ruler Ahuizotl (r. 1486–1502).

133. (*below right*) Interior of the temple at Malinalco, showing the skin of a feline carved on a bench and the eagle at the center of the chamber, with a hollow in its back.

130. (*opposite top*) The site of Calixtlahuaca, located in the Valley of Toluca in the State of México, was originally a Matlatzinca settlement. A masterful statue of Ehécatl-Quetzalcóatl was found in the temple seen here.

131. (*opposite bottom*) One of the most important markets in the central Altiplano was held at Tlatelolco, which was located on the same island as Tenochtitlán. The two cities were rivals until the Aztec ruler Axayacatl (r. 1469–1481) conquered Tlatelolco after a long siege and reportedly killed its ruler Moquihuitz himself. The plaza at Tlatelolco has been the site of further bloody episodes in Mexican history, such as the massacre of student protesters on October 2, 1968, and a devastating building collapse caused by the earthquake of September 19, 1985.

discovered near the pyramid in October 2006. The Templo Mayor is also remarkable for the diverse offerings that were found there, many from very distant territories. David Carrasco, one of the most distinguished scholars of this period, has interpreted these offerings in terms of the concept of center and periphery: the delivery of tributes from the periphery of the Aztec empire to the temple at its center symbolically unified the empire, and ensured the economic dominance of its capital. Matos's work has also shown that this ceremonial precinct was not only the center of Tenochtitlán but of the entire Aztec empire, with all the ideological burden that this implies.

We may also learn much about Aztec architecture from sites outside Tenochtitlán. For example, the remains of the mountaintop sanctuaries at Mount Tlaloc (plate 128) and Tetzcotzingo have yielded evidence of rituals linked to water and of processions that recalled the migrations that gave rise to the royal houses of the Mexica cities.[21] And during the reign of Ahuizotl, the construction of Aztec temples and administrative buildings was extended to sites

on the periphery of the empire, such as Tepoztlán in the Valley of Morelos. The Aztecs staked their claim to this site by building a temple on El Tepozteco, the mountain that overlooks it (plate 132); Ahuizotl's name appears in an inscription in the temple chamber.

The Aztecs also built atop the mountains that dominate the Matlatzinca region, which had been subjugated by the ruler Axayacatl (r. 1469–1481) in 1476.[22] One of the most important of these mountain sites was at Malinalco, a place that had a mythico-historical importance for the Aztecs, who believed it had been settled by the goddess Malinalxóchitl after she was separated from her brother Huitzilopochtli during the migration. The temple at Malinalco may be thought of not only as architecture but also as a work of sculpture, since it is carved out of the living rock (plates 129, 133). Like certain other Mesoamerican buildings, its entrance is adorned with the giant jaws of a feline or serpent; this might indicate that the temple was a site of initiation, in which the participant was "swallowed" by a supernatural being. Inside is a long bench with carvings of two birds and, on the central axis, a feline. At the center of the building, at a lower level than the bench, is a monumental sculpture of an eagle. This pairing of the feline and eagle, possibly in the context of initiation ceremonies, may allude to the jaguar and eagle warriors. These were Aztec military orders, frequently mentioned in documentary sources and also depicted in sculpture, that followed a strict disciplinary code. Ahuizotl apparently visited Malinalco in the first year of his reign, and perhaps celebrated some propitiatory ceremony inside the temple. Furthermore, according to Townsend, the orifice located between the eagle and the feline was used to pour offerings of blood into the earth. All this evidence suggests that the temple was devoted to a set of complementary practices—the offering of the blood of the ruler, propitiatory rituals, and divination—that celebrated the brotherhood of the two military orders and were restricted to a very select circle, including the ruler and his closest lieutenants. Malinalco is also noteworthy for its astronomical associations.

Another Matlatzinca settlement with Aztec remains is Calixtlahuaca. This site has a circular Aztec temple that is believed to have been dedicated to the worship of Ehécatl, Quetzalcóatl in the guise of the wind god (plate 130), because a magnificent statue of that deity was found inside it. There are evident similarities between El Corral at Tula and the temple at Calixtlahuaca.

With this site, which illustrates the deep connections through time and space that exist in Mesoamerican architecture, we will end our tour of the central Altiplano. At times, the sites in this region present us with difficulties of interpretation, either because of the complexity of the archaeological deposits resulting from the prolonged occupation of a single place, as at Cholula, or because ancient buildings have been obliterated by post-Conquest construction, as in Mexico City. Nevertheless, the great variety and high artistic quality of the Pre-Columbian architecture of the central Altiplano is still very much apparent.

134. Standard bearers on the stairway to the sanctuary of Huitzilopochtli, Templo Mayor, Tenochtitlán.

6
WESTERN MEXICO

VERÓNICA HERNÁNDEZ DÍAZ

The western part of Mesoamerica is expansive, and its geography is highly varied; it comprises what are now the states of Sinaloa, Nayarit, Jalisco, Colima, Michoacán, Guanajuato, and southeastern Zacatecas (figure 25). The peoples who inhabited this region during its long Pre-Columbian history created singular architectural works, such as elaborate chamber tombs and compounds with concentric circular layouts. Indeed, the societies of the west are characterized by the originality of their architecture and other cultural expressions. Precisely for this reason, there still exists a certain prejudice that has caused their legacy to be ignored or misunderstood, and has even contributed to its mass destruction.[1] Here we will offer a brief survey of the architecture of some of the principal western cultures, focusing on the forms most characteristic of the region, such as the chamber tombs and circular compounds, as well as certain types of ornament. Our examination of the forms, techniques, materials, functions, and symbolism of this architecture will not only reveal the ways in which it is unique, but also how it fits into the broader panorama of Mesoamerican art.

SPACES IN THE UNDERWORLD

Over the course of two thousand years, from around 1500 BC to AD 600, the inhabitants of the west maintained a rich funerary tradition, providing the dead with offerings of masterful sculptures and ceramic vases—among other objects—and interring them in subterranean spaces (plate 135). They developed a funerary architecture—not visible on the surface—whose forms, method of construction, and locations reveal a radical unity in the mortuary customs and religious beliefs of the El Opeño and Capacha cultures, as well as the so-called shaft tomb culture.

Funerary structures were uncommon in other parts of ancient Mexico, where direct burials beneath the floors of residential areas predominated. And even among the tombs that we do find elsewhere in Mesoamerica, those of the west stand alone on account of their method of construction: they did not have walls or vaults built from stone blocks or slabs, but were dug entirely out of the *tepetate*—a hard layer of subsoil composed of volcanic tuff—which was left exposed in the interior of the tomb. These architectural works may be conceived of as negative spaces,[2] because they were created by hollowing out a solid mass until the desired forms were

135. Reconstruction of a shaft tomb located in Zapopan, Jalisco. Museo Regional de Guadalajara.

attained. Given that wooden or stone tools were used, this process was extremely laborious, especially in those tombs that achieve colossal dimensions. Another distinctive feature of this class of tombs is that they were sometimes grouped into cemeteries, that is, areas dedicated exclusively to the burial of the dead. Some were even reused over the course of centuries, in the manner of family crypts.

The archaeological evidence indicates that the first manifestations of this tradition date to 1500 or 1300 BC, at the site of El Opeño in Michoacán,[3] where a complex and organized pattern of funerary practices can be traced over a long period of time. At this site a line of twelve tombs descend the gentle slope of Cerro Curutarán, near Zamora (figure 27).[4] Although their dimensions vary, they all follow the same general plan, consisting of a passageway with three to nine steps leading down to the tomb chamber through an opening that was sealed with one or more slabs (figure 28). The chamber is roughly rectangular in plan, with a vaulted roof. The floor is uneven, with benches on the north and south sides, also carved into the *tepetate*. The entrance is always oriented toward the west, the direction in which the sun sets, starting out—according to Mesoamerican beliefs—on its path through the underworld, in close contact with the world of the dead. As far as dimensions are concerned, those of the largest tomb—number 7—are surprising: its passageway is 6½ feet (2 meters) wide, 40 feet (12 meters) long, and more than 23 feet (7 meters) deep; the chamber is 30 feet (9 meters) long, 13½ feet (4.1 meters) wide, and up to 7 feet (2.1 meters) high.[5]

Around 800 BC, the basic model of the tombs dug out of the *tepetate* changed: they were no longer entered through a passageway with stairs, but rather through a well or vertical shaft that opened onto one or more chambers at the bottom. Several tombs of this date, and with these characteristics, have recently been discovered in the Mascota Valley, Jalisco; they are associated with the Capacha culture.[6]

THE ARCHITECTURE OF THE SHAFT TOMB CULTURE

Despite the gaps in our knowledge, we may assume that this subterranean architecture continued in the following centuries. We do know for certain that a boom took place between 300 BC and AD 600, when the shaft tomb culture developed, expanding throughout the southern half of Nayarit, Jalisco, Colima, southeastern Zacatecas, and western Michoacán.[7] Across this vast territory, the construction of shaft tombs was a massive phenomenon. Not only members of the elite were buried in this manner, but the general population as well,[8] although the design and size of the tombs indicate hierarchical differences among their occupants and perhaps variations in people's tastes over time and from place to place; that is to say, changes in fashion. Out of these sepulchres have come the most famous ceramic art of the west.

The shaft tomb culture presents a stylistic complex comprising four art forms that take the earth as their material: clay sculptures in a naturalistic style, ceramic vases decorated with geometric compositions that recall cosmograms, a subterranean architecture whose organic forms recall the maternal womb, and a surface architecture whose geometric forms may be interpreted as a representation of the cosmos.[9]

THE NATURALISTIC AND THE GEOMETRIC

Peter T. Furst has compared the form of the shaft tombs with the maternal womb: the shaft is the vagina, and the chamber, the uterus; thus this method of burial signifies a "rebirth," or an inverse birth.[10] (In Mesoamerican cosmology, the earth is conceived of as a source of fertility, birth, and death.) This interpretation may also be applied to the tombs with stairways at El Opeño, since they too consist of a narrow passage leading to a burial chamber.

Given the organic, feminine form of these tombs and the fact that they are excavated in the bowels of the earth, they might be seen as artificial caves. This interpretation would confer a sacred character on these sepulchres, because in Mesoamerica caves were associated with places of origin and with communication with the ancestors. Even though *tepetate* tombs are almost exclusive to the west,[11] it is evident that their makers shared certain fundamental concepts with the rest of Pre-Columbian Mexico.

In the region where the shaft tomb culture flourished, we find many variations on the basic model that we have described (figure 29). The shaft of the tomb may have a circular or quadrangular cross section, and is generally about 3 feet (1 meter) wide and 6½ to 10 feet (2 to 3 meters) deep, although there is one tomb that reaches a depth of 72 feet (22 meters).[12] They frequently possess a single chamber (figure 29a), but sometimes will have two (figure 29b). There is an extraordinary case of a tomb with five chambers and a shaft 49 feet deep (15 meters), a true subterranean complex (figure 29c).[13] Another singular example presents three shafts with two chambers (figure 29d). In terms of form, the shaft can be located in the center of the chamber's ceiling (a bottle-shaped tomb; figure 29e), or to one side (a boot-shaped tomb; figure 29a); some shafts have steps, as at El Opeño, albeit without an entry passageway (figure 29f). After the dead and their offerings were deposited in the burial chamber, the entrance to the chamber was sealed with slabs or pots, and then the shaft was filled with layers of fine soil.[14] The chamber may have an elliptical, rectangular, or quadrangular layout; the floor is flat, sometimes with low outcroppings like "shelves"; the ceilings are vaulted, ranging from quite low to over 6½ feet (2 meters) high in some cases.

We may gain a better idea of this architecture of the underworld from a description of the deepest and most complex shaft tomb to have been the subject of a detailed archaeological excavation.[15] This tomb is located in El Arenal, in the town of Etzatlán, Jalisco (plates 136, 137 and figures 26 and 29g). It has a quadrangular shaft with perfectly vertical walls, measuring 3 feet (1 meter) per side and reaching a depth of 52 feet (16 meters). At its base, two tunnels or passageways lead to their respective burial chambers, one of which is connected to a third chamber. All three rooms are very spacious and have quadrangular plans (the largest measuring 13 feet 11 inches by 12 feet 10 inches, or 4.24 by 3.9 meters), with floors paved with stone slabs, shelves carved in the walls, and vaulted ceilings (the highest measuring 9½ feet, or 2.89 meters).

In the central part of Jalisco, among the foothills of the Tequila volcano, we find tombs with more elaborate designs and greater dimensions. According to certain purely materialistic explanations, these characteristics may be attributed to the quality of the subsoil in this area. However, it is clear that the social rank of their occupants was taken into account in the construction of these tombs: even where the terrain is favorable, only a minority of them are colossal.

136, 137. The tomb at El Arenal, Etzatlán, Jalisco, studied by José Corona Núñez in 1955: views of the shaft and one of the three chambers. Late Formative–Early Classic.

I believe that throughout the shaft tomb region—Nayarit, Jalisco, Colima, and bordering areas in Zacatecas and Michoacán—the variations among tombs obeyed local modes and tastes, and distinctions of rank were indicated through architectural features and the quantity and quality of offerings, among other means. I would nevertheless emphasize the collective character of this architecture, which follows the same basic model and was used by the community as a whole, reflecting shared concepts, beliefs, and related practices. The importance of these uterus-tombs was such that they were built even in zones where geological conditions were unfavorable due to a lack of compactness in the soil. In these cases, a cavity might be excavated and given walls and a ceiling of slabs, creating a tomb with a well and a lateral chamber (figure 29h);[16] another solution was to dig a tomb with the desired shape, deposit the bodies, and finally, to avoid possible collapse, fill both the chamber and the shaft with earth.[17]

In other parts of Mesoamerica there are only isolated cases of tombs dug into the *tepetate*. However, they are abundant in South America, in Colombia, Ecuador, and Peru. According to the current data, this architectural type appeared first in western Mesoamerica, as the tombs at El Opeño in Michoacán and in the Mascota Valley in Jalisco show. However, in both the Americas, the datings are scarce and hardly represent an adequate sample. Meanwhile, it is a fact that various cultures of northwest South America constructed this kind of funerary architecture simultaneously with the shaft tomb culture of western Mesoamerica, although in the former region the practice persisted until the Spanish Conquest, for example among the Incas.[18] Some indigenous groups in Colombia and Peru even buried their dead in shaft tombs with lateral chambers as late as the 1960s.[19] The precise origin of the shaft tomb has long been sought, but ultimately it is best to leave aside diffusionist theories that rely on the concept of unique invention and consider instead the varied elements that so eloquently indicate historical links between far-flung societies.

138. Los Guachimontones, Teuchitlán, Jalisco, a site of the shaft tomb culture. Late Formative–Early Classic.

Returning to the shaft tombs of western Mesoamerica, aside from being grouped together in cemeteries, they are found beneath ceremonial surface structures that have a concentric circular plan. In this union between the worlds of the dead and the living, architecture displays two formal schemes: a naturalistic one for the dead, and a geometric one for the living. According to my interpretation, these are distinct yet complementary artistic languages that present an integrated vision of the cosmos, in which the subterranean and the aboveground are linked. In particular, the geometric layout of the surface architecture expresses the concept of a perfect, dynamic arrangement of the universe.

A CIRCULAR ORDER

The pattern of ceremonial architecture typical of the shaft tomb culture consists of a central terraced building with a circular plan and a flat top, surrounded by a ring-shaped patio that is in turn bordered by a circular bench supporting a series of eight, ten, twelve, or sixteen rectangular platforms (figures 30, 32). One variation exhibits four platforms surrounding the central mound in a cruciform arrangement (figures 31, 33); another variation presents a rather small central building. This type of complex is usually called a *guachimontón*; hence the site where the most exemplary remains of this kind are found, in Teuchitlán, Jalisco, is called Los Guachimontones (plates 138, 139). Its exploration may be considered recent, since it began in 1969 under Phil C. Weigand,[20] who with his attentive gaze was able to discover this site and reject the traditional prejudices which maintained that the western cultures before AD 600 had not created a formal architecture using nonperishable materials.

The concentric circular arrangement of these structures is unique in ancient Mexico, in contrast with the predominantly orthogonal design of other cultures' pyramids, patios, and plazas. Moreover, they are distinguished from other buildings with circular layouts—such as

139. One of the circular complexes at Los Guachimontones. Late Formative–Early Classic.

those of Cuicuilco and Xochitécatl in the central Altiplano or those in the Huastec mountains of the northeast—in that they are not individual structures, but part of a larger concentric complex. The Central Building of Los Guachimontones is also unique in that it has no stairways or ramps and was not surmounted by a temple.

Various other *guachimontones* are found at the same site, with different numbers of surrounding platforms. They are not separated from each other, but rather interact gracefully: frequently they share a section of the circular bench and one of the rectangular platforms that rests on it. This original arrangement also incorporates a pan-Mesoamerican architectural type: the *guachimontones* are often associated with ballcourts with an I-shaped plan, that is, with platforms on both sides and on both ends (plate 140). As is well known, the ballgame was one of the most important Mesoamerican rituals, with strong political and religious overtones; the courts were typically located near the highest-ranking precincts, and the game was associated with the underworld, sacrifice, fertility, and the establishment of the equilibrium of the cosmos, and served as a way of resolving conflicts between communities, such as property disputes.[21]

Weigand, the principal investigator of this architecture and of related elements of the present-day landscape (such as zones of habitation and resource exploitation, and hydraulic works)—which as a whole he calls the "Teuchitlán tradition"—has found numerous sites with *guachimontones* on the central high plains of Jalisco, in the vicinity of the Tequila volcano.[22] Outside of this area, in the rest of the shaft tomb territory, the distribution of circular complexes appears to be sparse and irregular.[23] This could be due to the fact that this is an enormous territory where there is still much to be learned, particularly about this kind of architecture whose discovery is so recent, and a great deal of which has surely been destroyed.

140. Ballcourt at Los Guachimontones. Late Formative–Early Classic.

In my judgment, the various evidence that we do have allows us to attribute the construction of *guachimontones* to the shaft tomb culture in general.[24]

Among the sites where circular complexes have been recorded, Los Guachimontones is the only one whose structures have been cleared and restored, and which is officially open to the public (plate 141). The site, whose peak period of construction was from AD 1 to 350, occupies 50 acres (20 hectares) and presents two ballcourts and nine concentric circular compounds of various sizes. The total diameter of the largest is around 425 feet (130 meters); its main building, which is impossible to reconstruct because of destruction and looting, was originally perhaps 60 feet (18 meters) high and is surrounded by a ring-shaped bench that supports twelve platforms, each one of which measures 50 by 65 feet (16 by 20 meters) on average.[25]

Behind the platforms on the southwest side there is a plaza in the shape of a half moon, parallel to the curvature of a hill that is terraced like an amphitheater. This amphitheater, which underlines the ceremonial and public character of the architecture of Los Guachimontones, would have permitted a large number of spectators to witness the ceremonies that took place at the site: it offers a panoramic view that, among other things, allows us to appreciate more easily the concentric circular arrangement of the *guachimontones*, and it has excellent acoustics.

In other *guachimontones* that have been restored at this site, we can see the terraced body of the main building, each step of which is about 1½ feet (50 centimeters) high. The longer of the two ballcourts—300 by 30 feet (90 by 9.5 meters)—is located in the central part of the site, between three *guachimontones* (two of which are the site's largest), some of whose rectangular platforms serve as the sides of the ballcourt.

That this was an earthen architecture, constructed with stone fill and successive layers of compacted clay,[26] underscores the radical importance of the earth in this culture's various

141. View of three circular complexes at Los Guachimontones. Late Formative–Early Classic.

artistic creations. We have already mentioned that *guachimontones* have been found above shaft tombs, although the design of this surface architecture was unfortunately not recognized before Weigand's discovery. For example, the impressive sepulchre at El Arenal, Jalisco, described in the previous section, was located beneath one of the rectangular platforms surrounding the circular mound of a *guachimontón*. Twenty-one more tombs were found beneath this same complex,[27] which shared a rectangular platform with another *guachimontón* next to it.

ARCHITECTURAL REPRESENTATIONS OF THE COSMOS

The ceremonial architecture of the shaft tomb culture offers multiple levels of interpretation that, together, form an integral vision of the cosmos. The structures were intentionally designed to express symbolic messages.[28] On the vertical axis, they created a duality that can be understood in various ways. On the one hand, there are the uterus-tombs of Mother Earth, which belong to the underworld, the place of the dead that is, at the same time, the place of the genesis of life; and on the other hand, there are the *guachimontones*, which belong to the world above ground, the place of the living, with the heavens overhead. This scheme creates a bilateral symmetry of opposites: feminine/masculine, dark/light, death/life, below/above. While these pairs of elements are antagonistic, they also complement each other and form part of the same whole.

On the horizontal plane, the design of the *guachimontón* presents a noteworthy central element, whose circular plan lends it a permanently dynamic character, as no angles interrupt the movement around its perimeter. Toward its surroundings, the circle radiates an expansive visual force that is materialized by the ring-shaped patio and bench, though it transcends these boundaries; toward its interior, the circle creates a powerful point of convergence—the beginning, the origin, the nucleus of the universe.[29] Considered in three dimensions, the central building repeats the concentric circular plan of the complex in the ascending movement of its terraced tiers.

Meanwhile, the surrounding platforms mark the four cardinal directions and the intermediate points,[30] and divide the surface symmetrically, into wedge-shaped segments that radiate outward from the center of the complex. It is easy to see that this structure corresponds to a universal cosmic diagram known as the quincunx.[31] Because several *guachimontones* may be found at a single site, it is worth considering that each one represented a cosmic replica and served as the ceremonial center for a different group within the same community. We may also infer that some of the complexes had a higher status than others.

On the ceramic vases that were offered to the dead in shaft tombs, the quincunx is also represented, in an abstract geometric style that recalls the forms of the surface architecture. Here I am referring in particular to certain boxes and bowls from the central part of Jalisco, although the same design or type of decoration is also found in vases from other areas, thereby revealing the unity of this culture and the conceptual integration of its arts. These ceramics have images painted on their inner and outer surfaces that I would interpret as cosmograms, that is, as graphic representations of the universe as this society conceived of it.[32]

One variation on the quincunx consists of a central square from each of whose vertices projects a line that curves to the right (figure 34). These lines allude to the cardinal directions and

142. (*left*) Hollow ceramic architectural model, Ameca-Etzatlán style, Jalisco. Shaft tomb culture. Late Formative–Early Classic. Museo Regional de Guadalajara.

143. (*right*) Ceramic model of a concentric circular architectural complex with a ritual scene, Ixtlán del Río style, Nayarit. Shaft tomb culture. Late Formative–Early Classic.

also to the dynamics of the universe, given that they suggest a continuous rotation; moreover, the composition is inscribed within a circular space clearly indicated by the outline of the vase, thus recalling the circular form of the *guachimontones*. The hemispheric shape of the vase also contributes to the cosmic character of the image, in that it imitates the celestial vault.

Another work modeled on this basic scheme, combining circular and quadripartite elements, is a hollow sculpture in the Ameca-Etzatlán style (plate 142). Around a central circular opening are arranged four arms, from each of which rises a structure with a quadrangular plan and a four-sided roof. The notable height of the Greek cross adds a subterranean dimension to the cosmic-architectonic design, linking it to the realm of the dead. Doubtless this piece refers to the *guachimontones*, particularly those that have four platforms surrounding the central mound; in fact, it completes our image of these compounds, because it shows the buildings that were found atop the ring-shaped benches.

We also have other clay sculptures that represent the original appearance of the *guachimontones*. The famous architectural models in the Nayarit style from Ixtlán del Río are remarkable for their fidelity.[33] One of them (plate 143) has a circular base 17 inches (43 centimeters) in diameter, on which are placed four buildings with rectangular plans, three of them having a rear entrance to a lower chamber, similar to a basement.[34] Atop this lower level are two parallel walls that support a high, four-sided roof. In the middle of the complex is a circular building with four terraced levels.

The artists of the shaft tomb culture also modeled a large number of human and animal figures that re-create the events that took place inside, around, and even above the structures. There are groups of musicians, men and women embracing, and people lost in contemplation;

others converse or eat, lie down, move about, or perform erotic acts. Dogs circulate among the people, and birds perch on the rooftops. Despite this variety of scenes, the architectural configuration indicates that the main event took place in the central building. According to the archaeological evidence[35] and certain of the clay sculptures, a post was erected atop this structure (figure 35), and rituals similar to that of the *palo volador* (flying pole) were celebrated, in which an individual with birdlike attributes ascended and descended this *axis mundi*, symbolizing the union between the upper and lower levels.[36] The placement of this vertical axis on the *guachimontón* reaffirms the ideas that we have already described regarding the visual conception of the cosmos expressed in the surface and subterranean architecture.

The two architectural environments, each with its own style (naturalistic or geometric) and functions (funerary or for the living), suggest a spherical model of the universe, in which the three-dimensionality of the architecture transcends the division between what rises from the surface and what penetrates the subterranean space. According to my interpretation, the art forms, their aesthetic integration, and the contextual elements allude to a circular conception of time and space.[37]

SCULPTURAL REPRESENTATIONS OF OTHER STRUCTURES
The artists of the Ixtlán del Río area also re-created ballcourts (plate 144). On a slab base they modeled the platforms that formed the sides of the court, which sometimes have stairways. The two opposing teams may be clearly distinguished by their position and outfits, while the animated and attentive spectators sit on the platforms and at court level on both ends. On the surface of the court are some protuberances that acted as markers.

144. Ceramic model of a ballcourt with players and spectators, Ixtlán del Río style, Nayarit. Shaft tomb culture. Late Formative–Early Classic. Museo Diego Rivera Anahuacalli.

In addition to the complexes with platforms, we have clay models of a variety of other buildings, whose occupants or users are also represented (plate 145). Hasso von Winning has proposed a typology that includes simple structures with a floor and two walls, leaving the front and back sides open, and other more elaborate buildings with terraced foundations, walls or columns supporting the roof, two stories, stairways at the center or on the sides, and various annexed rooms (figure 36).[38]

The roofs of these structures, like those of the *guachimontones*, are high and four-sided, or pyramidal; their form resembles two trapezoids joined at the shorter parallel side and crowned by two triangular projections. They are also ornamented, giving us indirect evidence of the existence of mural painting. The archaeological studies in Teuchitlán have revealed that the walls of these buildings would have been made of woven *otate* (a kind of bamboo) tied together with *ixtle* (agave) fibers, with pine or oak posts; the roof would have been thatched, and the entire structure, including the platform, would have been covered with layers of clay and red and white paint.[39]

145. Ceramic model of a building with occupants, Ixtlán del Río style, Nayarit. Shaft tomb culture. Late Formative–Early Classic. Museo Diego Rivera Anahuacalli.

MURAL PAINTING

As in most cultures of the world, in that of the shaft tombs ornamentation was an integral part of architecture and contributed to its multiple functions. Since polychromy is one of the features of the Ixtlán del Río ceramic style, its architectural models provide us with an interesting record of the mural painting of this people. We see designs painted in simple combinations of red, yellow, cream, and to a lesser degree, black; frequently they cover most of the exterior of the building. The motifs are linear and geometric in style, and the repertoire is very limited: straight, wavy, and zigzagging lines, and dots, triangles, and rhombuses. Strangely enough, despite its importance in the architectural configuration of the *guachimontones*,[40] the circle is absent from these two-dimensional expressions. The motifs are repeated in series and without much variation on roofs and walls, always in vertical, symmetrical arrangements.

Three or four concentric rhombuses are very common; this is a design that is repeated in many other cultures of the world, among them the Wixárika or Huichol.[41] This indigenous group, which currently resides in Jalisco and Nayarit, preserves a rich tradition of Pre-Columbian origin. By wrapping yarn over two perpendicular sticks, they create rhombus-shaped objects called *tsikiri* (God's eye). The metaphor is suggestive, given that the form of the concentric rhombus, like that of the *guachimontones*, creates a quincunx that recalls the five directions of the universe (the four cardinal directions and the center). The *tsikiri* has a sacred character, and is offered to the deities. It is also one of a number of objects that symbolize the *nierika*, a hollow or orifice that acts as a two-way portal between worlds, allowing the ancestors to see inside the world of human beings, and the shamans to communicate with the ancestors.[42] This leads us back to the funerary origin of the ceramic architectural models we have seen, and reinforces the intimate relationship between the living and the dead, the core concept that gave rise to the several aesthetically integrated art forms of the shaft tomb culture.

OTHER ARCHITECTURAL FORMS

THE SUNKEN PATIOS OF EL BAJÍO

Outside the shaft tomb region, compounds with concentric circular layouts are found in southwestern Guanajuato, at sites like Peralta II, Plazuelas, and La Gloria.[43] Although the influence of the shaft tomb culture in this area has not been studied, it may be inferred that for some three centuries the *guachimontones* existed alongside a tradition of sunken patios built on platforms.

In the greater part of what is today the state of Guanajuato, Efraín Cárdenas has counted 174 sites with sunken plazas or patios, dated around AD 300 to 650 (figure 37).[44] This architectural model extended throughout the complex of ancient basins known as El Bajío, which also includes part of southern Querétaro.[45] Enclosed patios are common in other parts of Mesoamerica, but those of El Bajío display certain unique characteristics: they are built on a platform with an orthogonal plan (rectangular or T-shaped, for example), in such a way that the patio is sunken with regard to the platform itself, or with regard to a long bench that circumscribes the patio, but is higher, in most cases, than the surrounding terrain. The patios are quadrangular or sometimes circular, and in rare cases they present a central sanctuary or altar; some platforms have two sunken patios. Frequently the pyramidal foundations of temples are built atop the platform, as well as series of rooms, in such a way that these elements form a structural whole, in contrast with other enclosed patios that consist of a pyramidal foundation and a U-shaped platform. The sunken patios were not entered at their corners, but rather by means of staircases that communicated with the surrounding bench or platform.[46]

Besides Plazuelas, Guanajuato (which we will describe below), another site with this style of architecture that has been restored and opened to the public is Cañada de la Virgen.[47] At this splendid sanctuary, a pond is integrated with the architectural works, which include a great avenue that leads to a nearby canyon, as well as a sunken patio with a pyramid at one corner and several rooms on the surrounding platform.

THE INFLUENCE OF TEOTIHUACÁN AFTER ITS FALL
Unlike other parts of Mesoamerica, such as the Gulf Coast and the Maya and Zapotec regions, the west was not much influenced by the expansive culture of Teotihuacán. From the standpoint of material culture, we have only isolated evidence of interaction that in no way indicates the existence of strong ties.[48] However, around AD 600, the construction of shaft tombs and *guachimontones* ceased, and some fifty years later the tradition of sunken patios ended in El Bajío. The collapse of the thousand-year-old shaft tomb culture coincided with that of Teotihuacán, and it is from this point on that the western region followed, with local modifications, certain architectural models that had flourished in the great city of central Mexico. The *talud-tablero* or slope-and-panel system of construction is emblematic, as can be seen in certain phases of buildings at Tinganio, located in Tingambato, Michoacán, and El Iztépete, in the metropolitan area of Guadalajara. But it is the site of Plazuelas, which developed between AD 600 and 900, that stands out from the rest.

PLAZUELAS: ARCHITECTURE AND ITS IMAGE
The diversity of its architectural forms makes Plazuelas an extraordinary site. Here, unique local expressions converged with different cultural traditions: that of the sunken patios, that of Teotihuacán, and that of the shaft tombs, via its complexes with concentric circular layouts. Plazuelas is located in southwestern Guanajuato, very close to Michoacán. Its structures extend across three hillsides separated by two ravines; on the east side is found a *guachimontón*. The archaeological work to date has concentrated on the central hillside, where, according to Carlos Castañeda and Jorge Quiroz,[49] the buildings were constructed on a vast plaza that was artificially leveled by means of a complex system of terraces ranging in height between 6½ and 100 feet (2 and 30 meters). The most noteworthy complex, called Casas Tapadas (plate 147), underwent four stages of construction, through which it maintained a general symmetry and an orthogonal plan (figure 38). At first its configuration was of the sunken patio type, built on a platform and with three pyramidal foundations on the north, south, and east sides. Later the complex expanded outward, creating more patios bordered by benches, with various staircases allowing access to the compound; also, the eastern pyramidal foundation was enlarged, and two new T-shaped foundations were constructed. While the profiles of the foundations changed in each phase of construction, the *talud-tablero* system was present from

the beginning. Another reference to the art of Teotihuacán can be appreciated in the decoration of one of the foundations: its walls were adorned with sculptures shaped like split snails, a reference to Quetzalcóatl.

The buildings of Plazuelas are surrounded by rocky outcroppings on which various forms were engraved or carved in bas-relief. Among a variety of geometric motifs, such as lines of small circular cavities, perhaps indicating routes, architectural images stand out: stairways, pyramids, sunken patios, ballcourts, circular buildings, and also ring-shaped structures surrounded by ten or twelve platforms that recall *guachimontones*. Even whole complexes of

146. (*above*) Carvings on a rocky outcropping depicting an architectural complex similar to the nearby Casas Tapadas. Plazuelas, Guanajuato. Late Classic.

147. (*left*) The Casas Tapadas complex, Plazuelas. Late Classic.

148. (*opposite*) Tzintzuntzan, Michoacán, a site of the Tarascan culture. In the local Purépecha language, the structures shown here are known as *yácatas*. Late Postclassic.

buildings are represented, including, among others, Casas Tapadas (plate 146). This rock carving may be a representation of the finished complex or a preliminary model: it depicts the five pyramidal foundations, the enclosed patios, the long benches, and the stairways that make it up. In summary, the hundreds of forms carved into the rocks of Plazuelas would seem to be the product of a consolidated school of architects, and they constitute an outstanding legacy within Mesoamerican art.

THE ARCHITECTURE OF THE AZTATLÁN CULTURE

Between AD 900 and 1300, the Aztatlán culture achieved a certain level of regional unification in the west;[50] its expansion encompassed Sinaloa, Nayarit, Jalisco, and the basin of Lake Chapala in Michoacán. This culture was characterized by strong ties with central Mexico, in particular with that region's religious iconography; with Tula, Hidalgo; and with the famous Mixteca-Puebla pictorial style. Its ceremonial architecture includes monumental structures with elongated platforms, ballcourts, rectangular plazas, pyramids, and avenues. Among the sites with well-known or well-preserved structures is Amapa, in Nayarit, a large settlement with some two hundred mounds constructed mainly of clay.[51] In the contiguous coastal zones of Nayarit and Jalisco, interesting remains have been found in Punta Mita, Puerto Vallarta, and the Valley of Tomatlán.[52] However, the only site belonging to this culture where architecture has been restored is Los Toriles, located in the municipal area of Ixtlán del Río, in southeastern Nayarit.[53]

This place has a long sequence of occupation that goes back to the era of the shaft tomb culture, although no burials have been found in the ceremonial center of Los Toriles. Its buildings, which at one time were covered with plaster, are constructed of stones joined with mud mortar. One outstanding structure has a circular plan that links it to Quetzalcóatl in the guise of the wind god Ehécatl. It underwent three stages of construction; today we can see the footprint of the third stage and, within it, the more completely preserved second one. This consists of a foundation with two pyramidal altars facing each other on top of it; the upper walls of the foundation have cross-shaped apertures, which once more recall Quetzalcóatl, in his role as Venus or the Morning Star. The circular temple presents four stairways that connect to cobblestone roads, only one of which is now visible, leading to the main plaza of the complex. Here and in other parts of the site there are rectangular platforms, some with square plans fronted by rows of columns that, together with the walls, held up the roof.

PURÉPECHA ARCHITECTURE

Today, in Michoacán, the Purépecha recognize themselves as direct descendants of the people of the powerful Tarascan state, which the Aztec empire was never able to vanquish and was still in existence at the time of the Spanish invasion. Recent studies trace the cultural background of this people back to the last few centuries BC and indicate its links to the northern Chalchihuites culture, and to the Hohokam of the southwestern United States.[54] This northern, or Toltec-Chichimec[55] heritage, which spread throughout Mesoamerica after AD 900, manifested itself in various ways in the architecture of the Purépecha.[56] Thus, in the initial phase of the Tarascan state's formation, from AD 750 to 900, rooms with columned cloisters were built at the sites of Cerro Barajas (in southwestern Guanajuato) and San Antonio Carupo (in central northern Michoacán; figure 39).[57] This model, which has Chalchihuites antecedents, combines closed and open private spaces. It consists of hypostyle galleries laid out in a quadrangular plan around an open central patio, which possessed a basin to collect rainwater. These areas, whose use was mostly likely restricted, would have allowed a large number of people to gather away from the public gaze and carry out actions that probably involved the heavens.[58]

After 1300, the Tarascans built their capital cities in the basin of Lake Pátzcuaro: Ihuatzio, Pátzcuaro, and Tzintzuntzan. The latter was the most important, extending across 450 acres (180 hectares).[59] Its ceremonial center was located on the side of Cerro Yahuarato or Yahuarán, where a monumental artificial platform, measuring 800 by 1,500 feet (250 by 450 meters), was constructed (figure 40). This platform was ascended by a terraced ramp some 330 feet (100 meters) wide.

On a large rectangular foundation within this ceremonial center, we find a row of five terraced buildings separated from each other by narrow passageways. Each building's plan combines a rectangle with a semicircle on the rear side, which faces the lake (plate 149). In the Purépecha language, these buildings, and any Pre-Columbian mound, are called *yácatas*. Those of Tzintzuntzan reached 39 to 43 feet (12 to 13 meters) in height; on top of them were temples made with perishable materials, such as wood and straw. Thanks to the *Relación de Michoacán*, a document of the sixteenth century, we may assume that these were dedicated to the supreme Tarascan deity, Curicaueri, a god of sun and fire. We also know that they were the site of funeral ceremonies for rulers, who were buried at the foot of the *yácatas*.[60]

149. (*opposite above*) Another view of the *yácatas* of Tzintzuntzan. Late Postclassic.

150. (*below*) *Janamus* (basalt slabs) with geometric designs, used as architectural ornaments at Tzintzuntzan. Late Postclassic.

151. (*opposite below*) This *janamu* from Tzintzuntzan, bearing a bas-relief of a flute player, was reused in the nearby San Francisco Convent, built in the sixteenth century.

ARCHITECTURAL DECORATION AND CULTURAL CONTINUITY

One common characteristic of Tarascan architecture is that the pyramids were sheathed in basalt slabs. These polished stones, cut with precision at right angles, are known in Purépecha as *janamus*. Some are engraved or carved in bas-relief, mostly with geometric shapes, such as various kinds of spirals and circles combined with different lines (plate 150); only a few represent the human form. In the ancient ceremonial center of Tzintzuntzan, there are several engraved slabs.[61] Very near the archaeological zone is a convent dedicated to Saint Francis of Assisi, constructed in the sixteenth century. As is well known, Pre-Columbian architectural elements were frequently reused after the Conquest, and this is what happened with the *janamus*. In the new ceremonial center of the site, now devoted to the European Christian tradition, these slabs retained their function as architectural facings: the engraved *janamus* are distributed among the structures of the convent complex.[62]

In both contexts, the Pre-Columbian and the viceregal, this architectural decoration seems to be haphazard, without apparent order.[63] However, given the use of these slabs in ceremonial centers of great importance, their placement on every building, and the images carved on them, I would propose that they were closely linked to the symbolic function of the structures, and that their reuse was an intentional act on the part of the Tarascans, one that went beyond the practical consideration of conserving construction materials. From an iconographic exploration, we can deduce that the geometric motifs on the *janamus* might have had a polysemous character, with deep meanings and symbolisms, referring to the sun, Venus, wind, water, lightning, or constellations; migration away and back, the return to the origin, images of the universe, the center of the world, the place where fire is born. In particular, one of the figurative designs recalls the historical relations established by the Purépecha with northern cultures: this is the flute player (plate 151), a mythical sacred figure characteristic of the indigenous cultures of the southwestern United States. Its portrayal on this *janamu*—as an asexual figure, hunched without actually being hunchbacked—is similar to those found in the art of the Hohokam of Arizona. This is an image from the historical memory of the Purépecha that evokes their ancient contacts with the societies of the north, as well as the continuity of the Purépecha cultural tradition within the context of New Spain.[64]

FINAL NOTES

Some other very important examples of architecture were not included in this brief essay, such as those of La Campana and El Chanal in Colima, or Huandacareo and San Felipe los Alzati in Michoacán. In fact, hundreds of sites with ancient architecture have been recorded in western Mexico, although, unfortunately, only a small fraction of them have been stabilized and restored, and only a few are open to the public. Moreover, research has focused mostly on ceremonial buildings, and there is still much to be learned about the structures where daily life took place. But even in the abbreviated panorama of western architecture presented here, we can appreciate many unique creations that contributed to the heterogeneity of Mesoamerica, and which demonstrate the great creativity exercised by its peoples in their effort to integrate themselves into the larger cultural scene while still maintaining their differences. For the ancient indigenous peoples of the west, architecture was a vital art form due to its intimate relationship with human existence, even after death. These cultures used architecture to express their conceptual images of the cosmos and their relationship to their natural surroundings. They constructed spaces that were physically and symbolically appropriate to their ceremonies and traditions, their ideologies, and their shared art forms, and which reflected their links to societies in other latitudes of the Americas.

7

NORTHERN MEXICO

VERÓNICA HERNÁNDEZ DÍAZ

Ancient northern Mexico presents us with splendid examples of architectural works integrated with nature. Buildings do not compete with their environment; rather, they adapt to it. In much of this region, diffuse settlement patterns allow us to appreciate the surrounding landscape as a majestic protagonist, just as it was conceived of and experienced by its inhabitants. In comparison with southern Mesoamerica, we are presented with different conceptions of constructed volumes and spaces. The cultural landscapes of the north express distinctive tastes and ways of life, traces of which still enrich the artistic styles and indigenous cultures of Mexico. Nevertheless, this is—along with the west—one of the most unknown and even disdained regions of the country. Broadly speaking, it has been difficult to recognize the true qualities of the different societies of nomadic and sedentary peoples, of hunter-gatherers and farmers, who have coexisted closely here through the ages, giving rise to varied cultural phenomena.

There predominates the mistaken notion of an arid territory, lacking in resources and culturally backward, occupied by the Chichimec, a word commonly associated with savage, wandering warriors. However, the north is rich in contrasts and offers us an extraordinary natural complexity even in its desert landscapes, to say nothing of the broad array of ecological niches to be found along its coasts, and also in the mountains of the Western and Eastern Sierra Madre that traverse it. The term *Chichimec* refers, in a pejorative manner, to diverse ethnic groups who speak different languages and represent various cultures, including those sedentary ones whose warlike character influenced the Mesoamerican peoples from AD 900 until the time of the Conquest. Chichimec was also the name given to the northern indigenous groups who fought ferociously against the Spaniards, resisting their dominion for many years.

THE REGION

Various criteria have been used to demarcate northern Mexico.[1] For the purpose of this brief essay, I will define this region according to cultural considerations, taking the present-day Mexican border as an upper limit; hence I will refer only to certain sites located in what are now the states of Durango, Zacatecas, northern Jalisco, Querétaro, Tamaulipas, Chihuahua, and Sonora (figure 41).[2] It goes without saying that the contemporary political boundaries do not correspond to those that existed in the past. For example, with regard to more recent times, in the first half of the nineteenth century northern Mexico encompassed territories that are now part of the southwestern United States.[3]

In general terms, three basic cultural areas can be distinguished in the vast region of northern Mexico. The first may be considered the northern part of Mesoamerica, since it was colonized in various waves by societies that migrated from the south from the last few centuries BC until AD 1150, when these settlers turned back and the northern border of Mesoamerica retreated with them, to the south of the Moctezuma and Lerma rivers. This first cultural area encompasses the states of Durango, Zacatecas, northern Jalisco, Aguascalientes, southeastern San Luis Potosí, Querétaro, and Tamaulipas.[4] After being abandoned by the "typical Mesoamericans," it continued to be occupied by the nomadic groups who had lived there in the past. The second cultural area comprises northwestern Chihuahua and northeastern Sonora. This territory gave rise to the so-called Casas Grandes culture, which is associated with the Mogollon culture that was also present in parts of New Mexico and Arizona.[5] Meanwhile, Baja California, Coahuila, and Nuevo Léon[6] make up a third cultural area, which was solely a base for nomads or communities of hunter-gatherers whose material remains are sparse or barely legible, the most evident being cave art. Of their architecture, which must have been of a seasonal nature, we have no physical testimony.[7] The following tour through the spectacular architecture of the north makes no pretense of being exhaustive, but will only show a few examples of the variety of these structures integrated with the landscape.

THE TERRACES OF CERRO DE TRINCHERAS

The far northwest corner of the state of Sonora is home to the Trincheras (Trenches) tradition.[8] Its members preferred to build on hillsides and construct their walls from undressed stone without mortar. An antecedent of this tradition, and also a sign of cultural continuity in the area, is the construction of pit houses, which began around AD 200 (figure 43). At first they were grouped into small villages, and later into large settlements. These dwellings are semi-subterranean, since the floor was excavated beneath the level of the soil, which forms the lower part of the wall. Their plan may be circular or square with rounded corners, with an entryway or antechamber, a hearth on the floor, and an adjacent hole for the ashes; frequently there are dividing walls in the interior space. This kind of architecture is shared with the American southwest and is found in the stages leading up to the peak of the Casas Grandes culture.

Between AD 800 and 1300, terraces or "trenches" began to be built on hillsides. Recent investigations indicate that their function was not exclusively defensive, as was previously believed, since there were huts on the terraces, and in some cases, rooms with circular or quadrangular plans and stone walls. Some of these hills have a rectangular structure at their base, while on top of others there are walls that form enclosures with restricted entrances.

During the phase from 1300 to 1450, the hills with trenches became more abundant in the Altar Valley. At some residential sites, oval mounds 20 feet (6 meters) long, 13 feet (4 meters) wide, and 5 feet (1.5 meters) high have been found.

The monumental structures on the Cerro de Trincheras were built during this phase. No doubt this site was selected because it stands out in the landscape (plate 152): it is an isolated

152. (below) The northern slope of Cerro de Trincheras, Sonora. Postclassic.

153. (opposite) La Cancha, the public ceremonial area at the foot of Cerro de Trincheras, Sonora. Postclassic.

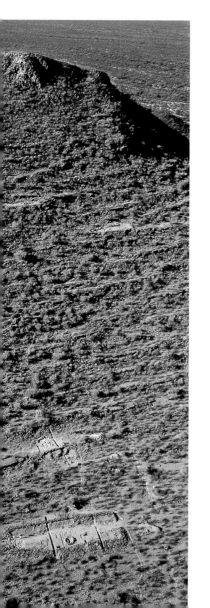

volcanic hill in the valley of the Magdalena River, with a surface area of about 250 acres (100 hectares) and an elevation of almost 500 feet (150 meters). Here we find over 900 terraces, ranging in height from 1½ to 10 feet (0.5 to 3 meters), most of them on the northern slope. Pit houses are distributed irregularly over the terraces, along with several hundred circular and quadrangular structures with drystone walls almost 3 feet (1 meter) high. La Cancha (plate 153), a rectangular structure located at the foot of the hill's northern slope, was constructed by the same technique; its low walls enclose an area of 49 by 187 feet (15 by 57 meters). It has been suggested that the terraces on the hillside served as an amphitheater for witnessing ceremonies, performances, or perhaps the characteristic Mesoamerican ballgame.

A unique building at the same site is El Caracol (figure 42), access to which may have been limited, since it is positioned on the eastern edge of the hill's crest. Its plan is similar to a spiral (although it can also be interpreted as the outline of a bird's head seen in profile), with stone walls more than 5 feet (1.5 meters) high, and it is surrounded by several circular structures. Cerro de Trincheras was abandoned in 1450.

CASAS GRANDES: ARCHITECTS OF THE EARTH
Among the sites belonging to this cultural development, Paquimé or Casas Grandes, Cuarenta Casas, Cueva de la Olla, and Huapoca, all located in Chihuahua, stand out. Their remains exhibit links to the traditions of both Mesoamerica and the American southwest, but in terms of style their architecture is more akin to that of the Pueblo Indians of the latter region, such as those who inhabited Chaco Canyon and Mesa Verde.

PAQUIMÉ, A CLAY CITY ON THE RIVER

This beautiful and elaborate urban area developed principally between AD 1200 and 1400;[9] since 1997 it has been catalogued as a World Heritage Site by UNESCO. It is located in the valley of the Casas Grandes River, whose flow is intermittent today. The city center, consisting of intricate orthogonal complexes, is laid out in a U shape around the great East Plaza (figure 44; plates 154, 155). The most important complexes, or those associated with powerful groups, can be seen on the western side; here, two kinds of structures have been identified: the residential compounds, workshops, and storerooms; and the ceremonial buildings.

Like, for example, Pueblo Bonito in Chaco Canyon, New Mexico, Paquimé presents architectural units with multiple contiguous rooms connected by doors and with more than one

154. View of Paquimé, Chihuahua. Postclassic.

story, perhaps up to four. However, the building materials differ: at Pueblo Bonito, sandstone walls predominate; and in the so-called Casas Grandes culture, those of adobe.

The architects of Paquimé enclosed ample interior spaces with thick clay walls—between 1½ and 4½ feet (0.5 and 1.4 meters) wide—that were molded with planks and then dressed with a coat of fine clay, whitewashed, and painted. This building technique proved to be well suited to the extreme temperatures of the area, since the thickness of the walls slowed the buildup of heat during the day and the loss of it at night. The ceilings, or mezzanines in cases where the structures had two or more stories, consisted of wooden beams covered with branches, grass, and clay. The entrance openings, which are just over 3 feet (1 meter) tall, have a distinctive T shape, the upper part being trapezoidal and elongated, and the lower, rectangular (plate 156). The walls occasionally have small windows; the rooms had interior stairways and were also connected by passageways. These compounds are distributed around plazas, some of which have porticoes with columns.

Among the buildings of a ceremonial nature, the so-called Bird Mound stands out on account of its plan, which resembles a decapitated bird. There is also a structure that has been identified as an astronomical observatory, the so-called Cross Compound, which consists of four arms that point, with a slight deviation, toward the cardinal directions. Each arm is associated with a platform with a circular base. As direct evidence of the Mesoamerican tradition, there are two ballcourts at the site, laid out in the shape of an I with rounded corners; other ballcourts have also been found in the area.

The architectural works went hand-in-hand with engineering works. The city's hydraulic system was impressive: its channels, lined with and covered by stone slabs, distributed water that was collected in the mountains by an intricate system of terraces and dams. In each plaza, there was also a drain and a channel that gathered rainwater in order to carry it to lower-lying parts of the city. Possible drainpipes have also been found.

155. The interior of a building at Paquimé. Postclassic.

156. Detail of the walls of Paquimé, showing
a typical T-shaped entryway. Postclassic.

157. (*top*) Cliff dwelling at Rancherías, Chihuahua. Postclassic.

158. (*bottom left*) Cliff dwelling at Cueva de la Olla, Chihuahua. Postclassic.

159. (*bottom right*) Cliff dwelling at Las Jarillas, Chihuahua. Postclassic.

Figure 160 illustration area

LIVING ON THE ROCKS

The architects of the Casas Grandes culture have left beautiful creations not only on the plains, but also in the mountains. In the rock shelters in the vertical walls of the nearby Western Sierra Madre, they built in another mode that is also linked to the traditions of the American southwest, as can be seen in the hollows of Canyon de Chelly in Arizona, among other sites. Toward the end of the nineteenth century, during his journey through the Tarahumara mountains, the famous Norwegian ethnologist and explorer Carl Lumholtz noted that some people there still lived in cliff houses, which were no doubt difficult to access.

Set within the impressive landscape of the Western Sierra Madre, the cliff dwellings at Cuarenta Casas, Huapoca, and Cueva Grande (in the municipal area of Madera) show a very close integration between nature and the works of humankind (figure 45; plates 157–60). At these sites we find the same style of construction as at Paquimé, down to the last detail: series of quadrangular rooms with walls of molded or poured clay covered in plaster, and with roofs of wooden beams that frequently supported two or three stories. The stairways were made of wood, and the doorways exhibit the characteristic T shape. As at Paquimé, clay was used to make stoves, beds, and storage containers.

In Sonora, the Casas Grandes culture is represented in the cliff buildings in the town of Bacerac and the Valley of Bavispe.[10]

160. Cliff dwelling at Cueva Grande, Chihuahua. Postclassic.

BALCÓN DE MONTEZUMA: A TASTE FOR THE CIRCULAR

Toward the southwest of the state of Tamaulipas, on a stretch of the Eastern Sierra Madre, is found Balcón de Montezuma, a site dated around AD 400 to 500, although its occupation may have continued until AD 1500.[11] The style of its artifacts and architecture show that its inhabitants were influenced by the Huastec culture. One of the most outstanding qualities of the architecture is its formal unity: grouped around the site's two plazas are a large number of structures that all have circular foundations, and whose distribution and orientation—as indicated by their entrances—manifest the power of the center.

The settlement, which has a closed, defensive character (figure 46), occupies the upper part of a hill surrounded by steep cliffs, with the exception of the western flank, where a very wide staircase with more than eighty steps was built. It was constructed, like the foundations of the other structures, from slabs of sedimentary limestone laid horizontally without mortar. The hilltop covers about 17 acres (7 hectares) and was leveled so as to form two plazas of irregular outline, around which are concentrated almost ninety circular foundations, whose height ranges from a few inches to over 6½ feet (2 meters), depending on the relief of the terrain.

In keeping with this taste for circles, the concept of the center was also considered important, as can be seen from the fact that each foundation has an entrance facing its respective plaza. In the lower foundations, the entrance is indicated by a gap in the circle of stones that make up the wall, while the more elevated foundations present one or more steps that form an

161, 162. (*above and opposite*) Ranas, Sierra Gorda, Querétaro. Classic.

elegant fan-shaped stairway. Atop these foundations were structures made of perishable materials, perhaps cylindrical huts with wattle-and-daub walls and posts that supported thatched palm roofs (figure 47).

Three kinds of buildings have been recorded: residential, religious, and surveillance. The first type measured from 30 to 36 feet (9 to 11 meters) in diameter; in these structures are found hearths, as well as fragments of ceramics and evidence of the development of a lithic industry. Burials have also been discovered directly beneath the floors of the residential buildings, in accordance with a practice that was common throughout Mesoamerica. The religious structures measure some 10 feet (3 meters) in diameter, and there is no evidence of reinforcements for posts, nor any burials, in their interior; one such building is located in the center of Plaza 2. The so-called surveillance posts are strategically positioned on the great stairway and near the sides of the hill.

Another feature that points to the restricted nature of the site, which was perhaps elitist or defensive, is the extreme proximity of the structures: they are separated by as little as a few inches, and no more than a few feet. Thus, access to the plazas was quite limited; like the individual buildings, they have only a single entrance each, an opening about 6½ feet (2 meters) wide: in Plaza 1 this was located between foundations 2 and 17, and in Plaza 2, between foundations 49 and 50.

THE BALLGAME SANCTUARIES OF THE SIERRA GORDA

The present-day state of Querétaro was the seat of several cultural traditions,[12] only one of which we will discuss here. Ranas and Toluquilla are the principal ceremonial and political centers of the so-called Serrana (Mountain) culture, whose territory was the southern end of the intricate Sierra Gorda mountain chain, in the northeast of Querétaro.[13] The two centers are believed to have been contemporary; the chronology of Toluquilla indicates two major periods of construction, one from 300 BC to AD 600, and the other, more intense, from the latter date to AD 1400. From an economic standpoint, this culture is noteworthy for its exploitation of red mercuric sulfide, or cinnabar, and for its links to the Gulf Coast and central Mexico. Its beautiful architecture, built on narrow hilltops, is equally outstanding, both for its characteristic ballcourts and for the delicate sensibility of its craftsmanship, which can be appreciated in the care with which the stones are laid in the walls, in the details of the profiles and especially the stairways of the buildings.

In order to maintain control over the mines, the lower-ranking sites in surrounding areas, and the entrances to the mountain chain, Ranas and Toluquilla were built in strategic positions, separated by a distance of 2 miles (3 kilometers) as the crow flies. They are located on mountainous heights surrounded by steep cliffs, in a forested terrain (figures 48, 49). The topography was a determining factor in the pattern of the architecture (plate 161), which was, however, elaborately planned: where the terrain was very broken, it was leveled in order to create a broader surface, and terraces or platforms reinforced with retaining walls were built on the hillsides (plate 162). The naturally elongated space of these sites dictated the linear ar-

163. El Cerrito, Querétaro, a site with Toltec affiliations. Epiclassic–Early Postclassic.

rangement of the structures. We can tell that the ballgame was a fundamental activity, since the main axis of the urban plan is defined by the ballcourts, which are I-shaped, with a pyramidal temple at one end. Other elements that can be seen are rectangular compounds for residential or public use, a number of semicircular structures, avenues, alleyways, patios, balustrades, the openings of doorways, and walls over 6½ feet (2 meters) high.

Scholars of the Serrana culture recognize various influences in its architecture: for example, the *talud-tablero* foundations are reminiscent of Teotihuacán, the flying cornices of El Tajín, and the semicircular stairways of Balcón de Montezuma. The system of construction at Ranas and Toluquilla took advantage of the abundant local materials: the buildings had a core of stone and mud and were finished with slabs of cut limestone, whose faces were retouched by percussion and, in certain cases, polished in order to round the edges. This lends a certain softness to the composition, especially in the numerous semicircular stairways at Ranas. Moreover, the slabs were selected for uniformity of size and laid in carefully leveled rows. The result was a finely crafted facade, perhaps with the stones left exposed, since it appears that no finish was applied, with the exception of the floors of houses and temples, which were covered with packed earth or layers of stucco.

SOME PARTICULAR FEATURES
Although Ranas and Toluquilla exhibit the same architectural style, there are differences between them. Recent research suggests that Ranas may have been dedicated to political and administrative activities, as its plazas and other spaces, which are larger and more open to

164. La Quemada,
Zacatecas. Classic.

circulation, may indicate. Toluquilla, meanwhile, may have been centered on religious activities, but of a restricted nature, given the lack of plazas where a large number of people could gather.

Toluquilla was settled on an elongated butte with a north-south orientation. Along this axis were constructed four ballcourts with markers on their surfaces and, parallel to them, a central avenue and two side streets. A total of about 120 buildings have been recorded there. Ranas, on the other hand, occupies the upper part of two connected hills that form a vertex with an east-northeast orientation. It possesses about 150 structures, divided into three sectors: in sector I, three ballcourts stand out; in sector II, the considerable unevenness of the terrain is alleviated by retaining walls and platforms, on top of which are found pyramidal foundations; and in sector III is a vestibule that provides access to the site. Ranas is also distinguished by the variety of ways in which the stairways are integrated with the buildings.

WAR AND THE SACRED IN CHALCHIHUITES ARCHITECTURE

At its maximum extent, the Chalchihuites culture encompassed what are now the states of Durango, Zacatecas, and the far north of Jalisco; it flourished principally in the first nine centuries of our era.[14] In the complex eastern relief of the Western Sierra Madre, as well as in the now semiarid valleys of the region, we find multiple scattered settlements with different ranks and characteristics, adapted to the diverse topography. Two fundamental conditions

165. View of La Quemada, with the ballcourt and the "votive pyramid" in the foreground, and in the background the terraced hill with its ceremonial and residential structures. Classic.

determined the location of this people's dwellings: proximity to water sources and the suitability of the terrain for defense against attacks. Thus they built on elevated buttes or other mountainous formations surrounded by cliffs or precipices, which would provide a bird's-eye view.[15] Some common elements of their villages, hamlets, and ceremonial and political centers are terraces supported by retaining walls, defensive walls, and houses and patios with a square plan. The patios tend to be closed and sunken, with stairways on all four sides; sometimes they have a central altar or are surrounded by residential compounds. Another common feature is the open-ended ballcourt with low benches on both sides. The system of construction was based on piles of stones, and at the larger centers the structures were faced with finer slabs, which were adhered with mortar.

The sites of the Chalchihuites culture include Hervideros, Zape, and La Ferrería in Durango; Alta Vista, Chalchihuites, and Teúl de González Ortega in Zacatecas; and El Huistle in Jalisco. However, the dominant center was La Quemada, Zacatecas, which has been described as an acropolis and is thought to have been a regional sanctuary visited by numerous pilgrims from all over the vast Chalchihuites territory. Its architecture and location indicate that it had defensive, residential, and religious functions (figure 50; plate 164).[16]

The terraces of La Quemada sit on a long and imposing hill, oriented north-south, in the Malpaso Valley.[17] The cliffs on this hill were faced with stone slabs, in the manner of buttresses, which served to protect the site and support its terraces (plate 167). The entrance to the monumental precinct is located in the lower section to the south; this is easily accessed, with broad open spaces that would have allowed for massive public ceremonies, while the upper levels would have been reserved for the private rituals and living quarters of the principal leaders, warriors, and priests. The buildings, whose stones are exposed today, would have been covered by layers of clay and of polished lime.

The entrance is marked by an enormous avenue more than 1,300 feet (400 meters) long and 80 feet (25 meters) wide, which is bordered by two lateral walls some 14 inches (35 centimeters) high, made of stone slabs and boulders. The surface of the road was filled in with slabs and paved with clay and pebbles. From this avenue springs a 60-mile (100-kilometer) network of lesser roadways, constructed in a similar fashion, that communicate with more than 220 villages throughout the valley. Within La Quemada, the great avenue leads to a sunken plaza associated with a hall of columns with a portico and central patio (plate 166); the only access to this room was through a single door. Originally its columns supported a roof, which would have made it one of the largest covered spaces in Mesoamerica. It is thought that the central portion was open, similar to a cloister.

166. (below) The Hall of Columns, La Quemada. Classic.

167. (opposite) View of the buttresses and terraces of La Quemada. Classic.

This combination of a hypostyle hall and plaza is a contribution to the architectural repertoire of ancient Mexico that, following the collapse of this culture, was disseminated with great success by the Tolteca-Chichimeca, even to sites as far away as Chichén Itzá. In the Chalchihuites culture, this architectural form generally combines an open public space (the plaza) with a private space (the hypostyle hall) that is at once enclosed—by its walls and roof—and open, because of the interior patio. It has been proposed that this kind of enclosure was the setting for rituals carried out by the rulers in their role as warrior-priests; this is supported by the fact that human sacrifices took place in the patios, as is shown by the remains of *tzompantlis*, or skull racks.[18]

Continuing our tour of La Quemada, to the north we find another outstanding feature, a ballcourt, which is oriented north-south and has an I-shaped plan with benches 230 feet (70 meters) long (plate 165). Farther to the north rises the so-called "votive pyramid," which is distinguished by its nearly vertical slopes. To the west, a great stairway leads to the second level, where there is a group of rooms with the remains of adobe walls, and a small pyramid annexed to a large platform that is, in turn, joined to the rocky hillside. Here there was found a plentiful ossuary whose skulls showed signs of having been hung on a *tzompantli*. On the third level is another sunken patio and hall of columns, but this time the patio has a central altar and a pyramid to one side. On the fourth level, only the remains of walls are preserved. Continuing along the hilltop, we arrive at its northern end, whose slope is protected by a long rampart over 13 feet (4 meters) high and 10 feet (3 meters) wide. On the plateau in this area we find two architectural units that, once again, consist of a sunken, enclosed patio that has a central altar and a pyramid to one side, and which is associated with a large hall that once had a hypostyle roof. Here there is also a second ballcourt, of smaller dimensions than the one below. Before it stands a building with a stairway on its northern side that crosses the great rampart.

Around AD 1000, in some parts of the eastern foothills of the Western Sierra Madre—such as at La Joya in the Mezquital region of Durango, or at Las Ventanas in the Juchipila municipal area in southern Zacatecas—dwellings with adobe walls were constructed in cavities in the rock walls of cliffs.[19] These structures, along with certain other elements, link the Chalchihuites culture to certain settlements in the American southwest, and to Paquimé.

THE UNDISCOVERED NORTH

A great deal of the bibliography on Mexico's indigenous past—and here we are thinking in particular of the maps these works contain—presents us with a northern region almost devoid of references, with only a few sites marked. Of course, this is not the result of a shortage of cultural remains, but of a lack of research and of projects devoted to consolidating, restoring, and opening sites to the public. Nevertheless, as we have seen, the ongoing efforts of the scholars of this region do allow us to appreciate some of the complex traditions that developed here. In the diverse cultural landscapes of the north, especially those created by sedentary societies, architecture coexists intimately with nature. The bellicosity of the northern peoples, as well as their particular ways of life and conceptions of the sacred, are expressed in the beautiful, even delicate structures that they built in these environments. Passing through their trenches, acropolises, cliff dwellings, and cities of clay and stone, we spontaneously find ourselves contemplating the landscape, because we are immersed in it.

8
CENTRAL VERACRUZ

ANNICK DANEELS

INTRODUCTION

Any mention of the Mesoamerican architecture of central Veracruz immediately evokes the Pyramid of the Niches at El Tajín (plate 168). Doubtless this is one of the greatest achievements of the ancient builders of this region, due to its balanced proportions, the alternation between slopes, niches, and cornices, and the play of chiaroscuro created by the niches beneath the tropical sun. Dated around the end of the Classic period, it is evidently the result of a long tradition of architecture. However, little is known about its antecedents, except that they may ultimately be traced back to the packed-earth architecture of the late Olmec era. We will describe the examples of this earthen architecture found at the sites of Cerro de las Mesas, El Pital, La Joya, and El Zapotal, identifying the ways in which it reflects typical Mesoamerican

168. The Pyramid of the Niches at El Tajín, Veracruz, AD 800–1000.

canons, as well as the ways in which it is unique. Afterward, we will analyze El Tajín as the culmination of the architectural trajectory of central Veracruz, and the focal point of the diffusion of a particular style in the Late Classic period. In the Postclassic, a series of cultural changes took place, probably as a result of migrations, which are reflected in architecture as a stylistic dichotomy: in the zone occupied by the Totonacs, the tradition of cornices and niches continued, whereas in the areas conquered by the Nahuas, the style of the central Altiplano was imposed, as at Castillo de Teayo, Zempoala, and Quauhtochco (figure 51).

THE ORIGIN: EARTHEN ARCHITECTURE

The earliest monumental sites identified so far in central Veracruz date between 300 BC and AD 100. They were inspired by the late Olmec model of the Grijalva-Tonalá Basin, which developed before 400 BC at sites such as La Venta, El Mirador, La Libertad, and Plumajillo. These are great monumental centers with quadrangular plazas surrounded by pyramids and large platforms that are oriented toward the cardinal directions. The core of the site is typically bordered by cisterns or artificial lakes that double as borrow pits and as both real and ritual architectural barriers. A characteristic feature of central Veracruz is the recurring presence of ballcourts in association with the plazas and pyramids of the most important centers. This preoccupation with the ballgame is also reflected in the presence of polished stone objects such as yokes, axes, and palms, interpreted as ritual representations of a player's protective equipment (plates 169–71).

The cities of central Veracruz emerged at the same time as other great centers that would go on to become the capitals of the Classic world, such as El Mirador and Calakmul in the Maya jungle, Izapa in Chiapas, and Cantona, Xochitécatl, Cuicuilco, and Teotihuacán in the central Altiplano. The early buildings at all these sites have cores of packed earth faced with stone (where it was available), stucco, or simply fine clay. This form of construction gives the taller buildings a characteristic squat profile: because of the lack of containment systems able to control the internal pressure of the amorphous fill, the walls have very pronounced inclines. However, this inconvenience could be overcome by the Mesoamerican tradition of periodically reconstructing and enlarging existing buildings, since the substructures acted as buttresses, containing the lateral pressure of the earthen fill and permitting the construction of increasingly vertical walls.

Cerro de las Mesas is the best-known early center in southern central Veracruz. Studied in the 1940s by the team of Stirling and Drucker under the auspices of the Smithsonian Institu-

169, 170. (*top*) Bas-reliefs on the northeast part of the south ballcourt at El Tajín, depicting ballplayers wearing the yoke, axe, and palm for protection, AD 600–900.

171. (*above*) The south ballcourt at El Tajín, AD 600–900, runs the entire length of the south side of Building 5. The depressions along the center line are modern drains.

tion and the National Geographic Society, it drew attention for the size of its buildings and the presence of dated stelae that were originally grouped around a secondary plaza annexed to the main one. The site's architecture has many points of resemblance with that of Izapa, its contemporary. It is necessary to recall that central and southern Veracruz, the isthmus, and Chiapas all used the Isthmian script, which suggests that at least the elite of this broad region spoke the same language (plate 172), as did the Zoquean ethnic group.[1]

The structures of Cerro de las Mesas, built completely from packed earth, are organized around a large central pyramid 85 feet (26 meters) high, which is 23 feet (7 meters) higher than the Pyramid of the Niches at El Tajín. This earthen pyramid dominates four plazas arrayed in the cardinal directions, plus another two toward the southeast—the so-called Plaza of the Monuments—and the southwest, where the ballcourt is located. The eastern plaza yielded early evidence of the volute style, and of the decapitation ritual associated with the ballgame and with the use of yokes.[2]

Because this site was not explored until the 1940s and since then has been looted and affected by urban growth, we know little else, aside from the fact that it was a principal center of the lower basin of the Blanco River from the Late Formative through the entire Classic period.[3] However, in many aspects of its design and technique, its architecture was similar to that of La Joya, a site belonging to the same cultural sphere and located just 25 miles (40 kilometers) away, which is currently the object of extensive excavations.

The chronology of La Joya is similar to that of Cerro de las Mesas, and although La Joya was smaller, it was a principal center or capital of its region. Situated in the lower basin of the Cotaxtla River, it was built around two main plazas. The east plaza, larger in size and bordered by three monumental platforms and a pyramid, is the older of the two, probably dating to AD 100 to 200 (although the North Platform is even earlier; plate 173, figures 53, 55). The south plaza was configured in what has come to be called the standard plan, which is a constant in the coastal area of southern central Veracruz:[4] the small, square plaza is bordered on the north by a pyramid, on the south by a ballcourt, and on the east and west by asymmetrical, elongated platforms. Three cisterns separate these main structures from the residential mounds distributed around them (figure 54).

La Joya is currently on the verge of disappearing due to the extraction of earth for the manufacture of bricks. However, recent excavations of the pyramid and two of the monumental platforms have shed crucial light on the construction techniques, function, and chronology of the site's earthen architecture.

The substructure of the pyramid, dated to the second century AD, has been reconstructed as a square building of at least nine tiers with a total height of around 36 feet (11 meters), with four stairways almost 20 feet (6 meters) wide, finished with balustrades 4 feet (1.25 meters) wide (figure 56). This type of pyramid, which serves as a monumental representation of the

172. (*bottom left*) Stele 6 at Cerro de las Mesas, Veracruz, bearing the long count date 9.1.12.14.10 1 Oc, AD 468 (Miller 1991), and glyphs in the Isthmian script.

173. (*bottom right*) Stairway on the North Platform at La Joya, Veracruz, c. AD 300.

quadripartite Mesoamerican worldview, is less common than those with one or two stairways; it occurs with greater frequency and duration in the Maya zone (from the Late Formative, at Uaxactún, to the Postclassic, at Mayapán). In the La Joya pyramid's second stage of construction, in the Late Classic, it reached a height of more than 65 feet (20 meters).[5] The average height of the principal pyramids of central Veracruz—about 65 feet—may be related to the height of the local vegetation, since it can be verified that the summits of these pyramids protruded from the forest canopy, permitting visual contact between the centers not only by day but also by night, using fires in braziers. The same phenomenon may be observed in the Maya area, although there the pyramids are taller, given the greater height of the Petén jungle.

The monumental platforms measure some 300 feet (100 meters) on a side and 15 to 30 feet (5 to 10 meters) in height; their volumes exceed 350,000 cubic feet (10,000 cubic meters). In the cases of Chalahuite[6] and La Joya, their origin predates our own era. They have been interpreted as palatial residences due to their formal similarity to the Maya acropolises,[7] and this hypothesis has been confirmed by the excavations at La Joya. At this site, the platforms went through five or six stages of construction, spanning the first millennium AD. Each stage represents a repetition of the preceding one on a larger scale, with a combination of public areas accessible from the plaza and areas enclosed by perimeter walls that gave access to administrative buildings (council rooms with benches that have a sloped base), ritual buildings (terraced foundations), elite residential areas (spacious rooms), and service rooms (small spaces with kitchen areas). These structures are generally built atop low foundations accessed by stairways of two to four steps, with or without balustrades (figure 52). The walls are made of adobe blocks of a standardized size: 30 inches (80 centimeters) long, 12 or 16 inches (30 or 40 centimeters) wide (apparently depending on whether the wall is load-bearing or not), and 4 inches (10 centimeters) high; they are joined with mud plaster and finished with layers of clay, sometimes painted red. At La Joya, as well as in the complex of sites in the lower Jamapa-Cotaxtla Basin,[8] there is no evidence of the use of stucco in the Classic period, unlike at Cerro de las Mesas, where floors, stairways, and *taludes* of packed earth finished with stucco have been reported.[9]

The roofs, as far as we can tell from the cane imprints on mud walls burned in a fire at La Joya, were flat: branches or reeds about an inch (2 or 3 centimeters) in diameter were laid atop the walls and then covered with clay. The spaces roofed in this manner were up to 8 feet (2.5 meters) wide. There is evidence of circular columns and rectangular pilasters, also constructed of adobe blocks, that were set into the walls, perhaps to reinforce the roof beams.[10] The combination of stepped pyramids likely of ritual use with residential and administrative buildings is more similar to the Maya acropolises than to the palaces of central Altiplano sites like Xochicalco or Cacaxtla, or the great residential compounds of Teotihuacán, such as Atetelco, Tepantitla, or Zacuala.[11]

El Pital is another of the large early sites that have been studied recently (plates 174, 175; figure 57).[12] Located on the banks of the Nautla River, to the north of the Sierra de Chiconquiaco, this center consists of a series of plazas dominated by three main pyramids over 65 feet (20 meters) high. There are at least eight ballcourts, whose placement follows the two most common patterns in northern central Veracruz: to one side of a plaza, or to one side of a pyramid. (The same patterns are frequently found in the region of El Tajín, as we will see below.) The site seems to have reached its peak between AD 1 and 300, when the greatest amount of

174, 175. Two views of El Pital, Veracruz, c. AD 300.

construction took place, although it remained a capital through the entire Classic period.[13] Unlike at Cerro de las Mesas and La Joya, at El Pital the cores of earthen fill were faced with stone before being stuccoed, but this indicates easy access to the raw material rather than an architectural tradition different from that of the sites to the south.

CONSTRUCTION OFFERINGS

As elsewhere in Mesoamerica, in central Veracruz there is evidence that important offerings, including human sacrifices, were made in order to dedicate or terminate a stage of construction. It is noteworthy, though, that most of the objects offered were figurines of fired clay, of the kind that were used for domestic worship in other Classic cultures. Each construction stage of the East Platform at La Joya has yielded offerings of figurines of the "big-nosed god" (*dios narigudo*), which are associated with male burials, generally in a seated position.

One famous example of this type of activity was found at El Zapotal.[14] In a low platform bordering the eastern side of the site's main plaza, extensive excavations revealed the existence of a sanctuary accessible from the north by a stairway of nine steps. This sanctuary, an open room bordered by benches with sloped bases and decorated with mural paintings on its interior and exterior walls, contained a statue of a skeletal figure of natural size wearing an elaborate headdress—the death god Mictlantecuhtli—looking north toward the summit of the site's 79 foot (24 meter) tall pyramid (plate 176; figures 58, 59). Beneath the sanctuary was found a construction offering of clay figurines and vases from the Early Classic. In the Late Classic, following an elaborate ritual, the sanctuary was intentionally sealed off, which explains why the polychromed statue of raw clay was so well preserved. The termination offering consisted of rows of monumental female figures with closed eyes and open mouths, which have been interpreted as *cihuateteos*, or women who died in childbirth. There were also various burials in a seated position; most were of adult women, and some were accompanied by offerings of smiling figurines. Given that they were all interred at once, it is difficult to believe that these individuals died of natural causes; instead, they were probably sacrificed. The compound was then partially dismantled: the walls were cut down to the height of the statue of Mictlantecuhtli, and the space was filled with fine mud until the sanctuary was covered, leaving a flat surface above, which was later buried by another stage of construction.

These same practices were also observed at La Joya; indeed, such offerings are common across the entire region, a fact that has led to much looting and to the presence of figurines from central Veracruz in public and private collections of Mesoamerican art around the world.

THE UNIQUE FEATURES OF CLASSIC ARCHITECTURE IN CENTRAL VERACRUZ

So far we have seen that the early architecture of central Veracruz, both in packed earth and in stone, shares many elements with the rest of Mesoamerica: its configuration around plazas, the dominating height of the pyramids, astronomical orientations, the presence of offerings commemorating the beginning or end of a cycle, foundations accessed by stairways with balustrades, and mural paintings (as at El Zapotal, El Tajín, and Las Higueras). Other characteristics are more closely related to Maya canons: plazas integrating sculpture as a type of political and religious discourse, particularly in the form of dated stelae with glyphic inscriptions (such as the early stele of La Mojarra); palatial residences with multiple functions on raised foundations, like acropolises; pyramids with four stairways; and the presence of benches. However, it must be recalled that all of these features originated in the late Olmec tradition of the Grijalva-Tonalá Basin, and that they generally appeared in central Veracruz before they did in the Maya zone or the central Altiplano.

Nevertheless, there are two characteristics that set this region apart from the rest: the recurring association of the ballcourt with the main plaza at the larger sites, and the use of niches.

176. Polychromed sculpture of raw clay representing the death god Mictlantecuhtli, found in a U-shaped sanctuary with sloped benches along the wall. El Zapotal, Veracruz, AD 600–900.

The ballgame seems to have been an important factor in architectural arrangements over the entire course of the Classic period. Although there is already evidence of the ballgame being linked to the decapitation ritual, yokes, and volutes at the beginning of our era, in the early centers there was no ballcourt associated with the main plaza, which was typically large (on the order of 2½ acres—a hectare—or more) and bordered—but not enclosed—by three or four large pyramids or platforms, it not always being clear which of them was the most important. During the Classic, this pattern changes: the plaza is smaller and better defined, and is clearly dominated by the main pyramid and associated with a ballcourt. This paradoxical evolution, from larger plazas in an era of lower population densities to smaller plazas at the time when populations peaked, is noteworthy. It has been calculated that in the second half of the Classic, the capitals of this region had more than 2,500 people per square mile (or more than 1,000 per square kilometer)—a population density similar to that of the Maya zone in the same era[15]—so that the inhabitants of a site could easily have filled the plaza. In the case of the early centers, however, the plazas provided much more space than the local population would have required. The inference is that the plaza also accommodated foreign visitors, or served

purposes other than a purely congregational one (perhaps being used for markets, dances, processions, or other activities that required more space). The plaza's reduction in size would therefore seem to suggest changes in the social interactions that took place there.

Thus, by the second half of the Classic, the aforementioned arrangement—in which the ballcourt is placed opposite the pyramid, and on axis with it—predominated in the main plazas of sites in the coastal zone of central southern Veracruz. These main plazas definitely had ritual functions: according to the epigraphic, iconographic, and historical evidence, the pyramid was the foundation of the temple dedicated to the center's principal divinity, while the ballgame was associated with a fertility ritual that included human sacrifice by decapitation. Moreover, the plaza's lateral platforms may have been used to observe the solstices, in the manner of the Maya E Groups.[16]

The main plaza was always associated with a subordinate plaza that was annexed to it and possibly served administrative or commercial purposes; with a large platform, perhaps the ruler's residence, located a certain distance away; and with one or more cisterns that border the site center. The settlements with this standard plan are thus multicomponent, multifunctional centers that ranked high in the regional hierarchy. Generally they have a single ballcourt, but it is not unusual for them to have more than one, or even up to five, especially in those entities interpreted as segmented states that emerged in the second half of the Classic.[17]

The standard plan is limited to a coastal area in southern central Veracruz. In the rest of the region, we find a series of variations on it, although the association of the ballcourt with the main plaza at sites of greater importance was a constant throughout central Veracruz

177. Buildings 17 and 27 at El Tajín, AD 600–900, which form one of the city's seventeen ballcourts.

in the Classic period. In northern central Veracruz, in the Nautla Basin (at the aforementioned site of El Pital) and the region of El Tajín, and along the Arroyo Tlahuanapa (at Cerro Grande and Morgadal Grande),[18] we find ballcourts that are perpendicular or parallel to the pyramid, or on one side of the plaza. There is a greater variety at El Tajín, the site in central Veracruz with the most ballcourts, seventeen having been identified to date (plate 177). Here they are found next to pyramids or at the sides of plazas, but some may also have belonged to plazas built on the standard plan, and others may have stood alone. The only Mesoamerican city with more ballcourts than El Tajín is Cantona, Puebla, which has twenty-four. These were placed in the same positions as were common in central Veracruz: on axis with the pyramid (as in the standard plan), or to one side of it.

EL TAJÍN: THE *TALUD*, NICHE, AND FLYING CORNICE

Despite being known since the eighteenth century,[19] El Tajín has just begun to reveal its history (plate 178; figure 60). The first studies were carried out by Agustín García Vega (1934–36) and José García Payón (1938–77). The Tajín Project (1984–95), directed by Jürgen Brüggemann, and Arturo Pascual Soto's investigations (1996–98) of sites on the periphery of El Tajín and, more recently, of the western hill of the center itself have contributed much information about the pattern of settlement, absolute chronology, and architectural interpretation of the site.

Several studies agree that the earliest stage of the site's visible architecture (which belongs to the Late Classic) is represented by the buildings located on the plain between the arroyos,

178. (*above*) View of El Tajín, AD 600–1000.

179. (*overleaf*) The Pyramid of the Niches at El Tajín, AD 800–1000, with a ballcourt beside it.

180–85. The architecture of El Tajín, AD 600–1000, is characterized by a wide variety of niches, some adorned with a pattern of thin stone slabs.

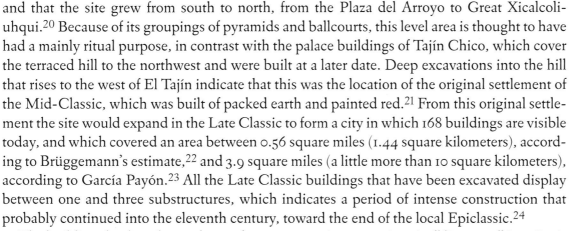

and that the site grew from south to north, from the Plaza del Arroyo to Great Xicalcoli-uhqui.[20] Because of its groupings of pyramids and ballcourts, this level area is thought to have had a mainly ritual purpose, in contrast with the palace buildings of Tajín Chico, which cover the terraced hill to the northwest and were built at a later date. Deep excavations into the hill that rises to the west of El Tajín indicate that this was the location of the original settlement of the Mid-Classic, which was built of packed earth and painted red.[21] From this original settlement the site would expand in the Late Classic to form a city in which 168 buildings are visible today, and which covered an area between 0.56 square miles (1.44 square kilometers), accord-ing to Brüggemann's estimate,[22] and 3.9 square miles (a little more than 10 square kilometers), according to García Payón.[23] All the Late Classic buildings that have been excavated display between one and three substructures, which indicates a period of intense construction that probably continued into the eleventh century, toward the end of the local Epiclassic.[24]

The building that has always drawn the most attention, ever since its "discovery" in 1785, is the Pyramid of the Niches (plate 179; figure 61). It came last in the sequence of construction, being built with an aberrant orientation[25] in a space that had been left open at the foot of the great retaining wall of Tajín Chico. In order to urbanize the plaza to its east, stairways were added to the northern side of Pyramid 5 and the rear facade of Pyramid 4, and an altar was placed in front. Formed of six tiers with a total height of 60 feet (18 meters), the Pyramid of the Niches has a seventh level that served as the foundation of the temple. The tiers are adorned with square recessed niches and crowned with flying cornices, each tier having three fewer niches per side than the one below it: 22, 19, 16, 13, 10, and 7. Multiplied by all four sides, this gives us 348 niches, to which we may add the 17 on the temple foundation (five on three sides and two in front) for a total of 365, one for each day of the solar year. (This is not counting the niches on the pyramid's stairway.)[26] Each niche is constructed of ten slabs of shale cut to measure, and the pillars and cornices are made of faced blocks of sandstone or limestone.

The pyramid was built without mortar, being stabilized instead by a precise distribution of the load. Afterward the entire structure was finished with stucco—which would be reapplied several times over the years—and painted red and black.[27]

El Tajín offers an almost infinite number of variations on the niche, which was a favorite theme of the site (plates 180–85): they may be rectangular, as on Building 5; decorated with a mosaic of stone slabs, as on Buildings 13 and 14; or porticoed, as on Building 10. The principle remains the same: the niched building was constructed of faced stone and then covered with painted stucco, creating a play of light and shade that makes the structure appear less heavy by breaking up the visual planes of its mass. The reflection of the tropical sun from the smooth surfaces of the stuccoed buildings is particularly hard on the eyes, as archaeologists find when they make drawings of these structures.

The niche first appears as an architectural element in the Late Formative, at Tlalancaleca, Tlaxcala, on the central Altiplano.[28] In the Early Classic, it is found at Teotihuacán[29] and Tikal,[30] with variants at Monte Albán (the so-called scapular niche).[31] Its presence in central Veracruz is recorded by the Mid- or Late Classic, in the Sierra de los Tuxtlas[32] and in the upper basin of the Blanco River, at Maltrata (where it is depicted on the monolith of the same name) and Toro Prieto.[33] The people in the region of El Tajín adopted the niche and made it one of the main elements of their architectural style, spreading it throughout much of northern central Veracruz, from the immediate vicinity of the site[34] to the area of Tuxpan in the north, and to the Sierra Madre in the east and southeast, at Yohualichan (plate 190)[35] and Banderilla.[36]

Another interesting building at El Tajín is Pyramid 16, which dominates the Plaza del Arroyo on the northern side. The excavations directed by Mario Navarrete in the 1990s revealed that in the last three stages of its construction this pyramid had 366 niches. In order to arrive at this number, a platform was added to a section of the pyramid's east side, thereby

reducing the number of niches on the first tier. It is noteworthy that the site thus has two buildings whose number of niches is clearly related to the days of the solar year (a normal year and a leap year).

On Tajín Chico, unlike the ritual area on the plain, we find residential buildings grouped together on different steps terraced into the natural elevation. There appear to have been audience halls surrounded by benches (such as Buildings Y, Q, and I, which are the first you encounter when you ascend onto Tajín Chico) and living areas (such as Buildings A, B, and C; plates 186, 187). On the summit stands the Building of the Columns (plate 189), which has been interpreted as the palace of the ruler 13 Rabbit, whose life and deeds are depicted on the three sculpted columns that adorn the entrance portico.[37] The interior spaces of these buildings had flat roofs of mortar (lightened by the inclusion of potsherds and pumice), supported by walls, columns, and pilasters constructed of faced blocks joined with mortar and covered with stucco. These roofed spaces were up to 11½ feet (3.5 meters) wide, which was greater than the typical span of the corbelled arch used by the Maya.

Finally, we must mention what is called the Great Xicalcoliuhqui. Located on the plain to the north of the site, this is a raised plaza with a surface area of approximately 2½ acres (1 hectare), surrounded by an impressive wall with monumental niches that forms a spiral 1,194 feet (364 meters) long (plate 188; figures 62a, 62b). Inside are two small ballcourts, the more central one being configured in a standard plan.

Access to this raised plaza is restricted to nine narrow doors, which makes us wonder about the nature of the ballgames celebrated in such an exclusive space, invisible to those circulating outside. The human cost of building the plaza must have been enormous: it is calculated

186. (*above*) Building A on Tajín Chico, El Tajín. AD 600–1000.

187. (*opposite*) Building B on Tajín Chico, El Tajín, AD 600–1000.

188. (*above*) The Great Xicalcoliuhqui, El Tajín, AD 600–1000.

189. (*below*) The Building of the Columns on Tajín Chico, El Tajín, AD 600–1000, the palace of the ruler 13 Rabbit.

that the monolithic blocks that were used weigh between 0.5 and 3 tons, and the visual impact makes the spectator feel small.[38] This structure is also important for another reason: its excavation revealed that it was affected by a catastrophic flood that left deposits of boulders and pebbles 6½ feet (2 meters) thick in some areas. This same flood damaged Building 22 and the ends of Buildings 17 and 27.[39] The flood deposits were never removed, which suggests that the inhabitants either decided not to do so or had already abandoned the site. Whether this catastrophic flood was the cause or the result of the site's abandonment is a question that has yet to be resolved. In any case, rubble from the buildings began to accumulate over the flood deposits, and on top of this there appeared crude circular or oval structures, which were made of stones recovered from the ruins and were associated with ceramics related to Totonac or Huastec groups.

As we have seen, the architectural style of El Tajín was distributed across a large part of northern central Veracruz. However, it also seems to have influenced the Late Classic architecture of the Huastec area during the Tanquil phase,[40] in the area of Río Verde in San Luis Potosí,[41] and at sites like Ranas and Toluquilla in the Sierra Gorda.[42] In these places there appeared structures of stone slabs with *taludes* crowned by counter-*taludes* (this is, with cornices that project from the top of the *talud*), with or without niches, as well as ballcourts and yokes, and interwoven volutes on stone and ceramic objects. This apparent diffusion of elements of the architecture and culture of El Tajín toward the north and west between AD 600 and 900 might explain what occurred in the Postclassic in northern central Veracruz.

190. (*below*) Yohualichan, Puebla, AD 600–1000, a site whose architectural style was influenced by that of El Tajín.

THE POSTCLASSIC SITES

In the transition from the Classic to the Postclassic, major changes took place in central Veracruz. In order to understand them, we must recall that population movements were taking place throughout Mesoamerica at this time. At the end of the Classic, groups from northern Mexico began to move back toward the central Altiplano, creating a demographic pressure.[43] In some cases, these immigrant groups were able to settle peacefully; in others, they occupied the land by force, killing or displacing the original inhabitants. The latter scenario is probably what occurred in central Veracruz, when Totonacs who had originally settled in Puebla (in the area of Zacatlán) were compelled to descend toward the coastal zone between the Cazones and Antigua rivers. Meanwhile, Nahuas from the central Altiplano and Tlaxcala entered the area from both the north (along the Necaxa and Tuxpan rivers) and the south (along the Cotaxtla River). These two groups related to the coastal inhabitants in very different ways, and this is reflected in the region's architecture.

191. (*below left*) The cemetery at Quiahuiztlán, Veracruz, AD 900–1500.

192. (*below right*) The Eastern Complex at Quiahuiztlán, AD 900–1500.

193. (*above*) Building A, Paxil, Veracruz, AD 900–1200.

194. (*below*) Patterned niche at Vega de la Peña, Veracruz, AD 900–1500.

Many characteristics of the Classic architecture of central Veracruz survived in the area occupied by the Totonacs, as part of the new culture: slab construction, *taludes* and counter-*taludes*, and occasionally niches and flying cornices, as well as interlaced meanders and volutes (although the latter do not appear in stone, but rather painted on fine paste ceramics of the Isla de Sacrificios type). The construction of ballcourts also continued, now with the novelty of *tlachtemalacatl*, or goal rings. There are many sites in the foothills of the Sierra de Chiconquiaco, such as Sollacuauhtla, Vega de Alatorre, Misantla, Los Ídolos, and Vega de Aparicio, but very few have been studied. Only three have been the object of recent investigations: Paxil (plate 193; figure 63),[44] Vega de la Peña (plate 194; figure 64),[45] and Quiahuiztlán. At these sites, ballcourts continued to be built near the main plaza and the great pyramid, suggesting that the ballgame retained its importance in Totonac society. However, the rules of the game had changed: it seems that the sculptures of yokes, axes, and palms were no longer being made, which could mean a change in the associated ritual; meanwhile, the introduction of a

goal ring indicates a new form of scoring, since the sources inform us that when the ball passed through the ring, it was a total victory, and the game was over.

The buildings, particularly the pyramids, are generally not as tall as they were in the Classic, a phenomenon that can also be observed in the Nahua area of central Veracruz, and in Mesoamerica as a whole. This has been related to the growing secularization of society during the Postclassic. But the architectural components remained very similar: foundations of *taludes* crowned by counter-*taludes*.

In the case of Quiahuiztlán, the first stage was built in the traditional style, employing slab construction with counter-*taludes* and niches, and with a ballcourt placed near the great pyramid in the Eastern Complex (plate 192). In the second stage, called Toltec by the archaeologist in charge,[46] the earlier building of the cemetery complex was covered by nearly vertical slopes of quarried stone, with stairways featuring balustrades finished with cubes. To the north and west of this foundation are grouped miniature temples that cover burials, for which reason they have come to be called mausoleum tombs (plate 191). They are built in the style of the central Altiplano, with smooth, nearly vertical walls and stairways with balustrades also topped by cubes. These mausoleum tombs have been recorded in at least eleven sites in the Sierra de Chiconquiaco and on the eastern slope of the Eastern Sierra Madre, which corresponds to the Totonac area, meaning that this adoption of the Altiplano style may be a case of cultural syncretism.[47]

In the area under Nahua control, the break with the Late Classic tradition was absolute, and the region as a whole adhered to the canons of the central Altiplano. The best-studied Nahua sites in central Veracruz are Castillo de Teayo (plate 199) in the north, Zempoala (plates 195, 197) and Oceloapan in the center, and Quauhtochco (figure 67) in the south. It is thought that Castillo was a Nahua outpost on the Tuxpan River, and that Quauhtochco and Cotaxtla (plate 196) were initially occupied by the Tlaxcaltecan Nahuas and then later conquered by the Tlatelolcans and Aztecs. The Totonac area south of the Sierra de Chiconquiaco, including the dominions of Zempoala (to which Oceloapan belonged) and Quiahuiztlán, was subjugated by the Triple Alliance, which is why the late architecture at these sites reflects the style of the central Altiplano rather than that derived from El Tajín.[48]

195. (*above*) The Templo Mayor, Zempoala, Veracruz, AD 900–1500.

196. (*below*) Calendar stone from Cotaxtla, Veracruz, AD 1300–1500.

197. (*above*) The so-called House of Moctezuma, Zempoala, AD 900–1500.

198. (*right*) The Temple of Ehécatl, Zempoala, AD 900–1500.

And the imported style was very different: its pyramids had *taludes* that were nearly vertical and covered with smooth stucco, creating great white planes that stood in sharp contrast to the surfaces of the local type, articulated horizontally and vertically by niches and cornices and adorned with balustrades topped by cubes. Even in those areas previously characterized by earthen architecture—due to the scarcity of stone—the walls of Postclassic structures were covered with stone and a stucco made of shell lime.

New kinds of buildings emerge as well: pyramids with double sanctuaries and rounded temples of Ehécatl (plate 198). On the other hand, ballcourts seem to have been absent. In order to demarcate the main areas, instead of cisterns or watercourses, perimeter walls, or *coatepantli*, were used, which may or may not have acted as fortifications, a reflection of the insecurity of those times.

The layout of the sites also changes: instead of a more or less concentric distribution, with the larger buildings at the center and the smaller ones around them, the sites occupied by the Nahuas are grouped into separate complexes, which are sometimes walled off (as, for example, at Zempoala, with its twelve walled compounds; figures 65, 66).[49] This pattern has been linked to the social organization of cities into neighborhoods (*calpulli*) and, more recently, with the *altepetl* political system.[50]

In sculpture, divinities are represented in the style of the central Altiplano, seated with legs folded in front of their chests, instead of with legs crossed or dangling from a high seat as was the custom in the Classic period. These statues are made of stone or clay, which indicates that the local technique of making monumental terra-cotta figures was transmitted to the new arrivals.

199. Castillo de Teayo, Veracruz, AD 1200–1500.

9
THE HUASTEC REGION

GUSTAVO A. RAMÍREZ CASTILLA

CUEXTLÁN OR XOCHITLALPAN, THE PLACE OF FLOWERS

That is how the ancient Mexicans referred to this region crowned with exuberant green foliage. They also knew it as Tonacatlalpan—the place of sustenance—where food and water were abundant, and where beautiful and finely crafted objects of cotton and clay were produced. And as Cuextecapan—the land of Cuextécatl, the ruler named for Ce Ácatl Topiltzin Quetzalcóatl—located to the east between the seashore and the mountains, where there lived women with hips up to four palms wide who adorned their hair with *cuextes* (buns) of colored ribbons. That was the idea, the perception of a faraway country, beautiful, rich, warm, and sensual; it was the paradisiacal vision of the Huastec region, of the province of Panoayan or Pánuco, Amichel, or Victoria Garayana, equally sought after by the Aztecs and the Spaniards who came later.

The Huastec region, or the Huasteca, located in northeastern Mexico, between the mouths of the Soto la Marina and Cazones rivers (figure 68), enjoys a privileged geographic situation. Basking in the sunshine of the Tropic of Cancer, it maintains warm temperatures for most of the year. It receives abundant rainfall, which makes the land fertile and feeds the enormous mirror lake of the Tamesí River and the coastal swamps. There are exceptional *cenotes*,[1] or sinkholes, formed by subterranean currents flowing between sheets of limestone. The humidity wafted in by the trade winds from the Gulf of Mexico sustains tropical forests and jungles, home to hundreds of animal species.

The limits of the Huastec region are set by the Eastern Sierra Madre, which runs northwest from the central coast of Veracruz. The landscape is enriched by wrinkles that conceal intermontane valleys, and by folds, fractures, landslides, lava flows, and karstic caverns that give rise to varied ecological niches and microclimates, the most important of which originates right in the seam between two great climatic zones, the nearctic and the neotropic.

The Huastec heights enjoy a temperate climate, with abundant rainfall, fog, and forests of pine and oak. All of these conditions favored the early occupation of the territory; the first evidence of sedentary agricultural settlements with pottery dates back to 1700 BC,[2] a time when different peoples established themselves in northern Veracruz, expanding toward the periphery in the centuries that followed. The presence of outside traditions in various eras is proven by finds of ceramics whose technique of manufacture and decorative style are markedly different.[3] Around AD 1200, a new style of ceramics, sculpture, and certain aspects of architecture unified the region's different material expressions, and perhaps also its ideas and traditions, shaping the culture that in archaeological terms is known as Huastec. Under this single material culture were amalgamated ethnic and linguistic groups as diverse as the Nahua, the Totonac, the Pame, the Tepehuan, the Otomi, and the Teenek. The latter spoke the Huastec language, which is related to Mayan, although the two tongues separated approximately 3,600 years ago.[4]

MATERIALS

The geological conditions of the Huastec region provided man with high-quality materials for the construction of earthen and stone foundations. The coastal plains were an inexhaustible source of the sandstone and shell conglomerates that were used in architecture and sculpture, as was limestone from the Sierra Madre, which was also converted into lime. Some of the lava flows provided basalt for construction, and also for the manufacture of *metates*, the flat mortars used for grinding corn.

The lagoons, rivers, and ocean provided the tons of shell that were used to manufacture another variety of lime through burning and pulverization. Shells were also employed as a construction material for elevations, fills, and simple mounds; meanwhile, earth, sand, and river cobbles were used to cover walls. On a lesser scale, asphalt, *muca* (coral), fired clay, potsherds, and the ashes or remains of plants, animals, and people were also utilized for building. And we must not forget that wood and foliage—the lost elements of architecture—were widely used in the construction of the walls, roofs, stairways, ornaments, and furnishings of civic-religious buildings and family residences.

TOOLS

When we contemplate delicately carved sculptures or precisely cut stone blocks, we may be inclined to think that their creators required a wide variety of tools; however, the archaeological evidence shows that these were limited to wooden wedges and hoes, axes, hammers, and chisels of hard stone. In the Huastec region, bronze was unknown until the thirteenth or fourteenth century,[5] and it still has not been confirmed whether axes and chisels of this metal were used in construction. The lime plaster must have been smoothed with trowels, as it was in the central Altiplano, where a wide variety of stone trowels have been found; in the Huastec region, these implements were perhaps made of wood, which would explain why none have been recovered. Finally, wide and fine-tipped brushes of vegetable fiber and animal, or even human, hair were used to give a colorful touch to temples, houses, and sculptures, but of the painter's tools there remain only fragments of the vases and palettes that held the prized pigments.

It is not known what instruments were used for the measurement and orientation of buildings; however, we can infer that a knotted rope may have served the former purpose, and a series of stakes aligned to a geographic or celestial reference point, the latter. In order to maintain vertical faces, the ancient builders may have used plumb lines, of which we have examples from other regions, while the horizontal alignment of the stone courses would have been achieved with a string or cord.

200. Mound at Rancho San Diego, Pánuco, Veracruz, that has been cut through the middle, exposing a core of dark earth covered by layers of lighter earth. Late Formative.

LIMITATIONS

The absence of sufficient research makes it difficult to characterize Huastec architecture and its regional styles. Of the hundreds of existing sites, only a dozen have been excavated, and of these, barely one-third have been the object of extensive investigations with published results. Nevertheless, we will propose a general outline by assembling the few available fragments.

EARTHEN ARCHITECTURE

The HV-24 site at Altamirano, Veracruz,[6] boasts the earliest known sequence of occupation in the Huastec region. Its ceramics point to the Chajil cultural phase, dating from 1700 to 1300 BC.[7] The settlement was sited on a hilltop near the Pánuco River, on which two circular structures and other oval and quadrangular ones were erected.[8] The earliest were built entirely of earth, without stone, with a diameter of 20 to 23 feet (6 to 7 meters) and a height of about 3 feet (1 meter).[9] While we cannot claim that these were all constructed at the start of the Early Formative—since some of them are from later periods—they may be considered the most ancient buildings at the site due to their lack of stone facings and stairways,[10] although, as we shall see, this is not necessarily a determining factor.

We cannot say with certainty the exact date when low earthen mounds began to be built in Huastec territory; it is possible that in the beginning, the villages had neither mounds nor platforms, since they would have become necessary only after the arrival of cult practices and the establishment of residences for priests and rulers inside the ceremonial area.[11]

The first earthen buildings had circular plans and profiles in the shape of a dome or a slightly truncated cone, with cores of sod and charcoal—packed or burned earth. Excavations in mounds from the Late Formative at the sites 3–Crucitas, 12–Rubén Jaramillo, and others in San Luis Potosí[12] indicate that their cores were made of a mixture of earth and charcoal, which was then covered with a lighter-colored soil.[13] Another example of this may be seen in a mound at Rancho San Diego, Veracruz, that has been cut through the middle (plate 200).

The earth that was used for construction must have been broken up with stone hoes fitted with handles, transported in baskets, and then compacted with water and a wooden tamper—work that required an enormous number of man-hours. The extraction of earth left hollows that would later be used as water reservoirs, popularly known as *jagüeyes*.[14]

As construction techniques were perfected, the diameter and height of the buildings increased. Thus, in the compound of circular structures at Ébano, San Luis Potosí, erected on a platform surrounded by streams, the largest mound has a diameter of 89 feet (27 meters) at its base and is 10 feet (3 meters) tall.[15] Like those of HV-24, it lacks a stairway or any facing. On top of it were found the remains of a possible wooden structure,[16] which would mean that it was crowned with a temple. Ébano presents ceramics typical of Period I (500 to 100 BC). Chila,[17] another settlement in Veracruz from this period,[18] located on the banks of the stream bearing the same name, consists of twelve circular buildings and oval platforms made of earth; the largest mound measures 110 feet (33 meters) at its base and is 16 feet (4 meters) high.[19]

During the Classic period, the earthen structures of the Huastec region reached their greatest dimensions. At Tamtoc,[20] San Luis Potosí, builders took advantage of a group of hills that lay on a plain surrounded by a wide meander of the Tampaón River in order to model a series of ceremonial structures of enormous dimensions (figure 69).[21] Outstanding among these

are the pyramids known as Paso del Bayo and El Tizate, which are more than 100 feet (30 meters) high and 650 feet (200 meters) wide at the base (plate 201). El Tizate, located to the extreme west of the site, has on its eastern face a stone stairway, one of the first in the region on this type of building. At the center of the site there are three nearly parallel elevations that run south-southwest to north-northeast, occupying a quadrangle of 1,150 by 1,300 feet (350 by 400 meters): to the west is Cerro Tantoque, from which the site gets its name; in the middle is the Sunken Patio; and to the east is the Eastern Platform with the Great Corridor, a kind of rectilinear channel dug into the platform and ending at Cerro Piedras Paradas.[22] These structures were partially[23] shaped by man with cuts and fills of a whitish or chalky earth, apparently volcanic ash.[24] The architecture was then complemented by monumental sculptures and bas-reliefs of sandstone and limestone in the style of central Veracruz,[25] thus highlighting the ritual and political character of these compounds (plate 202). Tamtoc was abandoned after a brief period of use and would not be reoccupied until the Late Postclassic.[26]

In the same era as the ceremonial center at Tamtoc emerged, the island of Pitahaya, in Chairel Lagoon across from what is now Tampico, Tamaulipas, was enlarged with hundreds of tons of oyster shells[27] until it reached a size of 27 acres (11 hectares).[28] On the far northern part of the islet, a compound of twelve circular and elongated mounds was constructed entirely of heaped-up oyster shells and sand (figure 70);[29] the mounds are sheathed in vertical slabs of sandstone to a height of a few meters from the base,[30] a feature shared with another site, one with stone buildings, that was discovered in the Sierra de la Palma in 1873 and seems to date to a later era.[31] Ekholm identifies Pitahaya as a site characteristic of periods II and III, between 100 BC and AD 700.[32] A similar site is Isleta Chica, close to Pánuco, with its three mounds made of sand and debris.[33]

At the beginning of the Postclassic, earthen architecture underwent a revolution. The mounds clearly acquired the form of a truncated cone, were covered with a thick layer of mixed lime and sand, and in some cases had stairways with balustrades. The site of Las Flores in Tampico is a case in point. Reports from the early twentieth century describe up to twenty-two mounds with these characteristics.[34] An excavation of the only surviving mound, the Pyramid of the Flowers or Mound 1,[35] revealed five substructures with similar features, with stairways leading in different directions and coats of lime mortar, sometimes painted solid red or with parallel red lines.[36] The presence of twenty-six floors of mortar within the mound would seem to indicate an equal number of repairs or renovations (figure 71).[37] The core of the pyramid is

203. (*below bottom*) Altar with bas-reliefs, from Celaya, El Mante, Tamaulipas. Early Postclassic.

204. (*right*) The Great Mound of Vega de Otates, Veracruz. Late Postclassic.

made of sandy, compacted earth, with a few pebbles, and the stairways and balustrades are of the same material; thus each stage of the building was basically modeled by hand out of mud, then covered with a wet mortar of ground shell, lime, and sand,[38] and finally smoothed over. The heat of the sun was essential for the hardening of these materials. The mortar dries very hard but is easily resoftened by water,[39] which means that it would have required constant maintenance, as the numerous floors suggest.

Du Solier identifies two architectural traditions at Las Flores. In the first tradition, the foundations are surmounted by circular temples, and in the second and later one, by quadrangular temples.[40] Buildings made of sand and finished with mortar may also be found in the lake basin of the Tamesí and the lagoons of Pueblo Viejo and Tamiahua, but without stairways or balustrades.[41]

The final phase of earthen architecture is represented by the great Postclassic sites at Vega de Otates, Veracruz, and Celaya–El Triunfo II and Tancol, Tamaulipas; in addition to circular plans, quadrangular ones became widespread, with buildings reaching up to 33 feet (10 meters) in height, either on large platforms or distributed around four-sided plazas (figure 72). These structures, like the earlier ones, lack stairways and balustrades, even though these features were already common in contemporary stone architecture. Monumental stone sculpture no longer formed an integral part of architecture, but it was the central motif in the construction of temples and plazas. Two noteworthy reliefs were found at the Celaya site: one represents the Lord of Death, and the other is a quadrangular altar with a smooth center bordered by a frame of bas-reliefs in the style of central Veracruz (plate 203),[42] similar to Altar I of Cholula, Puebla,[43] from the Cholulteca II period (AD 900 to 1325; figure 73). Tancol and Vega de Otates offer clear proof that the construction of earthen mounds without stairways or balustrades continued until Period VI (AD 1250 to 1500) (plate 204). A test pit in Mound 5 at Tancol revealed two successive stages of construction, both finished with an earthen floor. The mound was built over an ancient mortar floor, and at the northeast edge of its base were found several blocks of a shell conglomerate, possibly an artificial stone made of ground shell and lime paste.[44] These blocks measured 16 inches (40 centimeters) on a side and were 4 inches (10 centimeters) thick.[45] At Vega de Otates, meanwhile, earthen mounds without stairways were erected atop large quadrangular platforms up to 16 feet (5 meters) tall. A late variation on the earthen mound is represented by certain examples with a core of boulders and mud, sometimes covered with mortar,[46] which are found in the area of Tampico Alto, Veracruz.

In the earlier phases, the compounds of earthen structures were built on hills close to water sources, generally in a scattered rather than a symmetrical pattern. In the Postclassic, however, several sites were planned in a concentrated, symmetrical fashion around quadrangular plazas, on flat plains far away from water.

STONE ARCHITECTURE

The earliest stone structures in the Huastec region would seem to be the mounds of piled stones that are distibuted across a wide area between Huejutla and Tepehuacán, Hidalgo. In this region, the raw materials for construction were provided by deposits of alluvial silt and sandstone, and by the streams and creeks that cross them. The mounds have a conical shape, although their plan is not entirely circular, and are 5 to 20 feet (1.5 to 6 meters) high and up to 65 feet (20 meters) in diameter. They are constructed entirely of medium- and large-sized boulders, sometimes with slabs of sandstone mixed in, but without earth or any other kind of binding material (plate 206). Since their surfaces were not covered with earth or otherwise smoothed, these mounds could not have served as the foundations of temples, and did not have stairways. They were built on flat plains or fields furrowed by nearby streams. One site, Chumaquico,[47] also presents a series of elevations rather like large, irregular platforms, varying in height between 2 and 2½ feet (60 and 80 centimeters).[48]

205. (*below left*) Tomb at Tetzacual, Huejutla, Hidalgo, with walls of monolithic blocks and a roof of four large slabs. Probably Late Formative.

206. (*below top*) Mounds of piled stone at Vinasco, Huejutla, Hidalgo, whose destruction has been hastened by the removal of the stones for use as construction fill. Late Formative.

207. (below bottom) A school has been built atop one of the two quadrangular stone platforms at Tetzacual.

208. (right) This stone road, which passes between the mounds of Tetzacual and connects more than ten communities to Huejutla, is still in use.

Inside some of the stone mounds, which are known locally as *tetzacualis*,[49] there have been discovered tombs that, unlike the mounds themselves, were carefully built. At Vinasco, Du Solier reported two tombs, which are distinguished by stairways that lead down to a small, unroofed antechamber;[50] one of them contained ceramics typical of the Late Formative, Period II (100 BC to AD 200).[51] Another tomb, Building A, located inside a sloping rectangular platform at Huichapa,[52] displays the same method of construction: it has walls of superimposed slabs carved on the visible face and set with mud onto a monolithic floor. The tomb chamber is covered by four slabs weighing nearly eight tons.[53] Another architectural variation is represented by a tomb recently discovered at Tetzacual (plate 205):[54] its walls were constructed entirely of enormous slabs about 3½ feet (or a little more than a meter) long and 16 inches (40 centimeters) wide and thick, and its roof consists of four wide slabs set perpendicularly over the walls. Unlike the tombs mentioned above, this one provides lateral access without a stairway, being open on its southeast side. It is set inside a mound identical to those already described, approximately 20 feet (6 meters) tall and located about 65 feet (20 meters) from the cliff that overlooks the river. In addition to numerous mounds, this site has two enormous quadrangu-

lar platforms, apparently from a later period (plate 207),[55] and a stone road almost 12½ miles (20 kilometers) long that connects numerous communities to Huejutla (plate 208).[56]

The *tetzacualis* have the characteristics of an incipient stone architecture: massive but crude, using no adhesive material and lacking stairways. They basically serve a funerary function, incorporating tombs whose walls of stone slabs or monolithic blocks were constructed with greater care.

The next stage in the development of an architecture of defined forms and structures took place at Tancanhuitz, San Luis Potosí.[57] Here, set atop a long hill, there is a compound of twelve buildings that have yielded figurines and burials, and which include a circular building contemporary with that of Cuicuilco.[58] The other buildings have quadrangular and apsidal, or horseshoe-shaped, plans, and are up to 20 feet (6 meters) tall. The circular structure, which is 40 feet (12 meters) in diameter and 10 feet (3 meters) high, was composed of three superimposed tiers with sloping sides, made of stone slabs set in mud and lacking stairways;[59] however, Du Solier suggests that these stone *taludes* served only to hold in the core of the structure, which was originally covered with another layer of material so as to give it the shape of a truncated cone.[60] There is another circular mound at Huichapa, Hidalgo,[61] with six stone tiers topped by two rectangular altars with rounded corners.[62] It represents the beginnings of the stairway without balustrades. Tancanhuitz shows how the stone structures of the Huastec region evolved from the circular plan to the apsidal one: to the principal facade of the circumference was added a straight segment, inspired by the rectangular buildings with rounded corners that came into fashion during the Classic. This progression is confirmed by changes in other aspects of construction,[63] and by a singular architectural group at Tampozoque, San Luis Potosí,[64] in which four originally circular buildings, with stairways lacking balustrades,

209. (*above*) The Ceremonial Plaza at Tamtoc. During the site's second stage of occupation, in the Postclassic, more than fifty buildings with circular, quadrangular, and apsidal layouts were built from cobblestones and slabs.

210. *(below)* Structure AN 2, the Corcovado Mound, at Tamtoc, built with inclined walls of cobblestones and slabs. Platforms that served as house foundations were added on top of it. Late Postclassic.

were absorbed within a large rectangular platform with stairways in front; the two rear structures were converted to an apsidal plan. At Tamtoc, the great Huastec ceremonial center of the Classic period, ancient circular stone buildings were also modified into an apsidal shape, apparently to serve as priestly residences.[65] This type of foundation would continue to grow more common.[66]

During Tamtoc's second occupation, in the Postclassic, gigantic structures were created by modifying natural hills, and more than fifty other mounds and platforms were constructed. They were distributed in an east-west direction, in seven groups surrounding more or less well-defined plazas or open spaces (plate 209).[67] The most noteworthy of these buildings is the Corcovado Mound (AN 2), 26 feet (8 meters) high and 154 feet (47 meters) long, which seems to have originally been an elongated hill that in later stages was covered with cobblestone walls and had three stairways added to its southern face (plate 210). Two terraces were afterward constructed on its summit, and over these was placed a third terrace, whose apsidal shape indicates that it was the foundation of a habitation. Although AN 2 had a ceremonial use, it has not been ruled out as the residence of the local ruler.[68]

Practically the entire architectural history of Tamtoc is represented in Group A, or the Ceremonial Plaza, which consists of twenty-three buildings. The earliest structures of its initial phase were low circular platforms with cobblestone walls that were used as habitations. It was also in this stage that the ballgame was introduced (building AS 5).[69]

In the second phase, the circular structures were expanded and converted to an apsidal plan. The quadrangular plan was introduced as well, in buildings with cobblestone walls and a *talud-tablero* profile[70] similar to that of Teotihuacán; there were also buildings with a low, straight, terraced profile (figure 74). Stairways were oriented toward the middle of the plaza,

except in two cases, that of AC 1—which, due to its central position, has two stairways oriented toward the east and west—and the Corcovado Mound. There are also faux stairways and ramplike balustrades.[71]

In the third phase, limestone slabs began to be used for the construction of walls and stairways. The difficulty of obtaining this material, which had to be carried on people's backs from the distant hills of Cuayalab and Agua Nueva,[72] seems to have limited its application mainly to stairways, cornices supporting the *tablero*, and the ornamental parts of walls; only four buildings on the Ceremonial Plaza were built entirely of limestone slabs.[73] Aside from limestone, *pudinga*—a conglomerate of round stones—was used to a lesser extent, as well as fragments of *metates* and sculptures.[74]

New explorations have revealed a stone workshop and a ritual channel in the northwestern sector of the site known as the Noria Group.[75] The channel leads to Los Patos Lagoon, whose waters flow from a spring at the foot of Monument 32, where there is a bas-relief representing a decapitation ritual related to water (plate 211).[76] An oval pit, lined with cobblestones and slabs of rock, seems to have served as a ceremonial basin; its walls are carved with bas-reliefs in the style of central Veracruz. It is believed that water was the central element of the religion of Tamtoc, as these structures dedicated to its veneration show.

Located a few miles south of Tamtoc, the Cerro de Agua Nueva preserves the remains of a magnificent city built entirely of stone slabs. Although its origins go back to the Late Formative (Tantuan II phase, 350 BC to AD 200), it reached its peak in the late Postclassic (Tamuín

211. Ritual channel at Tamtoc that guides the waters of a spring as they emerge from the foot of Monument 32, where an enormous bas-relief represents a decapitation ritual in which the divine water—blood—spouts from the headless necks. Early Classic.

212. The Great Southern Platform, Tamohi, San Luis Potosí. The positioning of the *tablero*, which is flush with the top of the *talud* rather than protruding from it, represents an architectural innovation in the Huastec region. Late Postclassic.

phase, AD 1200 to 1555).[77] Constructed on artificial terraces on the hillside, the city comprises seven architectural compounds of a civic-religious and residential character;[78] the structures from the final period are contemporary with with those of Tamtoc and Tamohi, sites with which they share architectural features. However, it is important to emphasize the presence of numerous circular buildings finished with stone slabs carved into a trapezoidal shape so that they fit perfectly around the circumference of the structure. This technical advance was applied at other sites, such as the La Campana ranch in Nuevo Morelos, and Tammapul and Sierra de la Palma in Tamaulipas (figure 75). Agua Nueva is also noteworthy for the use of the cornice with an inverted slope that is characteristic of El Tajín, although this feature had already been employed in Building A at Cuatlamayán, San Luis Potosí.[79]

Coats of lime-sand mortar were applied to walls not merely as whitewash, but as a support for mural painting. This art form may have been widespread in the cities of the Postclassic, but so far its traces have only been found at Tamtoc and Tamohi in San Luis Potosí.[80] At the latter site, located on the southern bank of the Tampaón River (figure 76), is preserved the most complete example of Huastec mural painting: executed over an altar, it depicts a procession of richly attired figures (figure 77). This mural reveals the introduction, around the fifteenth century, of a style of figurative art very different from the usual abstract and geometric symbols that covered the ceramics and sculpture of Period VI.

The architecture of Tamohi also shows evidence of external contacts, indicating the presence of the Aztecs in the central Huastec region. The best-explored part of this site is a section

of the Great Southern Platform, which is a rectangular structure 407 feet (124 meters) long and 20 feet (6 meters) high.[81] On top of it are six buildings distributed around a quadrangular plaza open to the west, where the stairways are located. Inside the plaza are three altars, a stuccoed channel, and a circular tank.[82]

The platform, like the other buildings mentioned, has an earthen core and a cobblestone *talud* crowned by a cornice of slabs that supports the cobblestone *tablero*.[83] Unlike at Tamtoc, the *tablero* does not project from the *talud* but rather stands flush with the top of it; this is a completely new feature in this architectural tradition (plate 212). The walls were covered with a thick coat of smoothed and painted mortar. The western facade of the platform presents two stairways, the main one located in the middle, and the narrower one at the southern end (plate 213). These stairways are flanked by thick balustrades in the form of ramps; other stairways in the compound have the same sort of balustrades, and are also crowned by a large cube, a feature that is novel in this region (plate 214). However, ramp balustrades finished with cubes are characteristic of certain pyramidal foundations of the central Altiplano, such as those of Tenayuca, Santa Cecilia Acatitlán, Teopanzolco, and the Templo Mayor of Tenochtitlán, as well as Zempoala, Quiahuiztlán, Castillo de Teayo, and Tuzapan on the Gulf Coast.[84] In a more slender and concealed form, these same cubes cap the balustrades on the Venus Platform and the Temple of the Warriors at Chichén Itzá.

The sanctuary at Tamohi attached to a polychromed altar (plate 215) is another example of the changes that took place in architecture as a result of the political restructuring of the

213. Stairway of the Great Southern Platform at Tamohi. The earthen core of the platform was faced with cobblestones and finished with a layer of lime mortar, which was then painted. Late Postclassic.

Altiplano. It consists of a small building with a quadrangular plan and rounded corners, with sloped walls and a stairway on the eastern face. Three of the walls, but not the entry wall, are crowned by a single battlement in the shape of an inverted T. These battlements establish a direct relationship with another sanctuary, at Quiahuiztlán, that is nearly identical, except that its stairway is oriented differently, the balustrades are finished with cubes, and there are not three battlements but six, which are shorter and terraced (plate 216). The privileged location of the sanctuary at Tamohi indicates that it was a sacred place,[85] as was the polychromed altar attached to it, which has an I-shaped plan (plate 218). In an initial stage, this altar projected from the stairway of the sanctuary and ended in a small platform shaped like a truncated cone; in the following stage, it was extended to reach a second platform with a biconical form, apparently a brazier. This unique type of altar is an original creation of the Huastecs of the final period, but its prototype seems to be represented in certain codices of the Nahua tradition, such as the Borgia, Fejérváry-Mayer, Vindobonensis-Mexicanus, and Borbonicus; on folio 34 of the latter, which represents the ceremony of lighting the New Fire, appears a structure exceptionally similar to the altar at Tamohi.[86]

214. The South Structure at Tamohi has a low *talud* that emphasizes the stair-ways, whose balustrades are finished with cubes, a feature that was common in the Late Postclassic.

The forms and ideas of the new order imposed by the Aztecs are reflected in one of the site's smallest structures, the *tzompantli*, which shares the sacred space between the polychromed altar and the South Structure. It is oriented to the west and topped by a level rectangle with four orifices, in which were perhaps inserted an equal number of posts that held heads obtained as trophies of war.[87] Despite the lack of detail, disproportion of forms, and absence

215. (*top*) Sanctuary attached to a poly-chromed altar at Tamohi. Late Postclassic.

216. (*bottom*) A sanctuary at Quiahuiztlán, Veracruz, whose design and battlement decorations closely resemble those of the sanctuary at Tamohi pictured above it. Late Postclassic.

217. (*below*) This I-shaped altar at Tamtoc differs in its dimensions and form from the poly-chromed altar at Tamohi, but it may have had a similar significance. There are several other altars of this kind at Tam-toc. Late Postclassic.

218. (*right*) The poly-chromed altar at Tamohi, with a plan in the shape of a double I, ends in a biconical platform that resembles an Aztec brazier, but without the characteristic hollow in the center. Late Post-classic.

of meaning in the architecture of Tamohi, its remains suggest a superficial copy of Aztec architecture, based on the deficient models that were to be seen in central Veracruz, such as at Zempoala and Quiahuiztlán, towns that were subject to and tributaries of the Triple Alliance.

We will return to this theme, but before we do, it is worthwhile to analyze certain contributions of Huastec architecture in its final period: the altars with an I-shaped plan, the stuccoed channels, the water tanks, and the miniature circular tombs. The I-shaped altar consisting of a rectangular platform with a circle at one end seems to have its prototype in the polychromed altar and stuccoed channels of Tamohi, which have similar forms. At Tamtoc, numerous examples of variable length were constructed from cobblestones, but unlike the polychromed altar of Tamohi, these are only a few inches high. The largest is a few dozen yards long and crosses the ritual channel of the Noria Group from west to east;[88] others display a rectangular stone inserted vertically into the center of the circular part, like a stele (plate 217).

The stuccoed channels, which present the same plan, were dug into the earth and then lined with smoothed mortar to make them impermeable. There are a couple of these at

219. (*above*) Circular water tank 33 ft. (10 m) in diameter, located at the northeast corner of the West Structure at Tamohi. Late Postclassic.

220. (*left*) This circular water tank in the Ceremonial Plaza of Tamtoc has what appears to be a bench, which could have seated several people at once. Postclassic.

Tamohi, one of them more than 195 feet (60 meters) long.[89] They may have been ritual channels for water, possibly modeled after the one at Tamtoc.

The stuccoed channels are related to the so-called water tanks, which are shallow circular depressions of variable diameter lined with polished mortar to make them watertight. At Tamohi, near the corner of the West Structure, there is one 33 feet (10 meters) in diameter (plate 219), and at Tamtoc, there is a curious example 6½ feet (2 meters) in diameter, whose funnel-shaped basin has an intermediate ring that could have seated several people at once (plate 220). These water tanks are found with greater frequency at other Postclassic sites in the Huastec region.[90] It has been suggested that they were water mirrors used to observe the moon,[91] but they might instead have been *jagüeyes*—true reservoirs for the water that was vital to the community. In any case, the water tanks indicate not only the close relations that existed between Tamtoc and Tamohi in the Late Postclassic, but the importance of water as a life-sustaining element: its representations in architecture and sculpture magically assured its permanence.

Finally, there are the small circular tombs a couple feet in diameter and some inches high, shaped like truncated cones and built of cobblestones, sometimes with a long vertical stone standing in the center. Several tombs of this type, and others shaped like miniature sanctuaries, may be found at Tamtoc, beside the great altar that crosses the ritual channel (plate 221). They may also be seen at Tamohi, at the base of the West Structure, where the sculpture known as the Adolescent was found.

221. Group of miniature tombs shaped like truncated cones and temple, located to one side of the large altar of the Noria Group at Tamtoc. Late Postclassic.

One exceptional Huastec structure is the square tower, 5 feet (1 meter) on a side and 26 feet (8 meters) tall, that stands on a platform at Rancho la Rosa in Hidalgo (plate 222).[92] It was built of regular limestone slabs, 10 inches (25 centimeters) long and 4 inches (10 centimeters) high on average, joined with a mortar of lime and sand. The slabs were laid in rows that were leveled with thin shims of stone in order to maintain their stability. Three sides of the tower are smooth, but the northern one has thirteen stones projecting from it, which may have served as rungs for climbing (plate 223). The construction of this building indicates a new and unparalleled technical advance in masonry and scaffolding. Its function is unknown, but it might have served as a watchtower, a border marker, an emblem after the Mayan fashion,[93] or even an astronomical or calendrical marker. The only comparable objects in the region are the quadrangular basalt stelae from Structure 12 at Órganos, Veracruz, which might also have acted as markers.[94] Rancho la Rosa has other platforms, topped by mounds, as well as large flat areas, perhaps artificially leveled; its dates of occupation have not been established.

By the mid-fifteenth century, the southern part of the Huastec region was dependent on the Triple Alliance. Castillo de Teayo was the spearhead of the Aztec advance toward the Gulf Coast. There are remains of buildings at the foot of the mountains, but only one—located in the town's main plaza—has been preserved in good condition (plate 225). This is a foundation in the form of a truncated pyramid, composed of three tall tiers with slightly curved *taludes*, although this may be a deformation caused by settling. It measures 46 by 82 feet (14 by 25 meters) at its base, and is 33 feet (10 meters) high, with a low platform projecting from its western side, over which rises a stairway flanked by balustrades finished with cubes. On either side of the stairway, there emerge from the facade two thick buttresses, terraced to match the main body of the structure. On top of the pyramid is a *teocalli* (narrow temple) with a rectangular plan and thick walls 13 feet (4 meters) high, whose vertical profile is widened at the base by a running *talud* finished with a horizontal molding (plate 224). Expansions carried out in order to stabilize the temple reduced the width of the doorway.[95] The pyramid and temple were constructed entirely of sandstone slabs laid in rows and joined with lime-sand mortar; each step of the stairway consists of three courses of stone.[96] The stone studs protruding from the walls supported the coat of lime that covered the building. The interior of the temple preserves a fragment of this finish, with two horizontal bands of red and black paint, suggesting how this sanctuary must have looked in its day.

The notable similarities between this building and those of Tenayuca, Teopanzolco, and the Templo Mayor, among others, indicate its Aztec affiliation; however, its details do not correspond exactly: it does not have a double central balustrade on its stairway, twin temples, or studs in the form of serpents or skulls, all features of Toltec origin[97] that were common among the Aztecs.[98] The inexactitude of the details and general forms, in the site's sculpture as well as its architecture, suggests that these works were copies made by Huastec hands, as at Tamohi. Numerous sculptures of Aztec deities from Castillo de Teayo display Huastec modeling, materials, and "style" (plates 226–28). The scarcity or absence of Aztec ceramics and the predominance of Huastec ceramics of Period VI reinforce this idea.

Two interesting sites that may have been related to Castillo de Teayo are Cacahuatenco and Tuzapan. The former, located on a mesa of the same name, stands out for its large foundation in the form of a truncated pyramid, with five tiers of different heights rising from a low, two-tiered platform (plate 229). The structure, whose total height is 52 feet (16 meters), has a

222. (*top*) The square tower at Rancho la Rosa, San Felipe Orizatlán, Hidalgo, stands 26 ft. (8 m) tall atop a large rectangular platform, although locals say it used to be higher.

223. (*bottom*) The thirteen stones projecting from the northern side of the tower at Rancho la Rosa may have been used for climbing, or to support scaffolding.

224. (*above*) The temple atop the pyramid at Castillo de Teayo has walls that are sloped at the base and traces of red and black paint in its interior. Late Postclassic.

225. (*right*) The pyramid at Castillo de Teayo recalls Aztec models in its general form, but appears to be of Huastec workmanship.

quadrangular plan with rounded corners and measures 148 feet (45 meters) on a side. At the center of its western facade is a stairway divided into seven sections and flanked by balustrades. On the north side is another stairway, with straight balustrades. The shape of the pyramid has been compared to that of El Castillo at Chichén Itzá.[99] It is enclosed on three sides by a *coatepantli*, or wall of serpents,[100] similar to those that guarded the sacred precincts of Tula, Hidalgo; Tenayuca, in the State of México; and the great temples at Texcoco and Tenochtitlán. In this case the *coatepantli* is finished with a parapet of fretwork or *xicalcoliuhqui*. Aside from the pyramid, Cacahuatenco has cisterns and artesian wells lined with stone, circular sanctuaries, and several more pyramidal foundations.[101] The site at Tuzapan or Tuzanapan, Puebla, has more than fifty rectangular buildings,[102] including one outstanding example with sloping walls, a central stairway finished with cubes, and on top, a temple or *teocalli* that recalls the style of the central Altiplano. The ceramics at the site are similar to those of the Cholulteca type.[103]

The Aztec expansion toward the coast was possibly the reason for the establishment of fortified villages in the mountains.[104] Among the most notable of these are Cerco de Piedra, on the mesa of Metlaltoyuca, Puebla; Yahualica, Hidalgo; and Tenanquilicango, Veracruz. All of them display structures faced with stone slabs, and Metlaltoyuca also has a wall more than 1¼ miles (2 kilometers) long on its northern side, pyramidal foundations, sanctuaries, and artesian wells lined with stone slabs.[105] Yahualica, for its part, was built in a place that was difficult to access, where the water of two streams could be controlled in the event of a siege. There we find preserved some circular buildings and a larger number of quadrangular ones, neither type having stairways.[106] Tenanquilicango is noteworthy for having a *coatepantli*.[107]

The arrival of outside influences affected the local architecture, which became more varied and technically complex, and incorporated forms, elements, and symbols that were different than the traditional ones. In addition to the changes already described, rounded corners began to lose ground against angular ones, which were sometimes carved into immense monolithic blocks, as at La Cebadilla, Veracruz.[108] Artesian wells were dug and lined with stone slabs not only at Metlaltoyuca, but also at Cacahuatenco, Órganos, Xochicuatepec, La Cebadilla, and Tumilco, among other sites.[109] The ballcourt was adopted as well, albeit only in a few places, such as Metlaltoyuca, La Mata, La Cebadilla,[110] Tambolon, and Tamtoc.[111]

CONCLUSIONS

Generally speaking, Huastec architecture of all eras lacks a distinctive style, unlike the ceramics and sculpture of the final period. Every site, and sometimes every building, presents different characteristics. The buildings were constructed with the raw materials that were immediately available: earth, sand, and shells. Only in the Classic did stone begin to be used, which was sometimes carried in from far away. The lime-sand mortar was rarely used to join stone slabs, serving mostly to cover buildings that were then painted, sometimes with murals depicting ritual scenes. Circular mounds of earth and stone predominated originally, and later quadrangular ones with rounded corners, passing through the apsidal plan—a hybrid, transitional form—along the way. Tombs, as spaces built expressly for the burial of dignitaries, were restricted to the region of Huejutla, Hidalgo; it is possible that the irregular stone mounds that contain them had a specifically funerary purpose. Small structures in the shape of truncated

226–28. (*opposite*) These statues from Castillo de Teayo represent Aztec forms, but with Huastec proportions, indicating that they are copies made by local craftsmen. Late Postclassic.

229. (*right*) Detail of the pyramidal platform at Cacahuatenco, Veracruz, whose shape and proportions have been compared to El Castillo at Chichén Itzá. Late Postclassic.

cones or miniature temples were used to mark burials at Tamtoc and Tamohi in the Postclassic; sometimes, as at Tamtoc, the truncated cones had a stele in the center. The expansion of the Triple Alliance to the Gulf Coast in the fifteenth and sixteenth centuries led to the copying and adoption of architectural elements alien to the local tradition, and also had an impact on other aspects of material culture, such as sculpture and ceramics.

Although Huastec architecture has been studied since the nineteenth century, very few sites have been described, much less excavated. Any treatment of the topic is therefore partial and incomplete. To arrive at a more accurate understanding, researchers will have to address other subjects as well, such as settlement patterns and orientations. They must also take into account that architecture basically reproduces the divine cosmos—dominated by gods, spirits, and vital energies—on a human scale. And they must make haste, because many of the sites mentioned here are being altered or destroyed through urban sprawl and human ignorance.

IO

OAXACA

MARÍA TERESA URIARTE

The challenge in writing about the Pre-Columbian architecture of Oaxaca is to convey its abundance and diversity, traits it shares with the landscape itself (plate 230).

The fertile valleys of Oaxaca and the variety of its ecosystems permitted intense cultural development from very early on. Authors like Joyce Marcus and Kent Flannery have even questioned the predominance of the cultures of the Gulf Coast—the core Olmec area—because they consider those of Oaxaca to have been at least as, if not more, important. It has become clear that the romantic notion of an Olmec "mother culture" can no longer be sustained, and that the artworks and other cultural expressions of Oaxaca possess their own personality and character, while still sharing common features with other parts of Mesoamerica (figure 78).

Perhaps the greatest contributions to our understanding of the art and culture of Oaxaca were made by the Mexican archaeologists Alfonso Caso and Ignacio Bernal, the preeminent scholars of this region. The most complete chronology of Oaxaca was originally formulated by Robert Drennan. Although other authors have proposed their own variations, there is a consensus regarding the dates of the following phases:

Tierras Largas: 1400 BC
San José: 1150 BC
Guadalupe: 800 BC
Rosario: 600 BC
Early Monte Albán I: 500 BC
Late Monte Albán I: 300 BC
Monte Albán II: 200 BC
Monte Albán IIIa: 200 AD
Monte Albán IIIb: 450 AD
Monte Albán IV: 600–700 AD
Monte Albán V: 950–1500 AD[1]

230. View of the hilltop city of Monte Albán, Oaxaca's most important archaeological site, which flourished between 500 BC and AD 900.

EARLY SETTLEMENTS

To the Tierras Largas phase (c. 1400 BC) belong the earliest settlements, which had about 25 to 50 inhabitants each. Some of the objects uncovered at these sites include parrot bones (*Ara militaris*) and a tortoise shell (*Dermatemys mawii*) from the coast that was used as a drum.[2] These finds are evidence of the exchange of sumptuary goods with distant regions, and the use of these articles for ritual purposes. From this we may infer the existence of organized trading networks that transported various goods, in this case ritual objects, over hundreds and perhaps thousands of miles; elites who demanded these trade goods; traders dedicated to carrying out such exchanges; and finally—what interests us here—spaces for celebrating the rituals in which these items were used.

Of the various settlements that shared these characteristics, perhaps the best known is San José Mogote. Here we find Structure 31 or Mound I (belonging to the Rosario phase, c. 600 BC), a circular platform similar to those that were built at La Venta, at Cuicuilco, and above all in the Huastec region. In his excavations at Monte Albán in 1992–94, Marcus Winter also discovered a portion of a semicircular wall 16 feet (5 meters) in diameter, belonging to the Monte Albán I phase, in structure 1192-A of the North Platform.[3] These structures confirm the con-

232. (*below*) A tomb at Yagul, Oaxaca, dating to the Monte Albán I phase (c. 300 BC). Instead of being decorated with murals, like the tombs at Monte Albán, this one displays reliefs whose geometric patterns anticipate the stone mosaics of Mitla.

ceptualization and construction of a circular ritual space, and I think it is significant that they are contemporaneous with examples from other parts of Mesoamerica.

In the patio of Structure 26 at San José was found the earliest example of a tomb with a separate chamber and antechamber,[4] a type of structure that would later become common in the region (plate 231; figure 81). This tomb shows that ancestor worship was part of the ideology of the community. Its occupant, or perhaps occupants, were removed when the site was abandoned. This would become a widespread practice in Mesoamerica, and particularly in Oaxaca, where tombs were reused, and in some cases repainted. If a group moved from one place to another, they would sometimes transfer the bones of their ancestors to their new residence. The sources tell us that this tradition was revived by the Aztecs, who called the people who transported the bones *teomama*, or carriers of gods.

As Arthur Miller points out,[5] it was no easy task to reopen a tomb, since one had to break through the patio floor of a residence, remove all the rubble that blocked off access to the tomb, and finally lift away the stone slab that sealed its entrance. And naturally all these steps had to be repeated in the opposite direction once the new remains were deposited and the corresponding offerings made. The walls of the tomb would also have to be repainted, since the motifs varied according to very local customs, almost specific to the clan or family, as Diana Magaloni indicates.[6] The reuse of tombs has sometimes made it difficult to date ceramics and other artifacts from Oaxaca, since objects from different periods ended up being buried together.

The tomb offering in Structure 26 included the elements that would be associated with burials of the ruling class at different sites over a long period of time: jade ornaments, weapons exalting the role of the warrior (which in this case included projectile points made of imported obsidian and coated with red ochre), and an instrument that may have been used for autosacrifice, allowing the ruler to offer his blood as a supreme gift to the deities who protected the community.

In the Rosario phase, community buildings began to gain the same importance in small villages as they enjoyed at larger sites like San José Mogote or Tomaltepec. In terms of residential architecture, although social differentiation is reflected in the relative richness and abundance of the offerings that accompanied domestic burials, the pattern of construction was nearly the same for all social classes: rooms organized around a patio, with family burials beneath the patio or one of the rooms. According to Marcus Winter, the simplest homes had thin walls of reeds covered in mud, similar to those that can still be seen in many Mexican villages, while houses of intermediate size had adobe walls. The largest houses, or palaces, displayed thick stone walls with foundations, as well as stairs that communicated between a sunken patio and the rooms surrounding it.[7] They also had larger and more elaborate tombs, the most magnificent examples of which include Tombs 104 and 105 at Monte Albán (plate 234) or the one at Suchilquitongo, also known as Cerro de la Campana or Huijazoo (plates 233, 235). This site has been called by three different names since its discovery in 1985, because it is located on Cerro de la Campana, which lies right on the border between the Santiago Suchilquitongo and Huijazoo municipal areas. It is not open to the public, but in the small town of Santiago there is a museum that exhibits some of the offerings.

Enclosures, stairways, and wall facings were sometimes constructed entirely of stone, and sometimes of a combination of stone, adobe, and wattle and daub made from woven reeds

233. (top) The antechamber of Tomb 5 at Suchilquitongo, AD 700–900. This is one of the most spectacular tombs in Oaxaca, depicting processions of ballplayers and of men and women of the local elite. Suchilquitongo was perhaps a dependency of Monte Albán in the great city's final phase.

234. (bottom) Tomb 105 at Monte Albán, dating to phase IV of that city (AD 600–700). The brilliant murals in this tomb, seemingly painted for the enjoyment of the departed, reflect the tradition of ancestor worship that was widespread in Mesoamerica.

235. (opposite) Tomb 5, Suchilquitongo.

covered with mud. The walls of these structures must have looked very different from the bare stones that we see today, because they were all covered with a whitewash of lime that could be polished to a gleaming white or painted with colors. Columns and lintels were sometimes made of wood, and a few have even been preserved.

THE DOMINANCE OF MONTE ALBÁN

We still do not understand why the settlements that had attained a greater degree of complexity in earlier phases, such as San José Mogote, declined in importance, while a previously uninhabited site, with little water and poor conditions for agriculture, but a topographic situation that dominated almost the entire Valley of Oaxaca, began to show signs of settlement: Monte Albán (figure 79).

This city had walls, which not only marked it off as a special precinct but also protected it from possible invaders. Blanton wonders, with good reason, who these enemies might have been, since the contemporary Mesoamerican world presented no real rivals to Monte Albán. The only possible threats to the city were the smaller communities nearby. It might seem surprising that Monte Albán was in conflict with its neighbors, because the site's inhabitants apparently included people from all three arms of the Valley of Oaxaca.[8] On the other hand, we do know that the rise of outlying settlements would eventually lead to the abandonment of Monte Albán. And the fact that the city was involved in armed conflict is confirmed by the bas-reliefs known as the Danzantes (Dancers), which—as Winter and Flannery suggest, following Coe—actually represent prisoners. These authors note that the poses of certain Danzantes who appear to be climbing stairs, as in Building L, would later be repeated by the Maya in their own depictions of prisoners, for example at Dzibanché.

236. (*below left*) The western side of the main plaza at Monte Albán. To the right is Building L, or the Temple of the Danzantes, first constructed in phase I of the city (c. 300 BC) and renovated in phase IIIa (c. AD 200).

237. (*below right*) Detail of the relief of the Swimmers on Building L, dating to Monte Albán I (c. 300 BC).

238. (*above*) The North Platform of Monte Albán, which was occupied over a long period of time and consequently has rich architectural remains.

MONTE ALBÁN I

Ignacio Marquina's classic *La Arquitectura prehispánica*, whose valuable plans and drawings have been reproduced countless times, still provides one of the best accounts of the early architecture of Monte Albán. Marquina notes that Building L, also known as the Temple of the Danzantes (plate 236, 237), was constructed differently than later buildings at the site: its walls were straight, consisting of alternating rows of enormous stones and smaller ones that penetrate deeper into the masonry. In front of Building L is found the clearest example of a delimited space for ritual activities belonging to the Monte Albán I phase.

According to Marquina, in the lowest stratum of the site's North Platform there is an edifice that was constructed in a manner similar to Building L and adorned with the head of a serpent whose body, modeled entirely of clay, extended all the way around the base of the structure.[9] Winter also found evidence of other buildings with the same large, straight walls on the North Platform, as well as what may be the highest-status tomb belonging to Monte Albán I: designated 1993-11, it had red paint on its walls, floor, and roof slabs.[10] The excavations of the North Platform have made it clear that one of the city's original cores of settlement developed in this area. The builders used the irregularities of the terrain to lend more height to

the structures, as they would later do in other parts of the main plaza. This demonstrates the conceptualization of the site as an urban space from a very early stage (plate 238).

During this phase, other sites of lesser importance developed in Oaxaca, such as Dainzú in the Tlacolula Valley (the eastern arm of the Valley of Oaxaca), which would eventually decline around AD 200 or 300. The stone reliefs at this site—which are an important component of the architecture, as at San José Mogote and Monte Albán—are dedicated to the ballgame, a highly symbolic activity that was practiced at various sites in Oaxaca from an early time (figure 80). It is difficult to understand the urban plan of Dainzú, since the site has not been intensively excavated, but it does possess a ballcourt and an interesting tomb with a supernatural being carved in relief over the entrance. There is also evidence of very early occupation at another site in the Tlacolula Valley, Yagul (plate 239). Here were found six tombs constructed of adobe that have been dated to Monte Albán I (plate 232).[11]

The mountain settlements of the Highland Mixtec culture, such as Monte Negro, Huamelulpan, Yucuita, and Yucuñudahui, developed in this era as well, along with Cerro de la Mina, a Lowland Mixtec center. The highland settlements were generally placed so as to enjoy vantage points over a wide territory, and the archaeological evidence indicates the occurrence of armed conflicts from this period onward.

Monte Negro, located on the outskirts of the town of Tilantongo on the crest of a mountain, was occupied in Monte Albán I and II (figure 82). It had numerous buildings with columns

239. View of Yagul, which flourished principally in the Early Postclassic. This city is thought to have been constructed with defensive purposes in mind, since the majority of its buildings were placed on a mountainside overlooking the valley.

made of stone drums. The structure known as Temple T was open on its east and west sides and had two chambers connected by a wide doorway; on the west side, the roof was supported by two columns. Like Monte Albán, where various cisterns used in different eras have been found, Monte Negro possessed well-designed systems for channeling rainwater.

Yucuita, which is not far from Monte Negro, has one of the longest sequences of occupation in Mesoamerica; like certain other favorably located archaeological sites in Mexico, it was repeatedly settled and abandoned from around 1500 BC to the colonial period.

Perhaps the most remarkable thing about Yucuñudahui is the preservation of a roof with beams of juniper wood, recorded by Alfonso Caso during his early explorations.

MONTE ALBÁN II

The most significant structure from the second phase of Monte Albán is Building J (plates 240–42). This edifice, which appears to have an earlier substructure belonging to Monte Albán I, seemingly combines two different buildings, one with a regular plan and a wide stairway flanked by balustrades, and the other shaped like an arrow. It is also oriented differently than the other structures in the center of the main plaza. Building J's closest analogue is found at Caballito Blanco, an early settlement located near Yagul in the Tlacolula Valley, and Marcus Winter informs us that there is also a similar structure at San José Mogote.

240. Building J at Monte Albán, dating to phase II of that city (c. 200 BC). The arrow-shaped plan of this building is unusual, but there is a similar structure at Caballito Blanco, near Yagul.

241, 242. (*left*) Two views of Building J at Monte Albán.

243. (*below*) System M at Monte Albán presents one of the best examples of the use of the "double scapular" molding on the *tablero*. Monte Albán IIIa (c. AD 200).

244. (*opposite*) Sunken patio on the North Platform of Monte Albán, dating to phase IIIa of that city (c. AD 200). The sunken patio is a characteristic form in Oaxacan architecture, particularly at Monte Albán.

At Building J we again find relief carvings of human figures that allude to the conquest of different sites. Although some authors believe that the reliefs simply represent peoples under the dominion of Monte Albán, the fact that the figures are depicted upside down in these examples suggests rather that they are captives who have been ritually humiliated and treated with contempt. In the later phases of the site, the reliefs of captives would follow the conventions of other parts of Mesoamerica; on the South Platform and various stelae in the plaza, for example, they are represented with their arms tied.

According to various authors, some of these reliefs would have commemorated conquests in the Cañada de Cuicatlán. However, there are hundreds of other settlements in Oaxaca that must be studied before we can truly understand the social, economic, and political complexities of this vast territory and the armed conflicts they gave rise to. We would also emphasize that the bellicose strain in the sculpture of Monte Albán is hardly unique in Mesoamerican art, and should not be our only basis for understanding this city.

245. (*below*) The Yellow Temple, Dainzú, Oaxaca, dating to Monte Albán I–II (AD 200–450). This is one of the earliest examples of the use of the column as a support in Oaxacan architecture.

MONTE ALBÁN III TO V

The greatest amount of construction took place at Monte Albán in phase III, when the population may have reached as high as 30,000. The North Platform was expanded, becoming more complex, and Building L was renovated, with Systems IV and M, two complexes very similar to one another—comprising a temple, patio, and altar—being constructed on either side of it (plate 246). Buildings I, G, and H, which sit next to Building J at the center of the main plaza, were all constructed in a relatively brief period of time. On the east side of the plaza were built the ballcourt, which has no exceptional features; a long platform; and several structures believed to have been elite residences: Building S, or the Palace, and Buildings P, Q, and U (plate 247). The South Platform was built slightly later; slabs portraying captives were placed on different parts of it over the years, in accordance with a political agenda, as Javier Urcid has demonstrated.[12]

In this period, the city's relationship with Teotihuacán became apparent, being manifested in ceramics, the use of mica, and above all in the adoption of the *talud-tablero* style. As at other

sites, this system of construction acquired distinctive local features, the most notable one in this case being a double molding (known as the "double scapular") on the *tablero* (plate 243). Columns also began to proliferate in Monte Albán III, although they had already appeared in the Yellow Temple at Dainzú, which belongs to the transition between phases I and II (plate 245).[13] The use of columns at Monte Albán differs from the practice at Teotihuacán, where square pillars were often employed instead.

Starting in Monte Albán III, most buildings were placed atop stepped platforms surrounding a sunken patio (plate 244). Balustrades became very wide, taking the form of a large *talud* finished at the top and bottom with a double molding in the manner of a *tablero*, and the entrances of the temples grew larger. The elite residences or palaces display the configuration we have already described, with magnificent tombs located beneath their central patios. Where the houses are more humble, the burials and their offerings follow suit.

246. System IV at Monte Albán displays the geometric decoration typical of Zapotec architecture. Monte Albán IIIa–b (AD 200–450).

Most of the stone used for construction was local, although green limestone from the valley was employed for certain buildings and stelae. According to Marquina, the roofs were flat, either thatched or made of wood cemented together. The tombs were covered with thick slabs whose appearance recalled the roof of a family home.

There are a large number of subterranean passageways in the city, some of which were perhaps used for ceremonies, allowing rulers to "magically" appear and disappear. There are also some more recent tunnels, the result of archaeological explorations.

The architecture of Monte Albán did not change much in phases IV and V, when innovations instead took place in the valley, at Yagul and Lambityeco, and later Mitla.

247. Buildings S, P, and U at Monte Albán were probably elite residences. Monte Albán IIIa–b (AD 200–450).

SUCCESSORS TO MONTE ALBÁN

Just as the abandonment of San José Mogote coincided with the settlement of Monte Albán, the latter city was itself later abandoned for reasons unknown to us, as other centers rose to dominance in the Valley of Oaxaca.

YAGUL

Spectacularly located on a mountaintop overlooking the Tlacolula Valley, Yagul was settled relatively early; we have already mentioned its adobe tombs, which belong to the Monte Albán I phase. However, following the gradual abandonment of Monte Albán beginning in phase IV, Yagul gained a greater importance in Oaxaca.

Even though it shares certain characteristics with other sites in the Tlacolula Valley, such as Dainzú and Lambityeco, Yagul may be considered an independent settlement; Joyce Marcus has even called it a city-state. The ancient city was divided into three sections, each of which has been looted. Bandelier wrote about this problem as early as 1884, noting that several structures had already been destroyed, partly by locals who used them as a "quarry"—a common problem at archaeological sites with good stonework.[14]

From the remains that survive, we can tell that Yagul's most important building was the Palace of the Six Patios, which is popularly known as the Labyrinth due to its large number of rooms and passageways (plate 248). It is likely that the patio toward its southern end, which is more exposed, was an administrative area, while its northern end served a residential purpose. The city also has a ballcourt, which displays the characteristic I-shaped plan and apparently dates to Monte Albán IV or V (plate 251).

As at Mitla, the *tableros* of certain structures at Yagul are decorated with stone mosaics. The two cities are also similar in that they demonstrate the coexistence of the two groups that dominated Oaxaca's mountains and valleys respectively, the Mixtecs and the Zapotecs: all the architectural remains at both sites display Zapotec characteristics, while nearly all the tombs have yielded Mixtec ceramics, as Bernal points out.[15]

248. The Palace of the Six Patios at Yagul, popularly known as the Labyrinth. Monte Albán IV (AD 600–700).

249. (*top*) The entrance to Tomb 6 at Lambityeco, adorned with the masks of Lord 1 Earthquake and Lady 10 Reed. Monte Albán IIIb–IV (AD 450–700).

250. (*bottom*) View of Lambityeco, which flourished in Monte Albán IIIb–IV (AD 450–700).

251. (*overleaf*) The ballcourt at Yagul. Monte Albán IV–V (AD 600–1500).

LAMBITYECO

Another important site in the Tlacolula Valley is Lambityeco (plate 250). Its buildings, which are arranged around patios in the usual fashion, are distinguished by the elegance of their decoration; in particular, the facades of tombs and temples are adorned with large stucco masks. Mound 190 presents perhaps the finest example of architectural sculpture known in Oaxaca: the *tablero* is made to appear as a kind of cave from which two heads of the deity Cocijo emerge, wearing impressive headdresses. These masks flank a stairway, which, together with the double molding of the *tablero*, produces an interesting play of volumes.

An equally attractive structure, and one that highlights the coexistence of the living and the dead in Oaxaca, is Tomb 6; its entrance is adorned with a double molding that still retains some of its red paint, as well as the masks of Lord 1 Earthquake and Lady 10 Reed (plate 249; figure 83).

MITLA

The names for Mitla in Nahuatl (*Mictlán*) and Zapotec (*Lyobaa*) apparently alluded to the mortuary practices of Oaxaca, showing that this city was dedicated to the worship of the dead. Today it is famous for its amazing stone mosaics, which, like the tesselations of Islamic art, were the result of an exactly conceived design in which every block had its place; surely they were produced by a group of master stonecutters who knew the entire process from start to finish (plates 254–56).

Mitla, which flourished in Monte Albán IV and V, does not seem to have been built according to a preconceived urban plan, although this is difficult to tell for certain, because the ancient city has been buried beneath colonial and modern construction. Here, as in many places across Mexico—with the Templo Mayor being perhaps the most prominent example—the Spanish conquerors deliberately planted a church on the Pre-Columbian site.

252. The facade of the Hall of the Columns at Mitla, Oaxaca, with intricate stone mosaics divided by double moldings. Late Postclassic.

The archaeological remains are divided into five complexes—the Adobe, Arroyo, Columns, Church (or Parish, as Marquina calls it), and Southern groups—some of which preserve very little of their original architecture. However, we can still see that two different styles of construction are represented at Mitla: the Adobe Group and the Southern Group display the type of arrangement found at Monte Albán, with a central patio surrounded by rooms, while the other groups have two or more patios with structures on only three of their sides.

The architecture of Mitla is outstanding for its visual solutions. These include not only the flawless stone mosaics that cover many of its walls, but also the double moldings that traverse the same walls in an alternating pattern. The moldings on the Hall of the Columns, for example, divide its facade into three sections both horizontally and vertically (plate 252). All these sections are covered by stone mosaics in different geometric patterns, which complement each

253. *(left)* After passing through the monumental triple doorway of the Hall of the Columns at Mitla, one enters a portico whose roof was supported by massive columns.

254. *(right)* Stone mosaics in the inner courtyard of the Hall of the Columns.

other as gracefully as the commonly paired glyphs for "earth" and "sky." In addition to having this complex design scheme, the walls of the building are tilted slightly outward, probably to compensate visually for the height of the structure, somewhat like the *entasis* of the Parthenon. Marquina notes the use of this outward inclination at other sites as well, particularly Tulum, Quintana Roo. Finally, we should point out the three wide doorways of the Hall of the Columns, crowned by massive stone lintels resting on wide pillars that repeat the *talud* and *tablero* of the facade (plate 253).

    Some of the largest tombs in Oaxaca have been found beneath the North and East buildings of the Columns Group. The one to the north has a cruciform plan with an antechamber; in an earlier era, its entrance was in the main patio. This tomb's main space is 23 feet (7 meters) long and about 6½ feet (2 meters) high, with a column that supports the roof, which may have collapsed during construction. The walls are decorated with stone mosaics. None of the other complexes at Mitla have such impressive tombs, nor such large and elaborate buildings, which suggests that the Columns Group was the residence of the most important group in the city. However, the Church Group is distinguished by the paintings preserved on its lintels, which apparently had an astronomical significance (plates 257, 258).

The architecture of Oaxaca cannot be classified by ethnic group, since the Mixtecs and Zapotecs coexisted at various settlements in the region's valleys and canyons. The Mixtec ceramics found at Zapotec sites may be one proof of this coexistence, the most noteworthy example being Tomb 7 at Monte Albán, which is no different in its form and construction than many

255, 256. *(opposite)* Details of stone mosaics at Mitla, Late Postclassic. These mosaics are testaments to the skill not only of the architect or designer, but also of the masons who cut the precisely fitted blocks.

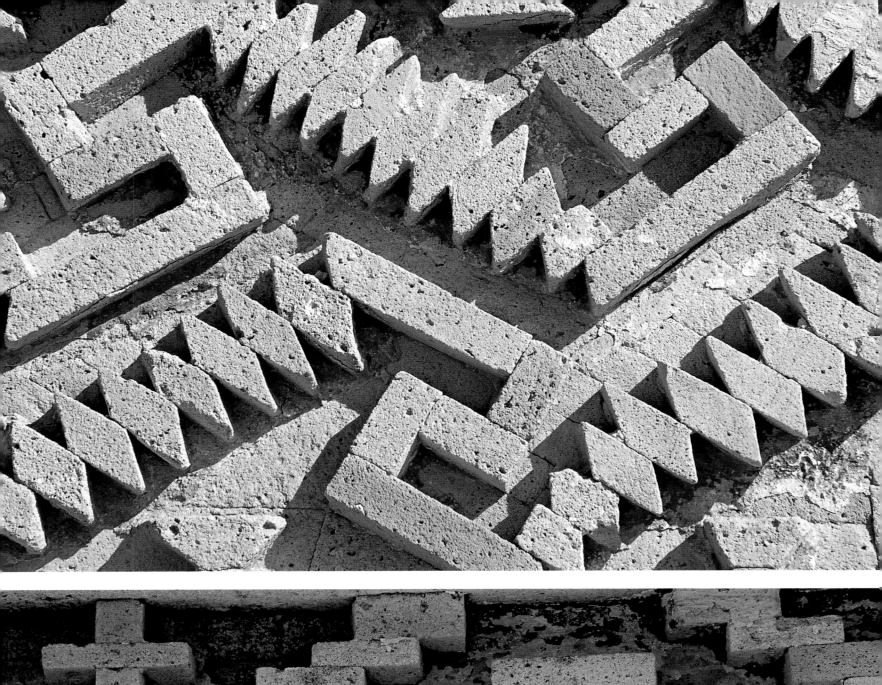

257. (*top*) With its triple doorway topped by a stone lintel and its stone mosaics, the Church Group is representative of the architecture of Mitla. Late Postclassic.

258. (*bottom*) This painted lintel in the Church Group at Mitla displays the Mixteca-Puebla style that was widespread in the Postclassic, appearing in the ceramics of Cholula, the Borgia group of codices, and the murals of the Maya city of Tulum and the Huastec city of Tamohi.

others at the site, but whose contents are typically Mixtec. According to some authors, this only shows that the tomb was reused by the Mixtecs after the Zapotecs abandoned Monte Albán, but the evidence is inconclusive in this regard.

We have deliberately refrained from going into greater detail about the tombs of Oaxaca, because these structures are distinguished mainly by their sculpture and painting, rather than their architecture per se. However, we should emphasize that the tomb chambers and antechambers of Monte Albán, Suchilquitongo, Zaachila, and Yagul—to name only a few sites—present some of Mesoamerica's most outstanding examples of the integration of visual art and architecture, demonstrating the imagination and technical skill of the ancient artists of Oaxaca.

II
THE MAYA REGION

MARY ELLEN MILLER AND CLAUDIA BRITTENHAM

Using a relatively small inventory of simple architectural forms, the ancient Maya built a vast array of cities, no two of which look alike, with towering temples that crested above the forest canopy and ample palaces that provided the spaces for royal and bureaucratic functions (figure 84). Elevated roads connected dense clusters of buildings within cities, often separated by *bajos*, or man-made reservoirs, and joined one city to another. At the same time, open plazas served as dramatic locations for rituals and processions and balanced the massive volumes of the buildings. Specialized buildings, including sweatbaths and ballcourts, were constructed at almost every site.

At the heart of this permanent architecture lies quarried stone, whether used or reused as rough rubble, finished into blocks, or refined to smooth veneer panels. The most common and widely found building material in the Maya region is limestone, and archaeologists have discovered dozens of ancient quarries. Limestone quality varies dramatically across the region, from the dense, fine-grained stone of Palenque that easily sheers into thin sheets for carved monuments or thick slabs for construction, to the rough, porous limestone, little more than compressed seashells and corals, that was found and used along the Caribbean coast. Regions with sandstone—particularly upland Chiapas and the Motagua drainage of Guatemala—used the local material; however, staircases at Toniná that feature both limestone and sandstone may point to the importation of limestone or perhaps its command appearance as tribute payment. In some regions, adobes—sun-dried bricks—were used; at Toniná, for example, adobes are found in elite structures of the eighth and ninth centuries AD—and this may have been the case elsewhere, although survival is extremely poor. At Comalcalco—where limestone does not occur—the Maya fired tens of thousands of bricks and set them in a mortar made from burned seashells.[1] In Honduras, the builders and sculptors of Copán worked exclusively with local tan, pink, and green volcanic tuff, which is easy to cut into uniform building blocks when quarried, but hardens when exposed to air. Local planners selected multicolored tuff for many buildings, but used imported limestone for some stone monuments; they also put aside tuff with nodules of chert for use in certain sculptures. That the Maya could commission the delivery of rare, imported stone for sculpture, if not for building material, is attested by Calakmul's "slate stele," which was probably brought from the Maya Mountains.

259. (above) Masks of
Chaak, the river god, decorating the exterior of the
Codz Pop' at Kabah, Yuca-
tán, 8th–11th century AD.

Maya builders laid out stone frameworks on the ground or dug deep into bedrock, filling
interstices with rubble, to create elevated floors for all but the most modest of domestic spaces.
At one extreme, they could repeat the process level by level, creating the setbacks of towering
pyramids. In their most prestigious buildings, they replicated the walls and roofs of perishable
domestic structures in stone, frequently multiplying the form almost beyond easy recogni-
tion. Throughout their realm, the Maya burned quarried limestone at best and seashells at
worst, consuming thousands of BTUs to produce a cement that could function as both mortar
and stucco. Reconstituted with water, this powdered cement became as hard and tough as
the original limestone. The Maya applied thin or thick layers of stucco to their buildings,
creating a smooth, durable surface for both painting (plate 261) and sculpting. Particularly
during the first millennium BC, they shaped huge architectural sculptures onto setbacks. The
predominant color in most Maya cities was red, easily available from local hematite-rich clays
and yielding powerful contrasts with the green forest and blue sky (plate 260). Using stucco,
artists created both massive imagery that could be seen at a great distance and life-size figural
sculptures meant to be viewed more intimately. All were brightly painted: the white or lichen-
covered walls of Maya cities today are the result of long exposure to the elements (plate 259).

260. (below) Vase from Dzibilchaltún, Campeche, reproducing an architectural structure in miniature. 7th–10th century AD.

261. (right) Structure 1, Bonampak, Chiapas, AD 792.

The Maya conceived of architecture through the metaphor of the body, which in turn was related to the larger natural world. They recognized doorways as analogous to both human mouths and entrances to a living, organic earth (figure 89). David Stuart notes that Structure 23 at Yaxchilán refers to "its opening" in a characteristically possessive form;[2] it is the building, on the one hand, and its human or divine owner, on the other, that contain these features. Structures from Copán in particular and Campeche in general have doorways configured as the mouths of mountains; that these natural forms are alive can further be understood from the eyes and noses that provide a full and often intimidating sense of nature as far larger than human life. Roofcombs function with respect to buildings much as headdresses do for humans or deities, identifying not only a name but also characteristics and aspects—and with their often vast scale, serving as billboards that proclaim their affiliations and identities (plates 262, 264). Temple 1 at Tikal may both embody the late king, in its tall and massive form, as well as portray his apotheosis in the afterlife through its elaborated roofcomb (plate 263). The Maya understood everything to be possessed, whether by the house itself or by its human owner. Dedications of buildings, from ballcourts to funerary temples, came to be among the most typical of ancient inscriptions.

From its inception, the simplest form, the one-room Maya house, formed a key building block of all architecture. Stone may be the physical material, but the house is the social and spiritual heart of Maya constructions (figure 85). At some of the earliest Maya sites, like Cuello in Belize or Uaxactún in Guatemala, archaeologists have found postholes laid out atop low platforms: these would have held the large timbers that supported house walls. Between the timbers, the Maya wove lesser branches, like the warp and weft of fabric, and then packed these walls with moist earth and straw, in the type of construction usually called wattle and daub. At about 6½ feet (2 meters) from the dirt floor, they framed a hip roof with long poles. A particular rainforest tree, the huano palm (*Sabal yapa*), served as the best thatching for the roof, and from this material the Maya wove a single continuous piece that straddled the roof peak and provided security against rain and storms. This basic type of house construction continues to be used in the Maya area to this day.

By 500 BC, Maya builders had extended the house into something more like a "longhouse"; shortly thereafter—although most such early constructions were subsequently destroyed or still remain buried within later buildings—a permanent and more massive stone architecture took root, using the house form for both single and multiple chambers, sometimes atop large platforms, and replicating the hip roof in the form of the corbelled vault. Workmen laid courses of stone to approach one another toward the peak until they could be spanned by a single stone, often setting in wooden cross-ties at irregular intervals to stabilize the construction. Later, the cross-ties served for hoisting stored goods into the peak, particularly seed corn and perishable costume items, such as feathers and fine cloth. The Maya also dug into bedrock to create tombs, capping these with corbelled vaults as well, as if to specify that they were houses for the dead.

262. (*below*) Aerial view of Tikal, Guatemala, showing the roofcombs of pyramids towering above the forest canopy. This city was continuously occupied between the 4th century BC and the 9th century AD.

263. (*opposite*) Temple 1 at Tikal, AD 734. This tall funerary pyramid houses the tomb of Ruler A (Jasaw Chan K'awiil), who governed Tikal from AD 682 to 734. Built entirely after his death, the pyramid is a testament to his lasting power and authority.

264. (*overleaf*) Temple 2 at Tikal. In the background are Temple 3 (to the left) and Temple 4 (to the right). 8th century AD.

265. (*page 229*) The Central Acropolis of Tikal was the city's royal palace complex between the 4th and 9th centuries AD.

The corbelled vault is inherently unstable: the weight at the top pushes down and out. The Maya could simply buttress the vault through mass, as they did when they made the narrow but very stable rooms at the top of Tikal's Temple 1. They also developed internal buttresses of the sort commonly seen in Yaxchilán buildings, solutions that once again consumed the internal space they sought to create. However, in the tropical Maya climate, many activities took place outdoors, in plazas or patios. Instead of maximizing interior space, the Maya added towering roofcombs on top of small and simple structures, increasing their long-distance visibility and creating new areas for stucco decoration.

Translated into stone, the house form not only served as the chamber at the pyramid's summit but was also multiplied and expanded to create noble residences and official palaces, as well as workshops and places for training and education. But regardless of how grand and expansive these stone buildings became, they seem to have always been called simply *na* or *otot*, both words for house among the Maya, reminding the viewer today that not only did the house function as the universe in miniature, but the "universe was considered a house."[3] Palenque's palace, along with Uxmal's ranging structures and many other buildings in the Puuc region, made explicit references to perishable structures. Although now darkened and stained by acid rain, Palenque's House E re-creates the ragged edge of thatch in sheets of thin limestone,

266. (*below*) The arch at Labná, Yucatán, 9th–10th century AD. On either side of this arch, which marks the entrance to a residential group, images of perishable thatched houses are made permanent in stone.

267. (*above*) House E,
Palenque, Chiapas,
AD 654. This palace of
King Pakal the Great
(K'inich Janaab' Pakal)
was called the *Sak
Nuk Nah* ("White Big
House"). The edge of
its stone roof imitates
thatching.

anchored to the sloping mansard roof edge by stone pins; the dedicatory text calls the structure *Sak Nuk Nah*, or "White Big House"[4] (plate 267). Miniature thatch-roof structures—some with elaborate snake adornments—appear in the architectural ornament at Uxmal, pointing to a lost custom of decoration. In the walls adjoining the Labná Arch, fancy carved stones are set among long thin ones that resemble thick branches, suggesting wattle and daub converted to limestone (plate 266). Although most surviving architecture had a stone roof, hybrid stone buildings were also constructed, with thatched roofs that spanned larger internal spaces than any stone roof could; such a building, for example, survives adjacent to the structure that houses the Bonampak paintings. Many other buildings, particularly palaces, have what are often thought to be curtain tie holes, but these may have supported substantial awnings, creating a temporary architecture and a transitional space between indoors and outdoors.

PALACES

Many palaces may have started out as perishable structures. The earliest suggestion of an extended range-type and open structure, as archaeologists have often labeled Maya palaces, comes from Uaxactún, where a building akin to a North American Indian longhouse, 59 feet (18 meters) long and 13 feet (4 meters) wide, sat atop several setbacks on a raised platform.[5] By 100 BC, such ranging structures became important foci at Maya cities: the elaborate paintings within a building at San Bartolo, Guatemala, may suggest that at least some of these relatively spacious structures served as centers of religious instruction. But like San Bartolo Pinturas Sub-1, these early buildings lie deep within later constructions and come to light only through extensive archaeological excavations. Much better known are palaces of the eighth and ninth centuries AD that were in use at the time of their abandonment; sculptures, paintings, and inscriptions articulate some of the functions that these structures had, especially as seats of administrative power. Over the course of the seventh and eighth centuries, easy access to the

268. (*above*) Central Acropolis, Court 6, Tikal. The palace of the fourth-century ruler Jaguar Claw (Chak Toh Ich'ak) lies at the heart of this royal residence.

private precincts of most Maya palaces had been closed off. At Uaxactún, what had been a temple precinct before AD 550, with the burials of kings, became a vast administrative compound, its seemingly open colonnades blocking the center of the compound by the time the city was abandoned in the early ninth century.

By the eighth century AD, Tikal's Central Acropolis had expanded to become one of the largest palace compounds extant (figure 86; plates 265, 268). The heart of the palace lies on the Central Acropolis's eastern end, in Court 6, where the fourth-century AD ruler Jaguar Claw built his palace and set his throne, with easy access to the East Plaza and its ballcourt, as well as what was probably the principal market of the city. Venerated for generations, the original throne room faced east and survived four hundred years of renovations and expansions to the complex. The various colonnades that face the Great Plaza offered an inviting facade but provided no easy entry to the courts within; the many small rooms along the plaza may have served for public receptions, tribute and tax payments, and possibly judicial proceedings. Archaeologists found a four-hearth kitchen adjacent to the palace reservoir, a rare discovery of institutional food preparation.

At seventh-century Palenque, architects and engineers began to explore some of the limitations of the vault, in what would lead to the most dramatic ancient Maya palace to survive today (plates 269, 270). First and foremost, in a solution that many other cities would adopt, they placed two corbelled vaults side-by-side, sharing the center wall—which then became secure, with force acting on it from two directions. The engineers of Palenque moved the roof-combs—the great billboards that announced the building's program—to these central load-bearing walls, offering yet greater stability, even as other cities piled greater weight directly onto the corbel itself. Because greater height could be achieved with lighter loads, at Palenque

269. (*right*) The Palace at Palenque, with its tower, 7th–8th century AD.

270 (*above*). Aerial view of Palenque, with the Palace at center, the Temple of the Inscriptions to the right, and the Cross Group in the background, 7th–8th century AD.

the builders made keyhole cutouts in both the Cross Group buildings and the Palace. In those same buildings they began to set a cross corbel to intersect the parallel ones: these intersections, hidden behind post-and-lintel doorways, opened up new types of interior spaces (figure 87). Although it is altogether possible that the solution of parallel corbels appeared elsewhere first, the other architectural innovations were limited to Palenque, suggesting a special role for engineers at the site. To control the Otulum River, they built a deep stone-lined channel for it, which was covered with corbels; where the aqueduct opens into a natural stream again, a final corbelled bridge spans the water.

The Palenque Palace served both as the setting for the royal throne and the locus of wealth for several generations of local kings in the seventh and eighth centuries. Personal royal residences grew up along the Otulum River downstream, with sweatbaths and sleeping rooms, as well as private courtyards and receiving rooms. Structure 16, behind the Cross Group, has an extensive warren of small rooms that could have served to house guests or as a school. Inscriptions record repeated attacks on the site until 654; King K'inich Janaab' Pakal may have then begun to set Houses E, B, and C atop the leveled rubble of earlier palaces (plates 271, 272), now seen only in the cool, dank subterranean chambers at the south end of the Palace and accessible only from courtyards and a single hidden staircase within House E. The two parallel chambers of House E increased the stability of the corbelled vault; the use of the stone "thatch" may have been an intentional appeal to the local population for support after political disruptions. A dedicatory text names House E the *Sak Nuk Nah*, the "White Big House," and unlike most other buildings at the site, which were eventually painted red, it remained white, with large yellow and blue flowers, through various repaintings. The doorway at the center of the front facade opens onto the throne, as indicated by the Oval Palace Tablet, still

271. *(below)* House E of the Palace at Palenque, with the Tower on the left and House C in the background, 7th–8th century AD.

272. *(right)* House B at Palenque, AD 661. This building within the Palace may have served as a council house.

in situ, which replicates an oval jaguar cushion of the throne back, a form unique in all of Mesoamerica. An interior stucco ornament over the northern doorway from House E to the Northeast Court would have framed a ruler within a celestial band.

Staggered doorways at House E's rear opened onto a small courtyard with House B. Although later subdivided, House B originally featured large, open rooms; the doorways, too, were wide and open, and particularly when seen from the Northeast Court, the mass of the facade begins to dissolve. The mansard ornament of woven mat may suggest the name *popol nah*, which in Colonial Yucatán referred to a council house; with its easy and private access to the throne room, House B would have served as an effective staging location for nobles and royal attendants. Bordered on two sides by Houses B and C, the Northeast Court not only acknowledged Palenque's defeats (on the steps of House C) but also recorded its later triumphs. Attendant lords from the plain to the north pay tribute in scenes carved on slabs; across the courtyard, captives in various states of humiliation took permanent form on huge slabs of various colors of limestone, some of which suggest reuse and importation.

Houses E, B, and C read like the spokes of a wheel; later buildings enclosed them within vast galleries that created closed courtyards. House AD's entry to the Northeast Court features a great ogee-shaped corbel archway that pierces the parallel north-south corbels. Keyhole-shaped cutouts in the sloping corbels lightened the load to be borne by the walls and vaults, allowing for narrow but cathedral-like spaces. A later throne, framed by the sculpture known as the Palace Tablet and facing to the north, replaced King Pakal's. The only Maya tower to survive (the example at Copán was washed into the Copán River in the nineteenth century) was the final eighth-century addition to the Palace, cramping House E's court; an architectural tour de force, the tower overlooked what had become valuable territory, the plain to the north. Throughout the Palace, small cutouts in the walls take the shape of the *ik'* glyph, meaning wind; these literal "windows" channel air and conversation throughout the structure.

Dissolving the mass of stone masonry in favor of internal space and volume became a goal of Palenque's architects in the late seventh and eighth centuries, culminating in the recently explored Structures 19 and 21. Destroyed in antiquity, the roofs of these buildings have not been fully reconstructed, but their rubble indicates that they were vaulted. Supported only by piers, these vaults would have created the largest interior spaces in the Maya area known to have had stone roofs—covering a space nearly 130 by 33 feet (40 by 10 meters) in the case of Structure 19. Set at some distance from the larger and more accessible courts associated with the Cross Group and the Palace, these sizable interior spaces would have been ideal for banqueting and feasting.

Sharing both the principle of privacy and the parallel corbelled vault with Palenque, Piedras Negras built a very different sort of palace on its West Acropolis, largely by using the topographic relief to stage successively higher courtyards (figures 90, 91). Despite its location along the Usumacinta River, the palace looks inward and inland, although the highest point of the complex opened onto vistas downstream. Although sweatbaths also occur elsewhere, the large ones found in the palace complexes of Piedras Negras played a greater role there than at any other Maya city over a several hundred year period, indicating the idiosyncrasy of Maya architecture and the way local cults and practices distinguished one center from another.

Local traditions also prevailed in the palace constructions at Yaxchilán. In contrast to the practice at all other large cities, the lords here constructed no large enclosed compound as an administrative center. Rather, small structures, most with three doorways, dot the plaza that follows the curve of the Usumacinta River and the steep hillside that rises up from it (figure 88); the massive assemblage of rock seen elsewhere is absent from Yaxchilán, although much of the hillside was finished with cut stone, as if to make the entire city seem man-made. Lady Xok' commissioned Structure 23 and the three lintels that acknowledge her role in King Shield Jaguar's regime (dedicated 724); subsequent buildings went up alongside (Structures 20 and 21) emulating her model, with important female dynasts featured in the sculptural program. At the same time, Shield Jaguar erected three-room structures at the highest crest, with what may have been the longest staircase in the Maya world leading down nearly 330 feet (100 meters); from Structure 41, at the top, the ruler would have surveyed not only the far side of the river but also a bridge or pier, whose remains can still be seen at times of low water. Shield Jaguar's son, Bird Jaguar the Great, selected a site partway down the slope for his palace, Structure 33 (dedicated 755), which looms over the plaza below (plate 273). Like most administrative buildings at Yaxchilán, the single-vaulted Structure 33 features three doorways with carved lintels and an open floor plan, with internal buttresses supporting the heavy roofcomb set atop the single corbel. This roofcomb includes a giant seated figure, tenoned into the mansard and finished with stucco ornament, that probably represents Bird Jaguar himself. The final step into the building is formed by a row of carved risers that depict the king and his predecessors playing the ballgame against flights of stairs; in some cases a bound captive is described on the surface of the ball. Unpublished tombs within the building may indicate that it was understood to be both temple and seat of authority. On axis with the central entry stands a carved stalagmite that the Maya moved into place, as if to set a cave below the seat of rulership. In

273. Structure 33, Yaxchi-lán, Chiapas. King Bird Jaguar the Great built this palace midway up the slope of the hill, dominating the plaza below. A carved stalagmite stands in front of the palace, which was dedicated in AD 755.

this way, the building acted as a metaphor of the "water-mountain," known centuries later in central Mexico by the term *altepetl*, a place of civilization and, by extension, a city.

Destroyed by a sudden devastating fire around 810, Aguateca preserved objects in use and persons in place within its palaces, although much was lost in the catastrophe. The royal family itself seems to have fled, securing valuable objects behind a hastily made wall. Very close to the royal palace, an elite residence contained shell, jade, and bone objects within a three-room structure that probably served as both workshop and home to a family of literate scribes. Across the Maya region, this social stratum of scribes and other courtiers gained the political and economic power to build increasingly elaborate palatial spaces over the course of the eighth century. Notable among such buildings is the House of the Scribes at Copán,

where sculptural busts of scribes with paintbrushes in hand emerge from huge serpent jaws on the main facade. A carved bench within the main chamber features some of the most florid hieroglyphic writing known—and this emulation of the royal throne serves as a measure of the challenge to royalty that wealthy nobles provided in the period. Like many buildings at Copán, the House of the Scribes has a perpendicular facade, rather than the sloping mansard common elsewhere.

All across the Puuc Hills, Maya lords erected low-lying palace buildings in the eighth and ninth centuries, usually without the centuries of underlying accretions that characterize Maya cities of the southern lowlands. When these ranging structures came to the attention of modern architects, they helped shape twentieth-century modernism, from the ranch house to Frank Lloyd Wright. Of the Puuc communities, Uxmal is both the largest and the best known (plate 274). Its early palace groupings—say, Las Palomas—took advantage of the structural integrity of parallel corbelled vaults but retained the roofcomb, setting it directly over the front load-bearing wall, in what is usually called a "flying facade." Structural innovations, especially the boot stone—an L-shaped stone with a tapered "foot" that offered enhanced stability—along with a local limestone that lent itself to thin and uniform veneer stones for shrouding a rubble core, supported the development of palaces throughout the region. The sloping mansard gave way to the cleaner lines of the vertical facade, in some cases with a slight "negative batter," or outward slope, lending buildings an appearance of lightness.

274. (*above*) View of Uxmal, Yucatán, 9th–10th century AD.

275. (*below*) Codz Pop', Kabah, 8th–11th century AD. The front facade of this palace is entirely covered with images of the rain god Chaak.

276. (above) The House of the Governor, Uxmal. This palace of Lord Chaak, the early tenth-century ruler of the city, is a tour de force of Puuc-style architecture.

At Uxmal, rulers planned palatial quadrangles on raised platforms, even though such structures may have taken a generation to complete. In the so-called Nunnery, the North Building, with its flying facade, went up first; the East and West Buildings may have been next, possibly replacing earlier structures, but one can see that the ornament previously adorning the roofcomb has been compressed to the vertical facade. Spaced doorways alleviate the tedium seen elsewhere, and double door frames, rarely found at other sites, underscore the lavish attention given the quadrangle. The designers completed the quadrangle with the South Building, whose archway provided the only foot access to the compound, despite the open space between buildings.

Lord Chaak built the House of the Governor, Uxmal's final palace, in the early tenth century (plate 276). Set upon a vast platform, this single structure with thirteen openings incorporated elements used in the Nunnery, but enshrined the great lord himself in an architectural ornament over the square central doorway. Subtle variations in the spacing of the attendant rectangular doorways emphasize the horizontal movement, and with its measurable negative batter the building seems to float from its supporting platform. Two pointed archways recede from the horizontal expanse, separating the outer sections of the building.

Just 11 miles (18 kilometers) away by elevated causeway from Uxmal, Kabah developed a distinct visual language using Puuc forms. The largest palace, known as the Codz Pop', is completely covered by continuous images of Chaak, the Maya deity of rain, lightning, and

277. (*left*) The Nunnery, Chichén Itzá, Yucatán, 9th–12th century AD. This hulking palace complex draws on Puuc-style architectural conventions and was the center of the early road network at the city.

278. (*below top*) The Group of a Thousand Columns, Chichén Itzá, 9th–12th century AD.

agriculture (plates 275). Long-snouted Chaak masks not only carpet the facade but serve as steps into the palace chambers—perhaps not only indicating the rain god's cult but also instructing the supplicant in chant or song.

Chichén Itzá's rulers built palaces in various styles over the years, including some resembling those of the southern lowlands. Among the earliest is the so-called Nunnery, in fact probably a royal residence and the focus of the city in its early centuries of occupation (plate 277). Like many palaces, it was subject to a complex series of renovations. In its final form, the Nunnery combined the materials and decorative style of Puuc-type buildings, especially in the almost baroque ornamentation of the freestanding Iglesia, whose tall, massive bulk is unusual in Puuc constructions (plate 280). One of the last structures to be built in the city, the misnamed Mercado was Chichén Itzá's grandest palace. Thirty-six doorways framed by alternating pillars and columns open onto a grand arcade that screened access through a single narrow doorway into the receiving rooms that surround a sunken patio, much like a Roman house (figure 93). Towering columns (over 16 feet, or 5 meters, high) of uneven number on the east and west sides of the patio allowed the occupant of the bench or throne centered on the east to have an unfettered and panoramic view of all activities within the enclosure. A large carved bench or throne remains in place in the colonnade, adjacent to the atrium entry; this may have been the principal place of business (figure 92).

279. *(below bottom)* Structure 25, Tulum, Quintana Roo, 13th–15th century AD.

280. *(right)* La Iglesia, Chichén Itzá, 9th–11th century AD.

Builders at Mayapán and Tulum adopted the colonnade from Chichén Itzá (plate 278) for what seem to have been largely administrative palaces. The structure at Mayapán known as the Hall of Masks underscores the references to earlier cities by physically incorporating Puuc Chaak masks into the structure—perhaps in homage, or perhaps as a tribute demand. Structure 25 at Tulum faces south adjacent to the site's large canoe landing area; its open colonnade could easily have served as a place for the receipt of trade goods and tribute, while the private rooms behind may have been for residence or storage (plate 279).

In the century before the Spanish invasion, wealthy nobles of distinct Maya groups across highland Guatemala—Pok'omchi, K'iche, and Cak'chik'el among them—built elaborate palace compounds that included ballcourts and temples within them, and which were usually situated on hilltops, like acropolises. Cak'chik'el lords allied themselves with the Spaniards, and their capital city, Iximché, accordingly survived, only to be inhabited by the invaders themselves, including Bernal Díaz del Castillo, whose chronicles would later become the best-known account of the Conquest. The two principal compounds, today known as A and B, housed separate lineages, as well as separate palaces, ballcourts, and temples, shedding light on the social organization of the Maya in their final years of independence.

PYRAMIDS

The difference between a palace and a temple is often one of size, scale, or number: how many chambers, how high the platform of the structure, how many doorways? The open, multidoorway structure on a relatively low platform argues for a dominant reading of palace over religious structure—yet these categories of modern humanity cannot address the overlapping of forms and functions in ancient Maya building. In Group A-V at Uaxactún, the funerary temples of fourth-century kings were covered by eighth-century administrative structures, with an attendant transition to modest burials of women and children—clear evidence that the Maya often decided to shift the function of a structure over time. Structures might also encompass different functions and meanings at a single moment: a funerary pyramid would also be a temple to the newly deified ancestor; the seat of accession rituals might also be dedicated to a particular god.

Maya architects used several strategies to create massive pyramids, taking advantage of the natural and built environment to add bulk to their structures. Early buildings were often used as the core for later construction, reducing the amount of materials and labor necessary to erect a giant pyramid. Among many other examples, the Mundo Perdido Pyramid at Tikal, the

281. (*opposite*) The Hieroglyphic Stairway, Copán, AD 710 and 755. The text on this stairway, one of the longest known Mayan inscriptions, recounts a history stretching back centuries, with the earliest events recorded at the top of the staircase. Like Temple 16 at Copán, the Hieroglyphic Stairway is built on top of significant earlier constructions.

282. (*above*) The Pyramid of the Magician, Uxmal, 8th–10th century AD.

Pyramid of the Magician at Uxmal (plate 282), and the Temple of the Warriors at Chichén Itzá (plates 283, 301) all have smaller substructures within them. Burying a building could have symbolic resonance—the earlier structure might persist in memory, adding to the meanings of the structure encompassing it. At Copán, two of the largest eighth-century pyramids on the Acropolis, Temple 16 and the Hieroglyphic Stairway (plate 281), were both built over uninterrupted series of buildings stretching back into the fifth century AD, each ritually terminated to make way for its successor. Instead of using previous constructions, the builders of other pyramids took advantage of dramatic topography: the Temple of the Inscriptions at Palenque or Structure 33 at Yaxchilán, for example, were terraced into the sides of mountains, creating the impression of great architectural mass. In light of these labor-saving techniques, pyramids that were built in a single stage of construction on purely flat land were especially powerful statements of royal authority. When a funerary pyramid of this type was erected after a ruler's death, like Temple 1 at Tikal, it spoke of power extending beyond the grave.

From the earliest times, Maya pyramids took on two distinct forms—axial, with a single principal staircase and an enclosed structure at the top of the platform, and radial, with staircases on all four sides. Although the two kinds of pyramids have vastly different distributions— radial pyramids remained a specialized form while axial pyramids became ubiquitous—they share similar trajectories, beginning as parts of formalized groups and later being deployed as independent architectural forms. Starting around the fourth century BC, radial pyramids

283. The Temple of the Warriors, Chichén Itzá. The use of colonnades was one of the great architectural innovations of the ninth and tenth centuries.

generally occurred as part of a specialized architectural complex called an E Group, named after the first such compound to be excavated, Uaxactún's Group E (plate 284). An E Group typically consisted of a radial pyramid and, to its east, a long platform parallel to the pyramid's north-south axis and topped with three small structures. The earliest examples were oriented so that the sun could be seen rising above the central structure of the long platform on the spring and autumn equinoxes and above the north and south structures on the summer and winter solstices. Although the ideal position for viewing this phenomenon—on the stairs or summit of the radial pyramid—was restricted to a few elites, there may have been visible effects of light and shadow from the plaza as well.[6] Later E Groups often replicated this basic plan, but did not function as solstice observatories: some mark twenty-day intervals from the zenith passage of the sun,[7] while others have no discernible alignment. Even the famous Uaxactún Group E ceased to function as an observatory after later renovations.[8] Form may have become more important than function in the later history of this architectural type.[9]

Although E Groups became less common after the sixth century AD, radial pyramids retained their association with solar movement and the measurement of time. On the spring and fall equinoxes, the rising sun blazes through the doors of the House of the Seven Dolls at Dzibilchaltún, which is unusual among radial pyramids for its distinctive superstructure (plates 285, 286). At Tikal in the seventh century AD, radial pyramids reemerged in the form of the Twin Pyramid Groups, erected every twenty years for over a century to commemorate

284. Structure E-VII-sub, Uaxactún, Guatemala, 1st century AD. This radial pyramid formed part of an E Group that could be used to observe solstices and equinoxes.

285, 286. (*left top and bottom*) The House of the Seven Dolls, Dzibilchaltún, Yucatán, 8th century AD. The sun rises directly behind this radial structure on the fall and spring equinoxes.

287. (above) El Castillo, Chichén Itzá, 10th–12th century AD. This radial temple is a chronographic marker of dazzling complexity. The serpent that appears to descend the staircase on the equinoxes is only one of this building's numerous calendrically significant features.

k'atun endings.[10] The Castillo at Chichén Itzá, a tenth-century revival of the radial pyramid form, is a monument to time (plate 287): as the sun sets on the equinoxes, the play of light and shadow on the north stair creates the illusion of a descending serpent. Calendrically significant numbers are built into the fabric of El Castillo: 365 steps (91 per side, plus 1 for the temple platform) count the days in the solar year, and 52 recessed panels on each side of the pyramid allude to the 52-year linking of the 365- and 260-day calendrical cycles. The Castillo has other meanings as well: its great feathered rattlesnake columns and balustrades mark it as a "serpent hill"—or in Nahuatl, a *Coatepec*—a pan-Mesoamerican place of origin, an association it seems to share with the early radial pyramid at Uaxactún, where huge snakes framed the principal stairway. A jaguar throne found inside the substructure of El Castillo suggests that it was also a seat of rulership, and this earlier structure was decorated with stucco jaguars and shields with martial overtones, although it likely replicated the equinox hierophany.[11] The Temple of Kukulcan at Mayapán, described by Diego de Landa as a copy of Chichén Itzá's Castillo, was also a Coatepec because of its serpent columns, but it has a different orientation, facing the December solstice, and its 260 steps link it to the Mesoamerican ritual calendar (plate 288).[12]

In contrast to radial pyramids, axial pyramids have a single staircase leading up a massive body composed of multiple setbacks, always topped with an enclosed building. Axial pyramids were far more widely distributed in time and space, becoming one of the most durable Maya architectural forms. In the first centuries of Maya monumental architecture, these pyramidal bases were often decorated with enormous painted stucco masks of deities, while in later centuries, the focus of ornament shifted to stone and stucco decoration on the temple building itself. At the summit of the earliest Maya pyramids were perishable structures or buildings with stone and stucco walls and thatch roofs. Soon vaulted stone structures took precedence, their upper cornices providing another area for stucco decoration. Roofcombs added on the top of these superstructures increased the pyramid's height and visibility, and became sculptural entities in their own right, being sometimes a solid modeled mass and, especially in the western Maya region or later in the Puuc region, sometimes an openwork lattice supporting brightly painted figural sculpture.

Early axial pyramids often occurred in what is called a triadic temple group, a ceremonial complex of three buildings arranged in a U shape. The central building was the largest, and the two subordinate buildings were oriented to face one another. This shape may evoke the three hearthstones set in place at the creation of the universe in Maya mythology,[13] forming a

288. (*opposite*) The Temple of Kukulcan, Mayapán, Yucatán, 12th–14th century AD, modeled on the Castillo of Chichén Itzá.

289. (*above left*) The Cross Group, Palenque, AD 692. Triadic temple groupings of this sort were an archaizing form by the late seventh century.

290. (*above right*) The Temple of the Foliated Cross, part of the Cross Group at Palenque.

set of spaces for interlinked rituals. Triadic arrangements were particularly typical of temples before AD 600. When the form occurs in the eighth or ninth centuries, as in the Cross Group at Palenque, it is likely an archaizing gesture (plates 289, 290). Here the three pyramids are freestanding like most late pyramids, rather than sharing a single pyramidal platform as was usually the case in earlier times. Extensive texts within the Cross Group temples reveal that each was a ritual space dedicated to a different patron god of the city and taking the form of a symbolic sweatbath.

Although excavations—and looter's trenches—usually do not encounter tombs inside early Maya temples,[14] they became an increasingly common feature in later centuries, when pyramids were often built to enclose royal burials, creating a space in which to worship a deified ancestor. The histories of such buildings could become quite complex, as later rulers returned to renovate the temples dedicated to their honored ancestors. At Tikal, for instance, most kings before the eighth century were buried in the North Acropolis, a royal necropolis of staggering architectural complexity created by successive additions of new tombs and renovations of royal ancestral shrines.

291. (*below left*) Temple 16 at Copán, AD 776, was the culmination of an uninterrupted sequence of construction dating back to the fifth century AD.

292. (*below right*) Altar Q at Copán, AD 776, located in front of Temple 16, records the city's dynastic history.

293, 294. (*right top and bottom*) The Temple of the Inscriptions, Palenque. Pakal the Great's nine-level funerary pyramid was largely completed before his death in AD 683, and finally dedicated by his son Kan Bahlam in 690.

At Copán, the fifth-century burial place of the dynastic founder, Yax K'uk' Mo', was a relatively modest structure (perhaps not even constructed as a tomb), but the slightly later structure, nicknamed Margarita, that was superimposed upon it and which contained the body of a woman, perhaps the founder's wife, was a far more elaborate affair: at least double the size, with brightly painted stucco decoration, and crammed full of rich ceramic and jade offerings. Later, in a gesture of ancestral piety by Copán's tenth ruler, both structures were enclosed within the magnificent Rosalila temple, which was enshrouded with a coating of white stucco before itself being buried under new construction. The final building in this sequence of construction was Temple 16, a massive pyramid dedicated by Copán's sixteenth ruler, Yax Pasaj Chan Yopaat (plate 291); Altar Q, placed directly in front of the monument, shows the entire sequence of Copán's dynastic kings, with the sixteenth ruler receiving his right to rule from the dynastic founder (plate 292).[15]

Many rulers must have spent considerable time planning their own funerary monuments; the clearest example is the Temple of the Inscriptions, the tomb of Palenque's greatest ruler, Pakal the Great, which was largely completed before his death in AD 683 (plates 293, 294). At the base of this nine-level pyramid is a tomb chamber containing a stone sarcophagus so massive that the entire temple must have been built around it; a vaulted stairway leading down to this chamber allowed the king's body to be placed there after his death.[16] By contrast, Temple 1 at Tikal, another nine-level funerary pyramid, is a solid mass over the tomb of Ruler A (d. 734), and must have been constructed by his son and successor as the first building project of his reign. Throughout the Maya area, one short-term result of death was new construction, especially to overlay burials and tombs; a new ruler, usually the son or brother of the previous king, would treat his predecessor with the reverence characteristic of a culture that worshipped ancestors.

However, not all tombs were located in stand-alone pyramids. Tombs or burials under palace floors blur the divisions between tomb, palace, and temple: are those Shield Jaguar's bones under the building of Lady Xok' at Yaxchilán?[17] Time and again, the Maya would dig into a staircase—sometimes reaching bedrock in the process—in order to fashion a tomb for a recently deceased member of the ruling family, or to revisit an ancient tomb, refreshing the "heat" of its owner.[18] This custom could replicate on a monumental scale the common practice of burying family members within household compounds. As archaeology has evolved into the twenty-first century, studies have revealed that women were honored as frequently as men, although fewer inscriptions point to their deaths or their tombs. At Caracol, for instance, both elite women and men were found buried within the Caana, the massive acropolis that was simultaneously the royal residence, administrative nerve center, and necropolis of the city. A plausible—and testable—hypothesis is that funerary temples were often incorporated into ranging structures. In some cases, the incorporation is subtle, as in J3, a nine-level pyramid—probably funerary—that lies within the West Acropolis complex at Piedras Negras. In others, the plan is direct and intentional, with the best examples coming from the Río Bec and Chenes regions. At Xpujil, Río Bec, Hochob, and elsewhere, massive towers pierce multiroom buildings that would otherwise seem to be palaces.[19] Fascinatingly, these towers feature architectural ornament that mimics stairways and doorways—but it is all just stucco over tenoned supports, some of which probably included human and divine actors in the simulacrum. Although unexcavated, these towers may hold royal tombs within. At ground level, the doorways function as the mouths of giant personified mountains, sometimes with a lower jaw extended like a welcome mat.

In other cases, rebuilding offered opportunities to turn functional chambers into tombs, and the process of accretive growth over centuries gave rise to hybridized structures incorporating aspects of palace, temple, and funerary pyramid. At Ek Balam (plate 295), for example, the lowest story of the main building features a long row of receiving rooms interrupted only by the main stairs. At the fourth level, to the west of the staircase, stand three chambers, the central one articulated by a great monster mouth, like those of Hochob, and the two that flank it reproducing in stone and stucco the Maya house, with the signature woven mat of the council house featured on the "roof." The middle room's monstrous personified mountain is the single richest example of such a face, articulated by three-dimensional stucco figures that serve as the pupils of its eyes or decorations on its ear flares. When the ruler who had built this structure died in the early ninth century, the room at the back of it became his tomb, and

295. The Acropolis of Ek Balam, Yucatán, 8th–9th century AD. This hybrid structure functioned as palace, temple, and funerary pyramid. On the fourth level, a building decorated with a stucco monster mouth entrance was later converted into a tomb.

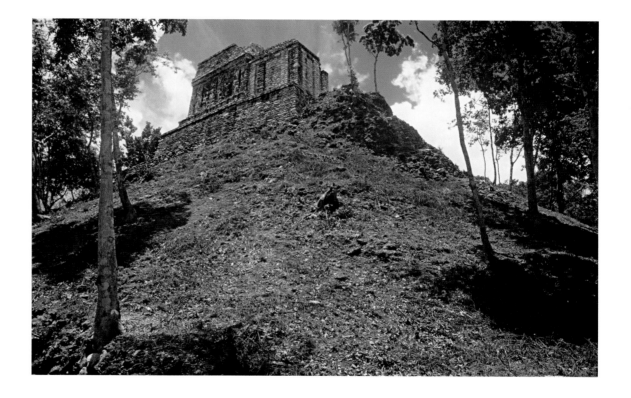

296, 297. (*above top and bottom*) The Temple of the Owl, Dzibanché, Quintana Roo, 3rd–9th century AD. This massive, accretive pyramid served multiple functions, from administrative structure to royal tomb.

his body was attended by rich offerings. The building itself was then buried, and the snout of the mask was stabilized by the construction of a column to underpin it; workers covered the three chambers with powdered limestone and rubble. The largest structures at many Maya sites were rarely limited to a single function; instead, buildings like the principal pyramid at Ek Balam, the Caana at Caracol, Structure II at Calakmul, the Temple of the Owl at Dzibanché (plates 296, 297), or the Acropolis at Toniná, to name just a few examples, were multipurpose spaces containing within them a record of centuries of use and modification.

SPECIALIZED STRUCTURES

Palace and pyramid alone did not define a Maya city: specialized structures with distinctive configurations were also part of the urban plan. Throughout Mesoamerica, the sweatbath served as a retreat for spiritual and physical cleansing, as well as a place of healing. Traditional peoples still maintain such sweathouses today, often with rigid guidelines for each gender, including healing rituals for newly delivered women. A sweathouse requires a small enclosed space for the firebox, where stones are heated; generally the place for the bathers is also small and windowless, to keep the temperature and humidity high. At Palenque and Chichén Itzá, such structures occur in smaller residential complexes away from the center of the site; an example at Copán forms part of what has been hypothesized to be a young men's residence.[20] At Piedras Negras, each generation of kings ordered grand examples with large dressing areas, their location within palace complexes underscoring their value to the court.

Ballcourts are among the most distinctive and unmistakable forms of Maya architecture. Two sloping parallel mounds may have been used as early as 1000 BC among the Olmec of Veracruz as a location for playing a game with a ball made of the resilient sap of the rubber tree. As archaeologists have learned to identify earthen architecture of the first millennium BC, they have found the game's hallmarks established by 500 BC.[21] The Maya included stone-faced courts in almost every city plan from at least AD 350 onward. While the ballcourt is defined by its regularity and specific geometry (the very notion of parallel lines can be seen otherwise only on the small scale, say, in the walls of a building, a road, or a room), no other architectural form better epitomizes the individuality of Maya cities. Local characteristics define the court at every city—from the large, dramatic structures that seemingly miniaturize the rest of the site and its setting at both Copán (plate 298) and Chichén Itzá (plate 299, 300) to the smaller courts at Yaxchilán and Piedras Negras that harmonize with the landscape without calling particular attention to their existence. The ballcourt is unmistakable but never exactly the same, like the

298. (*above*) The ballcourt at Copán is beautifully situated with respect to the mountains framing the surrounding valley. The latest version of this structure was dedicated in AD 738.

game itself, played by teams of three or four, as modern scholars hypothesize, with balls of different sizes and for stakes that ranged from modest bets to the greatest of all, one's own life.

Ancient architects laid out most principal ballcourts along a rough north-south axis, usually no more than 30 degrees west or east of north. At Copán, builders reconstructed the main court at least three times, adding a northern "end zone" with a stepped platform in the later phases; the stele atop this platform set the king in permanent review of the play in front of and below him. The building seems both to replicate the valley of Copán and to frame the sacred mountains to the north. Elaborate chambers top the sloping parallel structures, providing comfortable retreats for either noble observers or participants. Three stones marked openings to a supernatural realm in the court's alley: play in the court could pierce the membrane between the surface of the earth and a spirit world just beyond. At Toniná, huge "end zones" provided seating for hundreds of observers, though the actual playing court was smaller than Copán's. Architectural sculpture celebrated victory in battle and the humiliation of the defeated: three times on each side, tenoned three-dimensional bound captives protrude from the sloping walls atop two-dimensional representations of great war shields with hieroglyphic texts that enumerate Toniná's victories on the battlefield. Further associations between warfare and the ballgame can be seen in Chichén Itzá's Great Ballcourt, the largest to survive in Mesoamerica, and perhaps understood to be a place where the gods might come to engage in contest. Rings set 21 feet (6.5 meters) above the alley made scoring nearly impossible; viewers were confined to "end zone" temples with their own iconographic programs. Three sets of large carved panels on each parallel wall depict victorious Chichen warriors and their enemies, both teams of seven dressed in ballgame regalia; the victors decapitate the first defeated ballplayer, presumably as a prelude to dispatching the entire team.

299. (below) The Great Ballcourt at Chichén Itzá, 10th–12th century AD, is constructed on a monumental scale, perhaps intended for divine rather than human players.

When Bishop Diego de Landa visited Chichén Itzá in the sixteenth century, the local Maya elite described the platforms north of El Castillo as "dance platforms." Hieroglyphic inscriptions have revealed the importance of dance as both a local and an inter-city ritual for courtiers, and the radial platforms Landa identified may well have been loci for these performances. In their proximity to the Great Ballcourt as well as El Castillo, these platforms—known today as the Venus Platform and the Platform of the Eagles—contribute to the general sense that the main plaza at Chichén Itzá served for public theater and ritual entertainment. The Venus Platform falls directly on a line with the Sacred Cenote to the north, and its imagery consists of feathered serpents, Venus symbols, bundles of years, and descending creatures with warriors emerging from their maws. The smaller Platform of the Eagles is decorated with jaguars and eagles that consume human hearts, as well as a procession of warriors, suggesting that the dance on its surface celebrated heart sacrifice and solar rituals. Archaeologists gave a third platform, directly adjacent to the Great Ballcourt, the name Tzompantli, the term for Aztec skull racks, based on its architectural ornament of hundreds of skulls (plate 302). The dances on these platforms may well have celebrated the two principal forms of human sacrifice, decapitation and heart sacrifice.

Modern observers have eagerly sought evidence of Maya stargazing in architecture: after all, given that Maya inscriptions record extensive and sophisticated calculations regarding the

300. (*opposite left*) The Upper Temple of the Jaguars, Chichén Itzá, 10th–12th century AD. This elegant structure with serpent columns sits atop the east wall of the Great Ballcourt.

301. (*opposite right*) The chacmool on the Temple of the Warriors at Chichén Itzá, 10th–12th century AD. In the background are El Castillo and the Great Ballcourt.

303. (*below*) El Caracol, Chichén Itzá, 9th–10th century AD. This innovative round building may have functioned as an observatory. Inside El Caracol, two concentric vaulted passageways create a new kind of interior space, and a spiral staircase leads up to a small inner chamber.

302. (*above*) The Tzompantli, or skull platform, at Chichén Itzá, 10th–12th century AD.

sun, moon, Venus, Mars, and Jupiter, as well as eclipses, it has seemed as though observatories ought to exist. But the evidence is scant. House C at Palenque has a rooftop opening; one would gain access by ladder to a few steps that open through a great keyhole arch, presumably making it possible to stargaze in privacy. Any tower, or any temple roofcomb, would have enhanced the sense of proximity to the stars.

Although more traditionally called El Caracol, or "the snail," the round building at Chichén Itzá is commonly thought of as the Observatory (plate 303). Three tiny asymmetrical windows—of perhaps seven or eight in the original structure—survive in its second story, suggesting places for viewing astronomical alignments along the sight lines of the interior and outer jambs. Yet careful studies have been inconclusive, especially regarding the much-sought alignments with the movements of Venus.[22] Over time, the increasing collapse of the second story has yielded a more domelike form, also enhancing the modern reading of the building as an observatory. Made with finely finished limestone embedded over a rubble core, the structure was a tour de force of construction in its day. Rebuilt at least four times, El Caracol began as a round platform—perhaps nothing more than the round platform at Seibal—before taking a more elaborate shape. The plan of El Caracol lays out three concentric circles on the ground floor; a narrow passageway accessible by ladder connects to the upper story, spiraling like a great conch shell. The round building's main doorway does not align with the stairs on

its trapezoidal platform, enhancing the sense of movement, even disorientation, as if spinning within a conch shell—and associating the building with the wind gods, who wore a section of the conch shell on their chests. El Caracol inspired a series of imitations on a reduced scale, from the single-story round building at Mayapán, which replicates El Caracol's four doors and central core (plate 304), to even more modest buildings at sites like Uxmal, Paalmul, and Nohmul.[23]

CITY PLANNING

Maya city plans respond to the landscape, rather than imposing order upon it. The same basic elements—the house, the palace, the pyramid, the plaza, the ballcourt—were integrated into each Maya city, always in locally meaningful ways. Some of the earliest Maya architectural developments took place in locations that surprise modern observers, particularly when those locations offer no ready access to rivers, lakes, or coast, but rather feature swampy "bajos." But this very condition may have been most conducive to intensive agriculture, especially where the Maya could build raised fields or simple terraces. Ultimately, the Maya built great cities in these same regions, concentrating the heaviest and most monumental constructions in the areas of densest bedrock, and connecting clusters of buildings with raised causeways, called *sacbes* (literally, "white roads"). Farther west, cities were terraced into ridges on the sides of hills, using the natural features of the land to inscribe hierarchy and dominate the surrounding territory. In the north, city sites might be chosen for their proximity to cenotes, salt flats, or coastal trade (plate 305). The locations and plans of Maya cities also responded to a sacred landscape, drawing attention to the liminal places where the world of humans opened into other realms, particularly caves, springs, and mountains.

Maya cities were royal cities, each home to a *k'uhul ajaw*, or divine king, and his court. The fate of the city was tied to the fortunes of the ruling dynasty, and like the royal household itself, Maya cities were never static. Successive kings strove to leave their mark through massive construction programs. Older buildings were often used as a core for new construction,

304. Structure Q80, Mayapán, 12th–14th century AD. This round building is clearly modeled on El Caracol at Chichén Itzá, but built on a reduced single-story scale.

allowing dramatic increases in bulk with a lesser investment of labor; new structures were also built from scratch, demonstrating the potential to command extensive resources of labor and materials. The focal parts of the city, such as palaces and royal burial grounds, grew more massive and less accessible with each successive modification, but even within more modest architectural groups, function, scale, and access patterns could change dramatically over the years. At the same time, older buildings might be abandoned to neglect and decay.[24] The flexibility of Maya urban planning allowed cities to thrive for centuries, accommodating new construction, new kinds of construction, and even political transformations.

At the heart of every Maya city was a principal plaza, a space for public gatherings and the performance of civic rituals, typically large enough to accommodate the entire population of the city and its surrounding territories.[25] Although no rule holds for every Maya center, this plaza was often bordered on one side by the royal palace, whose centuries of accumulated growth formed an acropolis. Wide stairways often led from plaza to palace, terminating in large porticoed structures, as at Tikal, Palenque, or Piedras Negras. These porticoes gave an impression of accessibility and transparency not entirely supported by architectural reality: behind them, solid walls severely curtailed access to the private spaces of the palace beyond. As a constant reminder of the royal presence, stelae of rulers were erected in the plaza, eternal embodiments of the dances and rituals performed in this space.[26] A ballcourt was usually located near the principal plaza, representing another space where public contests and sacrifices were made permanent through architecture.

Pyramids towered above the central plaza, massive and tangible reminders of royal power. Funerary pyramids, such as Temple 1 at Tikal or the Temple of the Inscriptions at Palenque, continued the focus on the body of the ruler, the entire temple now legible as the deceased king buried within. Other prominent temples, like the Cross Group at Palenque, were dedicated to the patron gods of the city. Radial pyramids might occupy the center of a plaza, the better to be appreciated from all four sides, as at Uaxactún, Copán (figure 96), Seibal, or Chichén Itzá. From the early E Groups through El Castillo at Chichén Itzá, radial pyramids were associated with the observation of time, but the presence of a throne inside the inner substructure of El

305. The Sacred Cenote of Chichén Itzá. The Maya deposited countless offerings in this natural sinkhole.

Castillo suggests multiple meanings and functions for this prominent pyramid. Hieroglyphic stairways might also be located near the principal plaza, commemorating military defeats and victories stretching back far into the past, as at Copán, Yaxchilán, or Dos Pilas. Finally, administrative structures, long range-style buildings not associated with any residential function, were often found near the principal plaza as well.

In addition to the principal plaza, bordered by palace, ballcourt, stelae, and pyramids, most Maya cities had several secondary plazas, which might have some but not all of these elements. Often these spaces were records of factional and dynastic history; in some cities, the identification of the principal plaza shifted over time. Other open spaces might serve distinct functions, as spaces for markets or for particular local rituals, like the Twin Pyramid Groups commemorating twenty-year period endings at Tikal. Between groupings of monumental architecture were areas of lower urban density, home to elite palaces or even quite modest residential households, perhaps with fruit trees and kitchen gardens providing greenery within the urban setting.

The plaza or, on a smaller scale, the patio was the core of every important architectural group within the Maya city, from the principal plaza down to the humble house group. Just as the house was the fundamental building block of Maya architecture, the household lot, a loose group of buildings arranged around a central open space, was the basic unit of the Maya urban plan. No single organizational principle or alignment united all of the structures within a Maya city. Each group of buildings had its own internal, site-specific, and historically contingent logic. The interaction of site and landscape was an aesthetic focus of Maya urban plans.

In the Petén and the Yucatán, different monumental groups within the city were connected by roads that the Maya called *sacbes* (plate 306; figure 98). Like the house or the body, the road is an important structuring principle in Maya thought; in Classic Maya inscriptions, one expression for death is *och b'ih*, or "enter the road," while in modern Yucatec, the pleasantry *Bix a beel?* or "How are you?" literally inquires, "How is your road?" These straight raised roads, lined with stone and paved with lime, linked monumental centers within the city or the city epicenter with its outskirts. Sacbes had both practical and symbolic functions: they facilitated the movement of goods and people while also integrating different parts of a community and providing a space for ritual processions. Some sacbes even connected different cities: an extensive causeway system joined Nakbé, El Mirador, and Tintal by the first century BC,[27] and over a millennium later, a sacbe more than 60 miles (100 kilometers) long connected the cities of Cobá and Yaxuná. Like the urban plan itself, sacbe systems were flexible and adaptable. At Chichén Itzá, for example, Rafael Cobos has identified an early sacbe system centered around the palatial Nunnery complex beginning in the eighth century; these sacbes continued to be used as a new system of sacbes focused on the Great Plaza was built in the ninth and tenth centuries (figure 97).[28]

However, sacbes were not a consistent feature of Maya urbanism. In the mountainous terrain in the western part of the Maya area, cities along the Usumacinta River, like Piedras Negras, Yaxchilán, and Aguateca, as well as cities even farther west, such as Palenque and Comalcalco, did not use these roads.[29] In this region, height played a crucial role in the organization of urban space, and stairs may be as important as roads in linking different architectural groupings together. Cities like Toniná, Bonampak, Chinkultic, and Tenam Puente

take this kind of planning to an extreme (figure 101), converting the slope of a mountain into a massive stepped pyramid combining all kinds of civic structures, from palaces and temples to small plazas. Only a few civic buildings, usually ballcourts and administrative structures, lie on level ground, literally at the bottom of the architectural hierarchy (plate 307).

Like city centers, the boundaries of Maya urban areas displayed considerable variation. Some Maya cities were surrounded by walls or earthworks, which provided defensive fortifications while defining the extent of the city (figure 94). Many city walls enclosed just the central urban core, as at Becán, Uxmal, Mayapán, or Utatlán, but cities like Tikal included much larger areas within their systems of earthworks. Openings in the city walls were connected to an urban sacbe system, filtering traffic through a series of controlled checkpoints. These intersections could be marked by monumental architecture: a grand entrance interrupted the walls of El Mirador on the east, facing the causeway from the outlying La Danta Complex, while

306. Raised limestone causeways called *sacbes* (literally "white roads") connected spaces within Maya cities as well as linking cities as much as 60 mi. (100 km) apart. This sacbe at Labná connects two palace groups, 9th–10th century AD.

at Ek Balam, a freestanding four-way arch accessed by sloping ramps marked the entrance to the city core from the inner of the city's two concentric walls. For every Maya city that was bounded and defined by a wall, however, there was another that had no such definition. Some Maya cities extended over the landscape in a sprawl we might term suburban, like Caracol in Belize,[30] while topography was probably the primary line of defense at places like Palenque or Toniná, situated to have visual control over an extensive territory (figures 98, 99). In the Yucatán peninsula in the ninth and tenth centuries, walls were the exception rather than the rule,[31] but freestanding arches might mark important boundaries, like the terminus of the Uxmal–Kabah sacbe at the city of Kabah (plate 308) or the entrances to palace groups at Labná and Oxkintok. The boundaries of public works projects such as terraces, either residential and agricultural, or water management systems, could also serve to define city limits. In any Maya city, the sacbe system or its equivalent spatial logic offered visitors a carefully controlled introduction to the urban core.

Because of its flexibility, the Maya city plan was tremendously stable, lasting over a millennium through major changes in Maya civilization. All of the basic elements of this plan were in place by the third century BC. The first great cities, El Mirador and Nakbé, were remarkably similar in plan to cities like Tikal or Calakmul in the seventh century, or even Chichén Itzá in the eleventh century. All consist of focal clusters of civic structures, separated by areas of less dense settlement and interconnected by sacbes. Each city responds to the local geography, accommodating itself to its environment (figures 100, 102).

For all the stability of the basic urban plan, significant shifts did occur in the composition of Maya cities over time. Different kinds of buildings received particular emphasis during the successive phases of Maya history. Temples decorated with massive stucco masks, E Groups, and triadic building arrangements were particularly common in the first centuries of Maya urbanism, while rapidly multiplying palaces and funerary pyramids defined the urban landscape of the sixth to eighth centuries. Stone mosaics, raised quadrangles, and the use of the freestanding arch characterized eighth- to tenth-century city planning in the Puuc region, and the use of the colonnade at tenth- to eleventh-century Chichén Itzá and its successors was a striking addition to the urban fabric (plate 309). Over time, regional differences in topography also influenced Maya city planning. The earliest cities, founded in the swampy bajos of the Petén, made extensive use of sacbes to connect dispersed areas of settlement, a practice that continued until the end of urbanism in the region in the ninth century AD. To the west, an area which flourished between the sixth and ninth centuries, cities were often smaller and denser, making use of the mountainous terrain and constructing hierarchy through height. When the focus of Maya civilization shifted north to the flat limestone shelf of the Yucatán peninsula in the ninth and tenth centuries, the sacbe and the scattered urban form continued to be used in a radically different landscape.

The earliest Maya cities had at their core monumental temples, many erected in a single phase of construction. Royal palaces did exist, but they did not yet have the volume and prominence that they would later acquire. Certain kinds of structures, such as triadic groups or E Groups with radial pyramids, were particularly characteristic of early city plans. The larger cycle of ancient Maya history finds its analogue in architecture: the massive early temples at El Mirador and Nakbé were abandoned, never to be rebuilt after AD 100; what had been smaller cities, like Uaxactún, buried their early traces within structures of the first millennium AD. The

307. (*above*) The Acropolis of Toniná, Chiapas, a mountain that was converted into a pyramid over centuries of occupation, with the most elite structures placed at its apex. The last Maya inscription with a long count date, corresponding to AD 909, was found at Toniná.

308. (*below*) The Arch of Kabah, 9th–10th century AD, marking one end of the Uxmal–Kabah sacbe.

309. (*right*) The Temple
of the Warriors and the
Group of a Thousand
Columns at Chichén Itzá,
9th–12th century AD.

resilience of the Maya urban plan was tested in the fourth and fifth centuries AD by sustained contact—even conquest—from Teotihuacán in central Mexico. However, this episode left only modest architectural traces and a few rare examples of the hallmark *talud-tablero* architectural profile of the great city.

Warfare rent apart the Maya lowlands in the second half of the sixth century AD, but conquerors rarely occupied the cities they defeated, so when rebuilding took place, it was generally on local terms. In the case of Palenque—as, one might argue, in that of post–World War II Europe or Asia—architectural destruction opened opportunities for innovation. The vision of a single royal patron like Pakal at Palenque or Ruler A at Tikal could transform the city through massive reconstruction projects. Grandiose funerary pyramids that dominate the urban landscape were a reflection of these outsized ambitions. By the eighth century, wealthy nobles could compete with the royal family for economic resources, multiplying the resultant construction, and palaces both royal and elite had an increasingly prominent place in Maya city plans (figure 95). By the end of the eighth century, much of the southern lowlands was in demographic, economic, and political collapse—and most of the last datable architecture from the region is on a small scale, like the tiny one-chambered Structure 10 of Yaxchilán, dated 810, although Seibal saw a revival throughout the ninth century. While the defensive moat had been developed in the first millennium BC at Becán, the defensive wall, set with palisades, made an ineffective appearance in the eighth century.

The ninth century was the period of the greatest construction in the Puuc Hills, where the Maya successfully overcame the limitations imposed by a geography without surface water. By the tenth century, Chichén Itzá had become a magnet for what may have been a multiethnic population, resulting in new types of architecture and emphasizing colonnades, ballcourts, and radial platforms and pyramids. Forms introduced at Chichén Itzá reappeared at reduced scale and construction quality at both Mayapán and Tulum (plate 310), within walled cities that reflect the political and social fragmentation of the Maya in the years before the Spanish invasion. The Spanish recognized the nature of these last Maya cities, and there were in fact many similarities in plan between Maya and Spanish urbanism: the emphasis on the central

plaza, the enclosed household group organized around a patio, turning its back upon the street. The effects of this confluence can still be seen in modern Maya villages today. Like all Maya planning, that of today addresses space in ways that respond to local topographies and local politics.

In all such planning and building, from 500 BC until today, Maya geometry often seems rough, rather than precise. But from time to time, site builders working with the relationship between square and rectangle happened upon the golden rectangle, whose proportions are such that the removal of a square from its form yields another golden rectangle. Such understandings may have helped engineers design complex elevations, such as the Palenque Tower. Maya mastery of engineering also contributed to the stability and durability of their architecture, so that the earliest European travelers to the Maya region, from Bishop Landa in sixteenth-century Yucatán to John Lloyd Stephens and Frederick Catherwood in the nineteenth century, would marvel at buildings that silently spoke of cultural achievement. Today's visitor can experience a similar awe at these silent sentinels.

310. Aerial view of Tulum, Quintana Roo, overlooking the Caribbean Sea. This city was an important Maya commercial center between the 13th and 16th centuries AD.

12

ARCHITECTURAL TERMINOLOGY IN MAYA AND NAHUA TEXTS

ERIK VELÁSQUEZ GARCÍA

INTRODUCTION[1]

Although today we can find various definitions of the term "writing system," the classic view holds that such a system consists of conventionalized graphics that are used to record human language in a permanent and visible form.[2] This definition is based primarily on the fact that all deciphered or still-functioning writing systems from the Old World[3] represent, in their way, a spoken language. We now know that Chinese writing itself, considered since Athanasius Kircher (1602–1680) to be an "ideographic" system, is composed basically of lexical units (logograms) ordered in keeping with the syntax of the Chinese language.[4] In fact, the majority of specialists who work with writing systems from Africa, Asia, and Europe consider the category of "ideograms" to be unnecessary, since no known script represents ideas independent of the words for them.[5]

From this perspective, the only writing system from the New World in which we can read portions of spoken discourse are Mayan and Nahuatl; while it is possible to identify, for example, the glyph meaning "hill" in Zapotec or that for "ballgame" in Mixtec, it remains unclear what lexical unit they represent, or whether they are semagrams, phonetic signs, or auxiliaries. In fact, the simple iconic aspect of a sign is not enough to clarify its reading or meaning, because this can be arbitrary or conventional. Therefore we must take into account the information offered by other signs with which it interacts in different contexts, and seek phonetic evidence in the form of syllabic complements and substitutions.[6]

It is no coincidence that we have made such great advances in our comprehension of the Mayan and Nahuatl systems, given that in both cases we possess an abundant corpus of texts,[7] a long and uninterrupted tradition of studies that goes back at least to the nineteenth century, a certainty about the language or linguistic family represented, and one or several parallel texts, or "Rosetta stones," produced during the period of cultural collision with European civilization. In the case of the Maya, the principal such text is the so-called "Landa alphabet" (1566), while the Nahua have left us numerous glossed codices from the colonial period. Although we also possess glossed documents from the Mixtecs, the Zapotecs, and other indigenous groups, these have not been studied with the classic tools of epigraphy or the theory of writing; therefore I will not refer to them here.

MAYAN WRITING IN ARCHITECTURAL CONTEXTS

On the use of writing in architectural contexts, Fray Diego de Landa (1524–1579) is our most informative colonial source, just as he is on many other aspects of Maya civilization at the end of the Pre-Columbian period. He states: "On any of the Chen and Yax months, on the day indicated by the priest, they hold a festival they call *Ocna*, which means renovation of the temple…. Said festival is held every year…, and if necessary, they would remake the house or renovate it and put on the wall the memory of these things with their characters."[8] To partially cover an architectural facade with hieroglyphic texts was a common practice in the Classic and Late Postclassic; almost no public buildings were constructed without some kind of written ornamentation. It was believed that writing itself was invented by the supreme god Itzamna,[9] who was moreover the first priest, by virtue of which it was a sacred means of communication. On the other hand, David S. Stuart[10] has rightly pointed out that texts exhibited in public places, such as palaces, temples, or plazas, awarded the buildings an air of social prestige by their calligraphic appearance alone, independent of their content. They were probably also read aloud so that their messages, invested with an enormous political and ritual power, would reach the illiterate masses.

Especially illustrative are the architectural texts at Xcalumkin, on whose columns, lintels, and wall panels the very fact of possessing writing is emphasized. On Jamb 1 of the Initial Series Building (ill. 1) it is recorded that *'alay 'u[h]tiiy ['u]wo'jol [yu]xulil 'uk'aal Sajal 'Ulil(?) Chan 'A[h]k[u']l(?)*, "the glyphs of the engraving in the chamber of the Sajal 'Ulil(?) Chan 'Ahku'l(?) have already come to an end here." On the other hand, the text on Column 6 of the Southern Building of the Hieroglyphic Group (ill. 2) says *'uwo'jool Kit Pa['] 'I[h]kaatz Sajal 'Itz'aat*, "these are the glyphs of the Sajal Artist Kit Pa' 'Ihkaatz," a personage depicted on Panel 5 of the same building (ill. 3), accompanied by an inscription that says *k'a[h]l[a]j 'uwo'jool Kit Pa' Sajal*, "the glyphs of the Sajal Kit Pa' were presented." Like the scribes of Xcalumkin, those of Chichén Itzá emphasized the consecration of hieroglyphic inscriptions on architectural supports, as we may gather from the inscriptions on the Temple of the Four Lintels, one of which says (ill. 4): *'alay k'a[h]laj 'uxulnajal 'upakab' ti['i]l [y]otoot ['U]choch Yokpuuy*, "the engraving on the lintel of the door of the [god] 'Uchoch Yokpuuy was presented here," an explicit allusion to the sacred character of the building and its written texts. Finally, Lintel 1 of the building known as Red Hands at Kabah (ill. 5) records the existence of "houses of reading" (*xok naah*)[11] that were adorned with inscriptions: *yuxu[l] 'uxok naah yatoot Huk…t Sajal, 'utz'i[h]b'aal yatoot…suun*, "it is the engraving of the

house of reading, the house of the Sajal Huk…t; it is the decoration of the house of …suun."

The mentions of cities or urban spaces in Mayan hieroglyphic texts are few but substantial. To date, epigraphers have not found any term that directly denotes the concept of city, community, or population; rather, this idea was expressed by the diphrasism *'ukab' ch'e'n* (ill. 6a), literally "earth-cave,"[12] which is similar to the Nahuatl expression *āltēpetl* or *in ātl in tēpetl*, "the water and the hill," in that it probably alludes to the Mesoamerican belief that all cities were founded, at least ideally, around a sacred cave or mountain. In the Pre-Columbian Mayan texts we find different variants of this metaphor *kab' ch'e'n*, such as *ch'e'n* (ill. 6b), an abbreviation frequently used in contexts of war;[13] *tukab' tuch'e'n*, a variant employed in the codices; and probably *chan ch'e'n* (ill. 6c), "heaven-cave."[14] Alfonso Lacadena[15] has shown that this diphrasism was long in use, since it is also found in Yucatecan documents of the viceregal period, with the same meaning of city or people.

The expressions for "plaza" continue to be vague for epigraphers. At one time, it was believed that they could be identified with the cartouche T510b[501]:23,[16] which combines the glyph for "water" with a four-leafed portal (ill. 6d), similar to the one used by the sun god and the deified ancestors in Maya art. Scholars noted that the same four-leafed shape is embedded in the surface of the main plaza of Machaquilá,[17] which seemed to reinforce their interpretation of the glyph, and this led to conjectures that the Maya conceived of plazas as portals to the aquatic underworld.[18] However, Stuart and Houston[19] pointed out that in some inscriptions the logogram for "water" (**HA'** or T501) does not accompany the four-leafed sign (T510b), and it was afterward realized that T510b[501]:23 is actually the toponym of Machaquilá, reproduced in a larger size at the center of its plaza. Likewise, some researchers suggested that the locative phrase *ta[h]n ha' Pa' Chan*, "in the center of water of Yaxchilán" (ill. 6e), was a metaphorical allusion to the great plaza of this archaeological site,[20] but Lintel 25 in Structure 23 (U2–W2) makes it clear to us that *Ta[h]n Ha' Pa' Chan* was actually the city's toponym, since it is qualifed as the *kab' ch'e'n* of the ruler.[21] An analogous case is that of the phrase *'u[h]tiiy ta[h]n ha' B'aak[a]l*, "it has already taken place in the center of the water of Tortuguero" (ill. 6f), which appears on Monument 6 of this archaeological site and has also been interpreted as an allusion to its plaza.[22]

Mentions of paths or *b'ih* (ill. 6g) are relatively common in Mayan inscriptions, especially because they are found in intransitive phrases meaning death: *'ochb'iij*, "he entered the path." Page 41c of the Dresden Codex (ill. 7) illustrates the

Ill. 1

'a-'ALAY-ya 'UH-ti-ya ['u]-wo-jo-le
[yu]-xu-li-le 'u-k'a-li sa.ja-la 'u-²li?
IV-'AK?-la

*'alay 'u[h]tiiy ['u]wo'jol [yu]xulil
'uk'aal Sajal 'Uli[l](?)
Chan 'A[h]k[a]l(?)*

"the glyphs of the engraving in
the chamber of the Sajal 'Ulil(?)
Chan Ahkal(?) have already
come to an end here"

1. Jamb 1 of the Initial Series
Building at Xcalumkin: A1–A8
(Graham and von Euw 1992, 163).

Ill. 2

'u-wo-jo-li ki-ti-pa-'a 'i-ka-tzi sa-ja-la
['i]tz'a-ti

*'uwo'jool Kit Pa['] 'I[h]kaatz Sajal
'Itz'aat*

"these are the glyphs of the Sajal Artist
Kit Pa' 'Ihkaatz"

2. Column 6 of the Southern
Building of the Hieroglyphic
Group at Xcalumkin: A1–A5
(Graham and von Euw 1992, 178).

Ill. 3

K'AL-ja 'u-wo-jo-li ki-ti-pa-'a sa-ja-la

k'a[h]l[a]j 'uwo'jool Kit Pa' Sajal

"the glyphs of Sajal Kit Pa' were
presented"

3. Panel 5 of the Southern Building
of the Hieroglyphic Group at
Xcalumkin: A1–A4 (Graham and
von Euw 1992, 183).

Ill. 4

'a-'ALAY-ya K'AL-la-ja 'u-xu-lu-na
ja-la 'u-pa-ka-b'a ti-li 'OTOT-ti cho-
cho yo-ko pu-yi

*'alay k'a[h]laj 'uxulnajal 'upakab' ti['i]l
[y]otoot ['U]choch Yokpuuy*

"the engraving on the lintel of the door
of the [god] 'Uchoch Yokpuuy was
presented here"

4. Lintel 3 of the Temple of the
Four Lintels at Chichén Itzá:
A1–B5 (Krochock 1989, 12).

Ill. 5

yu-xu 'u-xo-ko NAH ya-to-ti VII-?-
?-ta sa-ja-la 'u-tz'i-b'a-li ya-'ATOT
?-su-na

*yuxu[l] 'uxok naah yatoot Huk...t Sajal,
'utz'i[h]b'aal yatoot...suun*

"it is the engraving of the house of
reading, the house of Sajal Huk...t; it is
the decoration of the house of ...suun"

5. Lintel 1 of the Red Hands
building at Kabah (Grube 2003, 351).

Ill. 6a

'u-KAB'-CH'EN

'ukab' ch'e'n

"it is his city"

Ill. 6b

CH'EN-na

ch'e'n

"city"

Ill. 6c

CHAN-CH'EN-na

chan ch'e'n

"city"

Ill. 6d

T510b[HA']-na

...n Ha'

toponym of Machaquilá

Ill. 6e

TAN-HA'-[PA']CHAN-na

Ta[h]n Ha' Pa' Chan

toponym of Yaxchilán

Ill. 6f

TAN-HA'-B'AK-la

Ta[h]n Ha' B'aak[a]l

toponym of Tortuguero?

Ill. 6g

b'i-hi

b'ih

"path"

Ill. 6h

SAK-b'i-hi

sakb'ih

"sacbe"

Ill. 6i

pe-TUN-ni

pe[pem] tuun

"stone bridge"

6. Terms related to urban spaces:
(a) *'ukab' ch'e'n*, "city," literally
"earth-cave" (Monument 83 at
Toniná: D2; Graham and Mathew
1996, 113); (b) *ch'e'n*, "city,"
literally "cave" (Monument 18 at
Dzibanché: A2; Nalda 2004, 51);
(c) *chan ch'e'n*, "city?," literally
"heaven-cave" (Stele 31 at Tikal:
H23; Jones and Satterthwaite 1983,
fig. 52); (d) *...n Ha'*, toponym of
Machaquilá (Stele 8 at Seibal: B7;
Graham 1996, 27); (e) *ta[h]n ha'
Pa' Chan*, "in the center of water of
Yaxchilán" (Lintel 25 of Structure
23 at Yaxchilán: I3; Graham and
von Euw 1977, 56); (f) *ta[h]n ha'
B'aak[a]l*, "in the center of the
water of Tortuguero" (Monument
6 at Tortuguero: F2; drawing by
Gronemeyer); (g) substantive
b'ih, "path" (Stele 1 at Piedras
Negras: C18; Stuart 2006a, 2); (h)
substantive *sakb'ih*, "white path"
(Stele 1 of Sacbe 1 of Cobá: A2;
Stuart 2006a, 1); (i) *pe[pem] tuun*,
"stone bridge" (Stele 40 at Piedras
Negras: C11; Stuart and Houston
1994, 40, fig. 42b).

Ill. 7

'u-CH'AB'-wa ta-b'i-hi cha-ki
KUTZ-WAJ

*'uch'a[h]b'[a]w ta b'iih Chaa[h]k
kutz[il] waaj*

"Chaak creates along the path, [his
omens are] turkey tamales"

7. The god Chaak contorts himself
on the path: *'uch'a[h]b'[a]w ta b'iih
Chaa[h]k kutz[il] waaj*, "Chaak
creates along the path, [his omens
are] turkey tamales" (Dresden
Codex, p. 41c; Thompson 1988).

relationship between the word *b'ih* and the imagery of the road: the god Chaak seems to seek an initiatory trance by contorting himself[23] over a double band with human footprints, an ancient Mesoamerican device for representing a road, while the text positioned above him says: *'uch'a[h] b'[a]w ta b'iih Chaa[h]k kutz[il] waaj*, "Chaak creates along the path, [his omens are] turkey tamales." Stuart[24] mentions four eroded expressions for *sakb'ih*, "white path" (ill. 6h), on blocks of stone found along the great *sacbe* that connects the cities of Cobá and Yaxuná; these are apparently inscriptions that record the dedication of the highway. A possible word for "crossroads" or "stone bridge" (*pe[pem] tuun*) has been identified recently by Erik Boot[25] in the nominal phrase of a lord of the sea that appears on Throne 1 and Stelae 12 and 40 at Piedras Negras (ill. 6i).

MEASUREMENTS AND MATERIALS

The most common materials in Maya architecture were stone (*tuun*) and wood (*te'*), and they are widely documented in the inscriptions by means of specific logograms (ills. 8a, b). It is well known that the builders of Comalcalco fired clay bricks due to the scarcity of stone; some of these bear texts of consecration or labels identifying them as *lak*, "brick(s)" (ill. 8c)—a word that also means plate, since it has been applied to various types of ceramic plaques.[26] In the inscriptions of the Classic period, the term for stucco seems to have been *luk'* (ill. 8d), while in the Yucatecan codices of the Postclassic, *sas* designated stucco, plaster, or finish (ill. 8e).[27]

All architectural traditions require a system of measurement. However, there are very few allusions to measurement in the Pre-Columbian Mayan texts. Robert F. Wald[28] has proposed that one was based on the verb *tek'* (ill. 8f), whose Yucatecan cognate, *chek'*, appears in the *Calepino Maya de Motul* with the meaning of "to measure by feet or footsteps."[29] On page 8c of the Dresden Codex (ill. 9) we find representations of the gods Itzamna and Kisin[30] measuring the size of a building by placing one foot in front of the other, while they count the number of steps on their fingers; the first three hieroglyphic cartouches from each scene say: *'utek'aj naah 'Itzamna'*, "'Itzamna' measured the house," and *'utek'aj naah B'uluk? Kisin*, "B'uluk? Kisin measured the house," while the omens indicate adverse and propitious days to construct a building. Taking measurements with a cord twenty steps long was a common practice among the Maya, one employed in the cosmogonic myths of the *Popol Vuh*[31] and the *Chilam Balam of Chumayel*,[32] in which the gods found time and space by measuring out a cornfield, which is what farmers did before they began to cut down trees.[33] A second unit of measurement was the *na[h]b'*, "fourth" or "palm" (ill. 8g), the distance between the tips of the thumb and the little finger of an extended hand (approximately 8½ inches, or 21.6 centimeters).[34] Its logogram consists of an extended hand (**NAB'**)

with the thumb open and opposed to the fingers. Markus Eberl and Victoria R. Bricker[35] propose that the cartouche for *na[h]b'* that often appears on representations of rubber balls in Maya art, accompanied by a numeral, refers to the length of the rubber strip used to construct the ball.

TECHNIQUES AND FINISHES

The percussion of stones is represented in the inscriptions by the logogram **B'AJ**, "to strike" or "to hammer" (ill. 10a), which iconically represents a fractured rock; *b'aj* belongs to a category of intransitive verbs called "affective" or "reiterative," because they express a repetitive action. Other important verbs associated with the decoration and finishing of buildings are *'uxul*, "to sculpt" or "to engrave" (ill. 10b),[36] as well as *jus* (ill. 10c) and *tak'* (ill. 10d), which mean "to stucco, to plaster, to cast" or "to affix."[37]

However, the principal verb for finishing is a logogram that is shaped like the woven rooftop of a Maya hut and is read **PAT**, "to form" or "to build" (ills. 10e–h, 35b). It constantly appears in the inscriptions and plays a major role in the texts that commemorate the construction of different buildings and sites, to such a degree that it might properly be considered as a verb of dedication. Its homophony with the noun for "service" or "tribute," *pat*, suggests that the erection of a public building was thought to be an obligation of service for Maya lords and dignitaries.[38] Most known examples of the verb have marks of derivation that identify them as "positional" verbs, a category of intransitives that describe the pose or position that a being acquires.[39] The inscriptions of the Classic period are so detailed in this regard that they allow us to trace the morphological evolution of the verb, from *pa[h]t[a]j* (proto-Ch'olan, fourth century) to *patlaj* (Eastern Ch'olan, sixth to eighth centuries) and *patwaan* (Western Ch'olan, seventh to ninth centuries).[40] On rare occasions the verb *pat*, "to build," is combined with the noun *tuun*, "stone," creating a compound nominal phrase that reads *pattuun*, "stone construction" (ill. 10h),[41] such as on Panel 1 of La Corona, which describes the dedication of the monument and the temple that contained it, possibly a stone pyramid called *wak mihnal*.[42]

Two additional verbs associated with the completion of construction are *laj*, "to finish, to finalize," and *mak*, "to close, to cover" or "to block up." The latter has been found in many inscriptions on the Yucatán peninsula, painted on the rectangular stones that close the upper parts of corbelled vaults; their setting into place, at the end of the building process, marked the dedication or completion of the room or habitation.[43] The so-called Tableritos in the subterranean chambers of the Palace at Palenque (ills. 11, 12) illustrate very well the relationship between the verbs *laj* and *mak* in the central lowlands: on June 9, AD 654, *laj 'umaytuuna['] naah cha' winikhaab' 'ajaw K'inich Janaab' Pakal, K'uh[ul]*

B'aak[a]l 'Ajaw, "the Maytuuna' house of the lord of the two k'atunes, K'inich Janaab' Pakal, Divine Lord of Palenque, was completed." Only two days, later ma[h]kaj 'uk'aal cha' winikhaab' pitziil, K'inich Janaab' Pakal, K'uh[ul] B'aak[al] (?) 'Ajaw, 'Ochk'in Kal[o']mte', "the enclosure of the two k'atunes, ballplayer, K'inich Janaab' Pakal, Divine Lord of Palenque, Kalo'mte' of the West, was closed." Thus was the work finished and, two days afterward, consecrated. K'inich Janaab' Pakal (AD 615–683) sponsored it, but the Tableritos seem to add (H1–H3) that it was carried out "through the work" (yeb'tej) of his priest 'Ajsul ('ajk'uh[u']n 'Ajsul), thereby giving us some indication of who played the role of architect at the Maya courts.

As we saw at the beginning of this chapter, the Yucatecan Maya practiced a "temple renovation" rite.[44] On Lintel 1 of Structure 1 at Yulá we find a verb of renovation that, although it refers to the renewal of an offering to a god, could be the same expression that was employed in architectural contexts: 'upaalkuna[j], "he renovated it". The verb is actually derived from the noun paal, "boy, youth" or "son," which by means of the inchoative morpheme -jal could also become "to renew" (paaljal), but through the causative suffix -kun was here transformed into the transitive expression paalkun, "to make new" (ill. 10i).[45]

ARCHITECTURAL TERMS

Among the architectural terms represented in the Mayan inscriptions, first and foremost is the word naah or naa' (ill. 13a, b), "house, structure, building" or "domestic group." Its meaning, as Stuart indicates,[46] can encompass a great variety of structures and contrasts with the word yotoot, "house, dwelling" or "domicile" (ill. 13c), in the same way that Nahuatl distinguishes between the concepts of kalli, "house," and chāntli, "house, dwelling" or "residence." The most characteristic feature of the logogram 'OTOT is the woven rooftop of a peasant hut. This is nearly always preceded by the phonogram yo-, which indicates the third person singular form of the prevocalic possessive pronoun: yo-'OTOT, yotoot, "his house." Nikolai Grube[47] noted that the early scribes of Oxkintok, around the late fifth century, introduced the lexical novelty ya-'ATOT-ti, yatoot, "his house" (ill. 13d), a possible archaism that could be linked to the proto-Maya 'atyooty.[48] During the Late Classic, the scribes of the northern Yucatán employed the form yo-to-che, yotooch, "his house" (ill. 13e), which could be a regional idiosyncrasy or an attempt to represent the Yucatecan enclytic -e.[49]

The "interiors, enclosures" or "rooms" received the name of k'aal (ill. 13f) or wa[h]y(?) (ill. 13g), the latter term having many other meanings, including "subterranean cavity," "to dream," and "to sleep." The noun "bedroom" was in fact wa[h]yab' or wa[h]y[i]b' (ill. 13h), since the instrumental suffix -ab' or -ib' has the function of nominalizing a verb;

Grube suggests that bedrooms were actually sanctuaries for the veneration of ancestors.[50] The openings of entryways received the name of ti', mouth or door (ill. 14a), a clear projection of the human body onto architecture.[51] Another way of referring to these openings was by the noun pasil, "door," which in turn is derived from the verb pas, "to open" or "to leave." On Lintel 23 of Structure 23 at Yaxchilán, the word pas enters into a relationship of partitive possession with the noun "house,"[52] indicating that it is an inherent possession: 'upasil yotoot, "the door of the house of" (ill. 14b).[53] A related term is pakab', "lintel" (ill. 14c), of which we encounter such variants as pakab' tuun, "stone lintel" (ill. 14d) and pakab' ti', "door lintel" (ill. 14e). The etymology of pakab' provides us with additional information regarding native architectural concepts, since it is derived from the positional verb pak, "to lie face down," plus the instrumental suffix -ab', which makes it into a noun; this suggests that for the Maya, objects could assume physical positions, and that lintels possessed a face that looked downward.

A stucco inscription from Toniná contains the word kot, "wall,"[54] a term that is also found in the mural painting covering the enormous bench of Group A of the North Acropolis of Calakmul (ill. 14f). This bench, which is 650 feet (200 meters) long and 5¼ feet (1.6 meters) high,[55] receives the name of Chi'[i]k Naa[h]b' Kot, "wall" or "enclosure of Calakmul."[56] Meanwhile, a block from Hieroglyphic Stairway 2 of Dos Pilas mentions the toponym Pa' Tuun, which means "wall" or "stone wall" (ill. 14g). Walls were sometimes adorned with engraved or sculpted panels whose name, as we see in Panel 2 of La Corona, was [h]eklib' (ill. 14h); Søren Wichmann[57] notes that heklib' is derived from the positional verb hek, "to nail, to hang" or "to affix," the participle -l-, and the instrumental grameme -ib', indicating that the Maya conceived of their mural panels as "objects inserted vertically," a concept opposed to that of pakab', or "lintel."

Boot[58] identified a possible word for "column" or "cylinder" (b'u, b'u[b']) on a hieroglyphic column from a private collection. On Stele 5 and Lintel 3 of Temple 4 at Tikal appears the toponym Yookman, which means "pillar" (ill. 15a); its etymology is uncertain, but it is undoubtedly derived from the noun 'ook, "foot," or "paw," confirming the somatization of certain architectural concepts.[59] Another architectural component identified in the inscriptions is mak, "limestones," (ill. 15b), a word found in the dedicatory text of a vault cover that once belonged to an unknown tomb at Chichén Itzá. Stuart[60] has proposed that in the eaves of House C at the Palace of Palenque there is a term for nu'ch', "roof projection" (ill. 15c). In an unpublished fragment from Calakmul there is also a term for po[h]p tuun, "slab,"[61] which literally means "mat" or "stone bedding."

The names for certain ritual buildings are also recorded in the inscriptions. The pyramidal platforms seem to have been

Ill. 8a

TUN-ni
tuun
"stone"

Ill. 8b

TE'
te'
"tree, wood" or "stick"

Ill. 8c

la-ka
lak
"brick, plate" or "terracotta plaque"

Ill. 8d

lu-k'u
luk'
"stucco"

Ill. 8e

sa-sa
sas
"finish, stucco" or "plaster"

Ill. 8f

te-k'a-ja
te[h]k'aj
"measured by steps"

Ill. 8g

NAB'-b'a
na[h]b'
"fourth" or "palm"

8. Materials and measures used by the Maya in construction: (a) substantive *tuun*, "stone" (fragment of a stucco panel from Temple 18 at Palenque; Schele and Mathews 1979, fig. 470); (b) logogram TE', "tree, wood" or "stick" (mirror from Tomb 49 at Topoxté; Grube and Gaida 2006, 61); (c) substantive *lak*, "brick(s)" (Shaped Brick 3 from Comalcalco: B5; Grube, Martin, and Zender 2002, II-46); (d) substantive *luk'*, "stucco" (fragment of a stucco panel from Temple 18 at Palenque; Schele and Mathews 1979, fig. 444); (e) substantive *sas*, "stucco" or "plaster" (Madrid Codex, p. 14a; Lee 1985, 91); (f) verb *te[h]k'aj*, "it was stepped" or "measured by steps" (engraved limestone panel at Dumbarton Oaks; Schele and Miller 1986, 275); (g) substantive *na[h]b'*, "fourth, palm" or "measure" (Step 10 of Hieroglyphic Stairway 2 at Yaxchilán; Zender 2004, 1).

Ill. 9

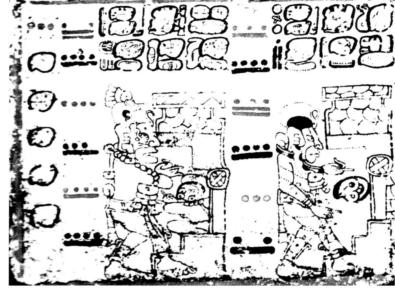

'u-te-k'a-ja NAH 'ITZAM-na
T24.533-li 'AJAW-le yo-T735-na
'utek'aj naah 'Itzamna' ...l 'ajawle[l]
yo...n
"'Itzamna' measured the house, [his omen is] ...l dominion, yo...n"

'u-te-k'a-ja NAH XI?-KISIN-ni
'u-mu-ka LOB'-b'a T31-MEN
'utek'aj naah B'uluk? Kisin, 'umu'k
lo'b',...men
"B'uluk? Kisin measured the house, his prediction is bad,...work"

Ill. 10a

B'AJ
b'aj
"to strike" or "to hammer"

Ill. 10b

'u-xu-lu
'uxul
"to sculpt" or "to engrave"

Ill. 10c

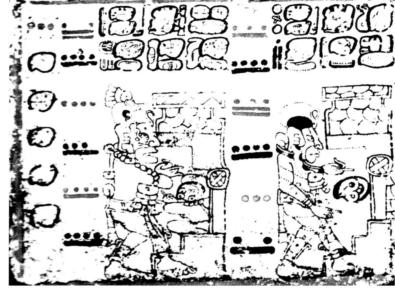

ju-su
jus
"to dress, to plaster, to stucco" or "to affix"

9. The gods D (Itzamna) and Q (Kisin) in the act of measuring a house with footsteps (Dresden Codex, p. 8c; Thomson 1988).

Ill. 10d

ta-k'a
tak'
"to dress, to plaster, to stucco" or "to affix"

Ill. 10e

PAT-ja
pa[h]t[a]j
"it was built"

Ill. 10f

PAT-la-ja
patlaj
"it was built"

Ill. 10g

PAT-wa-ni
patwaan
"it was built"

Ill. 10h

PAT-TUN-ni
pattuun
"stone construction"

Ill. 10i

pa-li-ku-na
paalkun
"to make new"

10. Glyphs associated with techniques and finishes: (a) affective verb *b'aj*, "to strike" or "to hammer" (Stair 5 of the western section of Hieroglyphic Stairway 2 at Dos Pilas: K2; drawing by Stephen D. Houston[?]); (b) transitive verb *'uxul*, "to sculpt" or "to engrave" (Emiliano Zapata Panel: D1; Miller and Martin 2004, 129); (c) transitive verb *jus*,

"to plaster" (Stele 1 at Aguateca: A8a; Graham 1967, 7); (d) transitive verb *tak'*, "to plaster, stucco" or "to cast" (Madrid Codex, p. 14a; Lee 1985, 91); (e) positional verb *pat*, "to be formed," with a Proto-Cholan derivation (Tikal, Stele 31: D27; Jones and Satterthwaite 1983, fig 52); (f) positional verb *pat*, "to be formed," with an eastern Cholan derivation (Lintel 3 of Temple 4 at Tikal: H3; Jones and Satterthwaite 1983, fig. 74);

(g) positional verb *pat*, "to be formed," with a western Cholan derivation (Altar G at Copán: A2; Schele and Mathews 1998, 172); (h) substantive compound *pattuun*, "stone construction" (Panel 1 at La Corona: Q2; drawing by Yuri Polyukovich); (i) transitive verb *paalkun*, "to renew, to make new" (Lintel 1 at Yulá: C7–D7; Grube 2003, 358, fig. 15).

Ill. 11

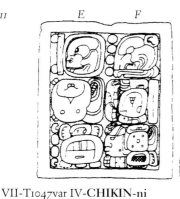

VII-T1047var IV-CHIKIN-ni
la-ja 'u-MAY-TUN-'a-NAH
II-WINIKHAB' 'AJAW-K'INICH-
ja-na-b'i-pa-ka-la K'UH-B'AK-
la-'AJAW 'u-k'a-li ye-'EB'TEJ-je
II-WINIKHAB' 'AJ-K'UH-na
'AJ-su-lu

*huk... chan chikin laj 'umaytuuna[']
naah cha' winikhaab' 'ajaw K'inich
Janaab' Pakal, K'uh[ul] B'aak[a]l
'Ajaw; 'uk'aal yeb'tej cha' winikhaab'
'ajk'uh[u']n 'Ajsul*

"[on] 7 Cimi 4 Xul the Maytuuna' house of the lord of the two k'atunes, K'inich Janaab' Pakal, Divine Lord of Palenque, was completed; his enclosure is [made] through the work of the worshipper 'Ajsul"

11. The verb *laj*, "to finish" or "to finalize," in the inscription of the Tableritos of the Palace at Palenque: E1–H3 (Schele and Mathews 1979, fig. 36).

Ill. 12

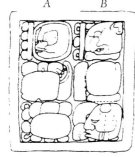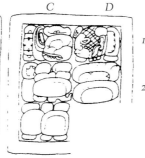

IX- ? VI-CHIKIN-ni ma-ka-ja
'u-k'a-li II-WINIKHAB' pi-tzi-la
K'INICH-ja-na-b'i pa-ka-la K'UH-
B'AK?-'AJAW-wa 'OCH-K'IN
KAL-ma-TE'

*b'olon... wak chikin ma[h]kaj 'uk'aal
cha' winikhaab' pitziil, K'inich Janaab'
Pakal, K'uh[ul] B'aak[al](?) 'Ajaw,
'Ochk'in Kal[o']mte'*

"[on] 9 Lamat 6 Xul the enclosure of the two k'atunes, ball player, K'inich Janaab' Pakal, Divine Lord of Palenque, Kalo'mte' of the West, was closed"

12. The transitive verb *mak*, "to close, to cover" or "to block up," in the inscription of the Tableritos of the Palace at Palenque: A1–D3 (Schele and Mathews 1979, fig. 36).

Ill. 13a

NAH-hi
naah
"house, building" or "structure"

Ill. 13b

na-'i
naa'
"house, building" or "structure"

Ill. 13c

yo-'OTOT-ti
yotoot
"his house, residence" or "dwelling"

Ill. 13d

ya-'ATOT-ti
yatoot
"his house, residence" or "dwelling"

13. Terms for houses and habitations: (a) substantive *naah*, "house, structure" or "building" (stucco cartouche of Temple 18 at Palenque; Schele and Mathews 1979, fig. 430); (b) substantive *naa'*, "house, structure" or "domestic group" (Paris Codex, p. 17b; Lee 1985, 154); (c) substantive *'otoot*, "house, dwelling" or "habitation" (Lintel 56 at Yaxchilán: H2; Graham 1979, 121); (d) substantive *'atoot*, "house, dwelling" or "habitation" (Lintel 15 at Oxkintok; Grube 2003, 355, fig. 12b); (e) substantives *'otooch*

Ill. 13e

yo-to-che
yotooch
"his house, residence" or "dwelling"

Ill. 13f

k'a-li
k'aal
"room" or "enclosure"

Ill. 13g

WAY?
wa[h]y(?)
"room" or "habitation"

Ill. 13h

WAY-b'i
wa[h]y[i]b'
"bedroom, sanctuary" or "temple"

and *'otoche*, "house, dwelling" or "habitation" (Column 4 of Xcalumkin: A3; Graham and von Euw 1992, 176); (f) substantive *k'aal*, "room" or "enclosure" (Jamb 1 at Xcalumkin: A5; Graham and von Euw 1992, 163); (g) possible substantive *wa[h]y* "habitation" or "room" (Vault Cover 1 at Ek Balam: C1; Staines 2004, 244); (h) substantive *wa[h]y[i]b'*, "bedroom" or "sanctuary" (Panel 12 at Piedras Negras: M1; Montgomery 1998).

called *ku'n* (ill. 16a) or *ku'nuul* (ill. 16b), while the term for temple was *yotoot k'uh[u']n*, apparently "his house of worship" (ill. 16c). It would seem that rulers held an undeciphered title (ill. 16d) whose main sign was shaped like a pyramid, and whose reading ended with the consonant -*n*. At times this is followed by the logogram NAH, "house," and its association with numerals suggests that it refers to the number of temples commissioned by the lord, e.g., "he of the five pyramids." The texts at Palenque frequently use the term *pib' naah*, "sweatbath" (ill. 16e)—literally, "subterranean cooking house"—to refer to the inner sanctuaries that sat atop the pyramidal platforms. These structures were probably conceived of as closed ovens, similar to those used to fire the incense burners that bore effigies of the gods.[62] Although archaeological remains of these burners have not been found, their names are written in the same inscriptions at Palenque: *chitin* (ill. 16f) and *wa[h]y[i]b'* (ill. 16g), the latter having the literal meaning of "bedroom" or "place of transformation."[63] Finally, among the ritual elements of architecture are found the recesses (caches), votive or commemorative hollows where the Maya placed a great variety of offerings;[64] the scribes of Copán called these hiding places *maab'* (ill. 16h), while those of Chichén Itzá simply referred to them as *mab'* (ill. 16i).

In the inscriptions there are also terms for "tombs" or "funerary chambers." The foundation of these expressions is a logogram with a stepped shape enclosing a human skull over a hatched background that presumably represents darkness;[65] its reading is MUK, "to bury, to hide," and it forms part of the nouns *muk[i]l*, "burial" (ill. 17a), and *muknal*, "place of burial" (ill. 17b). The codices use another term, *ch'e'nal*, which literally means "place of the well" or "of the cave" (ill. 17c).

There are also words for "stair" or "stairway." The most frequent is *'e[h]b'* or *'e[h]b'ul* (ill. 18a), but one atypical mention is found on Stair 2 of Hieroglyphic Stairway 4 at Dos Pilas: *k'a[h]n tuun*, "stone stairway" (ill. 18b). Among the Maya, there was a close relationship between the concept of the stairway and that of the ballgame. This is apparent in the very logogram for 'EB', "stairway" (ill. 18c), which frequently illustrates a ball descending the lateral stands of the court. The most typical variant of the logogram for ballgame (ill. 18d) still resists decipherment, although we know that its reading ended with the consonant -*n*. It represents a ballcourt seen end-on. Other terms related to the ballgame come from the northern Yucatán. On Lintel 1 at Yulá, for example, is found the expression *'alaw*, "ballgame" (ill. 18e), while at nearby Chichén Itzá there seems to be a form *jalaab'*, "ballgame" (ill. 18f), whose logogram includes the sphere and a possible marker; Boot[66] identified its likely Western cognate, *jalaw* (ill. 18g), on Hieroglyphic Step 1 at Uxmal. Altar 2 at Naranjo mentions a paved, polished, or whitewashed place, *b'ituun* (ill. 18h),[67] a term that seems to refer to the ballcourt.[68]

Finally, the famous ring at the Oxkintok ballcourt provides us with the Mayan name for these goals that were mounted on both sides of the court: *chiki[n] tuun*, literally "ear of stone" (ill. 18i).

THE CONSECRATION AND NAMING OF BUILDINGS
Maya scribes frequently painted or engraved texts commemorating the dedication of buildings, vases, earrings, jadeite plaques, bones, or other venerated articles. As Stuart affirms,[69] the essential function of such texts was to "mark the political, social, or ritual activation of an object or monument." Inscriptions of this type tend to contain the date of completion or consecration of the object, its proper name and common noun, certain details about its technique of decoration, and sometimes the theonym or anthroponym of its owner.[70] Michael D. Coe[71] was the first scholar to identify this type of inscription, which he called the primary standard sequence, but most of its components were not deciphered until the late 1980s and early 1990s.[72] More recently, Stuart[73] has proposed that we call this kind of text a dedicatory formula, which better describes their nature. The inscriptions engraved on architectural supports usually link several historic events within a narrative sequence that ends with the consecration of the building, emphasized by means of the dedicatory formula.[74]

The most typical dedicatory verb is *t'ab'*, which means "to ascend, to climb" or "to inaugurate" (ill. 19a); its logogram generally includes a stepped slope. A possible syllabic substitution is found in the dedicatory formula inscribed on Lintel 1 of the West Room of Structure 1 of Ikil, which reads (ill. 20): *'alay t'ab'aay 'uwa[h]yb'il k'uh[ul] 'ix[ik] 'Ix B'uluch 'Ajaw, 'Ix Chi. . .l*, "the bedroom of the divine lady 'Ix B'uluch 'Ajaw, she of th[e place] Chi. . .l, was inaugurated here."[75] Much farther southeast, a well-versed scribe recorded the consecration of structure 9N-82 at Copán on the hieroglyphic bench inside the building; the glyphs appear in their full-figure variants, including the logogram T'AB', which is presented as a hunchbacked old man:[76] *b'uluch 'ajaw 'u[h]x yax sijo'm t'ab'[aa]y yotoot Mak' Chan[a]l*, "[on the day] 11 Ahau 3 Yaax the house of Mak' Chanal was inaugurated" (ill. 21).

Other dedicatory phrases revolve around a nominal expression that, like the *pattuun* expressions (ill. 10h), is composed of a verb plus a noun; the result is a new, more complex noun:[77] *'ochnaah*, "house entrance," from *'och*, "to enter," and *naah*, "house" (ill. 19b); *'ochk'a[h]k'*, "fire entrance," from *'och*, "to enter," and *k'a[h]k'*, "fire" (ill. 19c); and *'elnaah*, "house burning," from *'el*, "to burn," and *naah*, "house" (ill. 19d).

According to Stuart,[78] *'ochnaah* is a cognate of the Yucatecan term *'oknah*, which, as we have seen, was described by Landa[79] as the "renovation of the temple" (*ocna*). The friar himself said that during these ceremonies "they renovated the

Ill. 14a

ti-'i
ti'
"door"

Ill. 14b

pa-si-li
pasil
"door"

Ill. 14c

pa-ka-b'a
pakab'
"lintel"

Ill. 14d

pa-ka-b'a TUN-ni
pakab' tuun
"stone lintel"

Ill. 14e

pa-ka-b'a-ti-'i
pakab' ti'
"door lintel"

Ill. 14f

ko-to
kot
"wall" or "enclosure"

Ill. 14g

[pa]TUN-ni
pa['] tuun
"wall" or "stone wall"

Ill. 14h

'e-li-b'i
[h]eklib'
"panel"

14. Terms associated with the entrances and walls of houses: (a) substantive *ti'*, "door" (lintel of the Akab Dzib building at Chichén Itzá: C1; drawing by Alexander Voss, from Boot 2005, 141, fig. 2.50); (b) substantive *pasil*, "door" (Lintel 23 at Yaxchilán: B2; Tate 1992, 207); (c) substantive *pakab'*, "lintel" (Lintel 1 of the Temple of the Four Lintels at Chichén Itzá: E3; Krochock 1989, 10); (d) substantive *pakab' tuun*, "stone lintel" (Lintel 3 of the Nunnery at Chichén Itzá: 7–8; Boot 2005, 327); (e) substantive *pakab' ti'*, "door lintel" (Lintel 2 of the Nunnery at Chichén Itzá: 7; Boot 2005, 326); (f) substantive *kot*, "wall" or "enclosure" (photograph by Jorge Pérez de Lara, from Carrasco Vargas and Colón González 2005, 45d); (g) substantive *pa' tuun*, "wall" or "stone wall" (Stair 4 of the western section of Hieroglyphic Stairway 2 at Dos Pilas: G2; drawing by Stephen D. Houston[?]); (h) substantive *[h]eklib'*, "panel" (Panel 2 at La Corona: I8; drawing by Linda Schele).

Ill. 15a

yo-ko-MAN-na
yookman or *yokman*
"pillar"

Ill. 15b

ma-ka
mak
"limestone"

Ill. 15c

nu-ch'a
nu'ch'
"roof projection"

15. Other terms referring to structural elements of buildings: (a) toponym *Yookman*, signifying "pillar" (Lintel 3 of Temple 4 at Tikal: H6; Jones and Satterthwaite 1983, fig. 74); (b) substantive *mak*, "limestone" (vault cover of an unknown tomb at Chichén Itzá: F); (c) substantive *nu'ch'*, "roof projection" (eaves of House C of the Palace at Palenque: B1; Grube, Martin, and Zender 2002, II-26).

Ill. 16a

ku-nu
ku'n or *kun*
"platform"

Ill. 16b

ku-nu-li
ku'nuul or *kunuul*
"platform"

Ill. 16c

yo-'OTOT K'UH-na
yotoot k'uh[u']n
"his house of worship"

Ill. 16d

'AJ-V-T685-NAH
'ajho' ...n naah
"he of the five pyramids (?)"

Ill. 16e

pi-b'i-NAH
pib' naah
"sweatbath"

Ill. 16f

chi-ti-ni
chitin
"oven"

Ill. 16g

WAY[b'i]
wa[h]y[i]b'
"oven?"

Ill. 16h

ma-b'i
maab'
"recess" or "cache"

Ill. 16i

ma-b'a
mab'
"recess" or "cache"

16. Terms associated with temples, sanctuaries, and ritual caches: (a) substantive *ku'n*, "platform" (jamb of the inner sanctuary of the Temple of the Foliated Cross at Palenque: B8; Stuart 2006b, 138); (b) substantive *ku'nuul*, "platform"

(west panel of the inner sanctuary of the Temple of the Cross at Palenque: C; drawing by Linda Schele, from Stuart 2006b, 110); (c) substantive *yotoot k'uh[u']n*, "his house of worship" (Vase K8009 of Cache 198 at Tikal: C–D (Culbert 1993, fig. 108); (d) title "he of the [#] pyramids" (Panel of the 96 Glyphs at Palenque: A4; drawing by Simon Martin, from Miller and Martin 2004, 124); (e) substantive *pib' naah*, "sweatbath" or inner sanctuary (balustrades of the Temple of the Foliated Cross at Palenque: G2; drawing by Linda Schele, from Stuart 2006b, 133); (f) substantive *chitin*, "oven" (Tablet of the Foliated Cross at Palenque: F2; drawing by Linda Schele, from Stuart 2006b, 146); (g) substantive *wa[h]y[i]b'*, "place of transformation" or "oven" (Tablet of the Sun at Palenque: F5; drawing by Linda Schele, from Stuart 2006b, 166); (h) substantive *maab'*, "recess" or "cache" (Altar G at Copán: C1b; Schele and Mathews 1998, 172); (i) substantive *mab'*, "recess" or "cache" (Lintel 2 of the Temple of the Four Lintels at Chichén Itzá: F4; Krochock 1989, 11).

Ill. 17a

MUK-li
muk[i]l
"burial"

Ill. 17b

MUK-NAL-la
muknal
"burial"

Ill. 17c

CH'EN-NAL
ch'e'nal
"burial" or "tomb"

17. Terms associated with funerary structures: (a) substantive *muk[i]l*, "burial" (Panel 2 of La Corona: H6; drawing by Linda Schele); (b) substantive *muknal*, "place of burial" or "tomb" (Tablet 5 of Seibal: DD1a; Graham 1996, 59); (c) substantive *ch'e'nal*, "place of the cave" (Dresden Codex, p. 48b [H3a]; Thompson 1988).

Ill. 18a

'EB'
'e[h]b'
"stairway"

Ill. 18b

K'AN-na-TUN-ni
k'a[h]n tuun
"stone stairway"

Ill. 18c

'EB'
'e[h]b'
"stairway"

Ill. 18d

?-na
...*n*
"ballgame"

Ill. 18e

'ALAW-la
'alaw
"ballgame"

Ill. 18f

JALAB'[b'i]
jalaab'
"ballgame"

Ill. 18g

ja-JALAW?-wa?
jalaw(?)
"ballgame"

Ill. 18h

[b'i]TUN-ni
b'ituun
"paved, polished"
or "whitewashed surface"

Ill. 18i

chi-ki-TUN-ni
chiki[n] tuun
"stone ear"
(ring from ballcourt)

18. Terms associated with stairways and ballcourts: (a) substantive *'e[h]b*, "stairway" (Stair 2 of Hieroglyphic Stairway 4 at Dos Pilas: J2; Houston 1993, 109); (b) substantive *k'a[h]n tuun*, "stone stairway" (Stair 2 of Hieroglyphic Stairway 4 at Dos Pilas: I2; Houston 1993, 109); (c) substantive *'e[h]b*, "stairway" (Stair 7 of Hieroglyphic Stairway 2 at Yaxchilán: Q2; Graham 1982, 160); (d) probable substantive for ballgame, ...*n* (Monument 141 at Toniná: C4b; Graham and Mathews 1999, 173); (e) probable substantive *'alaw*, "ballgame" (Lintel 1 at Yulá: D3; Boot 2005, 314); (f) substantive *jalaab'*, "ballgame" (Lintel 1 of the Temple of the Four Lintels at Chichén Itzá: C8; Krochock, 1989, 10); (g) substantive *jalaw*, "ballgame" (Hieroglyphic Step 1 at Uxmal: I1; Graham 1992, 117); (h) substantive *b'ituun*, "court" or "paved patio"

(Altar 2 at Naranjo: D4; Grube 2004, 208); (i) substantive *chiki[n] tuun*, "stone ear" or ballcourt ring (back surface of the Hieroglyphic Ballgame Ring at Oxkintok: K; drawing by José Miguel García Campillo, from Lacadena 1992, 179).

Ill. 19a

T'AB'[yi]
t'ab'[aa]y
"it was inaugurated?"

Ill. 19b

'OCH-NAH
'ochnaah
"house entrance"

Ill. 19c

'OCH-K'AK'
'ochk'a[h]k'
"fire entrance"

Ill. 19d

'EL-NAH
'elnaah
"house burning"

Ill. 19e

JATZ'
jatz' or *jaatz'*
"to beat" or "to hit"

PET-ta-ja-la
petjal
"it was made round"

19. Expressions associated with the dedication, consecration, and renewal of buildings: (a) transitive verb *t'ab'*, "to inaugurate" (vase K5362: B; Reents-Budet et al. 1994, 144); (b) substantive compound *'ochnaah*, "house entrance" (jamb of the inner sanctuary of the Temple of the Cross at Palenque: Ap6; Stuart 2006b, 114); (c) substantive compound *'ochk'a[h]k'*, "fire entrance" (Lintel 26 at Yaxchilán: H2; Graham and von Euw 1977, 58); (d) substantive compound *'elnaah*, "house burning" (Lintel 21 at Yaxchilán: A7b; Graham and von Euw 1977: 49); (e) transitive verb *jaatz'*, "to beat" or "to hit" (block from the Hieroglyphic Stairway at El Perú; Zender 2004, 8); (f) inchoative verb *petjal*, "it was made round" (back surface of the Hieroglyphic Ballgame Ring at Oxkintok: I; drawing by José Miguel García Campillo, from Lacadena 1992, 179).

'a-'ALAY-ya t'a-b'a-yi 'u-wa-ya-b'i-li K'UH-'IX 'IX-XI 'AJAW-wa 'IX-chi-?-la
'alay t'ab'aay 'uwa[h]yb'il k'uh[ul] 'ix[ik] 'Ix B'uluch 'Ajaw, 'Ix Chi...l
"the bedroom of the divine lady 'Ix B'uluch 'Ajaw, she of [the place] Chi...l, was inaugurated here"

20. Lintel 1 of the West Room of Structure 1 at Ikil: A–G (Grube 2003, 363, fig. 22).

XI-'AJAW III-YAX-SIJOM T'AB'[yi]-yo-'OTOT ma-k'a-CHAN-la
b'uluch 'ajaw 'u[h]x yax sijo'm t'ab'[aa]y yotoot Mak' Chan[a]l
"[on the day] 11 Ahau 3 Yaax the house of Mak' Chanal was inaugurated"

21. Hieroglyphic bench of Structure 9N-82 at Copán: A–D (Stuart 1998, 417).

'OCH-NAH VI-?-[CHAN]-na 'u-pi-b'i-NAH-li 'u-K'UH-li K'INICH-KAN[B'ALAM]-ma B'AK-WAY-la 'u-MIHIN-li K'INICH-[JANAB']PAKAL-la ya-'AL-la 'IX-TZ'AK-'AJAW-wa PAT-[la]ja LAKAM-HA'-CHAN-na-CH'EN-na
'ochnaah Wak ? Chan, 'upib' naah[i]l 'uk'uh[i]l K'inich Kan B'a[h]lam, B'aak[el] Wa[h]y[a]l, 'umihiin[i]l K'inich Janaab' Pakal, yal 'Ix Tz'ak[b'u'] 'Ajaw; patlaj Lakamha' chan ch'e'n

22. Eastern balustrade of the Temple of the Cross at Palenque (Stuart 2006b, 107).

'OCH-NAH-ja T225-K'AN-JALAL-NAH 'u-pi-b'i-NAH-li 'u-K'UH-li K'INICH-KAN[B'ALAM]-ma B'AK-WAY-la 'u-MIHIN-li K'INICH-[JANAB']PAKAL ya-'AL-la 'IX-TZ'AK-'AJAW-wa PAT-[la]ja LAKAM-HA'-CHAN-na-CH'EN-na
'ochnaah[a]j ? K'an Jalal? Naah, 'upib' naah[i]l 'uk'uh[i]l K'inich Kan B'a[h]lam B'aak[el] Wa[h]y[a]l, 'umihiin[i]l K'inich Janaab' Pakal, yal 'Ix Tz'ak[b'u'] 'Ajaw; patlaj Lakamha' chan ch'e'n

23. Southern balustrade of the Temple of the Foliated Cross at Palenque (drawing by Linda Schele, from Stuart 2006b, 133).

'OCH-chi-K'AK' K'AL-HUN-na?-NAH 'u-K'AB'A' III-K'IN-ni-ja-'a-ta yo-'OTOT-ti tzi-?-la-?-ni III-yo-HUN
'ochi k'a[h]k' k'alhu'n naah 'uk'ab'a' 'u[h]x k'in ja'at yotoot Tzi...l ...n Yohu'n

"the fire entered [into the] House of Coronation, it is the name of *'uhx k'in ja'at*, the house of Tzi...l ...n Yohu'n"

24. Tablet of the Palace of Palenque: R13–R16 (Robertson 1985, plate 258).

"it is the entrance of the Wak ? Chan house, sweatbath of the god of K'inich Kan B'ahlam, B'aakel Wahyal, the son of K'inich Janaab' Pakal, the son of 'Ix Tz'akb'u 'Ajaw; it was built [in the] city of Palenque"

"he entered the house ? K'an Jalal? Naah, sweatbath of the god of K'inich Kan B'ahlam, B'aakel Wahyal, son of K'inich Janaab' Pakal, son of 'Ix Tz'akb'u 'Ajaw; it was built [in the] city of Palenque"

IX-CHUWEN? IX-ma-MAK-ka 'OCH-K'AK' SAK-nu-ku-NAH ta-yo-'OTOT-ti K'INICH-[JANAB'] PAKAL V-WINIKHAB'-'AJAW
b'olon chuwen(?) b'olon ma[h]k 'ochk'a[h]k' Sak Nu[h]k Naah, ta yotoot K'inich Janaab' Pakal, ho' winikhaab' ajaw
"[on the day] 9 Chuen 9 Mac fire entered [into the house] of Sak Nuk Nah, into the house of K'inich Janaab' Pakal, lord of five k'atunes"

25. Panel of the 96 Glyphs at Palenque: B6–D2 (drawing by Simon Martin, from Miller and Martin 2004, 124).

'OCH-K'AK' SAK-MUK-li
'ochk'a[h]k' sak muk[i]l
"it is the entrance of fire [into the] white tomb"

26. Fragment of a monument at Toniná drawn by David S. Stuart (1998, 396).

VI-KAB' X-'UN-ni-wa 'OCH-chi-K'AK' tu?-MUK-NAL-la MO'-'o-B'ALAM-ma K'UH-?-'AJAW-wa
wak kab' laju'n 'uniiw 'ochi k'a[h]k' tumuknal K'an Mo' B'ahlam, K'uh[ul] ... 'Ajaw
"[on the day] 6 Caban 10 Kankin the fire entered the sepulchre of K'an Mo' B'ahlam, Divine Lord of Seibal"

27. Tablet 5 at Seibal: BB2–DD2 (Graham 1996, 59).

idols of clay and their braziers," which implies fire ceremonies, and in fact, fire and incense are central to the architectural rites described in the Mayan inscriptions.[80] Important *'och-naah* ceremonies were undertaken in the consecration of the inner sanctuaries of the Temple of the Cross (Wak Chan ?) and of the Foliated Cross (? K'an Jalal? Naah) at Palenque: *'ochnaah Wak ? Chan, 'upib' naah[i]l 'uk'uh[i]l K'inich Kan B'a[h]lam, B'aak[el] Wa[h]y[a]l, 'umihiin[i]l K'inich Janaab' Pakal, yal 'Ix Tz'ak[b'u] 'Ajaw; patlaj Lakamha' chan ch'e'n,* "it is the entrance of the Wak ? Chan house, sweatbath of the god of K'inich Kan B'ahlam, B'aakel Wahyal, the son of K'inich Janaab' Pakal, the son of 'Ix Tz'akb'u 'Ajaw; it was built [in the] city of Palenque" (ill. 22); *'ochnaah[a]j ? K'an Jalal?*[81] *Naah, 'upib' naah[i]l 'uk'uh[i]l K'inich Kan B'a[h]lam B'aak[el] Wa[h]y[a]l, 'umihiin[i]l K'inich Janaab' Pakal, yal 'Ix Tz'ak[b'u] 'Ajaw; patlaj Lakamha' chan ch'e'n,* "he entered the house? K'an Jalal? Naah, the sweatbath of the god of K'inich Kan B'ahlam, B'aakel Wahyal, the son of K'inich Janaab' Pakal, the son of 'Ix Tz'akb'u 'Ajaw; it was built [in the] city of Palenque" (ill. 23).

The most common dedicatory phrases relating to architecture in the Mayan texts are the *'ochk'a[h]k'* expressions.[82] One renowned example occurs on the Palenque Palace Tablet and records the consecration of House A-D, marking it as a hall of lordly investiture: *'ochi k'a[h]k' k'alhu'n naah 'uk'ab'a' 'u[h]x k'in ja'at yotoot Tzi…l…n Yohu'n,* "the fire entered [into the] House of Coronation, it is the name of *'uhx k'in ja'at*, the house of Tzi…l…n Yohu'n" (ill. 24). Even more famous is the dedication of House E, the only structure in the Palace painted white, which received the name Sak Nuk Nah, "White[-skinned] Big House."[83] According to the Panel of the 96 Glyphs, it was consecrated by Janaab' Pakal in AD 654 and acted as a throne room for three of his descendants: *b'olon chuwen(?) b'olon ma[h]k 'ochk'a[h]k' Sak Nu[h]k Naah, ta yotoot K'inich Janaab' Pakal, ho' winikhaab' 'ajaw,* "[on the day] 9 Chuen 9 Mac fire entered [into the house] of Sak Nuk Nah, into the house of K'inich Janaab' Pakal, lord of five k'atunes" (ill. 25).

According to Stuart,[84] the *'ochk'a[h]k'* expressions have a different meaning when they are associated with burial chambers. In this context, they do not seem to concern rites of dedication, but rather of renovation. Based on the archaeological, epigraphic, and iconographic data, I would argue that these ceremonies may have taken place during the night (*ti 'a[h]k'ab'*, "in the darkness"). They consisted in digging up (*pas*) or repositioning the skull and bones of the deceased, while at the same time fires or braziers were lit within the tomb. The participants may have personified the jaguar god of the underworld.[85] A typical example is the phrase *'ochk'a[h]k' sak muk[i]l,* "it is the entrance of fire [into the] white tomb" (ill. 26), found in a monument at Toniná, while the ruler of Seibal, Yihch'aak B'ahlam, introduced fire into

the tomb of his predecessor K'an Mo' B'ahlam: *wak kab' laju'n 'uniiw 'ochi k'a[h]k' tumuknal K'an Mo' B'ahlam, K'uh[ul]…'Ajaw,* "[on the day] 6 Caban 10 Kankin fire entered the sepulchre of K'an Mo' B'ahlam, Divine Lord of Seibal" (ill. 27).

It is worth mentioning that certain proper names for funerary buildings or chambers are frequently repeated in the Mayan texts,[86] such as B'olon 'Ajaw Naah, "House of the Nine Lords" (at Copán and Tikal); B'olon 'Eb'tej? Naah, "House of the Nine Labors?" (at Palenque); Wak Muyal Chanal, "Place of the Six Clouds of Heaven" (at Río Azul); and Ho' Janaab' Witz, "Mountain of the Five Flowers of Corn?" (at Cancuén and Piedras Negras). Their function as places of burial has been confirmed by the fact that they serve as the sites of action for the verbs *mu[h]kaj*, "he was buried," and *'ilaj*, "he saw it" or "he witnessed it," the latter referring to an unknown rite that, in this context, must have been associated with ancestor worship.[87]

The expression *'elnaah*, "house burning," seems to allude to a rite of dedication or renovation similar to that of *'ochnaah*, although the details of these ceremonies are not found in the inscriptions.[88] In at least one case (ill. 28) there is an allusion to the consecration of a building after its completion, rather than its renovation, and according to Stuart, when this ritual was associated with a burial, it was performed outside the tomb.[89] The logogram designating the verb 'EL, "to burn," deciphered by Stephen D. Houston in 1992, represents an incense burner,[90] which gives us an idea of the nature of the rite involved. A retrospective passage, written on Lintel 21 at Yaxchilán, records the dedication of a probable early version of Structure 22 in AD 454: *'elnaah Chan Suutz'nal yotoot K'a[h]k' 'Uwa't? Chan Chaa[h]k? Ja…Jol[o'm],* "it is the burning of the house Chan Suutz'nal, the house of K'ahk' 'Uwa't? Chan Chaahk?, Ja…Jolo'm" (ill. 28). Equally well-known is the consecration of Chahuk Naah or the "House of Thunder" (probably the palace chamber of Structure J-6), celebrated by Ruler 7 of Piedras Negras: *ho' 'ajaw 'u[h]x muwaan wi' ho'tuun 'elnaah Chahuk Naah yotoot Ya… 'A[h]k,* "[on the day] 5 Ahau 3 Muan is the final *ho'tuun*,[91] it is the burning of the house of Chahuk Naah, the house of Ya…'Ahk" (ill. 29).

The scribes who carved the frieze of the Red House at Chichén Itzá placed a special emphasis on their architectural dedication ceremonies, describing the act of boring sticks in order to light the fire: *tuju'n pis tuun ta ju'n 'ajaw joch'b'iiy 'uk'a[h]k' Te'? 'Uchook? 'uk'ab'a' [k'uh],* "on the first *tuun* in the [k'atun] 1 Ahau the fire of Te'? 'Uchook?, it is the name of the god, it was bored" (ill. 30). Stuart[92] suggests that these kinds of ceremonies were acts of renewal through fire within the temples, and that they reproduced the creation of the world by the gods, since the kindling of a fire was likened to the generative act of coitus[93] and implied the formation

Ill. 28

'EL-NAH IV-SUTZ'-NAL
yo-'OTOT-ti K'AK'-'u-wa-tu
CHAN-na CHAK-ja T674-JOL

*'elnaah Chan Suutz'nal yotoot K'a[h]k'
'Uwa't? Chan Chaa[h]k? Ja... Jol[o'm]*

"it is the burning of the house Chan
Suutz'nal, the house of K'ahk' 'Uwa't?
Chan Chaahk?, Ja... Jolo'm"

28. Lintel 21 at Yaxchilán: A7b–B8
(Graham and von Euw 1977, 49).

Ill. 29

V-'AJAW-III-MUWAN-ni WI'-V-
TUN-ni 'EL-NAH cha-hu-ku-NAH
yo-'OTOT-ti ya-?-'AK

*ho' 'ajaw 'u[h]x muwaan wi' ho'tuun
'elnaah Chahuk Naah yotoot Ya...
'A[h]k*

"[on the day] 5 Ahau 3 Muan is
the final ho'tuun, it is the burning of
the house of Chahuk Naah, the house
of Ya... 'Ahk"

29. Inscription on the right side of
Support 2 of Throne 1 at Piedras
Negras (Montgomery 1998).

Ill. 30

tu-I-pi-si TUN-ni-ta-I 'AJAW-wa
jo-ch'o-b'i-ya 'u-k'a-k'a TE'-'u-cho?-
ki 'u-K'AB'A'-'a-[K'UH]

*tuju'n pis tuun ta ju'n 'ajaw joch'b'iiy
'uk'a[h]k' Te'? 'Uchook? 'uk'ab'a
[k'uh]*

"on the first *tuun* on the [k'atun]
1 Ahau the fire of Te'? 'Uchook?, it is
the name of the god, it was bored"

30. Frieze of the Red House at
Chichén Itzá: 10–16 (Schele and
Freidel 1990, 360).

Ill. 31

JATZ'-na-ja III-'a-ha-li 'EB'

jaatz'naj 'u[h]x 'ahaal 'e[h]b

"the stairway of the three conquests
was struck"

31. Step VII of Hieroglyphic
Stairway 2 at Yaxchilán: Q1–Q2
(Graham 1982, 160).

Ill. 32

I-HA' XIX-SUTZ' ja-tz'a 'u-b'i-
TUN-ni K'AK'-TAK CHAN-na-
CHAK K'UH-SA'-'AJAW

*ju'n ha' b'olonlaju'n suutz' jatz'a[j]
'ub'i[h] tuun K'a[h]k' Tak[laj] Chan
Chaa[h]k, K'uh[ul] Sa[aal] 'Ajaw*

"[on the day] 1 Imix 19 Zodz the patio
[court] of K'ahk' Taklaj Chan Chaahk,
Divine Lord of Naranjo, was struck"

32. Altar 2 at Naranjo: F2–F5
(Grube 2004, 208).

Ill. 33

VIII-'IK' XIII?-?-T1046var PET-
ta-ja-la yu-xu-ja? 'u-chi-ki-TUN-ni
KAL-TE' I-? YOPAT

*waxak 'ik' 'u[h]xlaju'n? ...
petjal yuxul(?) 'uchik[in] tuun Kal[o'm]
te' Ju'n ... Yopaat*

"[on the day] 8 Ik 13? ...
the engraving on the ring of Kalo'mte'
Ju'n ... Yopaat was made round"

33. Front surface of the
Hieroglyphic Ballgame Ring at
Oxkintok: G–N (drawing by
José Miguel García Campillo,
from Lacadena 1992, 179).

Ill. 34a

yo-to-ti ma-ya 'IX chi-la-ni YAK?-ki
VII-TZIKIN-na me-je-na che-he-na
III-TAL-lo b'a 'i-V-K'IN-ni SAK-
TE'-NAL

*yotoot ma[h]y 'ix chilaan Yaak(?) Huk
Tzikiin Meje'n chehen Talo[l] B'aa'
Ho' K'in Sakte'nal*

"it is the house of the tobacco
of the interpreter [priestess]
of Yaak(?) Huk Tzikiin Meje'n,
it was told by Talol B'aa' Ho' K'in of
Oxkintok"

Ill. 34b

yo-to-ti

yotoot [mahy]

"it is the house of the tobacco"

34. Small bottles for tobacco
(called in Mayan *yotoot mahy*,
"houses of the tobacco"): (a) bottle
in the Chochula style from the
Puuc region (Grube and Gaida
2006, 190); (b) bottle in the codex
style from the northern Petén or
southern Campeche (Robicsek and
Hales 1981, 220).

Ill. 35a

yo-to-ti 'u-MAY-ya 'a-ku mo-'o

yotoot 'uma[h]y 'A[h]k Mo'

"it is the house of tobacco
of 'Ahk Mo'"

Ill. 35b

PAT-la-ja yo-'OTOT-ti 'u-ma-yi-ji
'AJ-k'a-xa

*patlaj yotoot 'umayij 'A[j]k'ax [B'ahlam
'Ajaw]*

"the house of the offering
[objects] of 'Ajk'ax [B'ahlam 'Ajaw]
was built"

35. Hieroglyphic labels on ceramic
bottles and wooden boxes that
describe them as houses: (a)
phrase *yotoot ma[h]y*, "house of
the tobacco," painted on a codex-
style flask (Grube and Gaida 2006,
191); (b) phrase *yotoot 'umayij*,
"the house of the offering [objects]
of," carved into a wooden box
originating in Tortuguero: S1–S5
(drawing by Gronemeyer).

of a new cosmological order after the flood.[94] As Sanja Sav-kic has recently indicated,[95] the kindling ceremonies (*joch'*) presented on pages 5b–6b of the Dresden Codex follow the depiction of the rain and earth lizard (*'Itzam Kaab' 'Áayin*) on pages 4b–5b, an omen of death and destruction.

Zender[96] has identified a possible verb for the ritual acti-vation of ballcourts: *jatz'* or *jaatz'*, "to beat, to hit" (ill. 19e), which probably alludes to the action of the rubber sphere on the court. Several ballcourts—at Copán, Naranjo, El Perú, and Yaxchilán—received the name *'u[h]x 'ahaal 'e[h]b'*, "stair-way of the three conquests" or "of the many victories," a term that seems to allude to myths and practices related to war and sacrifice.[97] The famous Step VII of Hieroglyphic Stairway 2 at Yaxchilán says, for example: *jaatz'naj 'u[h]x 'ahaal 'e[h]b'*, "the stairway of the three conquests was struck" (ill. 31).

The paved surfaces of the courts were activated through the verb *jaatz'*, according to Altar 2 at Naranjo.[98] A pas-sage states: *ju'n ha' b'olonlaju'n suutz' jatz'a[j] 'ub'i[h] tuun K'a[h]k' Tak[laj] Chan Chaa[h]k, K'uh[ul] Sa'[aal] 'Ajaw*, "[on the day] 1 Imix 19 Zodz the patio [court] of K'ahk' Taklaj Chan Chaahk, Divine Lord of Naranjo, was struck" (ill. 32).

Another way of consecrating a ballcourt seems to have been through the activation of the ring, which, in the inscrip-tions of the Puuc region, was expressed with the verb *petjal*, "it was made round" (ill. 19f), a form derived from the adjec-tive *pet*, "round," plus the inchoative pre-proto-Yucatecan suffix *-jal*,[99] which transforms it into a verb. The clear-est example is found on the front side of the hieroglyphic ring of the ballcourt at Oxkintok, which reads: *waxak 'ik' 'u[h]xlaju'n?...*[100] *petjal yuxul(?) 'uchik[in] tuun Kal[o'm]te' Ju'n...Yopaat*, "[on the day] 8 Ik 13?...the engraving on the ring of Kalo'mte' Ju'n...Yopaat was made round" (ill. 33), a curious conflation of manufacture, activation, and consecration.

VASES AND BOXES AS HOUSES

The term for house, dwelling, or room (*'otoot*) was applied not only to architectural structures, but to several types of ceramic and wood containers as well.[101] Of particular inter-est is a type of small bottle that comes from the Puuc region and the northern Petén (ill. 34). Archaeologists call them "poison bottles," because they resemble the glass flasks used for this purpose in the United States during the nineteenth century,[102] but they are labeled with inscriptions that refer to them as *yotoot [mahy]*, "houses of the tobacco of" (ill. 35a). This suggests that they were used to store the ground dust of that plant, which during the Pre-Columbian era was con-sumed in different ways and used by priests and shamans, since it alleviated tiredness and pain, cured several illnesses, and was credited with magical or supernatural powers, including that of warding off death. For these reasons, it came to be regarded as a god.[103]

Although most wooden objects did not survive the pas-sage of centuries in the humid tropical climate of the Maya lowlands, there are a few exceptions. On the lower part of a well-known wooden box that apparently originated in Tor-tuguero, there is a carved inscription that states: *patlaj yotoot 'umayij 'A[j]k'ax [B'ahlam 'Ajaw]*, "the house of the offering [objects] of 'Ajk'ax [B'ahlam 'Ajaw] was built" (ill. 35b). The key to this passage resides in the noun *may*, "gift" or "offer-ing,"[104] which, preceded by the pronoun *'u-*, in the third per-son singular, seems to acquire the form *'u-may-ij*. A similar box was found by David Pendergast in the cave of Actun Polbilche in Belize; its contents included a stingray stinger, a needle, and a bone pin, as well as an obsidian blade,[105] all instruments used in autosacrifice rituals. At Dzibanché and Yaxchilán, bone awls used to perform blood ceremonies have been found bearing inscriptions that describe them as *'umayij b'aak*, "bone offerer of."[106] This suggests that the wooden boxes called *yotoot 'umayij* ("house of the offering [objects] of") might have been used to store this kind of instrument.[107]

Some vases deposited in caches were called *yotoot k'uh[u']n*, "temples" or "houses of worship" of the gods (ill. 16c), a probable allusion to their ceremonial and sacred con-text, although their precise function is unknown. The most famous example is Vase K8009 from Cache 198 at Tikal. Its dedicatory formula states: *'alay t'ab'[aay] yotoot k'uh[u']n[i]l b'olon tz'akb'uul 'ajaw 'E[h]b' Xook Wak Chan Te'?; k'uh[u']n Chak Tok 'I[h]ch'aak, Mut[u']l 'Ajaw*, "the house of worship of the nine ordained lords of 'Ehb' Xook [of] Wak Chan Te'? was inaugurated here; Chak Tok 'Ihch'aak, Lord of Tikal, adored them" (ill. 36).

Certain of the vases that were conceived of as houses expressed cosmological ideas. Such is the case with Plate 13-LC-p2-162 from the Dumbarton Oaks collection. Its text states: *'ulak yotoot 'uk'inil 'uchan[i]l*, "it is the plate of the solar house, of the heavenly house" (ill. 37). As Karl A. Taube has noted,[108] this vase reflects the ancient conception of the world as a great platter,[109] but also as a great house.[110]

RECENT ADVANCES IN NAHUATL EPIGRAPHY

Although we possess many codices, maps, and colonial doc-uments with glosses of Nahuatl texts, and despite the fact that these documents have been used to study the calendar, anthroponyms, and toponyms at least since the nineteenth century—for example, by Antonio Peñafiel (1885)[111]—no research with a strictly epigraphic focus was carried out until very recently.[112] This was due in part to the German scholar Eduard Seler's proposal (1904)[113] that the phoneti-cism found in many colonial codices, especially from the area of Texcoco, was the product of various influences of

Latin writing on Nahuatl, and therefore does not reflect the Pre-Columbian writing system. To date most researchers have accepted this thesis,[114] and thus the indigenous writing of the Nahuatl tradition has been considered an ideographic or pictographic system[115] with little phoneticism, whose most "pure" examples are the Stone of Tizoc, the Cuauhxicalli of Moctezuma, the *Register of Tributes*, and a few other documents of Tenochcan-Tlatelolcan origin. The annexed glosses in Latin characters have simply been regarded as an interpretation, rather than a reading, of the hieroglyphic cartouches, with the frontier between logographic and phonetic signs not always being understood in detail, and many of the glyphs being interpreted iconographically.[116]

In the second half of the twentieth century, some scholars[117] finally began to consider the possibility that the phonetic glosses in certain colonial manuscripts might be derived from the resources of the Pre-Columbian scribes, rather than from Latin writing, although they did not take this argument any further. The task of developing these ideas, especially those of Joseph Marius Alexis Aubin (1849),[118] was taken on by Alfonso Lacadena,[119] who has renewed our understanding of the Nahuatl writing system, drawing on his experience in the field of Mayan epigraphy, as well as the methodologies used to study Old World writing systems. His ideas, which have begun to be used by other epigraphers and linguists,[120] may be summarized as follows: Nahuatl writing took up a minimal space in the codices and specialized in few themes—essentially numbers, dates, and place names. Its blocks of glyphs took the form of emblems, without a fixed order (but favoring readings from right to left and from bottom to top); it employed flat logograms—since the long vocalics ($\bar{a}$, $\bar{e}$, $\bar{\imath}$, $\bar{o}$) were not indicated—and phonograms with an open structure (vowel [V] or consonant plus vowel [CV]), which formed a true syllabary (thus making this a logosyllabic system). The Nahua scribes made use of various resources common to other writing systems of the world, such as the rebus,[121] phonetic complementation and substitution, and different types of abbreviation (syncope and suspension). Finally, the greater phoneticism that can be noted in certain codices of the colonial period is not the result of the influence of the European alphabet, but rather of the existence of different schools of scribes within the same writing system, whose traditions came from the Pre-Columbian era.

Taking the above into account, we must observe that there are no examples of Nahuatl hieroglyphic writing with a strictly architectural theme. Instead, the signs related to construction must be extracted from the anthroponyms, theonyms, and calendar terminology. On the other hand, most of the (predominantly colonial) documentary corpus has not yet been studied or published, which means that we are still far from identifying and quantifying the repertoire of signs. Thus, in the following pages, I will limit myself to

pointing out certain examples from well-known codices or monuments. The reading of several of these has been argued in Lacadena's articles, but an exhaustive study of Nahuatl architectural hieroglyphs is still to be undertaken.

MATERIALS AND TECHNIQUES

Like their Maya counterparts, the Nahua builders relied heavily on stone (*tetl*) and wood (*k^wawitl*). The sign for stone operated acrophonically[122] in the writing system as the phonogram **te** (ill. 38a), forming part of words (such as **te-so**, *Teso[k]*, "Tiçoçic," ills. 38b, 48j, and 50e) or acting as a phonetic complement to the logograms (**TISA-te-TEPE**, *Tīsatepē[k]*, "Tiçatepec" [ill. 38c]). However, we should be aware that the sign for stone is polyvalent and can sometimes act logographically: **TE** (ills. 38d, e),[123] although this seems to depend on the context.

The types of stone used in construction included the hard, porous white rock *tepetate*, which is represented in the codices by the sequence of signs **TE?-PETLA**, *tepetla[pan]* (ill. 38f) or by its logogram **TEPETLA** (ill. 38g), as well as the light and porous volcanic rock *tezontle*, written on page 5 of the *Register of Tributes* and 22r of the Codex Mendoza as a logogram shaped like a hill with blackish and yellow streaks: **TESON**, *Teson[yokān]*, "Teçoyuca" (ill. 38h).

Wood was represented by the logogram **K^wAW**, "tree, beam" or "stick" (ill. 39a), which forms part of numerous proper names, like that of Quauhtochco: **K^wAW-TOCH**, *K^wawtōch[ko]* (ill. 39b). The same sign can also behave as the syllabogram **k^wa**, as in the toponym of Quaguacan, where it operates as a phonetic complement to the logogram "eagle": **k^wa-K^wAW**, *k^wāw[a'kān]* (ill. 39c). A variant or allograph[124] of the sign for "tree" consists simply of a pair of wooden planks: **K^wAW** (ill. 39d). On folio 1v of the Codex Cozcatzin we find a logogram for "beam" or "crossbeam" (*we'pāmitl*) that forms part of the anthroponym Tlacaquépan: **TLAKA-WE'PAN**, *Tlākawe['']pān* (ill. 39e). Its syllabic variant (**we-pa**, *we[']pā[mitl]*) is found in trecena 8 of the Codex en Cruz (ill. 39f).[125]

There are references to the wood of some specific species that were used for construction. In the toponym **AWEWE-we**, *Āwēwē[pan]*, "Ahuehuepan" (ill. 39g), for example, the name of the *ahuehuete* or Montezuma cypress was written logographically as **AWEWE** and accompanied by a drum, the phonogram **we**, which acts as a phonetic complement. It is widely known that long stakes of another kind of cypress, *ahuejote*, were used to border the *chinampas*, and that these artificial fields were anchored by means of willow or cypress trees.[126] The name of the *ahuejote* occurs, for example, in the anthroponym of the mythic founder of the Huejotzincas as it appears on page 2 of the Codex Boturini—**WEXO-TZIN**, *Wexōtzin[katl]* (ill. 39h)—as well as in the toponym for Huejutla carved

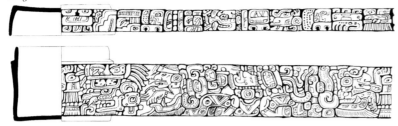

'ALAY-la-ya T'AB' yo-'OTOT
K'UH-na-li IX-TZ'AK-b'u-li-
'AJAW 'EB'-XOK VI-CHAN-na
TE'? K'UH-na CHAK-to-'ICH'AK
MUT-'AJAW

*'alay t'ab'[aay] yotoot k'uh[u']n[i]l
b'olon tz'akb'uul 'ajaw 'E[h]b' Xook
Wak Chan Te'?; k'uh[u']n Chak Tok
'I[h]ch'aak, Mut[u']l 'Ajaw*

"the house of worship of the nine ordained lords of 'Ehb' Xook [of] Wak Chan Te'? was inaugurated here; Chak Tok 'Ihch'aak, Lord of Tikal, adored them"

36. Unrolled inscription from Vase K8009 of Cache 198 at Tikal (Culbert 1993, fig. 108).

Ill. 37

'u la ka yo-'OTOT-ti 'u-K'IN-ni-li
'u-CHAN-li

'ulak yotoot 'uk'inil 'uchan[i]l

"it is the plate of the solar house, of the heavenly house"

37. Text painted on Plate 13-LC-162 at Dumbarton Oaks (Houston 1998, 350, fig. 13d).

Ill. 38a

te

Ill. 38b

te-so
Teso[k]
‹gloss: Tiçocic›
"Tizoc"

Ill. 38c

TISA-te-TEPE
Tīsatepē[k]
‹gloss: Tiçatepec›
"Tizatepec"

Ill. 38d

TE
te[tl]
"stone"

Ill. 38e

TE
te[tl]
"stone"

Ill. 38f

TE?-PETLA
Tepetla[pan]
‹gloss: Tepetlapā›
"Tepetlapan"

Ill. 38g

TEPETLA-TZIN
Tepetlatzin
‹gloss: Tepetlatzin›
"Tepetlatzin"

Ill. 38h

TESON
Teson[yokān]
‹gloss: Teçoyucā›
"Tizayuca"

38. Terms for stones used in Nahuatl architecture: (a) phonogram te (Codex Borbonicus, p. 18; Anders, Jansen, and Reyes García 1991); (b) anthroponym *Teso[k]* (Codex Telleriano-Remensis, p. 39r; Quiñones Keber 1995); (c) toponym *Tīsatepē[k]* (Codex Mendoza, p. 21v; Berdan and Anawalt 1992); (d) possible logogram TE, "stone" (Codex Mendoza, p. 28r; Berdan and Anawalt 1992); (e) possible logogram TE, "stone" (Codex Borbonicus, p. 5; Anders, Jansen, and Reyes García 1991); (f) the white rock *tepetate*, included in the toponym *Tepetla[pan]* (Codex Mendoza, p. 22r; Berdan and Anawalt 1992); (g) *tepetate*, included in the toponym *Tepetlatzin* (Codex Osuna, p. 11r; Zavala 1947); (h) the porous volcanic rock *tezontle*, included in the toponym *Teson[yokān]* (Codex Mendoza, p. 22r; Berdan and Anawalt 1992).

Ill. 39a

KᵂAW
kʷaw[itl]
"tree, beam" or "stick"

Ill. 39b

KᵂAW-TOCH
Kʷawtōch[ko]
‹gloss: Quauhtochco›
"Cuautochco"

Ill. 39c

kʷa-KᵂAW
Kʷāw[a'kān]
‹gloss: Quaguacan›
"Cuauhuacan"

Ill. 39d

KᵂAW
kʷaw[itl]
"tree, beam" or "stick"

Ill. 39e

TLAKA-WE'PAN
Tlākawe'pān
‹gloss: Tlacaquépan›

Ill. 39f

we-pa
we['] pā[mitl]
‹gloss: huepā›
"beam" or "crossbeam"

Ill. 39g

AWEWE-we
Āwēwē[pan]
‹gloss: Ahuehuepan›
"Ahuehuepan"

Ill. 39h

WEXO-TZIN
Wexōtzin[katl]
"Huejotzincatl"

Ill. 39i

a-WEXO
Āwexō[tla']
"Huejutla?"

39. Terms for woods used in Nahuatl architecture: (a) logogram KᵂAW, "tree, stick, wood" (Codex Mendoza, p. 13v; Berdan and Anawalt 1992); (b) substantive

"tree" or "wood," included in the toponym *Kʷawtōch[ko]* (Codex Mendoza, p. 8r; Berdan and Anawalt 1992); (c) symbol for tree or wood, operating as a phonetic complement in the toponym *Kʷāw[a'kān]* (Codex Mendoza, p. 5v; Berdan and Anawalt 1992); (d) another form of the logogram KʷAW, "tree, stick" or "beam of wood" (Codex Mendoza, p. 32r; Berdan and Anawalt 1992); (e) logogram WE'PAN, *we['] pām[itl]*, "beam" or "crossbeam," included in the anthroponym *Tlākawe[']pān* (Codex Cozcatzin, p. 1v; Valero de García Lascuráin 1994); (f) syllabic variant of the substantive *we[']pā[mitl]*, "beam" or "crossbeam": we-pa (Codex en Cruz, trecena 8; Dibble 1981); (g) the tree *ahuehuete*, included in the toponym *Āwēwē[pan]* (Codex Mendoza, p. 24v; Berdan and Anawalt 1992); (h) the tree *ahuejote*, included in the anthroponym *Wexōtzin[katl]* (Codex Boturini, p. 2; Ramírez 1952); (i) *ahuejote*, included in the toponym *Āwexō[tla']* (Stone of Tizoc; Dibble 1971, 327).

xa

xa-ko
Xa['kal]ko
⟨gloss: Xacalco⟩
"Jacalco"

40. Glyphs for adobe or brick: (a) phoneme xa (Lacadena's Nahuatl syllabary, 2006); (b) toponym *Xa['kal]ko*, which certainly includes the substantive *xa'kalli*, "house of straw" (Tepetlaoztoc Codex, p. 5, plate A; Valle 1994a).

Ill. 41a

TETLAPAN(A)
Tetlapāna[loyān]
⟨gloss: Tetlapanaloyā⟩
"Tetlapanaloya"

Ill. 41b

KʷAW–XIMA
Kʷawxīma[lpan]
⟨gloss: Quauximalpā⟩
"Cuajimalpa"

Ill. 41c

TLA'KIL
Tla'kil[pan]
⟨gloss: Tlaquilpā⟩
"Tlaquilpan"

Ill. 41d

TLA'KIL
tla'kil[li]
"whitewashed, polished" or "plastered"

41. Terms related to construction: (a) verb *tetlapāna*, "to extract stone," included in the toponym *Tetlapāna[loyān]* (Codex Mendoza, p. 29r; Berdan and Anawalt 1992); (b) verb *xīma*, "to work wood," included in the toponym *Kʷawxīma[lpan]* (Codex Mendoza, p. 5 v; Berdan and Anawalt 1992); (c) adjective *tla'killi*, "whitewashed, polished," included in the toponym *Tla'kil[pan]* (Codex Mendoza, p. 22r; Bernal and Anawalt 1992); d) logogram TLA'KIL, "whitewashed, polished, plastered" (Codex Osuna, p. 29r; Zavala 1947).

Ill. 42a

KAL
kal[li]
"house"

Ill. 42b

ISTA-a-KAL
Istaākal[ko]
⟨gloss: Istacalco⟩
"Iztacalco"

Ill. 42c

te-KAL-ko
Tekalko
⟨gloss: Tecalco⟩
"Tecalco"

Ill. 42d

te-TE-[PETLA]KAL
Tepetlakal[ko]
⟨gloss: Tepetlacalco⟩
"Tepetlacalco"

Ill. 42e

KALIMA?
Kalimāyān
⟨gloss: Caliymayan⟩
"Calimaya"

Ill. 42f

TLAKOCH-KAL
tlakōchkal[katl]
⟨gloss: tlacochcalcatl⟩
"captain" or "general"

Ill. 42g

TEKʷ-KAL
Tēkkal[ko]
⟨gloss: Tecalco⟩
"Tecalco"

Ill. 42h

TEKʷ-PAN?
Tēkpan
⟨gloss: Tecpan⟩
"palace"

Ill. 42i

pa-PAN?
[tēk]pan[nekatl]
⟨gloss: *tecpaneco/a*⟩
likely place of origin of Azcapotzalco

Ill. 42j

KAL-PIL?
Kalpil[ko]
⟨gloss: Calpilco⟩
"Calpilco"

42. Terms related to "house": (a) logogram KAL, "house" (Stone of the Sun); (b) substantive *kalli*, "house," included in the toponym *Istaākal[ko]* (Codex Cozcatzin, p. 16v; Valero de García Lascuráin 1994); (c) *tekalli* or "stone house," included in the toponym *Tekalko* (Tlatelolco Codex; Valle 1994b); (d) *tepetlakalli* or "tepetate house," included in the toponym *Tepetlakal[ko]* (Codex Mendoza, p. 20r; Berdan and Anawalt 1992); (e) possible logogram KALIMA?, "hamlet," included in the toponym *Kalimā[yān]* (Codex Mendoza, p. 10r; Berdan and Anawalt 1992); (f) *tlakōchkallo*, or "house of the darts," included in the title *tlakōchkal[katl]* (Codex Mendoza, p. 65r; Berdan and Anawalt 1992); (g) *tēkkalli* or "house of lords," included in the toponym *tēkkal[ko]* (Codex Mendoza, p. 20v; Berdan and Anawalt 1992); (h) substantive *tēkpan*, "palace" (Codex Cozcatzin, p. 15v; Valero de García Lascuráin 1994); (i) substantive *[tēk]pan*, "palace," which forms part of the gentilic *[tēk]pan[nekatl]* (Codex Azcatitlan, p. 3b; Graulich 1995); (j) *kalpilli*, "neighborhood, suburb?," included in the toponym *Kalpil[ko]* (Codex Cozcatzin, p. 9r; Valero de García Lascuráin 1994).

into the Stone of Tizoc: a-WEXO, *Āwexō[tla']* (ill. 39i).

There is also a sign shaped like two or three rows of bricks or adobes stuck together (ill. 40a). In the nineteenth century, Aubin[127] identified it as a possible phoneme **xa**, derived acrophonically from the word *xāmitl*, "adobe" or "square brick," an idea that seems to be confirmed in the toponym for Xacalco, which appears on signature 5, folio A of the Tepetlaoztoc Codex: **xa-ko**, *Xa['kal]ko* (ill. 40b).

I have been able to find few terms for construction techniques in the Nahua manuscripts. A possible expression for "extracting stone" (*tetlapāna*) can be found in the toponym of Tetlapanaloyā: **TETLAPAN(A)**, *Tetlapāna[loyān]* (ill. 41a); in it we can observe that the logogram **TETLAPAN(A)**, "to tear, to break," is iconically transparent, since it represents the act of percussion with stones. In the toponym for Quauximalpā we also find a term related to construction techniques: *xīma*, "to flatten, to polish" or "to work with wood," whose logogram is an ax with splinters, which in this case is embedded in the sign for "tree": **KᵂAW–XIMA**, *Kʷawxīma[lpan]* (ill. 41b). Finally, the adjective "whitewashed, polished" or "plastered" (*tla'killi*)[128] seems to be represented in the writing system by a mason's tool used to polish floors or walls (**TLA'KIL**), a sign that appears in the *Register of Tributes* and the Mendoza and Osuna codices (ill. 41c, d).

HIEROGLYPHS REFERRING TO ARCHITECTURAL CONCEPTS

Probably the most common architectural sign in the Nahuatl writing system is the logogram **KAL**, "house" (ill. 42a), which depicts the foundation, jambs, lintel, and roof of a structure. It also refers to the third day of the divinatory calendar (*tōnalpōwalli*) and forms part of multiple proper names, like that of Istacalco (*sic*): **ISTA-a-KAL**, *Istaākal[ko]* (ill. 42b). The Nahuatl hieroglyphic texts explicitly mention houses of different materials, principally stone (**te-KAL-ko**, *Tekalko*, "Tecalco" [ill. 42c]) or *tepetate* (**te-TE-[PETLA]-KAL**, *Tepetlakal[ko]*, "Tepetlacalco" [ill. 42d]), as well as huts made of straw or other perishable materials (**xa-ko**, *Xa['kal]ko*, "Xacalco" [ill. 40b]). There is also a possible logogram for "hamlet" (**KALIMA?**, *Kalimāyān*, "Caliymayan"), consisting of a pair of contiguous structures (ill. 42e).

Some terms for specific houses are found in the codices, especially the warehouse of darts or *tlakōchkalko*, alluded to in the title of an Aztec official: **TLAKOCH-KAL**, *tlakōchkal[katl]* (ill. 42f). The buildings intended for the high nobility tend to be written as **TEKᵂ-KAL**, *tēkkal[ko]*,[129] "audience hall for civil matters where justice is dealt out by the senators and elders" (ill. 42g),[130] a word derived from *tēkkalli*, "house of lords," or as **TEKᵂ-PAN?**, *tēkpan*, "royal mansion, palace" or "dwelling of a nobleman"[131] (ill. 42h). Although the hieroglyph for house also appears in the latter case, it remains unclear whether it has the reading **KAL** or **PAN?**, or simply acts as a semantic determinative for architectural structures. On page 3b of the Codex Azcatitlan, the word *tēkpan* is written with the sign meaning flag (**pa**) superimposed over that for house (ill. 42i), which suggests to me that the grapheme for house is read **PAN?** and that the flag acts as a phonetic complement (**pa-PAN?**, *[tēk]pan[nekatl]*, "tecpaneco").

There are other instances where the reading **PAN?** seems well applied to the hieroglyph for house, for example in the toponyms of Tepechpan (**TE-pe-PAN?**, *Tepe['ch]pan*, ill. 43a), Xaxalpan (**XAL-PAN?**, *[Xa]xālpan*, ill. 43b), and Tla-iacapa (**YAKA-PAN?**, *[Tla]yakapan*, ill. 43c), although it is necessary to study the behavior of this glyph in the rest of the documentary corpus before we can be certain. The possible reading of **PAN?** for the house sign would not contradict that of **KAL**, since the polyphony of certain characters is a common principle in other writing systems around the world that use context or phonetic complementation to clarify ambiguous readings.[132] However, I should emphasize that for the moment, the reading of the house sign as **PAN?** is still only a suggestion, and not without its problems. Another likely name for a building associated with the nobility is **KAL-PIL?**, *Kalpil[ko]*, "Calpilco" (ill. 42j), recorded on page 9r of the Codex Cozcatzin.

Some potentially deceptive depictions of houses occcur in the records of the Conquest in the Codex Mendoza (ill. 44a, b). In these instances, we find a drawing of a house on fire, its roof about to collapse. The annexed glosses transcribe the reading of the associated toponym (**pi-a**, *Pia[stlān]*, "Piaztlan," **E'EKA-TEPE**, *E'ekatepē[k]*, "Ecatepec," etc.), but none of them insinuates that the burning house has a pronunciation. This suggests that we are dealing with conceptual (pictographic) representations that belonged not to the writing system, but rather to the iconographic repertoire.[133]

Similar to the logogram **KAL** or **PAN?** is that of **CHAN**, "home, habitation" or "residence" (ill. 45), with the sole difference seeming to be that hieroglyphs identifying the inhabitant are placed in the entrance opening: an eagle in the case of **KᵂAW-CHAN**, *Kʷāw[tin]chan*, "Quauhtinchan" (ill. 45a), a saurian with a serrated back for **OXI**[134]-**CHAN**, *Oxichān*, "Oxichan" (ill. 45b), and a serpent for **KOA-CHAN**, *Kōā[tlin]chān*, "Coatlínchan" (ill. 51d).

The repertoire of Nahuatl hieroglyphs also contains expressions for the structural elements of buildings. There is *tepe'chtli*, "foundation" or "base of a house," which we have already seen in the case of **TE?-pe-PAN?**, *Tepe['ch]pan* (ill. 43a), as well as a possible logogram **TEPE'CH** (ill. 46a), which seems to be a digraph[135] formed by the signs for stone and a human leg. An alternative logogram consists of two stones enclosed within a rectangle: **TEPE'CH-PAN**, *Tepe'chpan* (ill. 46b). Finally, the word *tepāntli*, "wall" (literally "line of stones"), is represented by two horizontal rows of bricks in the toponym of Tetepanco (sic): te-te-TEPAN-tla, *Tetepāntla* (ill. 46c), as well as in that of Tetepantepetl, which appears on folio 27r of the Codex Telleriano-Remensis: TEPAN-pa-TEPE, *[Te]tepāntepē[tl]* (ill. 46d).

In another class of structures, there is a logogram for "granary" or "silo," represented symbolically by means of a covered earthenware jar for storing grain, which rests on a flat base supported by stones, as in the toponym Cuezcomatlyyacac: KᵂESKOMA-YAKA, *Kᵂeskomayaka[k]* (ill. 47).

On the Stone of Tizoc there is a logogram for TLATEL, "large mound of earth" (ill. 48a), a natural prominence of the sort that some Pre-Columbian pyramids were built on or were inspired by. The sign is relatively frequent in the codices of the Valley of Mexico, since it forms part of the toponym for Tlatelolco, which is written with a small syncope in the codex of that name: tla-TLATEL-ko, *Tlatel[ol]ko* (ill. 48b). On the other hand, a logogram likely meaning *tetelli?*, "rocky mound?," is found on page 48r of the Codex Mendoza: KᵂAW-TETEL?, *Kᵂawtetel[ko]*, "Quauhtetelco" (ill. 48c); the appearance of the sign TETEL? suggests that this is a man-made structure, and recalls the enigmatic hieroglyph for MOS, "altar" (ill. 48d), identified by Aubin in the nineteenth century.[136]

As for buildings of a ritual character, on page 6r of the Codex Mendoza we have an alleged logogram for TZAKᵂAL, "temple" or "pyramid" (ill. 48e), whose iconic aspect suggests a series of man-made terraced platforms. More certain is the logogram TEOPAN, *teōpān[tli]*, "temple" (ill. 48f), literally "wall, line" or "row of gods," which appears, for example, in the toponym for Quiyauhteopan: KIYAW-TEOPAN, *Kiyawteōpān* (ill. 48g), as well as the sign TEOKAL, "sanctuary" or "place of worship" (ill. 48h), literally "house of the god," which forms part of various toponyms, such as that of Teocalçinco: TEOKAL-TZIN, *Teōkaltzin[ko]* (ill. 48i). A partially phonetic variation was identified by Aubin[137] in the manuscripts from the area of Texcoco: te-o-KAL-TLAN, *Teōkal[ti]tlan*, "Teocaltitlan" (ill. 48j). It would seem that the only graphic distinction between the logograms TEOPAN (ill. 48f) and TEOKAL (ill. 48h) is the presence of the upper chamber in the latter.

The icon for sanctuary or place of worship may perhaps cause confusion when it is used to indicate conquest, as on folio 2r of the Codex Mendoza, which mentions the defeat of the Colhuacan people (KOL, *Kōl[wa'kān]* [ill. 49a]) and the Tenayucan people (TENAM, *Tenām[yokān]* [ill. 49b]). As with the Conquest pictograms that depict a burning house (ill. 44a, b), there is no gloss to suggest that the burning *teōkalli* with its roof collapsing was pronounced, which may indicate that it did not belong to the writing system, but rather to the iconographic repertoire. On page 5v of the same manuscript, the conceptual representation of conquest is reduced under the principle of *pars pro toto* to a flame with swirls

of smoke that emerges from the opening of the logogram TEOKAL, in the case of *Teōkal[wēyak]* (ill. 49c).

The altars with skulls or *tzonpāntli* (literally "rows, lines" or "walls of hairs") had a ritual character; their classic logogram consists of a low altar with two vertical posts, between which is a skull mounted on a horizontal stick, as in the toponym for Çonpahuacā: TZONPA-pa, *Tzonpā[wa'kān]* (ill. 50a). An alternate spelling is found on page 35r of the Codex Osuna, where the word is formed with the logogram for "hair" (TZON) plus that for "flag" (PAN), which acts as a rebus: TZON-PAN, *Tzonpān[ko]*, "Tzompāco" (ill. 50b). On the other hand, the logogram for ballgame (TLACH) normally consists of the I-shaped court painted with colors and with rings on both sides (ill. 50c), but on page 25 of the so-called Durán Codex it takes the form of the court's lateral stands (TLACH-KIYAW, *Tlachkiyaw[ko]*, "Tlachquiauhco" [ill. 50d]), recalling one of the variants of the corresponding Mayan hieroglyph (ill. 18f). Finally, we must mention the *tēmaskalli* or "sweatbath" (literally "house of cooking on the stove"), whose hieroglyphic cartouche appears on page 5 of the *Register of Tributes* and 21v of the Codex Mendoza, forming part of the toponym for Temazcalapā: TEMASKAL-a, *Tēmaskala[pan]* (ill. 50e), where the suffix -*pan* has been suspended or elided.

HIEROGLYPHS REFERRING TO OTHER CONSTRUCTION TERMS

Where Nahuatl toponyms designate settlements of a certain political rank, they may be associated with the word *āltepētl*,[138] "people" or "city," as in the case of the references to Texcoco (a-AKOL, *Ākōl[wa'kān]* [ill. 51a]) and Tlacuban (TLAKO, *Tlakō[pan]* (ill. 51b)) on pages 34r and 34v of the Codex Osuna; the reference to Tepetlaoztoc (PETLA-OSTO, *[Te]petlaōstō[k]* [ill. 51c]), written on sheet 42, folio A, of the codex of that name; and the reference to Coatlinchan (KOA-CHAN, *Kōā[tlin]chān* [ill. 51d]) that is found precisely at the center of the Map of Coatlinchan.[139] Evidently the glyphic composition of the phonogram a (acrophonic for *ātl*, "water") plus the logogram "hill" (a-TEPE, *āltepē[tl]*) alludes to the diphrasism *in ātl in tēpetl*,[140] which is linked to the ancient idea that cities were associated with mountains or sacred caves.

A possible term for "neighborhood" or "suburb" (*chināmitl*) appears in the codices in the form of a plot of earth from which a corn plant grows, since the primary meaning of *chināmitl* is "separation" or "cane fence," which alludes to a certain type of structure, as can be appreciated in the toponym for Chinamitlan: CHINAM-TLAN, *Chinām[i]tlān* (ill. 52a). On the other hand, there are various examples of urban structures with battlements, representing the logogram TENAM, *tenām[itl]*, "fence" or "city wall" (ill. 52b), which forms part of multiple toponyms, such as

TE-pe-PAN?
Tepe['ch]pan
‹gloss: Tepechpan›
"Tepechpan"

Ill. 43a

XAL-PAN?
[Xa]xālpan
‹gloss: Xaxalpan›
"Jajalpan"

Ill. 43b

YAKA-PAN?
[Tla]yakapan
‹gloss: Tlaiacapa›
"Tlayacapan"

Ill. 43c

43. Problematic contexts of the glyph for "house": (a) toponym *Tepe['ch]pan* (Codex Mendoza, p. 20r; Berdan and Anawalt 1992); (b) toponym *[Xa]xālpan* (Codex Mendoza, p. 20r; Berdan and Anawalt 1992); (c) toponym *[Tla]yakapan* (Codex Cozcatzin, p. 6v; Valero de García Lascuráin 1994).

pi-a
Pia[stlān]
‹gloss: Piaztlan›
"[conquest of] Piaztlan"

Ill. 44a

E'EKA-TEPE
E'ekatepē[k]
‹gloss: Ecatepec›
"[conquest of] Ecatepec"

Ill. 44b

44. Iconographic representations of houses in the context of war: (a) conquest of *Pia[stlān]* (Codex Mendoza, p. 15v; Berdan and Anawalt 1992); (b) conquest of *E'ekatepē[k]* (Codex Mendoza, p. 12r; Berdan and Anawalt 1992, fig. 45a).

KʷAW-CHAN
Kʷāw[tin]chān
‹gloss: Quauhtinchan›
"Cuauhtinchan"

Ill. 45a

OXI-CHAN
Oxichān
‹gloss: Oxichan›
"Oxichan?"

Ill. 45b

45. Examples of the logogram CHAN, "house, room" or "residence": (a) substantive *chāntli*, included in the toponym *Kʷāw[tin]chān* (Codex Mendoza 42r; Berdan and Anawalt 1992); (b) substantive *chāntli*, included in the toponym *Oxichān* (Codex Mendoza 49r; Berdan and Anawalt 1992).

TEPE'CH
Tepe'ch[pan]
‹gloss: Tepechpa›
"Tepechpan"

Ill. 46a

TEPE'CH-PAN
Tepe'chpan
"Tepechpan"

Ill. 46b

te-te-TEPAN-tla
Tetepāntla
‹gloss: Tetepanco›
"Tetepantla"

Ill. 46c

TEPAN-pa-TEPE
[Te]tepāntepē[tl]
‹gloss: Tetepantepetl›
"Tetepantepetl"

Ill. 46d

46. Expressions containing the terms for "foundation" and "walls": (a) substantive *tepe'chtli*, "foundation of a house," included in the toponym *Tepe'ch[pan]* (Codex Mendoza, p. 21v; Bernal and Anawalt 1992); (b) substantive *tepe'chtli*, "foundation of a house," included in the toponym *Tepe'ch[pan]* (document in the Archivo General de Indias, Justicia 164-2, maps and plans, Mexico, 664; Macazaga Ordoño, 1979, 146); (c) substantive *tepāntli*, "wall" or "stone wall," included in the toponym *Tetepāntla* (Codex Mendoza, p. 27r; Berdan and Anawalt 1992); (d) substantive *tetepāntli*, "wall" or "stone wall," included in the toponym *[Te]tepāntepē[tl]* (Codex Telleriano-Remensis, p. 27r; Quiñones Keber 1995).

KʷESKOMA-YAKA
Kʷeskomayaka[k]
‹gloss: Cuezcomatlyyacac›
"Cuezcomayacac"

Ill. 47

47. Logogram KʷESKOMA, "silo" or "granary," included in the toponym *Kʷeskomayaka[k]* (Codex Mendoza, p. 10v; Berdan and Anawalt 1992).

TLATEL
tlatel[li]
"earthen mound"

Ill. 48a

tla-TLATEL-ko
Tlatel[ol]ko
‹Tlatelolco›
"Tlatelolco"

Ill. 48b

KʷAW-TETEL?
Kʷawtetel[ko]
‹gloss: Quauhtetelco›
"Cuautetelco"

Ill. 48c

MOS
mos[tli](?)
"altar"

Ill. 48d

TZAKʷAL
Tzakʷal[li]
"pyramid" or "temple"

Ill. 48e

TEOPAN
teōpān[tli]
"temple"

Ill. 48f

KIYAW-TEOPAN
Kiyawteōpān
‹gloss: Quiyauhteopan›
"Quiahuiteopan"

Ill. 48g

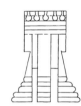

TEOKAL
teōkal[li]
"altar" or "sanctuary"

Ill. 48h

TEOKAL-TZIN
Teōkaltzin[ko]
‹gloss: Teocalçinco›
"Teocaltzingo"

Ill. 48i

te-o-KAL-TLAN
Teōkal[ti]tlan
‹gloss: Teocaltitlan›
"Teocaltitlan"

48. Expressions containing references to mounds and pyramids: (a) logogram TLATEL, "large mound of earth" (Stone of Tizoc; Dibble 1971, 327); (b) substantive *tlatelli*, "mound of earth," included in the toponym *Tlatel[ol]ko* (Tlatelolco Codex; Valle 1994b); (c) substantive *tetelli*, "rocky mound?," included in the toponym *Kʷawtetel[ko]* (Codex Mendoza, p. 48r; Berdan and Anawalt 1992); (d) possible logogram MOS, "altar" (Aubin 2002, 45); (e) possible logogram TZAKᵂAL, "temple" or "pyramid" (Codex Mendoza, p. 6r; Berdan and Anawalt 1992); (f) logogram TEOPAN, "temple" (Codex Mendoza, p. 37r; Berdan and Anawalt 1992); (g) substantive *teōpāntli*, "temple," included in the toponym *Kiyawteōpān* (Codex Mendoza, p. 8r; Berdan and Anawalt 1992); (h) logogram TEOKAL, "sanctuary" or "place of worship" (Lienzo de Tlaxcala, p. 21; Torre 1983): (i) substantive *teōkalli*, "sanctuary, place of worship," included in the toponym *Teōkaltzin[ko]* (Codex Mendoza, p. 23r; Berdan and Anawalt 1992); (j) substantive *teōkalli*, included in the toponym *Teōkal[ti]tlan* (Aubin 2002, 51).

Ill. 49a

KOL
Kōl[wa'kān]
‹gloss: Colhuacan.pueblo›
"Culhuacan"

Ill. 49b

TENAM
Tenām[yokān]
‹gloss: Tenayucan.pueblo›
"Tenayuca"

Ill. 49c

TEOKAL
Teōkal[wēyak]
‹gloss: Teocalhueyac›
"Teocalhueyac"

49. Iconographic representations of sanctuaries or places of worship in the context of war: (a) conquest of *Kōl[wa'kān]* (Codex Mendoza, p. 2r; Berdan and Anawalt 1992); (b) conquest of *Tenām[yokān]* (Codex Mendoza, p. 2r; Berdan and Anawalt 1992); (c) conquest of *Teōkal[wēyak]* (Codex Mendoza, p. 5v; Berdan and Anawalt 1992).

Ill. 50a

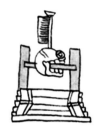

TZONPA-pa
Tzonpā[wa'kān]
‹gloss: Çonpahuacā›
"Tzompahuacan"

Ill. 50b

TZON-PAN
Tzonpān[ko]
‹gloss: Tzompaco›
"Tzumpango"

Ill. 50c

TLACH
Tlach[ko]
‹gloss: Tlachco›
"Taxco"

Ill. 50d

TLACH-KIYAW
Tlachkiyaw[ko]
‹gloss: Tlachquiauhco›
"Tlachquiauhco"

Ill. 50e

TEMASKAL-a
Tēmaskala[pan]
‹gloss: Temazcalapā›
"Temazcalpan"

50. Expressions which contain other terms for ritual structures: (a) substantive *tzonpāntli*, "row of hairs," included in the toponym *Tzonpā[wa'kān]* (Codex Mendoza, p. 35r; Berdan and Anawalt 1992); (b) substantive *tzonpāntli*, "row of hairs," included in the toponym *Tzonpān[ko]* (Codex Osuna, p. 35r; Zavala 1947); (c) substantive *tlachtli*, "ballgame," included in the toponym *Tlach[ko]* (Codex Mendoza, p. 31r; Berdan and Anawalt 1992); (d) substantive *tlachtli*, "ballgame," included in the toponym *Tlachkiyaw[ko]* (Durán Codex, p. 25; Durán 1967, vol. 2, plate 50); (e) substantive *tēmaskalli* or "sweatbath," included in the toponym *Tēmaskala[pan]* (Codex Mendoza, p. 21v; Berdan and Anawalt 1992).

Ill. 51a

a-AKOL-a-TEPE
Ākōl[wa'kān] ā[l]tepī[tl]
‹gloss: Tetzcuco›
"city of Acolhuacan"

Ill. 51b

TLAKO-a-TEPE
Tlakō[pan] ā[l]tepē[tl]
‹gloss: Tlacuban›
"city of Tacuba"

Ill. 51c

PETLA-OSTO-a-TEPE
[Te]petlaōstō[k] ā[l]tepē[tl]
‹gloss: Tepetlaoztoc›
"city of Tepetlaoztoc"

Ill. 51d

KOA-CHAN-a-TEPE
Kōā[tlin]chān ā[l]tepē[tl]
‹gloss: Coatlínchan›
"city of Coatlinchan"

51. Compound glyphs designating a "city, settlement" or "population" (a-TEPE, *āltepē[tl]*, "the water and the hill"): (a) toponym *Ākōl[wa'kān]* (Codex Osuna, p. 34r; Zavala 1947); (b) toponym *Tlakō[pan]* (Codex Osuna, p. 34r; Zavala 1947); (c) toponym *[Te]petlaōstō[k]* (Codex Tepetlaoztoc, p. 42, plate A; Valle 1994a); (d) toponym *Kōā[tlin]chān* (Map of Coatlinchan; Mohar Betancourt 1994).

Ill. 52a

CHINAM-TLAN
Chinām[i]tlān
‹gloss: Chinamitlan›
"Chinamitla"

Ill. 52b

TENAM

tenām[itl]

"fence" or "city wall"

Ill. 52c

TENAM-TZIN

Tenāmtzin[ko]

⟨gloss: Tenamtzinco⟩

"Tenantzingo"

Ill. 52d

TE-TENAM

Tetenām[ko]

⟨gloss: Tetenamco⟩

"Tetenango"

Ill. 52e

te-na-ko

Tenā[m]ko

"Tenango"

Ill. 52f

o

Ill. 52g

XIKO-ko-o

Xīko[']

⟨gloss: Xico⟩

"Xico"

Ill. 52h

TE?-PANO?/TEPAN?

tepanō['ayān]?

"Tepanoayan"

52. Terms related to urban structures: (a) substantive *chinámitl*, "cane fence, neighborhood" or "suburb," included in the toponym *Chinām[i]tlān* (Codex Mendoza, p. 46r; Berdan and Anawalt 1992); (b) logogram TENAM, "fence, city wall" (Codex Mendoza, p. 7v; Berdan and Anawalt 1992); (c) substantive *tenāmtli*, "city wall," included in the toponym *Tenāmtzin[ko]* (Codex Mendoza, p. 34r; Berdan and Anawalt 1992); (d) substantive *tetenāmtli*, "city wall constructed of stone," included in the toponym *Tetenām[ko]* (Codex Mendoza, p. 36r; Berdan and Anawalt 1992); (e) substantive *tenāmtli*, "city wall," included in the toponym *Tenā[m]ko* (Tepetlaoztoc Codex, p. 5, plate B; Valle 1994); (f) syllabogram o (Aubin 2002, 39); (g) anthroponym for *Xīko[']* (Codex of Santa María Asunción, p. 69v; Williams and Harvey 1997); (h) substantive *tepantli*, "stone bridge?," included in the toponym *tepanō['ayān]* (Stone of Tizoc; Dibble 1971, 327).

Ill. 53a

PANO

panō

"wade, pass" or "cross the river on foot"

Ill. 53b

KʷAWPAN

Kʷawpan[ōayan]

⟨gloss: Quauhpanoayā⟩

"Cuaupanoayan"

Ill. 53c

KʷAWPAN

Kʷawpan[ōayan]

⟨gloss: Quauhpanoayan⟩

"Cuaupanoayan"

Ill. 53d

KʷAWPAN-o

Kʷawpanō[ayan]

⟨gloss: road or path with 1 wooden bridge⟩

"Cuaupanoayan"

Ill. 53e

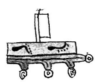

a-o-PAN

Āo[']pan[ko]

⟨gloss: Aochpanco⟩

"Auchpango"

Ill. 53f

ATZAKʷA

Ātzak[kān]

⟨gloss: Atzacan⟩

"Atzacan"

53. Expressions containing terms associated with hydraulic structures: (a) logogram PANO, "to ford or pass the river by foot" (Codex Mendoza, p. 38r; Berdan and Anawalt 1992); (b) and (c) substantive *kʷawpantli*, "wooden bridge," included in the toponym *Kʷawpan[ōayan]* (Codex Mendoza, pp. 32r and 10r; Berdan and Anawalt 1992); (d) "road or path with 1 wooden bridge" (Codex Mendoza, p. 64r; Berdan and Anawalt 1992); (e) substantive *āo'tli*, "canal" or "aqueduct," included in the toponym *Āo[']pan[ko]* (Codex Mendoza, p. 20v; Berdan and Anawalt 1992); (f) verb *ātzakʷa*, "to cover or to block the water and keep it from running," included in the toponym *ātzak[kān]* (Codex Mendoza, p. 18r; Berdan and Anawalt 1992).

those of Tenayuca (*Tenām[yokān]* [ill. 49b]), Tenamtzinco (*Tenāmtzin[ko]* [ill. 52c]), and Tetenamco (*Tetenām[ko]* [ill. 52d]). In this last case it seems to carry a horizontal row of stones, which apparently acted as the logogram TE?. Charles E. Dibble[141] has indicated a phonetic instance of Tenamco in the Tepetlaoztoc Codex: **te-na-ko**, *Tenā[m]ko* (ill. 52e), a form that elides the consonant *-m* because it comes before another consonant, a limitation of all writing systems that only link syllables CV-CV.[142]

Except in the term for "aqueduct," which we will analyze below, I cannot find any instance of the noun "road" (*o'tli*), although the Nahua scribes frequently used an acrophonic syllabogram **o** (ill. 52f) in the composition of proper names, as in **te-o-KAL-TLAN**, *Teōkal[ti]tlan*, "Teocaltitlan" (ill. 48j), or **XIKO-ko-o**, *Xīko[']*, "Xico" (ill. 52g). On the Stone of Tizoc there is a glyphic component that Dibble[143] interprets as Tepanoayan (**TE?-PANO?/TEPAN?**, *tepanō['ayān]?* [ill. 52h]), "stone bridge," but the reading of the sign above the stones is still very obscure.

The logogram **PANO**, *panō*, "to ford, to pass" or "to cross the river by foot" (ill. 53a), features a section of a channel marked by a human footprint. In other contexts, this footprint is the logogram **PAN**, "on, over," but when it is associated with water, it seems to form part of the digraph *panō*. Another compound logogram may be **KʷAWPAN**, *kʷawpan[tli]*, "wooden bridge,"[144] which consists of a footprint (**PAN** or **PANO**) on wood planks (**KʷAW**), which in turn are laid over a channel. We find this possible digraph in the toponym for Quauhpanoayan: **KʷAWPAN**, *Kʷawpan[ōayan]* (ills. 53b, c). A similar glyphic arrangement appears on page 64r of the Codex Mendoza (ill. 53d), where it is accompanied by a gloss that states: "road or street with 1 wooden bridge."

Another hydraulic structure that deserves mention is "channel, aqueduct" or *āo'tli*, which literally means "water road" and forms part of the toponym for Aochpanco: **a-o-PAN**, *Āo[']pan[ko]* (ill. 53e). Finally, among those terms that reflect the lake environment of the Aztecs, there is a logogram that apparently reads **ATZAKʷA**, *ātzakʷa*, "to block the water and keep it from running." The hieroglyph for this verb is iconically transparent, since, as Peñafiel[145] noted, it represents a hand raising or lowering a lid over water, and forms part of the toponym Atzacan (**ATZAKʷA**, *Ātzak[kān]* [ill. 53f]), which probably means "floodgate."[146]

FINAL REFLECTIONS

Using systems of logosyllabic writing, Maya and Nahua scribes recorded a repertoire of construction-related terms that reflected their cultural interests. The languages in which their respective hieroglyphic texts are written must have had much richer architectural vocabularies, but the words and phrases dealt with here reflect only the scant remains of two ancient textual corpuses, those documents that managed to survive the ravages of time, nature, and mankind. While the Maya *ah dziboob* ('*ajtz'ihb'o'ob'*) were especially interested in recording the names, construction, consecration, and activation of their buildings, these subjects were probably far from the thoughts of the Nahua *tlahcuiloque* (*tla'kwilo'ke*), who employed architectural words only within the narrow thematic margins of their writing.

It should be mentioned that although many architectural hieroglyphs may seem iconically transparent, this does not mean that they are read according to their appearance. Much help is provided by the glosses in Latin characters from colonial texts. Still, these glosses do not always precisely reflect the reading of the glyph (see, for example, ills. 46c and 51a), since they were sometimes the work of Spanish officials oblivious to hieroglyphic complexities, who hurriedly took dictation from indigenous scribes.[147] The decipherment of both writing systems must be based not on iconographic interpretations, but on the careful analysis of all the available documents in order to find the phonetic substitutions and complements that will allow us to derive epigraphic readings.

The adornment of certain walls and facades with hieroglyphic texts—taking advantage of their purely calligraphic aspect—suggests that one of the values appreciated by Maya artists was the visual impact of public buildings, closely linked to political and ritual prestige. The relative abundance of words associated with construction and materials attests to the fact that technical perfection was another of the ideals to which Maya and Nahua architects aspired.[148]

As the Mayan texts themselves suggest, the human body was the measure or model for many architectural terms: nouns like *chikin* ("ear"), *nuhk* ("skin"), *'ook* ("foot"), and *ti'* ("mouth"), are complemented with verbs that describe the position of the human body (*hek*, "to hang oneself," *pak*, "to lie facedown," and *pat*, "to form oneself") and with measurements based on the extremities (*nahb'*, "fourth" or "palm," and *tek'*, "to measure by foot or with footsteps"). It is possible that the inclusion of construction-related words in some Nahuatl anthroponyms also somehow reflects this identification of buildings with human beings.

One of the great preoccupations of the Maya was the activation and ritual renewal of buildings through ceremonies involving fire, smoke, and incense. These activities were considered sacred, since they seem to have evoked the hierogamy and the extraction of fire by the gods during the mythical night that followed the destruction of the world by flood, and marked the generation of a new cosmic order. The mere act of measuring out the land to be used as a cornfield or house was conceived of as a repetition of the actions undertaken by the gods during the creation of time and space. Behind these ideas lies the identification of the world with the structure of a house, a phenomenon that is reflected in the very political geography of Mesoamerica, where toponyms incorporate many architectural terms.

Given the evocation of cosmogonic myths in the rituals for the consecration of houses, as well as their decoration with sacred hieroglyphic texts and images of the divine kings and gods, there is no doubt that public buildings were far from being profane spaces. What little written testimony there is about the identity of the architects suggests that a certain kind of priest (*'ajk'uhu'n*) designed the buildings and supervised their construction. Some enclosures clearly belonged to specific gods, including the so-called poison bottles or flasks. Finally, the Mayan terms for certain sanctuaries of worship (*wahyib'* and *pib' naah*) or rites associated with tombs (*'ilaj*) suggest that they were intended to produce complex supernatural or mental experiences, which included dream transformation and the externalization of the spirit.[149]

MAPS AND DRAWINGS

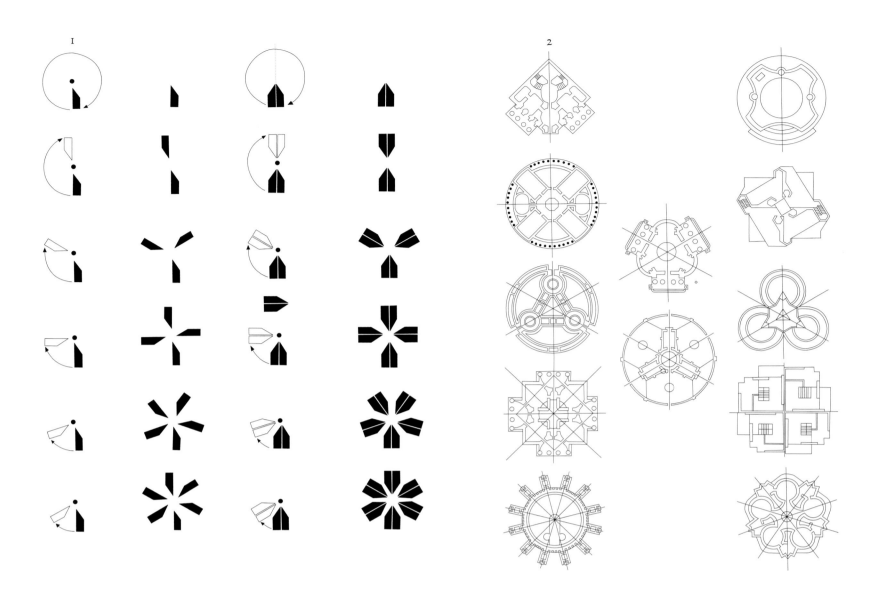

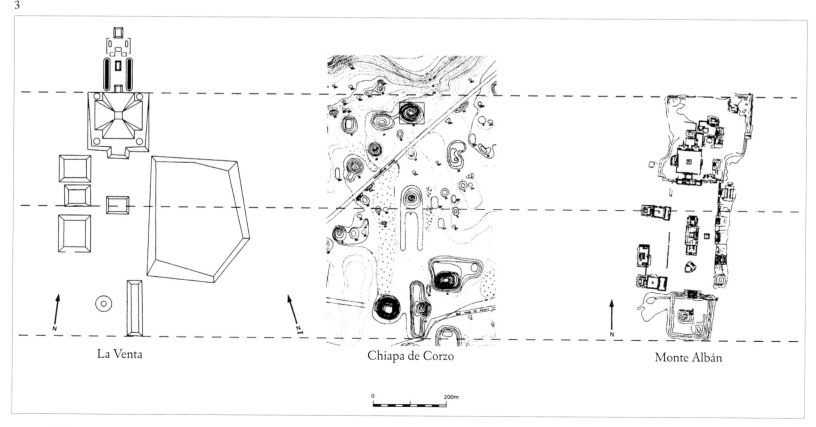

La Venta   Chiapa de Corzo   Monte Albán

0   200m

Chapter 1

ARCHITECTURE AS ART

1. Exercises in symmetry involving rotation around a fixed point, based on studies carried out by Leonardo da Vinci for the purpose of adding capitals and niches to buildings in a harmonious fashion. (Drawing by Arturo Reséndiz, after March and Steadman 1971, 57.)

2. The application of symmetry in certain European structures. In his *Ten Books on Architecture*, Leon Battista Alberti maintained that the ideal plan of a building was either round or polygonal, with six, eight, or ten sides, and various European architects have explored this concept. (Drawing by Arturo Reséndiz, after March and Steadman 1971, 57.)

3. A comparison of three Formative cities, showing that they are all about two times longer than they are wide, with a principal north-south axis and a secondary east-west one. (Clark 2001, 190.)

4. Profiles of *talud-tablero*, or slope-and-panel, buildings at Teotihuacán, State of México. This system of construction was traditionally ascribed to that city, but is now thought to have originated in the Valley of Puebla.

5. Plan of the Maya city of Pechal, Campeche, showing what may be an amphitheater.

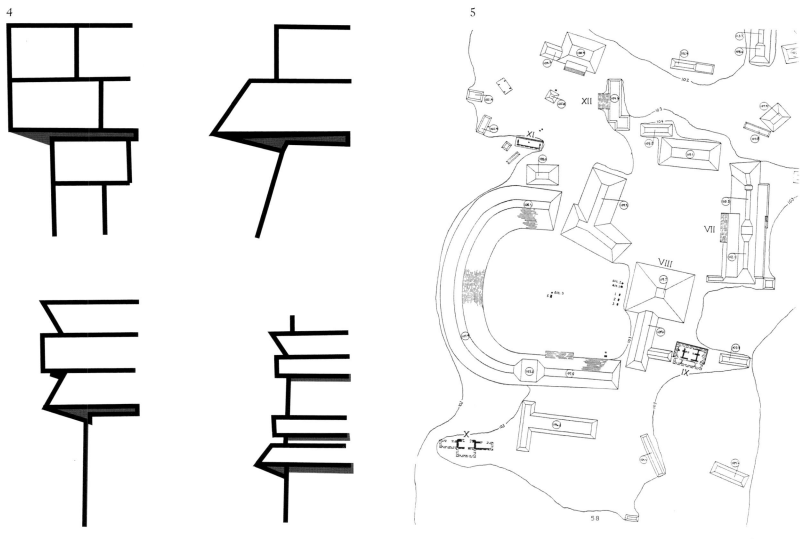

4

5

6

7

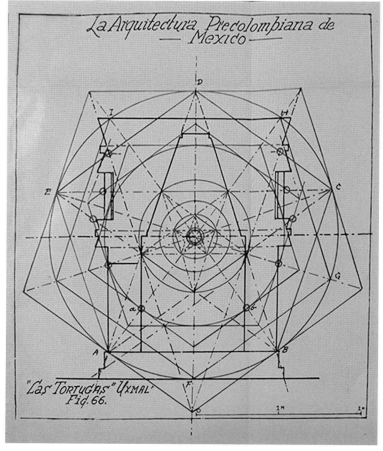

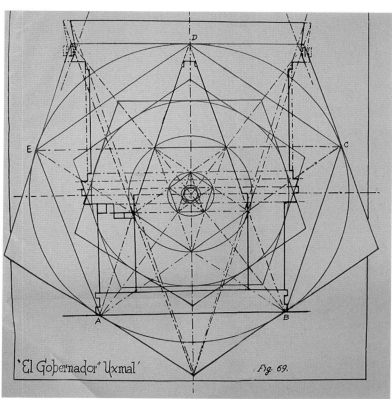

6. Drawing by Manuel Amábilis showing the application of geometric principles to the design of the Nunnery building at Uxmal, Yucatán (9th–10th century AD). Amábilis, a noted Yucatecan architect who had studied in Paris, won a prize from the Real Academia de Bellas Artes de San Fernando in 1930 for his study of the proportions of Pre-Columbian buildings.

7. Drawing by Amábilis of the House of the Turtles at Uxmal (9th–10th century AD). According to him, this diagram "shows the golden ratio in the most important proportions of the elevation, especially in the profile of the facade and in the interior."

8. Drawing by Amábilis analyzing the proportions of the House of the Governor at Uxmal (early 10th century AD). He proposes that the ancient architects used the seventh concentric circle seen here to find the optimal relationship between the moldings and their projections.

8

Chapter 4

PRE-OLMEC AND OLMEC ARCHITECTURE

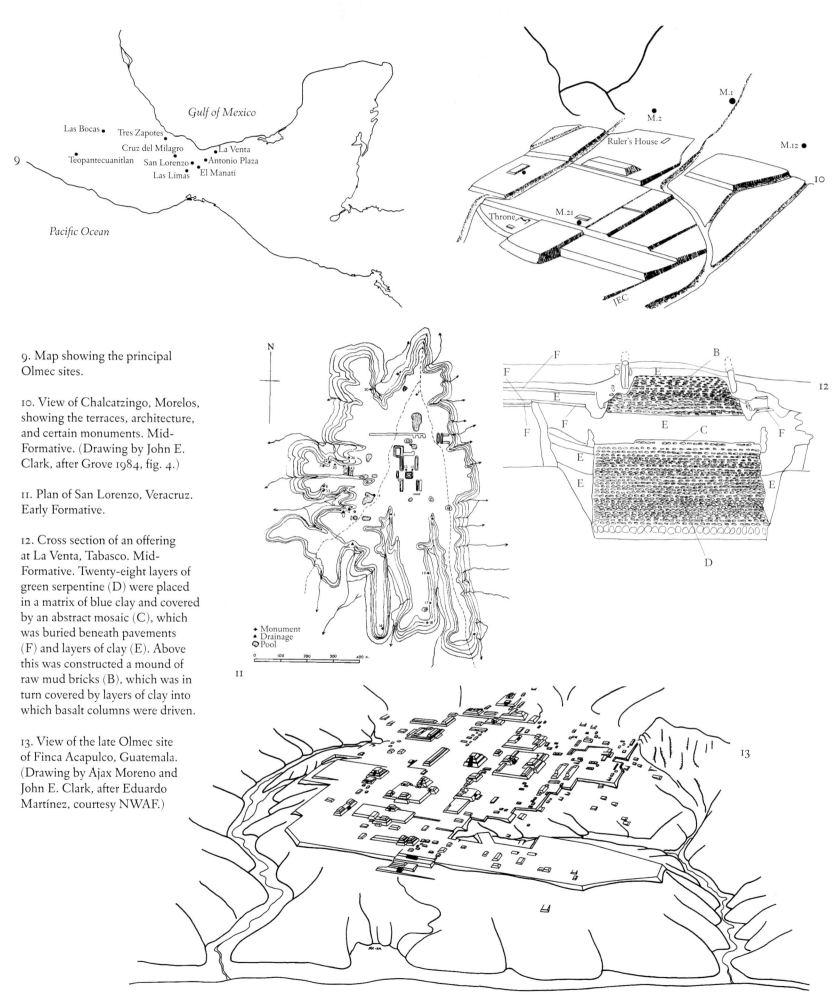

9. Map showing the principal Olmec sites.

10. View of Chalcatzingo, Morelos, showing the terraces, architecture, and certain monuments. Mid-Formative. (Drawing by John E. Clark, after Grove 1984, fig. 4.)

11. Plan of San Lorenzo, Veracruz. Early Formative.

12. Cross section of an offering at La Venta, Tabasco. Mid-Formative. Twenty-eight layers of green serpentine (D) were placed in a matrix of blue clay and covered by an abstract mosaic (C), which was buried beneath pavements (F) and layers of clay (E). Above this was constructed a mound of raw mud bricks (B), which was in turn covered by layers of clay into which basalt columns were driven.

13. View of the late Olmec site of Finca Acapulco, Guatemala. (Drawing by Ajax Moreno and John E. Clark, after Eduardo Martínez, courtesy NWAF.)

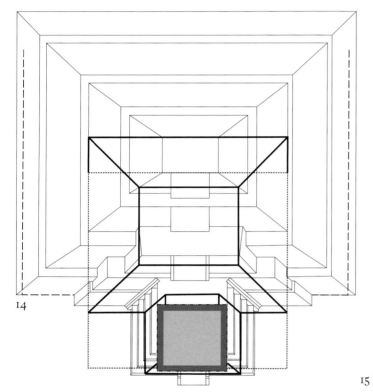

14

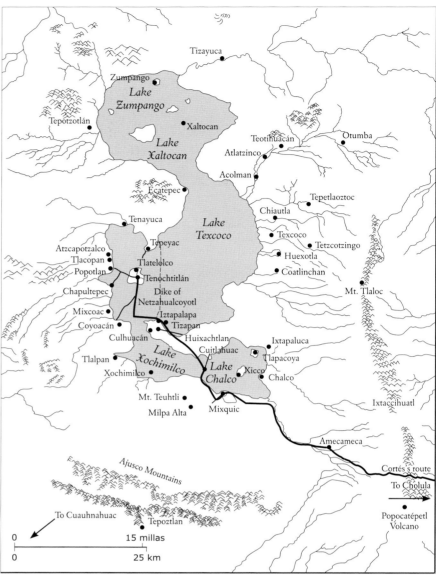

15

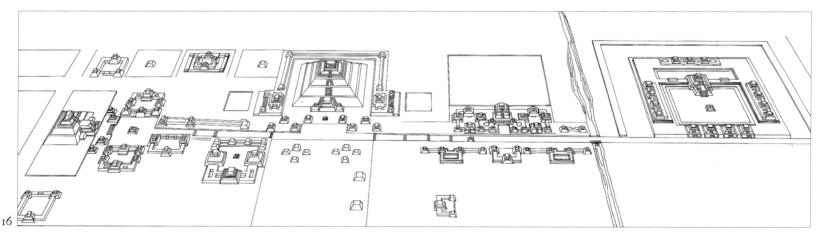

16

14. Plan of the Pyramid of the Moon at Teotihuacán, showing the successive phases of construction between AD 100 and 600 that were revealed by the excavations of Saburo Sugiyama and Rubén Cabrera.

15. Map of the Valley of Mexico indicating the principal archaeological sites. (Drawing by Arturo Reséndiz, after Townsend 1992, 27).

16. View of Teotihuacán with the Plaza of the Moon on the left, at one end of the Avenue of the Dead; the Pyramid of the Sun at top center; and the Ciudadela at top right. (Drawing by Ignacio Marquina, from Gamio 1922, fig. 12.)

17, 18. Plan and oblique view of the Great Pyramid of Cholula, Puebla, with the plan showing its successive phases of construction. Late

Formative–Postclassic. (Drawing by Arturo Reséndiz, after Solís et al. 2007, 77).

19. Reconstruction of the Great Pyramid of Cholula. (Drawing by Arturo Reséndiz, after ibid.).

20–22. Reconstruction of the Chapulines building, the second phase of the Great Pyramid of Cholula, based on the findings of

Gabriela Uruñuela and Patricia Plunket. The semiflayed heads painted on the facade have been described as grasshoppers or, more recently, as skulls. If they are indeed skulls, they are not human, because the bodies attached to them are not. As in the bas-reliefs on the Temple of the Feathered Serpent at Teotihuacán, the heads in these murals are depicted frontally, while the bodies unfold to one side. (Drawing by Arturo Reséndiz.)

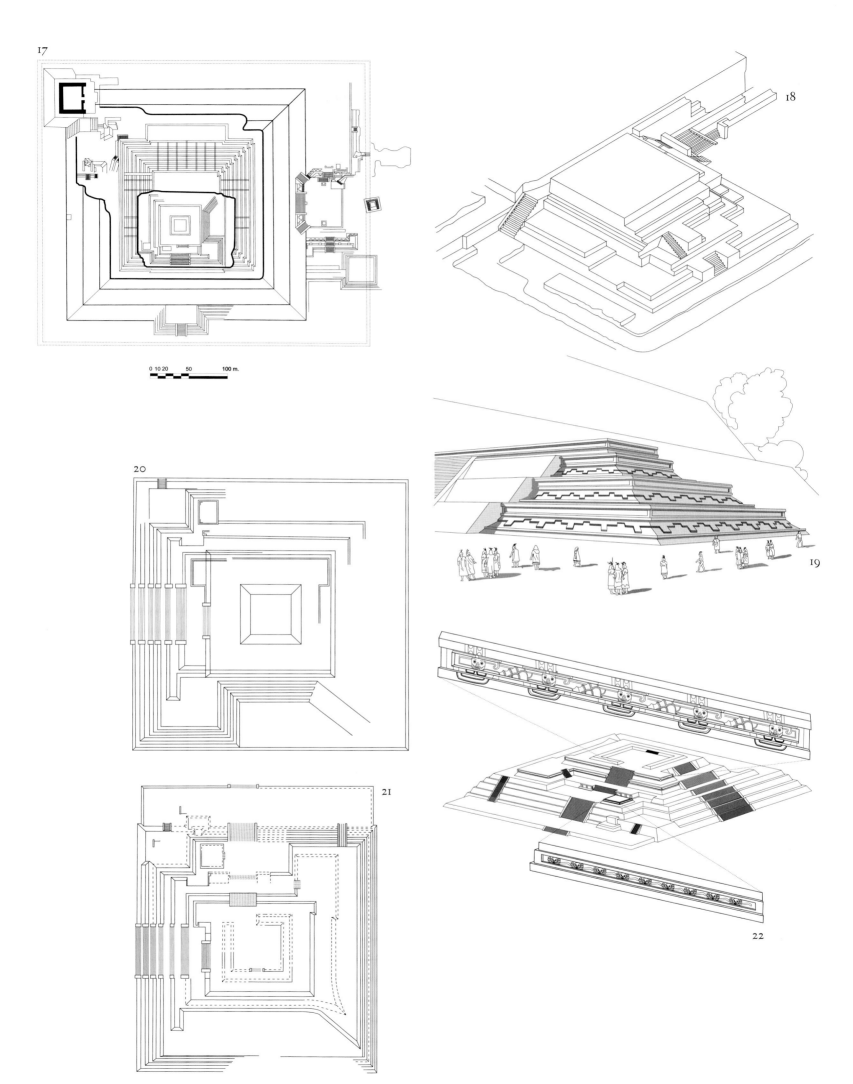

17

18

19

20

21

22

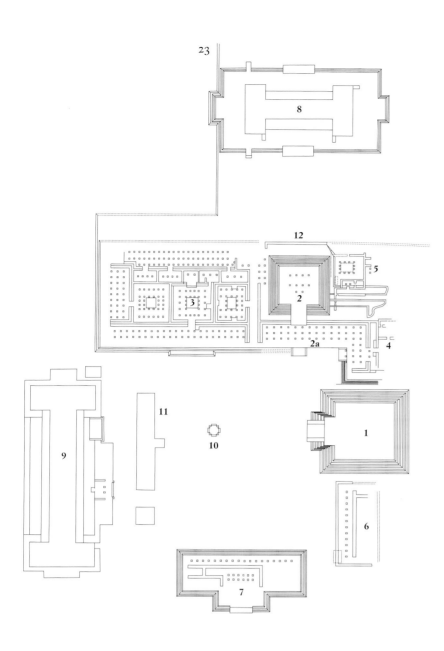

23

8

23. Plan of the principal sacred precinct of Tula, Hidalgo, AD 900–1200.
(1) Pyramid C
(2) Pyramid B
(2a) South Vestibule
(3) Burned Palace
(4) East Palace
(5) Palace of Quetzalcóatl
(6) Building J
(7) Building K
(8) Ballcourt 1
(9) Ballcourt 2
(10) Altar
(11) Tzompantli
(12) Coatepantli

24. View of the Burned Palace at Tula, with Pyramid B beside it. AD 900–1200.

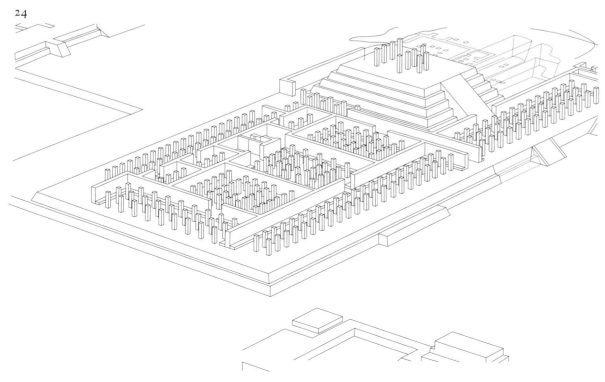

24

Chapter 6

WESTERN MEXICO

25. Map of western Mexico showing the principal archaeological sites.

26. Tomb at El Arenal, Etzatlán, Jalisco, investigated by José Corona Núñez in 1955: (a) shaft, (b) tunnel leading to Chamber 1, (c) and (d) interior views of two of the three chambers. Late Formative–Early Classic.

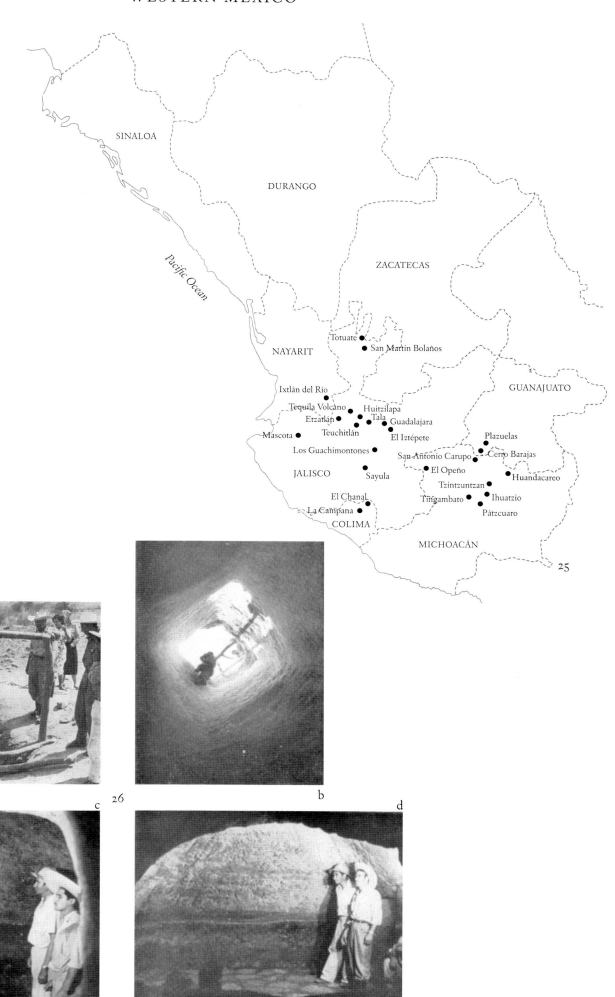

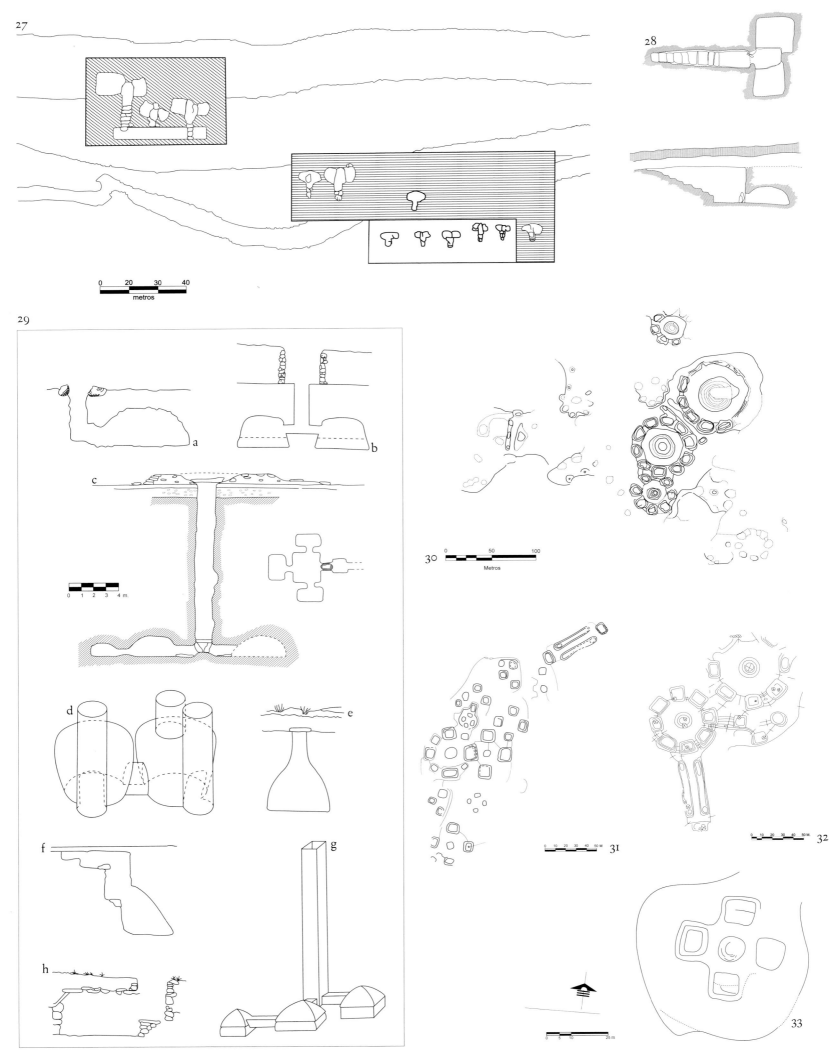

27

28

0 20 30 40
metros

29

a

b

c

0 1 2 3 4 m.

d

e

f

g

h

30

0   50   100
Metros

31

0 10 20 30 40 50 M

32

0 10 20 30 40 50 M.

33

0 5 10   25 m

27. Plan of the cemetery at El Opeño, Michoacán. Formative. (Drawing by Arturo Reséndiz, after Oliveros 2004, 30, fig. 4.)

28. Plan and section of Tomb 7 at El Opeño, Michoacán. (Drawing by Arturo Reséndiz, after Oliveros 2004, 31, fig. 6.)

29. Various types of shaft tombs: (a) Cardona, El Platanar, Colima; (b) Las Cebollas, Nayarit; (c) San Andrés, Jalisco; (d) Pisotita, Bolaños, Jalisco; (e) San Blas and Santa María del Oro, Nayarit; (f) Loma de Santa Barbara, Colima; (g) El Arenal, Etzatlán, Jalisco; (h) Amacueca, Jalisco. (Drawing by Arturo Reséndiz, after various publications.)

30. Plan of Los Guachimontones, Teuchitlán, Jalisco. Late Formative–Early Classic. (Drawing by Arturo Reséndiz, after Weigand 1993, 59.)

31. Plan of the Huitzilapa site, Magdalena, Jalisco. (Drawing by Arturo Reséndiz, after Weigand 1993, 191.)

32. Plan of the Mesa Alta site, Santa Quiteria, Jalisco. (Drawing by Arturo Reséndiz, after Weigand 1993, 193.)

33. Plan of La Noria site, Tala, Jalisco. (Drawing by Arturo Reséndiz, after Weigand 1993, 64.)

34. Ceramic vase painted with a quincuncial design. Shaft tomb culture, Jalisco. Late Formative–Early Classic. Tlallan Museum, Tala, Jalisco. (Drawing by Verónica Hernández Díaz.)

35. Ceramic model with *palo volador* (flying pole). Shaft tomb culture, Nayarit. Late Formative–Early Classic. Yale University Art Gallery. (Drawing by Arturo Reséndiz, after Townsend 1998, 144.)

36. Three kinds of buildings rendered in ceramics. Shaft tomb culture, Nayarit. Late Formative–Early Classic. (Drawing by Arturo Reséndiz, after Von Winning and Hammer 1972, figs. 3, 18, 34, 30.)

34

35

36

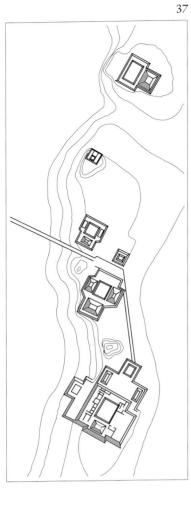

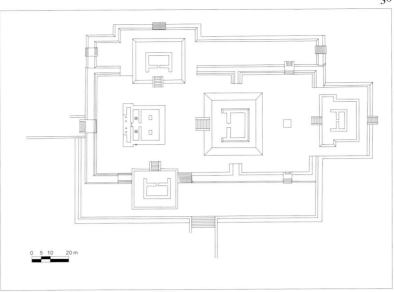

38

0 5 10 20 m

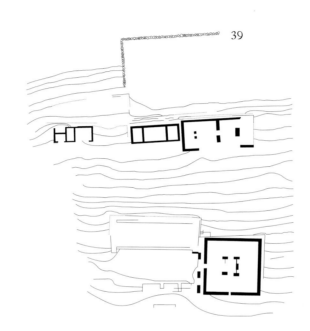

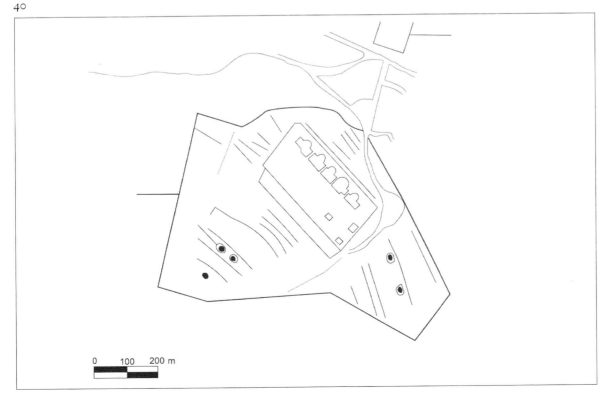

0 100 200 m

37. Architectural complex with sunken patios at San Bartolo Agua Caliente, Guanajuato. Classic. (Drawing by Arturo Reséndiz, after Cárdenas 1999, 65.)

38. Plan of the Casas Tapadas complex at Plazuelas, Guanajuato. Late Classic. (Drawing by Arturo Reséndiz, after Castañeda and Quiróz 2004, 149.)

39. Plan of San Antonio Carupo, Michoacán; at the lower right is a room with columns and an open patio. Late Classic. (Drawing by Arturo Reséndiz, after Faugère-Kalfon 1996, fig. 10.)

40. Plan of the archaeological zone at Tzintzuntzan, Michoacán. Late Postclassic. (Drawing by Verónica Hernández Díaz, after Cárdenas 1996, 31.)

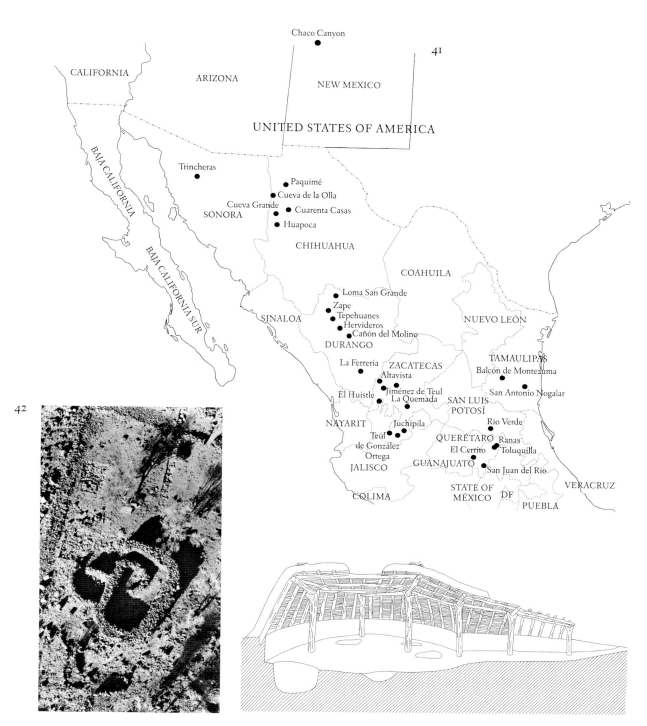

41

42

43

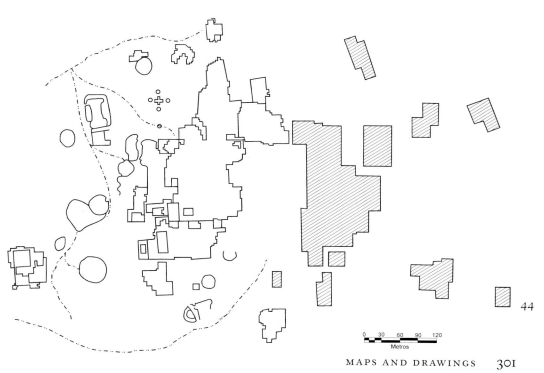

44

41. Map of northern Mexico
showing the principal archaeological sites. (Drawing by Arturo
Reséndiz.)

42. Aerial view of the structure
known as El Caracol at Cerro de
Trincheras, Sonora. Postclassic.
(Photo by Adriel Heisey, from
Braniff, *La Gran Chichimeca*
[2001], 232.)

43. Reconstruction of a pit house
in Sonora. (Drawing by Arturo
Reséndiz, after Plog 1997, 59.)

44. Plan of Paquimé, Chihuahua.
Postclassic. (Drawing by Arturo
Reséndiz, after Schaafsma and
Riley 1999, 97.)

45

46

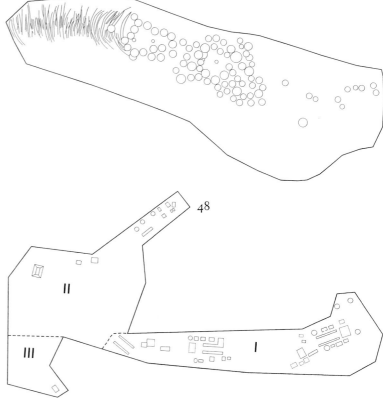

48

47

49

45. Cliff dwelling, Huapoca,
Chihuahua. Postclassic. (Photo
by Verónica Hernández Díaz.)

46. Plan of Balcón de Montezuma,
Tamaulipas. Classic. (Drawing
by Arturo Reséndiz, after Nárez
1992, 19.)

47. Reconstruction of one of the
circular structures at Balcón de
Montezuma, Tamaulipas. Classic.
(Drawing by Arturo Reséndiz,
after Nárez 1992, 22.)

48. Schematic plan of Ranas,
Querétaro. Classic. (Drawing by
Arturo Reséndiz, after Velasco
1991, 256.)

49. Reconstruction of Toluquilla,
Querétaro. Classic. (Drawing by
Arturo Reséndiz, after Mejía and
Herrera 2006, 41.)

50. Plan of La Quemada, Zacatecas. Classic. (Drawing by Arturo
Reséndiz, after Jiménez Betts
2004, 82.)

50

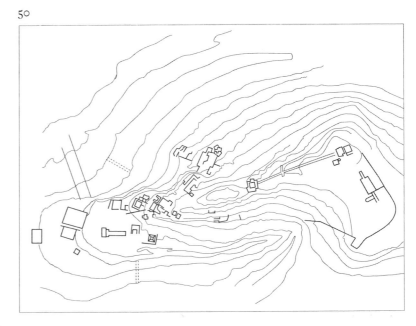

Chapter 8

CENTRAL VERACRUZ

51. Map of central Veracruz showing the principal archaeological sites: (1) Pánuco, (2) Castillo de Teayo, (3) El Tajín, (4) Cerro Grande, (5) Morgadal, (6) Yohualichan, (7) El Pital, (8) Vega de la Peña, (9) Cuajilotes, (10) Los Ídolos, (11) Paxil, (12) Misantla, (13) Vega de Aparicio, (14) Quiahuiztlán, (15) Chalahuite, (16) Zempoala, (17) Sollacuauhtla, (18) Banderilla, (19) Oceloapan, (20) La Joya, (21) El Zapotal, (22) Cerro de las Mesas, (23) La Mojarra, (24) Cotaxtla, (25) Quauhtochco, (26) Maltrata. (Drawing by Annick Daneels, 2008.)

52. Stairway to the North Platform at La Joya. (Photo by Annick Daneels.)

53. Reconstruction of an audience room from the second phase of the North Platform at La Joya. (Drawing by Annick Daneels.)

54. Plan of La Joya, a site of the Late Formative and Classic Periods. (Drawing by Annick Daneels.)

55. Room accessing the North Platform at La Joya, seen from above. (Photo by Annick Daneels.)

56. Reconstruction of the first phase of the main pyramid at La Joya, second century AD. (Drawing by Annick Daneels.)

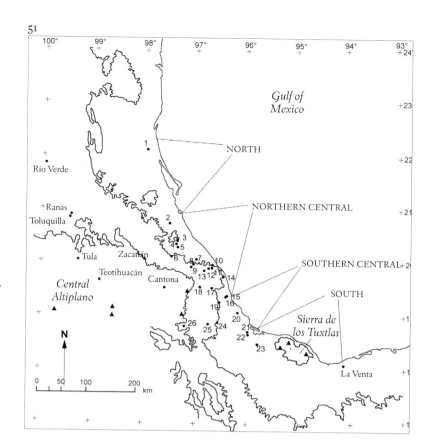

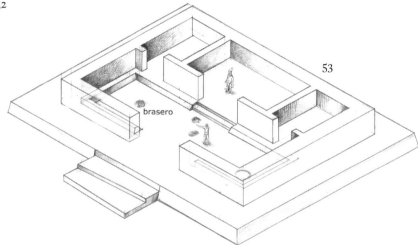

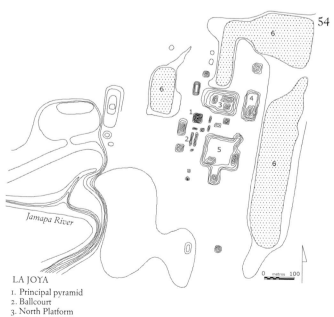

LA JOYA
1. Principal pyramid
2. Ballcourt
3. North Platform
4. Northeast Platform
5. East Platform
6. Cisterns

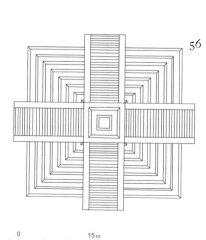

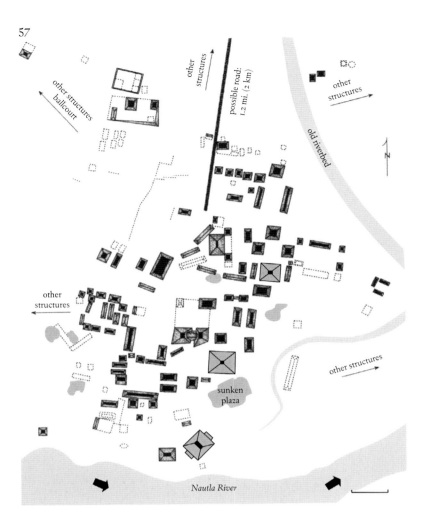

57

other structures
ballcourt

other structures

other structures

possible road: 1.2 mi. (2 km)

old riverbed

other structures

other structures

other structures

sunken plaza

N

Nautla River

57. Plan of El Pital. (Wilkerson 1994.)

58. Top: plan of the sanctuary of Mictlantecuhtli at El Zapotal, AD 600–900; bottom: section of the sanctuary and the nine-stepped access platform in front of it. (Torres et al. 1975.)

59. Reconstruction of the sanctuary at El Zapotal, showing its mural paintings and the terra-cotta *cihua-teteo* figures that were placed there as part of a termination offering. (María Eugenia Maldonado Vite 1996.)

60. Plan of El Tajín, AD 600–1000. Ballcourts (JP) 34–35, 13–14, and 17–27 are perpendicular to a pyramid; JP 11 and 5–6 are parallel to the side of a pyramid; and JP 24–25 is on one side of a plaza. There are even two possible instances of the standard plan, one in the Great Xicalcoliuhqui and the other composed of JP 13–14 and Pyramid 3, as well as isolated ballcourts (30–31 and 30–31 bis, 62–63). (After Wilkerson 1987, incorporating data from the Brüggemann Tajín Project and Pascual 2006.)

61. Plan of the Pyramid of the Niches at El Tajín. (Drawing by García Payón, from Marquina 1951.)

62. Perspective drawing (a) and section (b) of the Great Xicalcoli-uhqui at El Tajín. (Ortega 1995.)

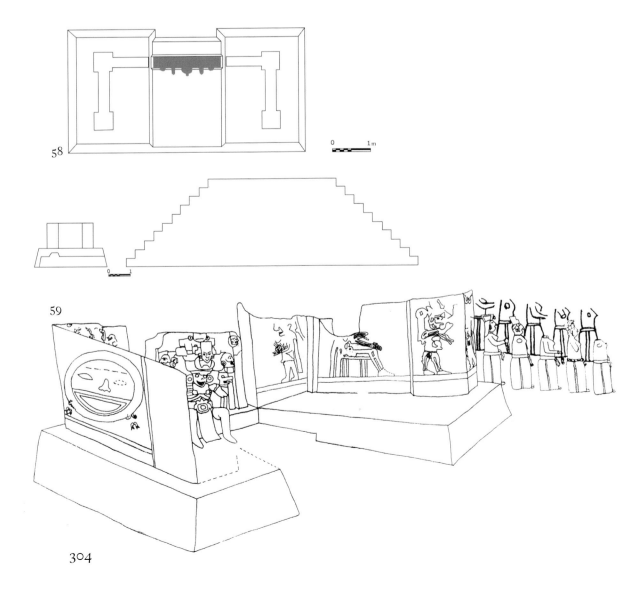

58

0   1 m

59

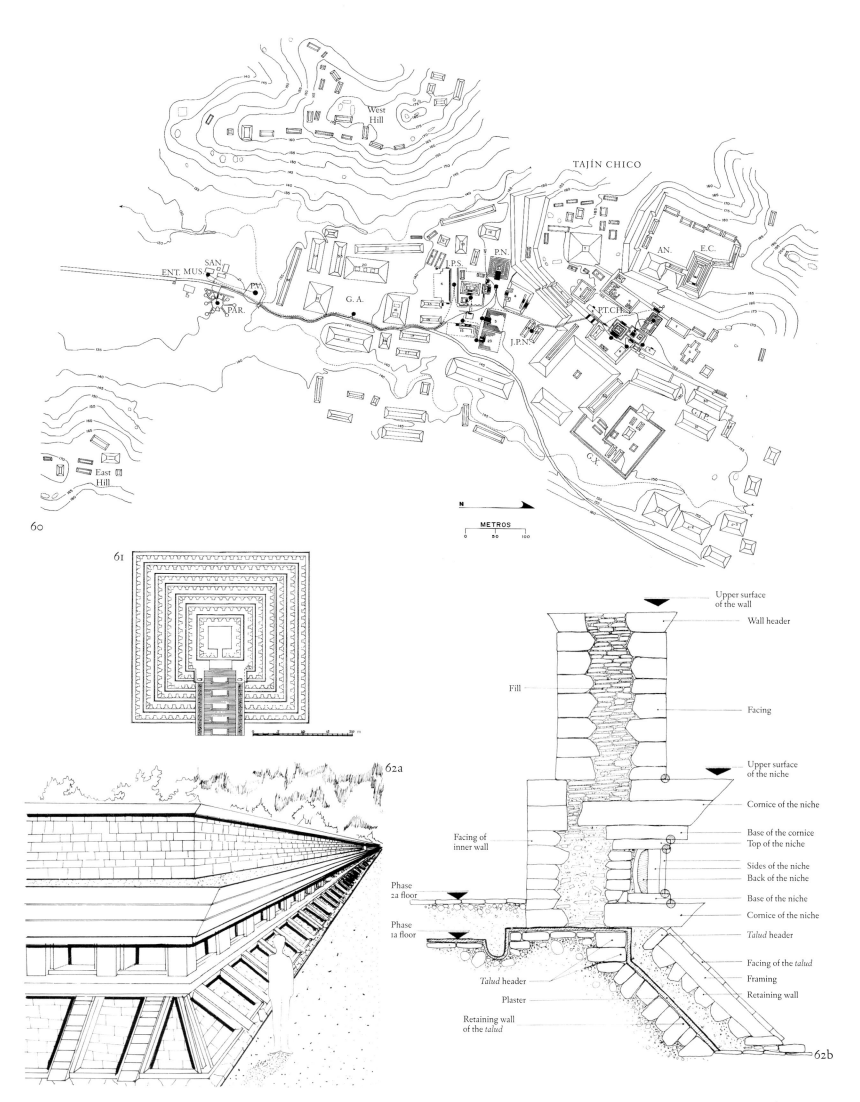

60

61

62a

Upper surface
of the wall

Wall header

Fill

Facing

Upper surface
of the niche

Cornice of the niche

Facing of
inner wall

Base of the cornice
Top of the niche

Sides of the niche
Back of the niche

Base of the niche

Phase
2a floor

Cornice of the niche

Phase
1a floor

Talud header

Facing of the *talud*

Talud header

Framing

Plaster

Retaining wall

Retaining wall
of the *talud*

62b

TAJÍN CHICO

West
Hill

East
Hill

N

METROS

0   50   100

ENT. MUS.   SAN.

PV.

PAR.

G. A.

L.P.S.

P.N.

AN.   E.C.

PT.CH.

J.P.N.

C.J.P.

G.X.

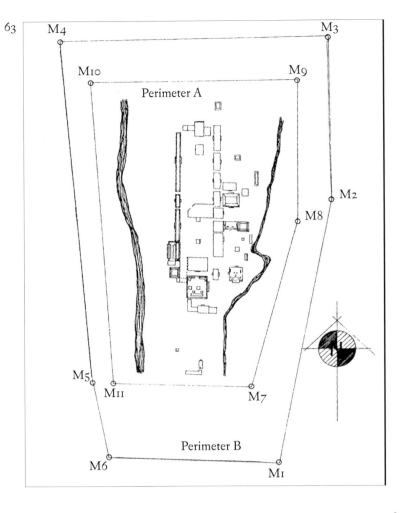

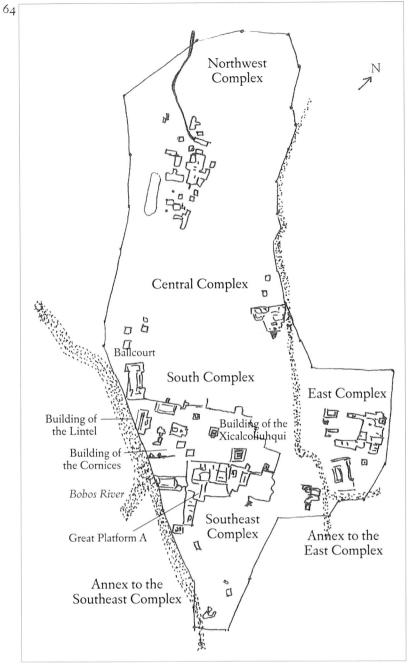

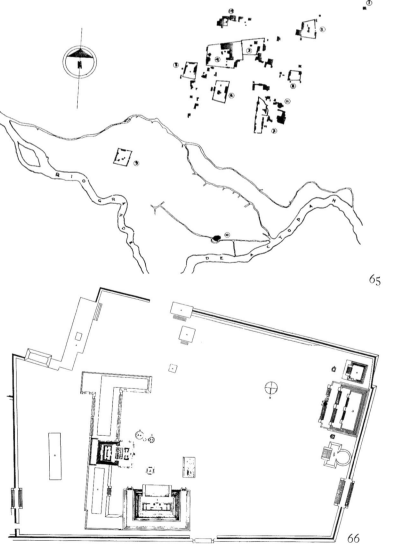

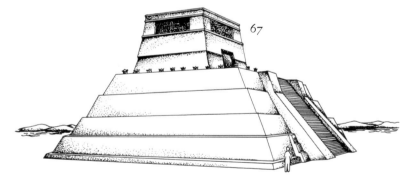

63. Plan of Paxil. Postclassic. (Ruiz 1999.)

64. Plan of Vega de la Peña. Postclassic. (Pérez, in Cortés 1994.)

65. Plan of Zempoala showing its twelve walled compounds. Postclassic. (Marquina 1951.)

66. Plan of the main compound at Zempoala. (Marquina 1951.)

67. Reconstruction of the pyramid at Quauhtochco. Postclassic. (Drawing by Guillermo Reyes, from Medellín 1960, plate 87.)

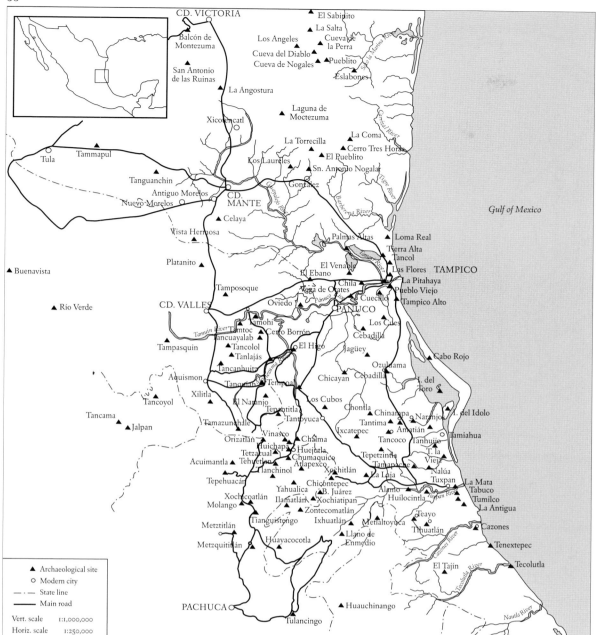

68. Map of the Huastec region, or the Huasteca, showing the principal archaeological sites. (Drawing by Sophie Marchegay, 2007.)

69. Plan of the central area of Tamtoc, San Luis Potosí. Classic. (Stesser Péan et al. 2001, fig. 30.)

70. Plan of the twelve mounds on the north part of the island of Pitahaya, Tampico, Tamaulipas. Excavations revealed that the mounds were composed entirely of oyster shells and compacted sand. Classic. (Drawing by Francisco Mayén, 2006.)

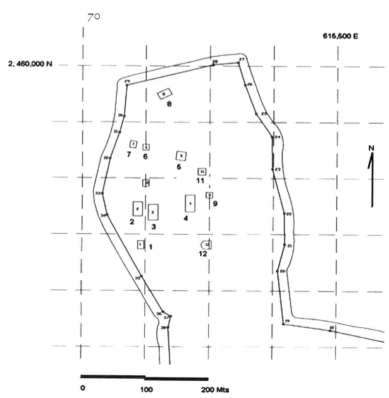

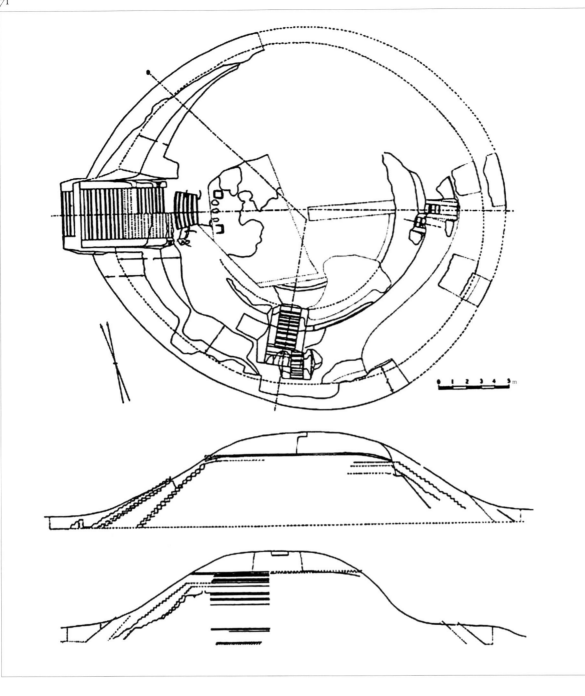

71. Plan and sections of the Pyramid of the Flowers at Las Flores, Tampico, Tamaulipas, showing its five substructures and twenty-six floors of mortar. Early Postclassic. (Ekholm 1944.)

72. Test excavations in Mound 5 at Tancol in Tampico, Tamaulipas, have revealed two phases of construction marked by floors of earth and shell. Late Postclassic. (Drawings by Gustavo A. Ramírez, Archivo Técnico INAH Tamaulipas, 1999.)

73. Altar 1 from Cholula, Puebla, AD 900–1325.

74. Profiles of three Postclassic buildings at Tamtoc. (Stresser Péan 2001.)

75. The Pyramid of La Palma, in the Sierra de la Palma, Altamira, Tamaulipas, as depicted in a lithograph published in 1873 by Alejandro Prieto.

73

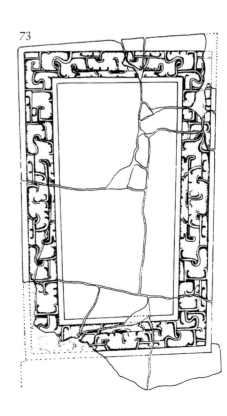

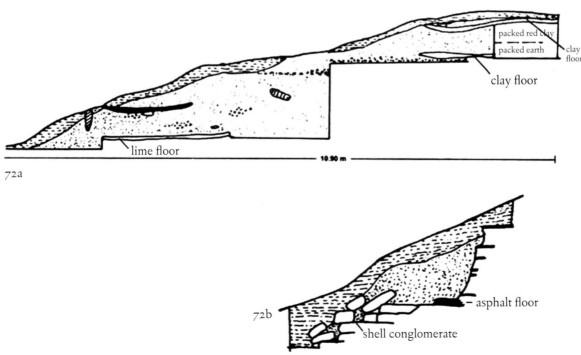

72a

72b

76. Plan of the Postclassic archaeological site of Tamohi, in the municipal area of Tamuín, San Luis Potosí. Of the numerous groups of buildings, only the Great Southern Platform has been extensively explored. (Zaragoza 2003.)

77. Polychromed altar at Tamohi, San Luis Potosí, representing a procession of richly dressed figures. Late Postclassic. (Meade 1962, plate 98.)

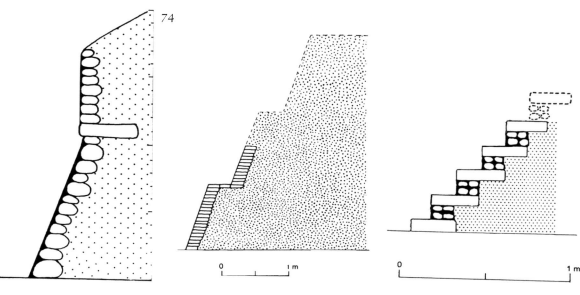

74

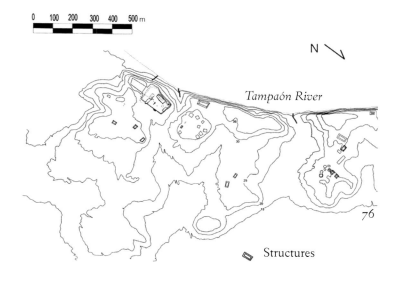

75

77

Tampaón River

N

0 100 200 300 400 500 m

Structures

76

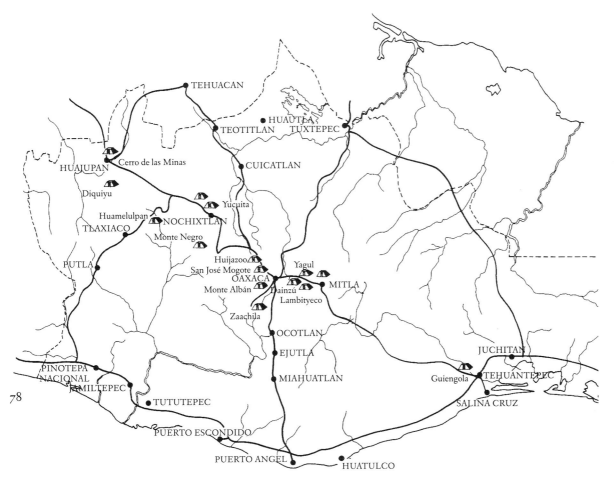

78

78. Map of Oaxaca showing the principal archaeological sites.

79. Plan of Monte Albán, which flourished between 500 BC and AD 900.

80. Relief from the Late Formative site of Dainzú, depicting ballplayers who wear helmets to protect their faces. This protective gear is also depicted in a relief at Monte Albán.

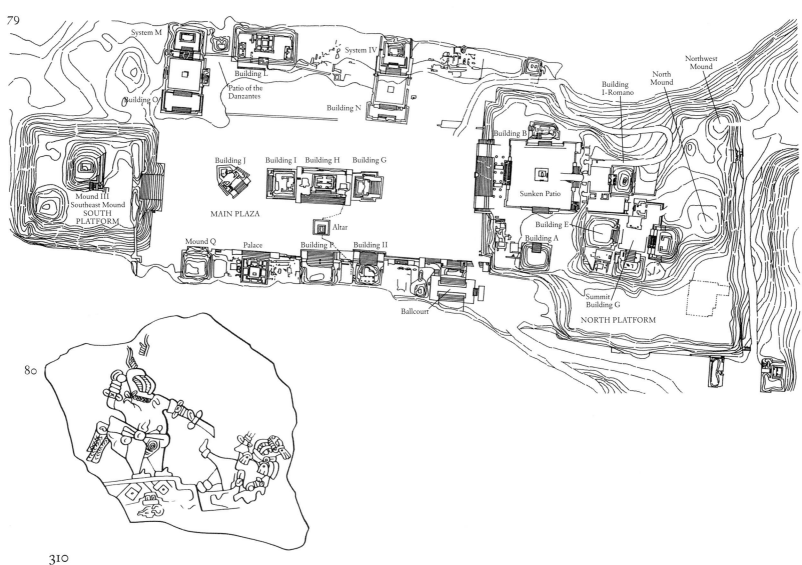

79

80

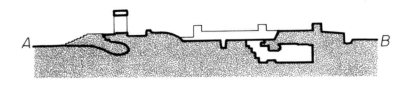

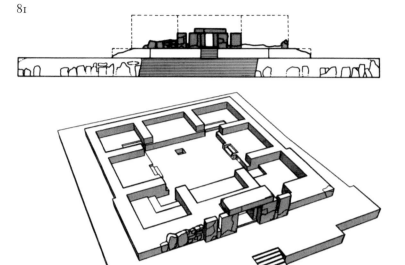

81. Section, elevation, and perspective view of an ancient Oaxacan house with a tomb located beneath the central patio.

82. Plan of Monte Negro, a Highland Mixtec site contemporaneous with Monte Albán, and drawings of two of its buildings. In their use of columns, these structures demonstrate the similarity between the architecture of the mountains and the central valleys of Oaxaca.

83. Section of Tomb 6 at Lambityeco, AD 450–700, showing its relation to the building above it. In Oaxaca, the spaces for the living were located directly above the dwellings of the ancestors.

81

82

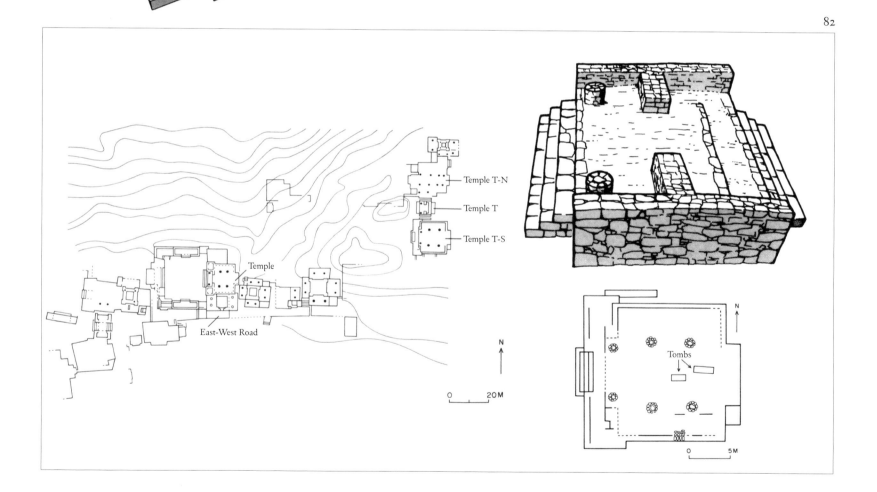

Temple T-N

Temple T

Temple T-S

Temple

East-West Road

0   20M

N

Tombs

N

0   5M

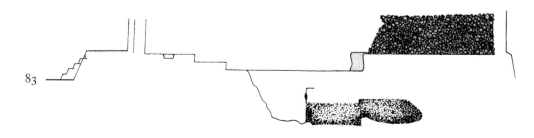

83

84

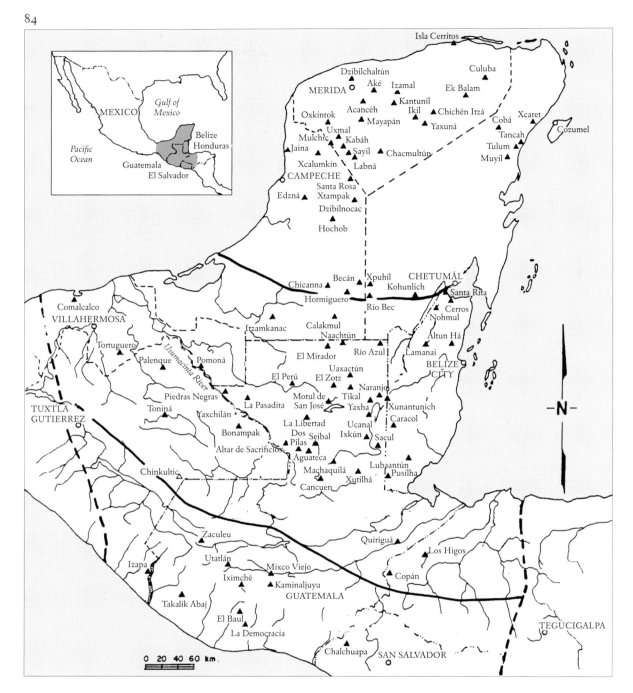

85. Typical Maya thatched house. This simple form is the basis of Maya monumental architecture.

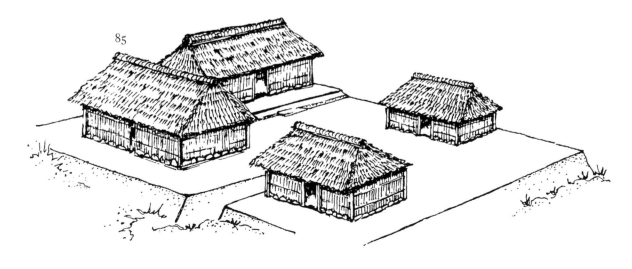

85

86. Plan of the Central Acropolis of Tikal, Guatemala. Over time, this palatial compound grew into a series of six interlocking court-yards, with broad porticoes border-ing the public plazas of the city and secluded spaces within.

87. Drawings of House A at Palenque, Chiapas, showing the innovative vaulting system used to create gracious interior spaces.

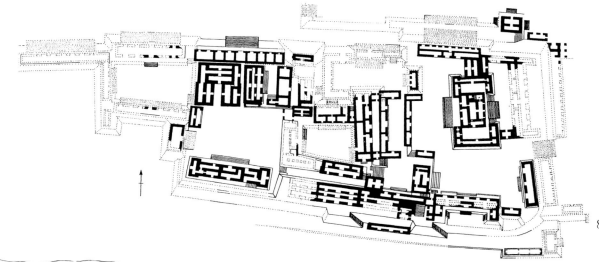

86

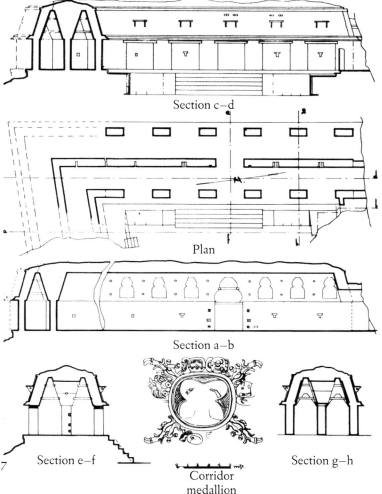

Section c–d

Plan

Section a–b

87   Section e–f

Corridor
medallion

Section g–h

88

88. Plan of Yaxchilán, Chiapas. This city's particular form of ur-banism focused on smaller palace structures, arrayed along the curve of the Usumacinta River and as-cending a steep hillside.

89. Building in the Chenes style. Its entrance is presented as the mouth of the living earth, with paired volutes suggesting eyes just above the door opening. On either side of the doorway, stone images of humble thatched houses are topped with human heads, another metaphor of the house as body. (Drawing by G. Ramírez.)

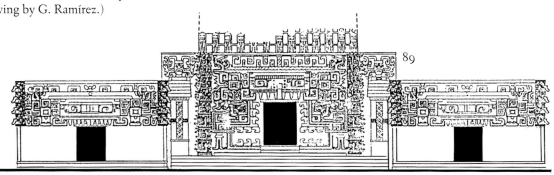

89

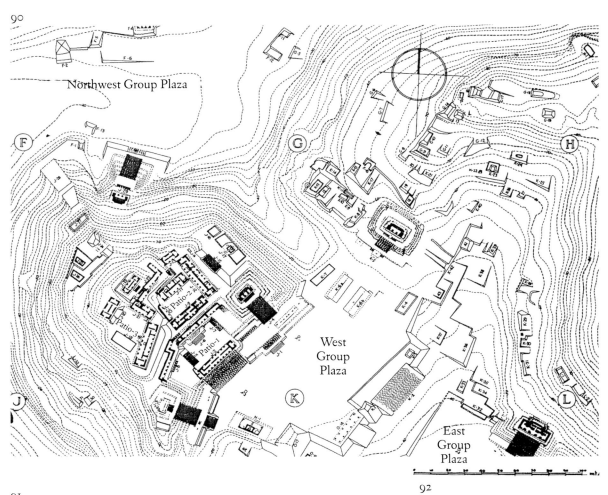

90

Northwest Group Plaza

West Group Plaza

East Group Plaza

90, 91. Plans of the northwestern and southeastern parts of Piedras Negras, Guatemala, a Maya city located on the banks of the Usumacinta River. (After Satterthwaite.)

92. This reconstruction of the Mercado at Chichén Itzá, Yucatán, gives a sense of how the outer colonnade, with its wide benches, would have looked when roofed. Although this building is called the "Market," it was probably one of the last palaces constructed in the city. (After Tatiana Proskouriakoff.)

93. Plan of the Mercado, Chichén Itzá, organized around an open sunken patio surrounded by graceful columns.

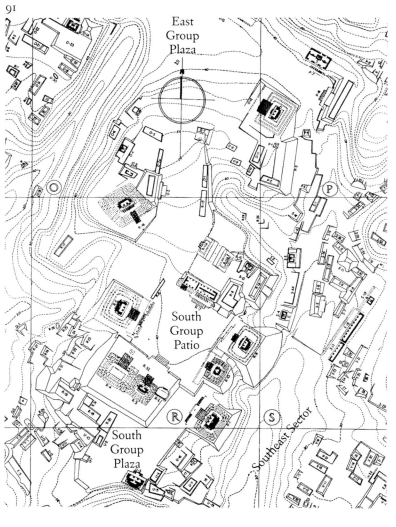

91

East Group Plaza

South Group Patio

South Group Plaza

Southeast Sector

92

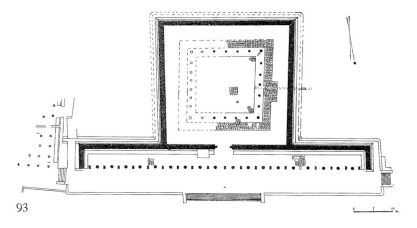

93

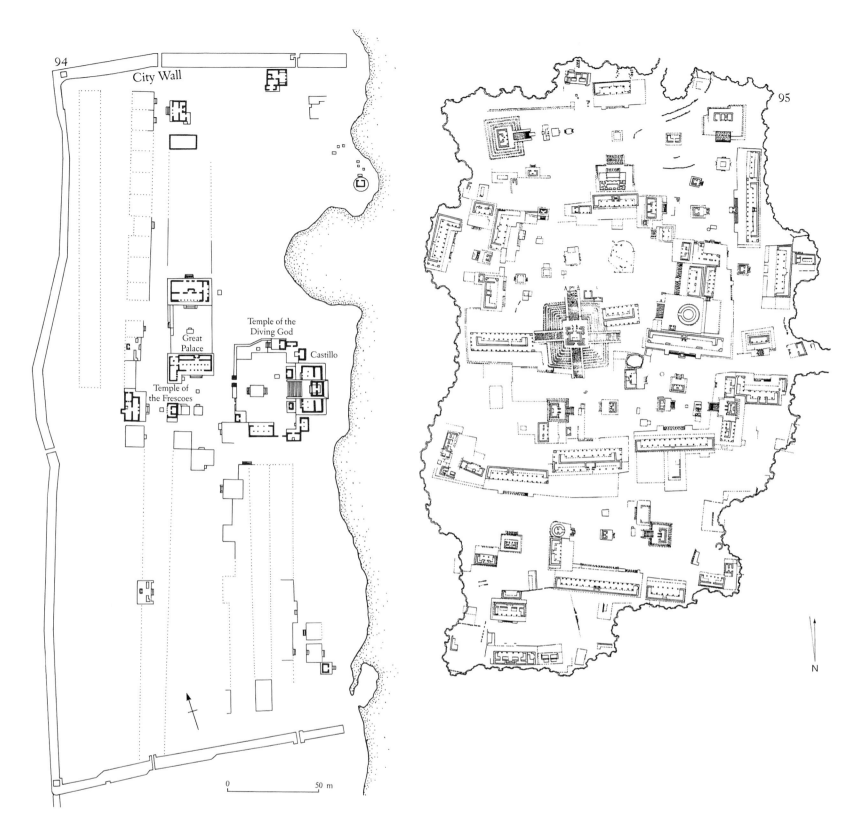

94

City Wall

Temple of the
Diving God

Great
Palace

Castillo

Temple of
the Frescoes

0   50 m

95

N

94. Plan of Tulum, Guatemala. The walls surrounding this city must have served as much to delimit a civic space as to provide defense; the beach within the city walls would have provided an excellent landing area for canoes.

95. Plan of Mayapán, Yucatán. The monumental center of this Postclassic city was surrounded by many residential complexes.

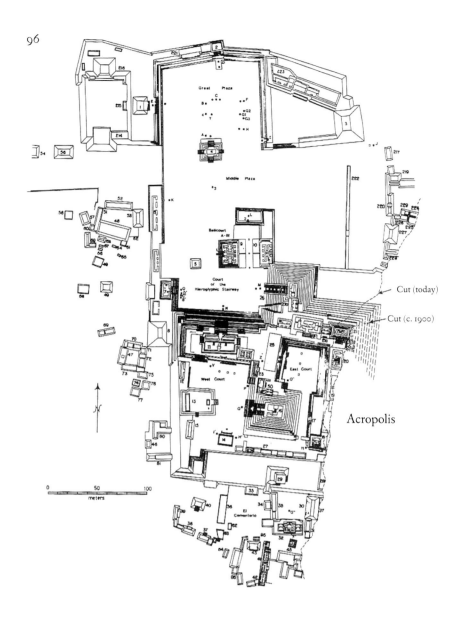

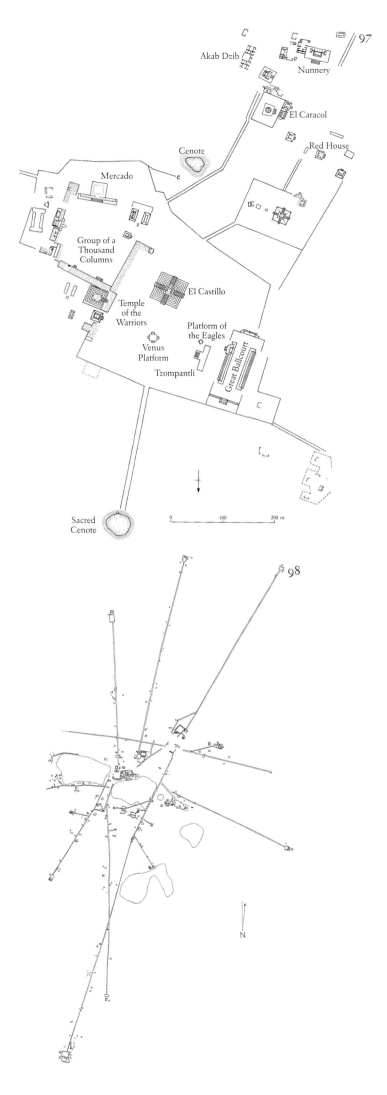

Acropolis

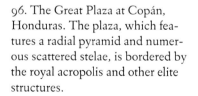

98

96. The Great Plaza at Copán,
Honduras. The plaza, which features a radial pyramid and numerous scattered stelae, is bordered by
the royal acropolis and other elite
structures.

97. Plan of Chichén Itzá. Networks
of sacbes centered around the Nunnery complex and the Great Plaza
connect distant parts of the city.

98. Plan of Cobá, Quintana Roo,
showing the city's sacbes.

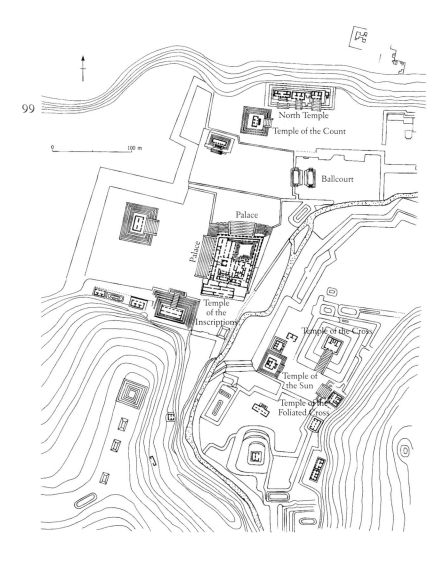

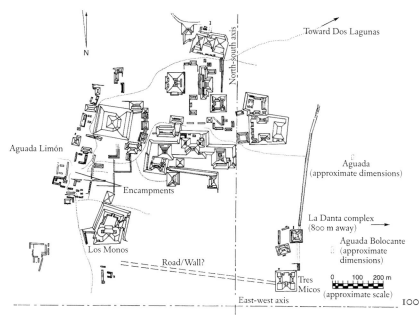

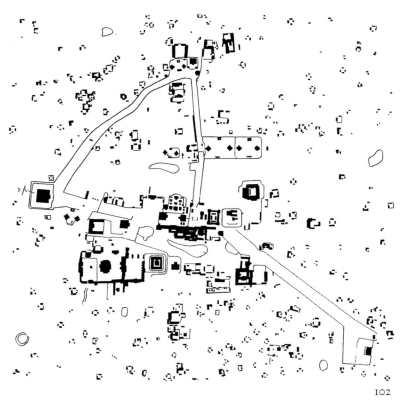

99. Plan of Palenque. Terraced into the side of a mountain with a strategic view of the plain below, Palenque's urban plan makes little use of the sacbes common farther east.

100. Plan of El Mirador, Guatemala, an early Maya city. Many of the key elements of Maya urban planning, such as plazas, sacbes, pyramids, and city walls, were already in place by the third century BC.

101. Plan of Toniná, Chiapas. Only a few structures, such as the ballcourts, are located on the plain; the rest are incorporated into the pyramid-mountain.

102. Plan of Tikal, showing the ceremonial center surrounded by residential structures. (After Kubler 1984.)

NOTES

Chapter 1
Architecture as Art

1. Preziosi 1998, 63.

2. Semper 1989.

3. Clark 2001, 183–209.

4. Marcus and Flannery 1996, 21.

5. The basic concepts of symmetry are *rotation*, such as the symmetry of a flower; *inversion*, such as the difference between the right and left hands; and the combination of these with linear movements in space. There are only a limited number of possible symmetries that can be obtained using regular figures: 230 in three dimensions, and 17 in two. However, by altering the scale of the figures, a greater number of internal harmonies may be obtained. Bernal 1971, 120.

6. Hansen 1998, 68.

7. Houston 1998, 25.

8. López Luján 2007.

9. Marcus 1983, 207.

10. Yoneda 1996, 154.

11. Hansen 1998, 66.

12. Cabrera Castro 2002, 195–217.

13. Marcus and Flannery 1996, 180.

14. Fash 1998.

Chapter 2
The Hidden Meanings of Architecture

1. Galindo Trejo 2002.

2. Heyden 1981, 1–39.

3. Martínez Donjuán 1994, 143–63.

4. Thompson 1983, 115–27.

5. Sotelo Santos 1988.

6. Sotelo Santos 1996.

7. Ponce de León 1982.

8. Galindo Trejo 1994, 121–89; Sprajc 2001, 201–38.

9. Malström 1991, 37–47.

10. Galindo Trejo 2001a, 295–98.

11. Sprajc 2001, 280–84.

12. Galindo Trejo et al. 1998, 179; Galindo Trejo 1999.

13. Aveni, Gibbs, and Hartung 1975; Galindo Trejo et al. 2001.

14. Galindo Trejo 2007.

15. Morante 1995; Galindo Trejo 2003.

16. Galindo Trejo 2000.

17. Galindo Trejo 2004.

18. Galindo Trejo 2003, 56.

19. Casares Contreras 2002, 142–45.

20. Ibid., 117–27.

21. Galindo Trejo et al. 2001.

22. Galindo Trejo 2001b.

23. Córdoba 1886.

24. Galindo Trejo 2007.

25. Morante 1995; Morante 2001.

26. Alcina Franch 1993, 185.

27. Galindo Trejo 2001c, 31; Galindo Trejo 2007.

28. Tichy 1978; Galindo Trejo 1994.

29. Galindo Trejo and Ruiz Gallut 1998.

Chapter 3
Architectural Function and Technique

1. Amábilis 1956, 62/63, 100.

2. Haselberger 1986.

3. Frankl 1945, 46–60.

4. Moessel 1931.

5. Taladoire 1981.

6. Uriarte 1992.

7. Garza Camino 2002.

8. López Austin 1984, 65.

Chapter 4
Pre-Olmec and Olmec Architecture

1. Pool 2007, 7.

2. Clark 1994, 31–43.

3. Hill et al. 1998, 878–79.

4. Lesure and Blake 2002.

5. Marcus 1996, 87–88.

6. Symonds et al. 2002.

7. Cyphers 1997a and b.

8. Drucker 1952; Drucker, Heizer, and Squier 1959.

9. González Lauck 1997.

10. Heizer, Graham, and Napton 1968.

11. Hirth 1987.

12. Fash 1987.

13. Prindiville and Grove 1987.

14. Neidelberger 2000, 173; Tolstoy 1989, 101.

15. Love 2002, 56–59.

Chapter 5
The Central Altiplano

1. For a more complete perspective on the geography of Mexico, see the *Atlas nacional de México*, edited by the Geographic Institute of the UNAM, and *México: Una visión geográfica* by Atlántida Coll de Hurtado.

2. For more on the interactions between the different regions of Mesoamerica, see Richard E. Blanton et al., *Ancient Mesoamerica: A Comparison of Change in Three Regions* (1993), and William T. Sanders and Barbara J. Price, *Mesoamerica: The Evolution of a Civilization* (1968).

3. Yamamoto 2001, 158.

4. Heizer and Bennyhoff 1957, 96.

5. Sanders and Santley 1983, 243–91.

6. Spence 1987, 434.

7. Sanders and Santley 1983, 243–91.

8. López Bajonero 2006, 9.

9. Rosas and Vega 1997.

10. Sugiyama and Cabrera Castro 2006, 16.

11. Sugiyama and López Luján 2006, 50.

12. Matos Moctezuma 2000, 189.

13. Garza Tarazona de González, forthcoming.

14. Uruñuela, Plunket, and Amparo Robles n.d., 183.

15. Plunket and Uruñuela n.d., 167.

16. In *Twin City Tales: A Hermeneutical Reassessment of Tula and Chichén Itzá* (1995), Lindsay Jones undertakes a very complete analysis of the similarities and differences between the two cities. Also interesting is Roger Bartra's *El Salvaje en el espejo* (1992).

17. Mastache, Cobean, and Healan 2002, 60.

18. Durán 1994, 43–44.

19. Pasztory 1983, 105.

20. Matos Moctezuma 1987, 32.

21. Townsend, 1992, 142.

22. Ibid., 101.

Chapter 6
Western Mexico

1. The ceramic art of western Mexico, especially the naturalistic sculpture from the shaft tombs, is emblematic of the uniqueness of this region within the Mesoamerican sphere. The renowned artistic quality of these ceramics, together with the limited investigation and institutional protection of its cultural contexts, has led to intense and prolonged looting and collecting, from at least the late nineteenth century to the present. Another factor that has contributed to the profound denial of this region's ancient indigenous past is the chaotic circumstances under which the Spanish Conquest took place: on their arrival in this vast territory, the invaders encountered an extraordinary ethnic and linguistic diversity, which complicated their rule. Indigenous rebellions and plagues decimated the original population, and there were political disputes between the conquistadores of this region and those of central Mexico. Finally, with regard to the sources, there are few colonial documents that describe the Pre-Columbian situation in the region (see Hernández Díaz, forthcoming a).

2. The concept of negative space in general is treated in Roth 2003, 54.

3. Oliveros and De los Ríos 1993, 47.

4. The archaeological excavations at the site have been directed by Eduardo Noguera and Arturo Oliveros (Oliveros 2004; in this work, see the appendix, 175–79, for Noguera's text on El Opeño, originally published in 1942).

5. Oliveros 2004, 33–35.

6. Joseph B. Mountjoy is the discoverer of the shaft tombs in Mascota, Jalisco, associated with the Capacha culture (Mountjoy 2004a, and Mountjoy and Sandford 2006, 326).

7. Many archaeologists have contributed to our understanding of the shaft tomb culture, including Isabel Kelly, Stanley V. Long, Peter T. Furst, José Corona, Joseph B. Mountjoy, Javier Galván, Ángeles Olay, Teresa Cabrero, and Gabriela Zepeda.

8. Other types of burial included rectangular and trapezoidal graves excavated in the *tepetate* (Disselhoff 1931, 532, fig. 1a–b), direct burials (i.e., in the topsoil) (Cabrero 2005, 196; Mountjoy and Sandford 2006, 316), and cremations, with the cremated remains buried in urns (Cabrero 2005, 19; Mountjoy and Sandford 2006) or directly in the ground (Mountjoy and Sandford 2006, 316).

9. The concepts of the artistic integration of the four art forms of the shaft tomb culture and the complementary nature of their naturalistic and geometric styles are derived from my Ph.D. dissertation (Hernández Díaz, forthcoming).

10. Furst 1966, 289.

11. In other regions of Mesoamerica there are only isolated examples of tombs in the *tepetate*, such as at Chilpancingo, Guerrero (Martínez Donjuán 1994, 153): Cuicuilco, Mexico City (Muller 1990); Coixtlahuaca and Jaltepetongo, Oaxaca (Bernal 1948–49 and Matadamas 1997, respectively); Huandacareo, Michoacán (Macías 1990, 153); and Guatemalan sites like La Lagunita, Los Cimientos, and Zacaleu (Ichon and Arnauld 1985). It should be noted that these tombs are simpler in form than those of the shaft tomb culture of western Mexico, and not all of them belong to the same period. Hollows carved in

the subsoil were more commonly used for storage or as garbage dumps.

12. Located in San Juan de los Arcos, in the municipal area of Tala, Jalisco (Weigand 1996, 16), this tomb was looted. In western Mexico, looting is a traditional occupation in which different schools of *moneros* or professional grave robbers are recognized. Implicated in this activity are sophisticated networks of merchants and collectors on a national and international scale, at times with the support of the local authorities.

13. This tomb is located in San Andres, Jalisco (Weigand and Beekman 1998, 40).

14. In the Valley of Banderas in Puerto Vallarta, Jalisco, human burials and offerings have been reported in the shafts (Mountjoy and Sandford 2006).

15. This tomb at El Arenal became known following a report of looting, and its contents had already been robbed when José Coroña Núñez made his scientific investigation (1955). Despite the efforts of the archaeologists who work in the region, very few shaft tombs have been found in their original state, and even fewer have undergone an exhaustive and multidisciplinary analysis of their contents.

16. As recorded in the basin of Sayula, Jalisco (Valdez 1998, 227).

17. See Galván 1991, 111.

18. Olsen Bruhns 1994, 368.

19. In northeastern Peru these are the Boro, Ocaina, and Huitoto; and in Colombia, the Ica and Kogui, of the Sierra Nevada de Santa Marta (Long 1967).

20. Weigand and Beekman 1998, 35–36. Weigand's breakthrough consisted in seeing what others did not. It happens that archaeological investigations had been concentrated on the search for unlooted shaft tombs, because the absence of surface architecture was taken for granted. Since 1969, Weigand has dedicated himself to the discovery and study of these sites, mainly in Jalisco. Other academics have joined this enterprise.

21. On the ballgame, see, among others, Taladoire 1994 and 2001, and Uriarte, ed., 1992.

22. Weigand 1993. The area around the Tequila volcano comprises the municipalities of Tequila, Magdalena, San Antonio Escobedo, Etzatlán, Ahualulco, Teuchitlán, Tala, El Arenal, and Amatitan.

23. Complexes with concentric circular plans have been located in the metropolitan area of Guadalajara (recorded by Javier Galván, in Gómez Gastelúm n.d., 22); in the extreme north of Jalisco, along the Canyon of Bolaños, at Totuate Totuate (Kelley 1974, 25; Hrdlicka 1903), Cerro de Colotlán, Cerro Prieto (Weigand 1993, 380–85), and Pochotitan (Cabrero 2005, 42); on the northeastern shore of Lake Chapala (Weigand and García 1996, 294); in Guaynamota, Nayarit (as noted in Weigand 1996, 25); at La Florida, Zacatecas (Jaramillo Luque 1995, 174); and at Comala, Colima (Serna 1991).

24. In his definition of the Teuchitlán tradition, Weigand postulates that the central high plains of Jalisco constituted a key economic area, which underwent a differential development that was imposed upon other regional or subregional cultures within the shaft tomb region (Weigand 2004, 218). In my opinion, this conclusion is too hasty, and I have preferred to emphasize the cultural unity of the communities that developed in this region (Nayarit, Jalisco, Colima, and bordering areas of Zacatecas and Michoacán) between 300 BC and AD 600, and which shared the characteristic architectural forms of the shaft tombs and the *guachimontones*, as well as a naturalistic style of ceramic art. Given our lack of data (due to the limited number of archaeological projects and the extensive destruction of ancient remains), rather than a simple hierarchy of center and periphery based on economic domination, for now it seems more convenient to speak of societies that shared basic cultural features such as religion or artistic expressions of their cosmology (Hernández Díaz, forthcoming b).

25. Weigand 2004, 222.

26. Weigand and García 2002, 134–37.

27. As seen in the plan of the site at El Arenal drawn by Stanley V. Long (1966), who studied in detail the funerary aspects of the shaft tomb culture in central Jalisco. It should be noted that Long marked the surface mounds in his plan; however, neither he nor the many other archaeologists who visited the site realized that they are arranged radially. That this could not be seen until the *guachimontones* were discovered is a clear symptom of the strong prejudices that completely denied the possibility of this architecture's existence.

28. On the symbolic function of architecture in general, see Arnheim 2001 [1975], 162–71.

29. For a general analysis regarding the center, see Arnheim, 1984.

30. This division into four parts, or a larger even number of segments (8, 10, 12, or 16 in the case of the *guachimontones*), has many cross-cultural meanings: the four ages of man (infancy, youth, adulthood, and old age), the four seasons, the four elements (earth, wind, air, and fire), the four evangelists, the twelve months, the twelve apostles (cf. Pajares Ayuela 2001, 241).

31. For a discussion of the quincunx in classical and medieval Europe, see Pajares Ayuela 2001.

32. Hernández Díaz, forthcoming b.

33. Aside from Ixtlán del Río, ceramic architectural models were made in various local styles in Jalisco and Nayarit. Almost all known examples were looted, and most are found in U.S. collections; their origin is presumed to be funerary.

34. Von Winning 1996, 284.

35. Weigand and García 2002, 143.

36. Von Winning and Hammer 1972, 23, 25.

37. Hernández Díaz, 2004 350–53.

38. Von Winning and Hammer 1972, 17–19.

39. Weigand and García 2002, 138–39.

40. Of the ceramic architectural models that I know of, only one is painted with circular forms, and these are negative spaces with some dots in the interior.

41. As noted by Von Winning and Hammer 1972, 17.

42. On the symbolism of this *Wixárika* art, see for example Fresan 2002 and Kindl 2003.

43. Sánchez and Marmolejo Morales 1990; Cárdenas 1999a.

44. Cárdenas 1999b.

45. See chapter 7 of this volume, on northern Mexico.

46. Cárdenas 1999b.

47. See Zepeda García-Moreno 2005.

48. Filini 2004 inventories the isolated signs of the presence of Teotihuacán in western Mexico, and confirms that the evidence of direct contact is flimsy. On the other hand, at Teotihuacán there have been found ceramic sculptures and vases that suggest the presence of people from Michoacán in the city (Gómez Chávez 2002).

49. Castañeda López and Quiroz Rosales 2004.

50. Carl Sauer, Isabel Kelly, Donald Brand, Gordon F. Ekholm, and Clement W. Meighan are among the pioneers in the study of the so-called Aztatlán culture, complex, or tradition. It should be noted that the archaeologists Gabriela Zepeda and José Carlos Beltrán set the beginning of Aztatlán culture at AD 700.

51. Meighan, ed., 1976.

52. Mountjoy 2004b, 361–64; Beltrán 2004.

53. Gabriela Zepeda has carried out the most recent archaeological work at Ixtlán del Río. She published the results of this exhaustive project, as well as those of previous investigations, in 1994.

54. Carot 2004.

55. See Hers 1989.

56. And likewise in other cultural and artistic expressions, such as the sculpted figure of the *chacmool*, the use of copper and turquoise rattles, and the skull racks or *tzompantlis* (cf. Hernández Díaz 2006b).

57. On Cerro Barajas, see Pereira, Migeon, and Michelet 2005; and on San Antonio Carupo, Faugère-Kalfon 1996, 39, 41, 134.

58. Hers 1995, 96–97.

59. Pollard 1993, 29.

60. Historical facts about the Purépecha are recorded in the voice of their elite, in an account attributed to Fray Jerónimo de Alcála (1988). Archaeological investigations have confirmed these elite burials (cf. Cabrera 1987, 560–64).

61. In the field I observed ten engraved *janamus* in the *yácatas*. Later bibliographical research has allowed me to add another six.

62. Hernández Díaz 2006b. I recorded the engraved *janamus* at Tzintzuntzan in 2000.

63. Archaeologists report that the *yácatas* were found in a ruinous state, with large quantities of rubble surrounding them. However, some engraved *janamus* were still embedded in the pyramids, indicating their scattered distribution (Acosta 1939; Cabrera 1987).

64. Hernández Díaz 2006a, b.

Chapter 7
Northern Mexico

1. Paul Kirchhoff's analyses give us some guidelines for the characterization of ancient northern Mexico. Among other works, Braniff 1996–97a [1975] and López Austin and López Luján 1996, 19–75, raise interesting questions about the definition and subdivision of this vast territory, also called the "Gran Chichimeca."

2. In a broader sense, this region should also include Nuevo León, Coahuila, San Luis Potosí, Aguascalientes, Guanajuato, and Baja California; however, there are several reasons to exclude these states from the present work.

Nuevo León, Coahuila, and Baja California were inhabited mainly by nomadic groups, whose material culture was not prolific and of whose architecture—which must have been perishable—little remains.

In San Luis Potosí, the sites with the most noteworthy Pre-Columbian architecture are associated with the Huastec culture, and therefore will be discussed in chapter 9 of this book. Another cultural development in this state is that of Río Verde, studied by Dominique Michelet; we have little formal data about its architecture, but the existence of many circular and quadrangular ceremonial structures, as well as some plazas and ballcourts, may be noted (Michelet 1996).

The archaeological data on Aguascalientes is simply too limited to discuss. As for Guanajuato, it belongs more to western Mexico—on which see chapter 6 of this volume—because the cultural developments that took place there (the Chupícuaro culture, the architectural tradition of the sunken patios, and settlements associated with initial stage of the Tarascan state) are connected to the history of that region, and to a certain extent even that of central Mexico. However, I do recognize the major reciprocal influences that existed between the ancient societies of Guanajuato and those of the northern region.

3. In 1835 and 1836, Texas seceded from Mexico and was a sovereign republic until 1845, when it was admitted to the United States. Shortly afterward, following its defeat in the Mexican-American War of 1846–48, Mexico ceded Alta California and New Mexico under the treaty of Guadalupe Hidalgo. In 1853, Mexico also sold Mesilla, a territory located in northern Chihuahua and Sonora, to the neighboring country. (For a synthesis of these and other interesting border incidents, see Aboites Aguilar 1997).

4. As previously noted, the state of Guanajuato may also be considered part of the northern region of Mesoamerica.

5. This area has been called Oasisamerica.

6. This territory, inhabited in antiquity by nomads, is identified as part of Aridoamerica (together with part of what is now the American Southwest); however, this characterization is problematic, given the varied cultural mosaic that this region presents (see López Austin and López Luján 1996, 27–28).

7. On the history and archaeology of the nomads, see *La gran chichimeca*, edited by Beatriz Braniff, a work that also discusses the sedentary cultures of ancient northern Mexico.

8. Our knowledge of the Trincheras tradition is based on the research directed by Randall H. McGuire and Elisa Villalpando. The data provided in the present text is based on Villalpando 2001.

9. Guevara Sánchez 1994–95, 341, based on the archaeological investigations of Charles Di Peso, who carried out the fundamental studies of the Casas Grandes culture. This brief text on Paquimé is drawn from the work of Guevara Sánchez, and Braniff 1997b.

10. Villalpando 2001, 226–28.

11. Balcón de Montezuma was investigated by Jesús Narez, on whose account (1992, 7–43) this section is based.

12. Aside from the mountain culture of Ranas and Toluquilla, at least another three cultural traditions can be distinguished in the state of Querétaro. In the northeastern part of the Sierra Gorda, the sites of Jalpan and Tancama belong to the Huastec sphere, and therefore will not be dealt with in this chapter. In central southern Querétaro, El Cerrito is clearly associated with the Toltec culture of Tula, Hidalgo. And in the valley of San Juan del Río, in the southern part of the state, several sites show links to the architectural tradition of the sunken patios that flourished in Guanajuato (see chapter 6, on western Mexico). On the ancient history of Querétaro, see Crespo and Brambila, eds., 1991.

13. The most recent archaeological investigations of Ranas and Toluquilla were carried out principally by Margarita Velasco Mireles, Elizabeth Mejía Pérez Campos, and Alberto Herrera Muñoz. Their work has also led to the consolidation and restoration of the monuments at these sites, and their opening to the public. The information in this text is derived from their works: Velasco Mireles 1990, 1991, and 2006; Velasco Mireles, ed., 1997; Mejía Pérez Campos 2001 and 2002; and Mejía Pérez Campos and Herrera Muñoz 2006. It should also be noted that the ancient mining activity in the Sierra Gorda has been studied by Adolphus Langenscheidt.

14. In Durango, the Chalchihuites culture developed between AD 600 and 1200 (Hers 2001a, 68). Based on her research, Marie-Areti Hers has proposed that we revisit the broader notion of the Chalchihuites culture, including its territorial extent and chronology (Hers 1989, 39–45). It should be noted that there have been many other studies of this culture, and likewise, a variety of interpretations. Among the most thorough archaeological investigations were those of Charles J. Kelley (1971).

15. See Hers 2001b, 131.

16. Hers 2001b, 139–47.

17. This account of La Quemada is derived principally from Jiménez 2004 and Hers 2001b.

18. Hers 1995, 104–5.

19. Hers 2001b, 150, 152.

Chapter 8
Central Veracruz

1. Miller 1991; Kaufmann and Justeson 2001.

2. Drucker 1943; Daneels 2008.

3. Stark 2003.

4. Daneels 2002; Stark 2003.

5. Eighty-two feet (25 meters), according to Escalona's 1937 report.

6. Lira 1991; Daneels 2005.

7. Stark 1999.

8. Andrade 2002.

9. Drucker 1943, 9, 12, 19–24.

10. See also Dirección 2003; Andrade 2002.

11. See Inomata and Houston 2001.

12. Wilkerson 1994.

13. Wilkerson 1994 and personal communication, 1998.

14. Torres 1972, 2004; Ortega 2000; Maldonado 1996; Wyllie 2008.

15. Daneels 2002.

16. Daneels 2002, 179.

17. Daneels 2002.

18. Jiménez Lara 1991; Pascual Soto 2006.

19. Márquez 1804.

20. García Payón 1976; Villalobos 1986; Wilkerson 1987; Brüggemann 1991, 1992b, 1994–95, 2001; Pescador 1992.

21. Pascual 2006, 149.

22. Brüggemann 1991, 81.

23. García Payón 1976: 9.

24. Wilkerson 1987; Brüggemann 1994–95.

25. Villalobos 1986; Brüggemann 1994–95.

26. García Payón 1976.

27. Wilkerson 1987; Ortega and García 1991.

28. García Cook 1981.

29. Marquina 1951.

30. Laporte 1989.

31. Fahmel 1991.

32. Valenzuela 1945.

33. Daneels and Miranda Flores 1998.

34. Jiménez 1991; Vásquez Zárate 1997.

35. García Payón 1971.

36. Arellanos and Beauregard 1981.

37. Lira in Cuevas et al. 1995; Ladrón de Guevara 1999.

38. Ortega Guevara 1995.

39. Daneels 1992, 2009; Navarrete Hernández and Ortega Guevara 1992.

40. Merino Carrión and García Cook 1987, 58.

41. Michelet 1984.

42. Mejía 2009.

43. Braniff 2001; Hers 2001.

44. Ruiz Gordillo 1985.

45. Cortés Hernández 1994.

46. Arellanos 1997.

47. García Payón 1950; Medellín Zenil 1960, 160–66; Izquierdo 1986.

48. García Márquez 2005.

49. Brüggemann et al. 1991.

50. García Márquez 2005.

Chapter 9
The Huastec Region

1. In the municipal area of Aldama, Tamaulipas.

2. Merino and García 1987.

3. Ekholm 1944; MacNeish 1954.

4. Manrique, in Ochoa Sálas 1990.

5. Hosler and Stresser Péan 1992, 1215.

6. On common land bearing the same name, in the township of Panuco, 3 miles (5 kilometers) south of Vichinchijol (Arias Melo Granados 1982, 90). The site was explored in the late 1970s by the Huastec Archaeological Project under the direction of Beatriz L. Merino Carrión and Ángel García Cook.

7. Merino Carrión and García Cook 2002, 2004.

8. According to the plan on page 93 of Arias Melo Granados 1982, 93. The number of mounds illustrated in this plan does not agree with the sketch of the same site included as figure 19 of this thesis, nor with the site description on page 95.

9. Arias 1982, 95.

10. Ibid., 183.

11. Some researchers believe that platforms and mounds were principally intended to protect dwellings from floods. However, there are early sites with large platforms and mounds located on high hilltops, far from any water.

12. In the municipal areas of Tamuín and Ebano, San Luis Potosí. Excavated during the L. T. Champayán–Anahuác Potencia Archaeological Salvage Project (Ramírez Castilla et al. 2001).

13. Ramírez Castilla et al. 2001.

14. Many Pre-Columbian *jagüeyes* continue to be used and maintained in order to water cattle.

15. García Payón 1978, 416.

16. Ochoa Sálas 1984, 57.

17. In the municipal area of Panuco, Veracruz, 9 miles (15 kilometers) west of Tampico.

18. Ekholm 1944, 420–21.

19. Meade 1942, 167.

20. In the municipal area of Tamuín, 11 miles (18 kilometers) south of the municipal headquarters.

21. There is an ongoing debate regarding the natural or artificial origin of these elevations.

22. Stresser Péan 2001, 77–88.

23. Patricio Dávila, who excavated Tizate, believes that this structure was constructed of earth from the ground up, like the pyramids at Cahokia, Illinois (Dávila Cabrera and Zaragoza Ocaña 1994 and 2002, 69).

24. Dávila Cabrera and Zaragoza Ocaña 1994 and 2002, 77, 89.

25. Stresser Péan 2005, 691.

26. Ibid., 778.

27. This mollusk was apparently a dietary staple of the river people, as well as an indispensable source of the lime used to cover buildings starting in the Late Classic.

28. Ekholm 1944, 421; Sanders 1971; Ramírez 2007, 224.

29. Mayén 2006.

30. Ekholm 1944, 421.

31. Twenty-five miles (40 kilometers) north of Altamira, Tamaulipas (Prieto 1873).

32. Prieto 1873.

33. Ochoa Sálas 1984, 69.

34. Fewkes 1903–4; Müelleried 1924; Muir 1926; Meade 1942.

35. Excavated by Gordon F. Ekholm and Wilfredo Du Solier in 1941–42 (Ekholm 1944).

36. Ekholm 1944, 384.

37. Ekholm only refers to them as construction phases, which he divides into nine stages (ibid., 386).

38. Ekholm 1944, 377; Littmann 1959.

39. Ekholm 1944, 377; Littmann 1959.

40. Du Solier 1945, 137.

41. Fewkes 1926; Ekholm 1944; Gutiérrez Mendoza 1996; Ramírez 2007.

42. Pérez et al. 2007.

43. Marquina 1970, 93–102.

44. Lorenzo Ochoa reports the use of similar blocks at Tabuco in Tuxpan, Veracruz, and at Chontalpa, Tabasco (Ochoa Sálas 1999, 122).

45. Ramírez Castilla 2007, 221–22.

46. Ochoa Sálas 1999, 69.

47. In the municipal area of Huejutla, located on the eastern side of the Mexico City–Huejutla highway, 650 feet (200 meters) south of the entrance to Chilcualoya.

48. Ramírez Castilla 2007b.

49. Tetzacuali is a Hispanization of the Nahuatl word *tetzacualli*, literally "pile of stones." Significantly, my informants stressed that this word also alludes to the fact that the mound has hollows and is hiding something inside.

50. Du Solier 1945, 145.

51. Located 1 mile (1.5 kilometers) east of Vinasco.

52. Du Solier 1945, 143.

53. Ibid., 145.

54. In the municipal area of Huejutla, 12 miles (20 kilometers) toward San Felipe Orizatlán. Information about its discovery was provided by archaeologist Carlos Hernández of the Centro INAH Hidalgo.

55. The town's church was built on one of these platforms seventy-five years ago. In one side of the church was embedded a fragment of a sculpture of the fertility goddess Teem, of typical Postclassic Huastec workmanship.

56. Ramírez Castilla 2007b.

57. In the municipal area of the same name. The site has been completely destroyed by urban sprawl.

58. Du Solier 1945, 127.

59. Ibid., 125.

60. Ibid., 127.

61. My efforts to locate this building have been unsuccessful, and no one in the area is familiar with it. Du Solier does not specify its exact location, although it seems to have formed part of the same site at Huichapa where he excavated the tomb, on lands owned by Mr. Salomón Monterrubio (Du Solier 1945, 141). It possibly corresponds to the El Chilar property, access to which is not permitted, but whose neighbors say it contains *cuecillos*.

62. Du Solier 1945, 145.

63. Ibid., 125.

64. Seventeen miles (28 kilometers) from Ciudad Valles, San Luis Potosí. The site has apparently not been relocated since the 1940s.

65. Stresser Péan 2001, 269.

66. Ibid., 270.

67. Referred to as follows: 1, Group A, or of the Ceremonial Plaza; 2, group B, or of the Northeastern Plaza; 3 Group C, or of the Northern Mounds; 4, Group D, or of the Northeastern Mounds; 5, Group E, or of the Mounds near the River; 6, Group F, or of the Southern Mounds; 7, Group G, or of the Eastern Mounds (Stresser Péan 2001, 93–102). The Tamtoc Project has recently discovered more funerary and ritual buildings, but the results of its explorations have not yet been published.

68. Stresser Péan 2001, 263.

69. Ibid., 293.

70. Ibid., 276.

71. Ibid., 277.

72. Ibid., 275.

73. Ibid.

74. Ibid.

75. The ritual channel was excavated and restored during the Tamtoc Project, under the direction of archaeologist Guillermo Ahuja.

76. Monument 32 of Tamtoc, identified by G. Ahuja Ormachea (2006) as an Olmec-style lunar calendar; its dating is still subject to debate.

77. Walz Caviezel 1991, 90–94.

78. Ibid., 90.

79. Du Solier 1945, 132–33.

80. The latter site, located in the municipal area of Tamuín, is also known as Tamuín or El Consuelo in the archaeological literature. Its current official name is Tamohi. However, there are also remains at Old Tamuín and El Consuelo Ranch, which sometimes makes its identification confusing. Minor traces of mural painting have been located in El Porvenir, San Jose del Tinto, and several other places.

81. Zaragoza Ocaña 2003, 92.

82. Ibid., 92.

83. Ibid., 89.

84. Orellana Tapia 1948, 3; Marquina 1951, 458; Zaragoza Ocaña 2003, 90.

85. Zaragoza Ocaña 2003, 108.

86. Ibid., 112.

87. Ibid., 115.

88. It was built at a later stage, following the disuse and filling in of the ritual channel.

89. Ibid., 117.

90. A very large one was preserved until recently at Tanquián, San Luis Potosí, and was used as a dance floor for the town. It was demolished to make way for the current gazebo (Juan Carlos Soni, personal communication, 2007).

91. Zaragoza Ocaña 2003, 117.

92. In the municipal area of San Felipe Orizatlán, 6 miles (10 kilometers) from San Martín Chalchicuauhtla, in the town of El Brasilar (Zaragoza Ocaña and Dávila Cabrera 2004, 2007).

93. The site was discovered by Patricio Dávila and Diana Zaragoza and explored in 2006 (Zaragoza Ocaña and Dávila Cabrera 2004).

94. Gutiérrez Mendoza 1996, 158.

95. Marquina 1951, 458.

96. Ibid.

97. Orellana Tapia 1948, 3.

98. García Payón 1944, 4; Ochoa Sálas 1984, 79.

99. García Payón 1944, 4; Ochoa Sálas 1984, 79.

100. Medellín Zenil 1956, 134–37; García Payón 1978, 418–19; Ochoa Sálas 1984, 78–79.

101. Medellín Zenil 1956, 134–37; García Payón 1978, 418–19; Ochoa Sálas 1984, 78–79.

102. Meade 1991, 16.

103. Ibid.

104. Ochoa Sálas 1984, 78.

105. Ochoa Sálas 1999, 119.

106. Ochoa Sálas 1984, 78.

107. Ibid., 80.

108. In the municipal area of Ozuluama, Veracruz.

109. Ochoa Sálas 1999, 119.

110. Ochoa Sálas 1984, 83.

111. García Payón 1978, 420; Stresser Péan 2001.

Chapter 10
Oaxaca

1. Blanton 1978, 29. See also Marcus and Flannery 1996, 25. Michael Lind (1994, 99) has proposed alternate names for these phases.

2. Marcus and Flannery 1996, 84.

3. Winter 1994, 10.

4. Ibid., 132.

5. Miller 1995, 3.

6. Magaloni 2007.

7. Winter 1989, 41.

8. Blanton 1978, 40.

9. Marquina 1951, 314.

10. Winter 1994, 12.

11. Chadwick 1966–70, 245–55.

12. Urcid 1994, 77–97.

13. Marcus and Flannery 1996, plate 9.

14. Bernal and Gamio 1974, 9.

15. Bernal 1966–70, 345–66.

Chapter 11
The Maya Region

1. Littmann 1948.

2. Stuart 1998, 379.

3. Ibid., 395.

4. Ibid., 378.

5. Wauchope 1934, 148–51.

6. Aveni et al. 2003, 173.

7. Ibid., 173.

8. Aveni and Hartung 1989, 451.

9. Guderjan 2006; Laporte and Fialko 1990.

10. Jones 1969, 93.

11. Aveni et al. 2004, n. 5.

12. Ibid., 130.

13. Hansen 1998, 80; Taube 1998, 432–46.

14. Hansen 1998, 89.

15. Argucia Fasquelle 1999, 2004.

16. Ruz Lhuillier 1973.

17. García Moll 2004.

18. Stuart 1998.

19. Piña Chan 1985.

20. Hohmann and Vogrin 1982.

21. Hansen 1998, 74.

22. Aveni et al. 1975.

23. Chase and Chase 1982.

24. Webster and Houston 2003, 443.

25. Inomata 2006, 810–15, table 1.

26. Stuart 1996.

27. Hansen 1998, 75.

28. Cobos and Winemuller 2001.

29. See Shaw 2001, figure 1.

30. Chase and Chase 1982.

31. Dahlin 2000, 294.

Chapter 12
Architectural Terminology in Maya and Nahua Texts

1. In this chapter, I will use the rules proposed by Alfonso Lacadena and Søren Wichmann (2004a; undated) for the transliteration and transcription of Maya hieroglyphs, and those of Lacadena (2003c; undated a; undated b; Lacadena and Wichmann 2004b) for Nahuatl glyphs. I am well aware, however, that vowel length in Mayan inscriptions is one of the ongoing debates of epigraphy. For Mayan words, I will use the following characters: a, e, i, o, u, aa, ee, ii, oo, uu, a'/a'(a), e'/e'(e), i'/i'(i), o'/o'(o), u'/u'(u), b', ch, ch', h, j, k, k', l, m, n, p, q, s, t, t', tz, tz', w, x, y, ', but for the names of Maya cities and languages, as well as calendar terms, I will try to stick to traditional usage, based on sixteenth-century orthography, whose initial attempts at adaptation to the Latin alphabet are probably due to Fray Luis de Villalpando (?–1552). For Nahuatl signs I will use the following characters: a, e, i, o, ā, ē, ī, ō, ch, k, k^w, l, m, n, p, s, t, tl, tz, w, x, y, ', following the vowel length proposed by Frances Karttunen (1992), except in the case of colonial glosses, whose orthography I will try to respect.

2. Woodard 2004, 2.

3. On the history of decipherment, from Egyptian to Mayan writing, I recommend the book by Maurice Pope (1999).

4. See Sampson 1985, 145–71; DeFrancis 1989, 89–121; Moore 2000.

5. See Hill 1967; Coe 1995, 23, 31; Robertson 2004, 20–21, 37 note 4, 38 note 7. Some authors, led by Elizabeth Boone and based on the concept of "semasiographia" by Geoffrey Sampson (1985, 26–45), have suggested the possible existence of Mesoamerican writing systems that transmitted ideas without the intermediation of language. However, their examples rely on iconic communications systems from the modern world (traffic or airport signs, computer icons, musical notation, etc.) that coexist with phonographic writing systems and do not invade their functions; moreover, they do not indicate the maximum number of signs or categories that a "wordless" system could have in its repertoire, which leads them to consider even the *quipus* of South America to be writing systems.

6. Stuart 1998, 387; "Today we know that there is no reason to assume that the representation of a sign has something to do with its meaning or phonetic value. For example, a sign representing a bat can signify 'bat' in some contexts, but can also act as a syllable, thus changing its role and conduct completely.... The modern methods of decipherment...pay less attention to the imagery of an unknown sign and concentrates on its possible placement in proportion to the signs with which it interacts" (Stuart 1995, 47). "But even the pictorial signs themselves are always read according to the obvious representation of their image" (Stuart 2001, 52).

7. In the case of the Maya, the corpus includes more than 15,000 hieroglyphic texts (Houston 2000, 131), including portable and monumental inscriptions, as well as those painted on ceramics, codices, or walls. The total number of codices, maps, or documents with Nahuatl writing (the vast majority from the colonial period) is still unknown, but we can probably speak of hundreds.

8. Landa 1994, 149–50. In an important article about architecture in Mayan hieroglyphic texts, David S. Stuart (1998, 374) was the first epigrapher to call attention to this passage.

9. López de Cogolludo 1996, vol. I, 352.

10. Stuart 2001, 52–53; see also Grube 2003, 351.

11. The most famous of these "houses of reading" is the one with the great stuccoed monster-facade in the Chenes style that is located on the acropolis of Ek Balam and in whose back room was found the funeral chamber of the city's dynastic founder, 'Ukit Kan Lek Tok' (late eighth century). The name of the structure was rendered on the cover of Vault 19 in Room 35 as **SAK xo-ko-NAH**, *Sak Xok Naah*, "White House of Reading" (see Lacadena 2003a, 25–26; 2005, 66).

12. Diphrasisms are literary figures of semantic equivalence that consist of the association of two words in order to denote a third meaning, broader than that of the two terms taken separately (Edmonson 1986, 19; Lacadena 2002, 7; Hull 2003, 135–42, 410–14; Martin 2004b, 108). On the diphrasism *kab' ch'e'n*, see Lacadena 2002, 7–8, 14–15; Hull 2003, 425–31; Martin 2004b, 106–9; and Velásquez García 2004b, 83–85.

13. Stuart and Houston (1994, 12–13, note 9) were the first scholars to show the locative nature of the expression that we read today as *ch'e'n*, "cave, well" or "crag."

14. Based on examples at Copán and Tikal, Alexander Tokovinine (2006, 28–29) suggests that the diphrasism *chan ch'e'n*, "heaven-cave," may have had a somewhat different shade of meaning, since it links the name of a place with that of the city containing it.

15. Lacadena 2002, 14.

16. Nomenclature from the Mayan hieroglyphic catalog by J. Eric S. Thompson (1962).

17. See Graham 1967, 59.

18. See Schele and Grube 1990, 2–3.

19. Stuart and Houston 1994, 33.

20. Schele and Grube 1990, 1; Martin 2004a, 2–3, note 5.

21. Alfonso Lacadena (personal communication, October 23, 2007). Nikolai Grube thinks that the word *yok[el]te'* or *yokte'[e]l*, which appears on Lintel 25 (I2), is the noun for "plaza" (personal communication, November 15, 2005). This reinforces the idea that the name of Yaxchilán was actually Tahn Ha' Pa' Chan, since on the same lintel *'uyok[e]lte' Ta[h]nha' Pa' Chan* could be translated as "the plaza of Yaxchilán."

22. Schele and Grube 1990, 4. All this discussion of *ta[h]n ha' Pa' Chan* y *ta[h]n ha' B'aak[al]* necessarily leads us to suppose that the four-leafed sign (T510b-na **HA'**) found in texts at Seibal, Dos Pilas, and Machaquilá had the logographic reading **TAN**, *ta[h]n*, "in, at the center of," a hypothesis that should be investigated.

23. On the meaning of the contorted posture in Mesoamerican art, see Tomás Pérez Suárez's article (2005).

24. Stuart 2006a.

25. Erik Boot 2007, 136–37, note 167.

26. Stuart et al., 2005, 125; during the colonial period, *lak* was also the generic name of the sculptures and clay figurines that the inquisitors of the Provisorato de Indios confiscated from apostate Maya (Chuchiak 2000, 324).

27. The identification of the term *sas*, "stucco, plaster," should be attributed to Stephen D. Houston (Alfonso Lacadena, personal communication, October 23, 2003).

28. Robert F. Wald 2004, 43, note 23.

29. Arzápalo Marín 1995, 235.

30. Gabrielle Vail (1996, 289) has demonstrated, in my opinion, that the logogram of the god Q reads **KISIN**, since it possesses the phonetic complements -ni and in the Madrid Codex (p. 87c) his name is written **ki-si-ni**.

31. Christenson 2003, 65.

32. Roys 1967, 116–19.

33. Velásquez García 2004a, 102.

34. Chuchiak 2000, 327, note 25; Eberl and Bricker 2004, 34; Zender 2004, 3.

35. Eberl and Bricker 2004, 36–43. In that same year, Marc U. Zender (2004, 1–5) argued that the hieroglyph for *nahb'* could be used to designate the circumference of the sphere, which suggested the existence of gigantic balls between 24⅜ and 37⅞ inches (61.9 and 96.2 centimeters) in diameter. In response, Eberl and Bricker cite archaeological, ethnohistorical, and ethnographic data to show that balls of those dimensions did not exist in ancient or modern times.

36. Identified by Stuart (1986).

37. Identification of the verb *tak'*, "to plaster, to stucco," can also be attributed to Houston. See note 27 above.

38. Stuart 1998, 384.

39. Houston, Robertson, and Stuart 2000, 330.

40. See Houston, Robertson, and Stuart 2000, 331–34; Lacadena and Wichmann 2000, 11–14; and Hruby and Child 2004.

41. David S. Stuart (personal communication, November 25, 2007).

42. Panel 1 at La Corona was found in a looters' trench (Guenter 2005, 15).

43. Staines Cicero 2004, 239, 247.

44. See note 8 above.

45. Lacadena 2004, 96, 98 note 26.

46. Stuart 1998, 376.

47. Grube 2003, 354–55.

48. Kaufman and Norman 1984, 127.

49. See Lacadena and Wichmann 2002, 287–88.

50. Grube 2003, 362–63.

51. See López Austin 1989, vol. I, 397; Houston, Stuart, and Taube 2006, 36.

52. Houston, Robertson, and Stuart 2001, 26–27.

53. It is possible that another term for "entrance" is found in the emblematic glyph of Piedras Negras: yo-ki-b'i, *Yokib'*, "throat, canyon," which seems to be derived from the proto-Mayan archaism *'ook*, "to enter" (Kaufman and Norman 1984, 127), plus the instrumental morpheme -ib'.

54. A term apparently identified by Yuri Polyukhovich (Alfonso Lacadena, personal communication, October 23, 2007).

55. Domínguez 2005, 14.

56. The reading is by Simon Martin. The word *kot*, "wall," also means "chamber," which might be suitable for *Chi'[i]k Naa[h]b' Kot*, since it designates an area inside Calakmul (Alfonso Lacadena, personal communication, October 23, 2007).

57. Wichmann 2001, 6.

58. Boot 2007, 35.

59. See note 51 above.

60. Stuart 1998, 379.

61. Boot 2007, 140.

62. An analysis of the ceramic pastes from which the compound braziers of the Cross Group at Palenque were manufactured has revealed that they were fired in closed ovens, with a reducing atmosphere and at high temperatures (Guillermo Bernal, personal communication, September 19, 2007).

63. Guillermo Bernal, personal communication, September 19, 2007. The ovens were conceived of as "places of transformation," probably because the Maya believed that when the raw vases were fired, they were transformed into the gods of which they were effigies. Moreover, simple observation demonstrates that in the firing process, the clay or paste is transformed into an entirely different material: ceramic (see Balfet, Fauvet-Berthelot, and Monzón 1992, 79–80 and note 6).

64. See Smith 1955, vol. I, 5.

65. Stuart 1998, 396.

66. Boot 2007, 76.

67. Grube 2004, 208; Grube and Martin 2004, 20, 38, 70.

68. Alfonso Lacadena (personal communication, October 23, 2007). See the lexicographic entries for the Cholti word *bitum*, "patio" (Morán 1695, 49), and for Yucatecan Maya word *betun*, "road or highway of stone" (Arzápalo Marín 1995, 83).

69. Stuart 1998, 374.

70. Houston 1989, 14.

71. Coe 1973.

72. See principally Grube 1990, 1991; Houston, Stuart, and Taube 1989; Houston and Taube 1987, MacLeod 1990, and Stuart 1989. Regarding the Primary Standard Sequence or Dedicatory Formula on architectural supports, see Stuart 1998.

73. Stuart et al. 2005, 114.

74. Stuart 1998, 375.

75. See Grube 2003, 362–64; Biro 2003.

76. Recently, David F. Mora-Marín (2007) has proposed that this logogram of the hunchbacked man (God N) does not have the logographic reading **T'AB'**, but rather **HU'**, "blowing (air)" or "sacred, power, authority." In the context of the consecration of monuments or portable objects, Mora-Marín suggests that this sign would mean "blowing air for healing or ritual dedication."

77. Stuart 2000b, 3; on the verbalization of this kind of complex noun, see Lacadena 2003b, 847–48, 855–57.

78. Stuart 1998, 402.

79. See note 8 above.

80. Houston 1989, 13; Stuart 1998, 402.

81. The reading of the glyphic compound T214:610 does not seem to have been fully proven. Stuart (2006b, 135) proposed that it had the logographic value **'AK**, "grass" or "straw," but seven months later Boot (2006) presented arguments in favor of the reading **JAL**, "cane" or "reed." For his part, Lacadena (personal communication, October 23, 2007) believes that Boot's reading might be corrected slightly, to **JALAL**, since the lexicographic entry for "cane" or "reed" is *jalal*.

82. Stuart 1998, 384–85.

83. Martin and Grube 2002, 163.

84. Stuart 1998, 396–99, 404–9.

85. On the mortuary rites recorded in Maya art and epigraphy, see the work of Marcus Eberl (2005, 96–119).

86. Stuart 1998, 381, note 4; Eberl 2005, 92–96.

87. Guenter 2002, 18. I suspect that the classic Maya rite of *'ilaj* was analagous to the contemporary Tzotzil practice of *il*, "seeing," which is based on the myth that the gods clouded the vision of the first men, since their powers of perception rivaled their own (see Christenson 2003, 197–201). Evon Z. Vogt (1979, 292) says that the Tzotzils believe that the first men "were capable of 'seeing' within the mountains where the ancestral gods lived," but that this capacity was now reserved to the seers (*h'ilol*). This is a kind of vision beyond the physical, since it allows the Maya shamans to attain understanding and full awareness

through the initiatory trance (Garza 1990, 172; also see Houston, Stuart, and Taube 2006, 167, 173).

88. John F. Chuchiak (2000, 399) quotes various colonial sources that describe the role of Yucatecan Maya priests (*ajk'iino'ob*) in the consecration of temples and oratories; all report that the buildings were sprinkled with "virgin water" (*suhuy ha'*), using a stick or sprinkler with a serpent's rattle on the end.

89. See Stuart 1998, 389–92, 399.

90. Braziers are generally represented by covered plates that bear the solar sign and from which emerge swirls of smoke or fire (see Stuart 1998, 389–90).

91. *Ho'tuun* is one-fourth of a *k'atun*, in other words, a period of five years of 360 days each.

92. Stuart 1998, 404.

93. Taube 1992, 39.

94. Stuart 2000a, 29; 2005, 68, 180; 2006b, 101; Velásquez García 2006, 4.

95. Savkic 2007, 106.

96. Zender 2004, 5–8.

97. On this subject, see Colas and Voss 2001, Tokovinine 2002, and Stuart 2003.

98. See note 67 above.

99. See Lacadena and Wichmann 2002, 284–86.

100. On the date of consecration of this ring (between November of AD 713 and October of AD 714) and the decipherment of its generic name (*chik[in] tuun*), see Lacadena 1992, 179–83.

101. Stuart et al. 2005, 132; also see Houston 1998, 349–50, and Grube and Gaida 2006, 188–91.

102. Coe 1973, 136.

103. On the use of tobacco among the Maya and Nahua, see De la Garza 1990, 95–100, 166–70, and also Thompson 1975, 137–59. Houston (1998, 349) notes that this conception of vases as the houses of gods parallels that of the modern Lacandons, who call their ritual containers *nahk'uh*, "house of the god." During the colonial period, the Yucatecan Maya called their idols, which took the form of braziers or vases, *lak*, "plate" (Chuchiak 2000, 324–29).

104. Houston, Robertson, and Stuart 2001, 17. See also the Cholti lexicographic entries *maii*, "present, gift, offering, thanksgiving" (Morán 1695, 23), and *quekchí*, *mayej*, and *majij*, "offering, sacrifice" (Sedat 1955, 105; Haeserijin 1979, 222), as well as the colonial Cakchiquel word *maih* "offering, generally the thing that is given in thanks" (Coto 1983, 378).

105. Coe 1973, 51.

106. I am grateful to Alfonso Lacadena (personal communication, November 17, 2005) for helping me to understand the syntactic structure of this kind of stamp, and its implications for translation.

107. I am grateful to David S. Stuart (personal communication, November 19, 2005) for helping me to understand that the expression *yotoot 'umayij* refers to a "house of offering [objects]." He also offered the astute observation that a box of wood similar to that of Tortuguero is supported by Yaxuun B'ahlam IV on Lintel 43 at Yaxchilán, while his wife Hiix Witz holds a basket with cords and other implements for autosacrifice. Interesting connections between the word *may* and the ceremonial bleedings of youths can be found in the texts of the Panel of the Cross (C3) and the Panel of the Palace (C18–F14) at Palenque, which describe the presentation of offerings (*k'almay y k'a[h]ljiiy may*).

108. Cited by Houston 1998, 349; see also Taube 1988, 198.

109. Among the riddles recorded in the books of Chilam Balam is the following: "'Bring me the Sun, my children,

to have it on my plate. The lance of the high cross must be stuck in the center of its heart, and on it must sit Yax Bolon, Green-jaguar, drinking blood. This is the speech of Zuyua.' This is what we ask of you: the Sun is a great fried egg and the lance with the high cross stuck in its heart to which he refers is a blessing, and the green jaguar sitting on top of it drinking blood is the green chili pepper when it begins to turn color" (Barrera Vásquez and Rendón 1984, 132). "He picks up for walking a true elongated gourd and enters it through the largest part, which is the edge of the Earth. This is the Kahlay of the Sun" (Mediz Bolio 1988, 66–67).

110. For more on the cosmogonic symbolism of the houses, see the article by Cecilia Klein (1982).

111. Peñafiel 1977.

112. These documents have been the subject of valuable studies of iconography, land tenure, history, religion, the calendar, aesthetics, genealogy, paleography, etc. This varied research has taken advantage of the glosses in Latin characters, but the structure and function of the glyphs have not been fully understood.

113. Seler 1904, 209.

114. For example, in Charles E. Dibble (1971, 331): "The writings from the middle of the sixteenth century can be considered a final result of a generation of colonial influence on the writing of Aztec hieroglyphics."

115. I believe that the term *pictographic* or *pictogram* does not designate any operative category of signs within a writing system, but simply alludes to their formal aspect. All known writing systems (including ours) function with logograms, phonograms (syllabic, consonantal, or vocalic signs), semagrams (semantic determinatives or radicals), and auxiliary signs. A logogram, phonogram, semagram, or auxiliary sign can be pictographic or not, depending on its figurative aspect, but this does not affect its function.

116. On the danger of doing this, see note 6 above.

117. Especially Nicholson 1973, Manrique Castañeda 1989, and Lockhart 1996.

118. Aubin 2002.

119. Lacadena 2003c; undated a; undated b; Lacadena and Wichmann 2004a.

120. See, for example, Zender 2006, 5.

121. By *rebus* we mean a clever use of logograms that represent homophone or nearly homophone words, with the objective of facilitating the expression of more abstract concepts. Illustrative examples are, for example, among the Maya, the use of a sign with the reading **TZAK**, "to grasp," in the representation of the word *tzak*, "to conjure," and, among the Nahuatl, the use of the sign **TZIN**, "anus, base, foundation," to write the diminutive or reverential suffix *-tzin*.

122. *Acrophony*, a principle common to many writing systems, is the derivation of phonetic signs from the first sounds of certain words. In Mayan writing, for example, the syllabograms **k'a**, **ch'o**, and **wi** originated respectively from the words "hand" or "arm" (*k'ab'*), "mouse" (*ch'oj*), and "root" (*wi'*), and retained the iconic appearance of those words, whereas in the Nahuatl system the acrophonic phonograms **kʷe**, **po**, and **we** are derived from the nouns "skirt" or "dress" (*kʷēitl*), "smoke" (*pōktli*), and "old man" (*wēwe'*).

123. Lacadena 2003c, 27, note 30.

124. An *allograph* is a sign that has the same phonetic or logographic value as another, although its formal appearance may be entirely different. In Mayan writing, for example, the graphemes T585a and T1029 are allographs between themselves, since they both have the phonetic value **b'i**, while in Nahuatl documents the glyphs for tree and jawbone are allographs, given that both of them can operate as the phonograms **kʷa**.

125. I am grateful to Alfonso Lacadena (personal communication, October 23, 2007) for having called my attention to these examples.

126. McLung de Tapia 1984, 35; Niederberger 1996, 46.

127. Aubin 2002, 48.

128. Of uncertain vocalic duration.

129. In this word and that of *tēkpan* the final consonant of the morpheme *tēkʷ* loses its labiality or is absorbed by the next labial consonant (Karttunen 1992, 217).

130. Siméon 1992, 442.

131. Siméon 1992, 450.

132. As has been widely recognized in Egyptian and Mayan writing and the cuneiform systems of Mesopotamia (Coe 1995, 248).

133. Alfonso Lacadena (personal communication, October 23, 2007).

134. The noun designating this reptile (*oxin?*) has not been recorded, as far as I know, in any Nahuatl dictionary, but I think it may be a very archaic word for "lizard," some traces of which (*ixin?*) remained in the *Vocabulary* of Fray Alonso de Molina (1992, 76): *texixincoyotl* and *tecouixin* [*sic*].

135. That is to say, a sign formed by the association of two other signs, with the phonetic or logographic value of the diagraph being different than those of either sign taken separately. If I am correct regarding the possible logogram **TEPE'CH** (Fig. 46a), it would seem to result from the combination of the logogram **TE?**, "stone," with the phonogram **xo**.

136. Aubin 2002, 45.

137. Aubin 2002, 51.

138. Valle 1998, 8.

139. Alfonso Lacadena (personal communication, October 23, 2007).

140. See note 12 above.

141. Dibble 1971, 329, fig. 3.

142. That is to say, consonant [C] plus vowel [V]. The Mayan writing system had similar problems, since the scribes frequently found it necessary to elide the consonants h, j, l, m, n, y, or ', as can be seen, for example, in the transliteration and transcription of "bowl" (**ja-wa-TE'**, *jawa[n]te'*) or "he was captured" (**chu-ka-ja**, *chu[h]kaj*) (see Lacadena 2001, 53).

143. Dibble 1971, 327.

144. The glyphic compound of a footprint on wood laid over water may consist of two logograms (**KʷAW-PANO**), but it is more likely to be a single one (**KʷAWPAN**) (Alfonso Lacadena, personal communication, October 23, 2007), an ambiguity that can only be resolved by the exhaustive and patient study of the Nahuatl corpus.

145. Peñafiel 1977, 68.

146. León-Portilla 2003, 24.

147. Lacadena 2003c, 6.

148. I am grateful to Leticia Staines (personal communication, October 25, 2007) for calling my attention to the ideals of visual impact and technical perfection sought out by Mesoamerican artists.

149. I would like to express my gratitude to María Teresa Uriarte for having invited me to contribute to this book, to Alfonso Lacadena García-Gallo and Leticia Staines Cicero for reading a preliminary version of this text and providing astute comments, as well as to Guillermo Bernal Romero, Nikolai Grube, and David S. Stuart, all of whom provided me with valuable information.

BIBLIOGRAPHY

Chapter 1
Architecture as Art

Bernal, J. D. *Art and the scientist* (1939). In Circle: International Review of Constructive Art. New York: Praeger Publishing, 1971.

Cabrera Castro, Rubén. "Teotihuacan Cultural Traditions Transmitted into the Postclassic According to Recent Excavations." In *Mesoamerica's Classic Heritage: From Teotihuacan to the Aztecs,* edited by David Carrasco, Lindsay Jones, and Scott Sessions, 195–217. Boulder: University of Colorado Press, 2002.

Clark, John E. "Ciudades tempranas olmecas." In *Reconstruyendo la ciudad maya: El urbanismo en las sociedades antiguas,* edited by Andrés Ciudad Ruiz, María Josefa Iglesias Ponce de León, and María del Carmen Martínez, 183–209. Madrid: Sociedad Española de Estudios Mayas, 2001.

Fash, William L. "Dynastic Architectural Programs: Intention and Design in Classic Maya Buildings at Copan and Other Sites." In *Function and Meaning in Classic Maya Architecture,* edited by Stephen D. Houston. Washington, D.C.: Dumbarton Oaks Research Library and Collection, 1998.

Hansen, Richard D. "Continuity and Disjunction: The Pre-Classic Antecedents of Classic Maya Architecture." In *Function and Meaning in Classic Maya Architecture,* edited by Stephen D. Houston. Washington, D.C.: Dumbarton Oaks Research Library and Collection, 1998.

Houston, Stephen D., ed. *Function and Meaning in Classic Maya Architecture.* Washington, D.C.: Dumbarton Oaks Research Library and Collection, 1998.

López Luján, Leonardo. "La Cuenca de México. El Clásico 150/600–650. El campo y la ciudad." In *Arqueología Mexicana.* Mexico: Editorial Raíces INAH, 2007.

March, Lionel, and Philip Steadman. *The Geometry of Environment: An Introduction to Spacial Organization in Design.* London: RIBA Publications, 1971.

Marcus, Joyce. "On the Nature of the Mesoamerican City." In *Prehistoric Settlement Patterns: Essays in Honor of Gordon R. Willey,* edited by Evon Z. Vogt and Richard Eventual, 207. Cambridge, Mass.: Peabody Museum of Archaeology and Ethnology, Harvard University, 1983.

Marcus, Joyce, and Kent Flannery. *Zapotec Civilization: How Urban Society Evolved in Mexico's Oaxaca Valley.* New York: Thames and Hudson, 1996.

Preziosi, Donald, ed. *The Art of Art History: A Critical Anthology.* Oxford: Oxford University Press, 1998.

Semper, Gottfried. *The Four Elements of Architecture and Other Writings.* Translated by Harry Frances Mallgrave and Wolfgang Herrmann. Cambridge, England, and New York: Cambridge University Press, 1989.

Sharer, Robert J. *La civilización maya.* Mexico: Fondo de Cultura Económica, 2003.

Yoneda, Keiko. *Migraciones y conquistas: Descifre global del Mapa de Cuauhtinchan núm. 3.* Mexico, D.F.: INAH (Colección científica 289), 1996.

Chapter 2
The Hidden Meanings of Architecture

Alcina Franch, José. *Calendario y religión entre los Zapotecos.* Mexico: IIH-UNAM, 1993.

Aveni, F. Anthony, Sharon Gibbs, and Horst Hartung. "The Caracol Tower at Chichén Itzá: An Ancient Astronomical Observatory?" *Science* 188 (1975): 977–85.

Aveni, F. Anthony, and Horst Hartung. "Archaeoastronomy and Dynastic History at Tikal." In *New Directions in American Archaeoastronomy,* 46th International Congress of Americanists, edited by A. F. Aveni, 1–16. Oxford, England: B.A.R., 1988.

Casares Contreras, Orlando. "Un estudio arqueoastronómico en Oxkintok, Yucatán." B.A. thesis in archaeology, Universidad Autónoma de Yucatán, Merida, 2002.

Córdoba, Fray Juan de. *Arte del idioma Zapoteco 1571.* Morelia: Imprenta del Gobierno del Estado de Michoacán, 1886.

Galindo Trejo, Jesús. "Alineación astronómica en la huaxteca. El caso de El Consuelo en Tamuín." *Ciencias* No. 54. Mexico: Facultad de Ciencias-UNAM, 1999: 36–40.

———. "Alineación calendárico – astronómica en Oaxaca prehispánica." In *La Pintura mural prehispánica en México,* edited by Beatriz de la Fuente. Mexico: IIE-UNAM, 2007.

———. "Alineación solar del Templo Mayor de Tenochtlan." *Arqueología Mexicana* VII, no. 41 (2000): 26–29.

———. "Alineamientos calendárico-astronómicos en Monte Albán." In *Procesos de cambio y conceptualización del tiempo, Primera Mesa Redonda de Monte Albán,* edited by N. M. Robles García, 271–84. Mexico, INAH, 2001b.

———. *Arqueoastronomía en la América Antigua.* Madrid: Editorial Equipo Sirius, 1994.

———. "La astronomía prehispánica en México." In *Lajas celestes, Astronomía e historia en Chapultepec,* 15–77. Mexico: INAH – Museo Nacional de Historia, 2003.

———. "Cocijo: deidad definitoria de una alineación calendárico astronómica." In *La pintura mural prehispánica en México. Boletín informativo,* Year VIII, No. 17: 22–28. Mexico: IIE-UNAM, 2002.

———. "La observación celeste en el pensamiento prehispánico." *Arqueología Mexicana* VIII, no. 47 (2001c): 29–35.

———. "Transfiguración sagrada de visiones celestes: Alineación astronómica de estructuras arquitectónicas en cuatro sitios Mayas." In *La pintura mural prehispánica en México,* edited by Beatriz de la Fuente, vol. II, tomo IV: 294–310. Mexico: UNAM, 2001a.

———. "Visiones celeste-calendáricas desde la Costa del Golfo." In *Muros que hablan, Ensayos sobre la pintura mural prehispánica en México,* edited by Beatriz de la Fuente, 453–65. Mexico: Colegio Nacional, 2004.

Galindo Trejo, Jesús, and M. Elena Ruiz Gallut. "Bonampak: Una confluencia sagrada de caminos celestes." In *La pintura mural prehispánica en México,* Part II, edited by Beatriz de la Fuente, 137–57. Mexico: IIE-UNAM, 1998.

Galindo Trejo, Jesús, M. Elena Ruiz Gallut, and Daniel Flores Gutiérrez. "La astronomía." In *Fragmentos del Pasado, Murales prehispánicos,* exh. cat., 167–81. Mexico: Antiguo Colegio de San Ildefonso, UNAM, 1998.

———. "Mayapán: De regiones obscuras y deidades luminosas. Práctica astronómica en el posclásico Maya." In *La pintura mural prehispánica en México II, Área Maya,* Part III, edited by Beatriz de la Fuente, 265–75. Estudios. Mexico: UNAM, 1999.

———. "Senderos celestes con visiones divinas: Un estudio arqueoastronómico del Templo Superior de los Jaguares de Chichén Itzá." In *La pintura mural prehispánica en México,* edited by Beatriz de la Fuente, vol. II, part IV: 258–64. Mexico: IIE-UNAM, 2001.

Heyden, Doris. "Caves, Gods and Myths." In *Mesoamerican Sites and World Views,* edited by Elizabeth Benson, 1–39. Washington, D.C.: Dumbarton Oaks Research Library and Collections, 1981.

Malmström, Vincent H. "Edzná: Earliest Astronomical Center of the Maya." In *Arqueoastronomía y etno-astronomía en Mesoamérica,* edited by J. Broda et al., 37–47. Mexico: IIH-UNAM, 1991.

Martínez Donjuán, Guadalupe. "Los olmecas en el estado de Guerrero." In *Los olmecas en Mesoamérica,* edited by John E. Clark, 143–63. Mexico, D.F.: Citibank, 1994.

Morante, López Rubén. "Las cámaras astronómicas subterráneas." *Arqueología Mexicana* VII, no. 47 (2001): 46–51.

———. "Los observatorios subterráneos." *La palabra y el hombre* 94 (April-June 1995), 35–71.

Ponce de León, H. Arturo. *Fechamiento arqueoastronómico en el Altiplano de México.* Mexico: DDF, 1982.

Sotelo Santos, Laura Elena. "La ciencia en torno al tiempo." In *Los Mayas, Su tiempo antiguo,* edited by Gerardo Bustos and Ana Luisa Izquierdo. Mexico: UNAM, 1996.

———. *Las ideas cosmológicas Mayas en el siglo XVI.* Mexico: UNAM, 1988.

Sprajc, Iván. *Orientaciones astronómicas de la arquitectura prehispánica del centro de México.* Mexico, D.F.: INAH (Colección Científica 427), 2001.

Thompson, Donald E. "Buildings Are for People: Speculations on the Aesthetics and Cultural Impact of Structures and Their Arrangement." In *Prehistoric Settlement Patterns: Essays in Honor of Gordon Willey,* edited by Evon Z. Vogt and Richard M. Leventhal, 115–27. Cambridge, Mass.: Peabody Museum of Archaeology and Ethnology, Harvard University, 1983.

Tichy, Franz. "El calendario solar como principio de organización del espacio para poblaciones y lugares sagrados." *Proyecto Puebla-Tlaxcala, Comunicaciones* 15 (1978): 153.

Chapter 3
Architectural Function and Technique

Amábilis, Manuel. *La arquitectura precolombina de México.* Mexico: Editorial Orión, 1956: 62/63, 100.

Frankl, Paul. "The Secret of the Medieval Masons." *Art Bulletin* 27 (March 1945): 46–60.

Garza Camino, Mercedes de la. "El templo dragón de la acrópolis de Ek'Balam." In *Estudios Mesoamericanos.* Mexico, UNAM, Revista del Posgrado en Estudios Mesoamericanos, 2002.

Haselberger Lothar. "Planos del Templo de Apolo en Dídyma." *Investigación y ciencia* 113 (February 1986).

López Austin, Alfredo. *Cuerpo humano e ideología: Las concepciones de los antiguos nahuas.* Mexico: UNAM, 1984, vol. I: 65.

Moessel, Ernst. *Urformen des Raumes als Grundlagen der Formgestaltung.* Munich: C.H., 1931.

Taladoire, Eric. *Les terrains de jeu de balle.* Mexico, D.F.: Mission archeologique et ethnologique francaise au Mexique, 1981.

Uriarte, María Teresa, ed. *El juego de pelota en Mesoamérica: Raíces y supervivencia.* Mexico: Siglo Veintiuno Editores, 1992.

Chapter 4
Pre-Olmec and Olmec Architecture

Clark, John A. "Antecedentes de la cultura olmeca." In *Los olmecas de Mesoamerica,* edited by John A. Clark, 31–43. Mexico: Citibank, 1994.

Cyphers, Ann. "La arquitectura olmeca en San Lorenzo Tenochtitlán." In *Población, subsistencia y medio ambiente en San Lorenzo Tenochtitlán,* edited by Ann Cyphers, 91–117. Mexico, D.F.: UNAM, 1997a.

————. "Olmec Architecture at San Lorenzo." In *Olmec to Aztec: Settlement Patterns in the Ancient Gulf Lowlands*, edited by Barbara Stark and Philip Arnold, 96–114. Tucson: University of Arizona Press, 1997b.

Drucker, Phillip. *La Venta, Tabasco: A Study of Olmec Ceramics and Art*, Bureau of American Ethnology, No. 153. Washington, D. C.: Smithsonian Institution, 1952.

Drucker, Phillip, Robert F. Heizer, and Robert Squier. *Excavations at La Venta, Tabasco, 1955*. Bureau of American Ethnology, No. 170. Washington, D.C.: Smithsonian Institution, 1959.

Fash, William. "The Altar and Associated Features." In *Ancient Chalcatzingo*, edited by David Grove, 82–94. Austin: University of Texas Press, 1987.

González Lauck, Rebecca. "Acerca de pirámides de tierra y seres sobrenaturales: observaciones preliminares en torno al edificio C-1 de La Venta, Tabasco." *Arqueología*, 2ª época (Mexico: Coordinación Nacional de Arqueología. INAH) 17 (1997): 79–97.

Grove, David. *Chalcatzingo: Excavations on the Olmec Frontier*. New York: Thames and Hudson, 1984.

Grove, David, and Jorge Angulo. "A Catalog and Description of Chalcatzingo's Monuments." In *Ancient Chalcatzingo*, edited by David Grove, 114–31. Austin: University of Texas Press, 1987.

Heizer, Robert F., John A. Graham, and Lewis K. Napton. "The 1968 Investigations at La Venta." In *Contributions of the University of California Archaeological Research Facility*, No. 5, 127–205. Berkeley: University of California, 1968.

Hill, W. D., M. Blake, and J. Clark. "Ball Court Design Dates Back 3,400 Years." *Nature* 392 (1998): 878–79.

Hirth, Kenneth G. "Formative Period Settlement Patterns in the Río Amatzinac Valley." In *Ancient Chalcatzingo*, edited by David Grove, 343–67. Austin: University of Texas Press, 1987.

Lesure, Richard, and Michael Blake. "Interpretive Challenges in the Study of Early Complexity: Economy, Ritual and Architecture at Paso de la Amada, Mexico." *Journal of Anthropological Archaeology* 21 (2002): 1–24.

Love, Michael. *Early Complex Society in Pacific Guatemala: Settlements and Chronology of the Río Naranjo, Guatemala*. Provo: Brigham Young University (Papers of the New World Archaeological Foundation, 66), 2002.

Marcus, Joyce. *Zapotec Civilization: How Urban Society Evolved in Mexico's Oaxaca Valley*. New York: Thames and Hudson, 1996.

Martínez Donjuan, Guadalupe. "Teopantecuanitlán." In *Primer coloquio de arqueología y etnohistoria del estado de Guerrero*, 55–80. Mexico, D.F.: INAH and Gobierno del Estado de Guerrero, 1986.

Niederberger, Christine. "Ranked Societies, Iconographic Complexity, and Economic Wealth in the Basin of Mexico toward 1200 B.C." In *Olmec Art and Archaeology in Mesoamerica*, edited by John E. Clark and Mary E. Pye, 169–91. New Haven: Yale University Press; Washington D.C.: National Gallery of Art, 2000.

Pool, Christopher A. *Olmec Archaeology and Early Mesoamerica*. Cambridge and New York: Cambridge University Press, 2007.

Prindiville, Mary, and David Grove. "The Settlement and Its Architecture." In *Ancient Chalcatzingo*, edited by David Grove, 63–81. Austin: University of Texas Press, 1987.

Symonds, Stacey, Ann Cyphers, and Roberto Lunagómez. *Asentamiento prehispánico en San Lorenzo Tenochtitlán*. Mexico, D.F.: UNAM, 2002.

Tolstoy, Paul. "Coapexco and Tlatilco: Sites with Olmec Materials in the Basin of Mexico." In *Regional Perspectives on the Olmec*, edited by Robert J. Sharer and David C. Grove, 85–121. New York: Cambridge University Press, 1989.

Chapter 5
The Central Altiplano

Alcina Franch, José, Miguel León-Portilla, and Eduardo Matos Moctezuma. *Azteca Mexica: Las culturas del México Antiguo*. Barcelona: Lunwerg Editores, 1992.

Atlas nacional de México. Mexico: Instituto de Geografía, UNAM, 1990–91.

Bartra, Roger. *El salvaje en el espejo*. Mexico: UNAM, Ediciones Era, 1992.

Benson, Elizabeth, ed. *The Art and Iconography of Late Post-Classic Central Mexico*. Washington, D.C.: Dumbarton Oaks, 1982.

Blanton, Richard E., et al. *Ancient Mesoamerica: A Comparison of Change in Three Regions*. New York: Cambridge University Press, 1993.

Broda, Johanna, Davíd Carrasco, and Eduardo Matos Moctezuma, eds. *The Great Temple of Tenochtitlan: Center and Periphery in the Aztec World*. Berkeley: University of California Press, 1987.

Carrasco, Davíd. *City of Sacrifice: The Aztec Empire and the Role of Violence in Civilization*, Boston: Beacon Press, 1999.

Clendinnen, Inga. *Aztecs: An Interpretation*. New York: Cambridge University Press, 1991.

Coll de Hurtado, Atlántida. *México: Una visión geográfica*. Mexico, D.F.: Instituto Geografía, 2000.

Davies, Nigel. *The Toltecs: Until the Fall of Tula*. Norman: University of Oklahoma Press, 1977.

Durán, Fray Diego. *Historia de las Indias de Nueva España e Islas de Tierra Firma*. Mexico: CONACULTA, 1995.

————. *The History of the Indies of New Spain*. Translated, annotated, and with an introduction by Doris Heyden. Norman: University of Oklahoma Press, 1994.

Garza Tarazona de González, Silvia. "Xochicalco." In *La pintura mural prehispánica en México: El Altiplano después del abandono de Teotihuacán*. Mexico: UNAM, IIE, forthcoming.

Heizer, Robert F., and James A. Bennyhoff, "Archaeological Excavations at Cuicuilco, Mexico, 1957," *National Geographic Research Reports 1955–1980*, 96.

Heyden, Doris, and Paul Gendrop. *Pre-Columbian Architecture of Mesoamerica*. New York: Electa/Rizzoli, 1980.

Hill Boone, Elizabeth, ed. *Painted Architecture and Polychrome Monumental Sculpture in Mesoamerica*. Washington, D.C.: Dumbarton Oaks, 1985.

Jones, Lindsay. *Twin City Tales: A Hermeneutical Reassessment of Tula and Chichén Itza*. Niwot, Col.: University Press of Colorado, 1995.

López Bajonero, Raúl Manuel. "La concurrencia del derecho y la historia del arte: El caso de Cuicuilco." Mini-thesis published to enter the art history degree program, Facultad de Filosofía y Letras, 2006.

López Luján, Leonardo, Robert Cobean, and Guadalupe Mastache. *Xochicalco y Tula*. Milan: Editorial Jaca Book, 1995.

Marquina, Ignacio. *Arquitectura prehispánica*. Mexico: INAH-SEP, 1951.

Mastache, Alba Guadalupe, Robert Cobean, and Dan Healan. *Ancient Tollan: Tula and the Toltec Heartland*. Boulder: University Press of Colorado, 2002.

Matos Moctezuma, Eduardo. *Los aztecas*. Milan: Editorial Jaca Book, 1989.

————. "From Teotihuacan to Tenochtitlan. Their great temples." In *Mesoamerica's Classic Heritage: From Teotihuacan to the Aztecs*, edited by David Carrasco, Lindsay Jones, and Scott Sessions. Boulder: University Press of Colorado, 2000.

————. "The Templo Mayor of Tenochtitlan: History and Interpretation." In *The Great Temple of Tenochtitlan: Center and Periphery of the Aztec World*, edited by Johanna Broda, David Carrasco, and Eduardo Matos

Moctezuma. Berkeley: University of California Press, 1987.

Matos Moctezuma, Eduardo, and Leonardo López Luján. "La diosa Tlatecuhtli de la casa de las Ajaracas y el rey Ahuízotl." In *Arqueología Mexicana* XIV, no. 83 (January-February 2007): 23–29.

Pasztory, Esther. *Aztec Art*. New York: Harry N. Abrams Inc., 1983: 105.

Plunket, Patricia, and Gabriela Uruñuela. "Testimonios de antiguas formas de vida." In *La gran pirámide de Cholula*, edited by Felipe Solís et al., 167. Mexico: CONACULTA, INAH, Editorial Azabache, n.d.

Rosas, Romel, and Héctor Vega. "Ocupación prehispánica del Altiplano y fundación de México Tenochtitlán." Dissertation presented to the graduate studies division of the architecture faculty of the UNAM, Mexico, August 1997.

Sanders, William T., and Barbara J. Price. *Mesoamerica: The Evolution of a Civilization*. New York: Random House, 1968.

Sanders, William T., and Robert S. Santley. "A Tale of Three Cities: Energetics and Urbanization in Pre-Hispanic Central Mexico." In *Prehistoric Settlement Patterns: Essays in Honor of Gordon R. Willey*, edited by Evon Z. Vogt and Richard M. Leventhal, 243–91. Cambridge, Mass.: Peabody Museum of Archaeology and Ethnology, 1983.

Spence, Michael W. "The Scale and Structure of Obsidian Production in Teotihuacan." In *Teotihuacán: Nuevos datos, nuevas síntesis, nuevos problemas*, edited by Emily McClung de Tapia and Evelyn Childs Rattray. Mexico, D.F.: UNAM, 1987.

Sugiyama, Saburo, and Rubén Cabrera Castro. "El proyecto pirámide de la Luna 1998–2004: Conclusiones preliminares." In *Sacrificios de consagración en la pirámide de la Luna*, edited by Saburo Sugiyama and Leonardo López Luján, 16. Mexico: CONACULTA, INAH, Museo del Templo Mayor; Arizona State University, 2006.

Townsend, Richard F. *The Aztecs*. London: Thames and Hudson, 1992: 142.

Uruñuela, Gabriela, Patricia Plunket, and María Amparo Robles. "Nueva evidencia sobre los inicios de la Gran Pirámide de Cholula." In *La gran pirámide de Cholula*, edited by Felipe Solís et al., 183. Mexico: CONACULTA, INAH, Editorial Azabache, n.d.

Yamamoto, Yoko S. "Central Mexico." In *The Oxford Encyclopedia of Mesoamerican Cultures: The Civilizations of Mexico and Central America*, edited by David Carrasco, 158. New York: Oxford University Press, 2001.

Chapter 6
Western Mexico

Acosta, Jorge R. "Exploraciones arqueológicas realizadas en el estado de Michoacán durante los años de 1937 y 1938." In *Revista Mexicana de estudios antropológicos* (Mexico: Sociedad Mexicana de Antropología) vol. III, no. 2 (May-August 1939): 85–98.

Alcalá, Jerónimo de. *La relación de Michoacán*. Prologue, paleographic version, separation of texts, colloquial ordering, preliminary study and notes by Francisco Miranda. Mexico: Secretaría de Educación Pública, 1988.

Arnheim, Rudolf. *La forma visual de la arquitectura*. Barcelona: Gustavo Gili [1975] 2001.

————. *El poder del centro: Estudio sobre la composición en las artes visuales*. Translated by Remigio Gómez Díaz. Madrid: Alianza, 1984.

Beltrán, José Carlos. "Los concheros y el desarrollo cultural en Nayarit, la tradición Aztatlán." In *Introducción a la arqueología del Occidente de México*, edited by Beatriz Braniff Cornejo, 397–409. Mexico: Universidad de Colima, INAH, 2004.

Bernal, Ignacio. "Exploraciones en Coixtlahuaca, Oaxaca." *Revista Mexicana de Estudios Antropológicos* (Mexico: Sociedad Mexicana de Antropología) vol. 10, 1948–49.

Cabrera Castro, Rubén. "Tzintzuntzan, décima temporada de excavaciones." In *Homenaje a Román Piña Chan*, edited by Barbro Dahlgren et al., 531–65. Mexico: UNAM, Instituto de Investigaciones Antropológicas, 1987.

Cabrero, María Teresa. *El hombre y sus instrumentos en la cultura Bolaños*. Mexico: UNAM, Instituto de Investigaciones Antropológicas, 2005.

Cárdenas, Efraín. "La arquitectura de patio hundido y las estructuras circulares en el Bajío: desarrollo regional e intercambio cultural." In *Arqueología y etnohistoria: La región Lerma*, edited by Eduardo Williams and Phil C. Weigand, 41–73. Zamora: El Colegio de Michoacán; Guanajuato: Centro de Investigación en Matemáticas, 1999a.

———. *El bajío en el clásico: Análisis regional y organización política*. Zamora: El Colegio de Michoacán, 1999b.

———. "Pátzcuaro, Ihuatzio y Tzintzuntzan." In *Arqueología Mexicana*, 28–33, Mexico: INAH (Raíces, no. 19), 1996.

Carot, Patricia. "Arqueología de Michoacán: nuevas aportaciones a la historia purépecha." In *Introducción a la arqueología del occidente de México*, edited by Beatriz Braniff, 443–74. Mexico: INAH, Universidad de Colima, 2004.

Castañeda López, Carlos, and Jorge Quiroz Rosales. "Plazuelas y la tradición Bajío." In *Tradiciones arqueológicas*, edited by Efraín Cárdenas García, 141–59. Zamora: El Colegio de Michoacán, Gobierno del Estado de Michoacán, 2004.

Corona Núñez, José. *Tumba de El Arenal, Etzatlán, Jalisco*. Mexico: INAH, Dirección de Monumentos Prehispánicos, 1955.

Disselhoff, H. D. "Note sur le résultat de vuelques fouilles archéologiques." In *Revista del Instituto de Etnología de la Universidad de Tucumán*, edited by A. Métraus, 525–37. Tucumán: Universidad Nacional de Tucumán, vol. 2, 1931.

Faugère-Kalfon, Brigitte. *Entre Zacapu y río Lerma: Culturas de una zona fronteriza*. Mexico: Centre français d'études mexicaines et centraméricaines (Cuadernos de Estudios Michoacanos, 7), 1996.

Filini, Agapi. "Interacción cultural entre la cuenca de Cuitzeo y Teotihuacan." In *Tradiciones arqueológicas*, edited by Efraín Cárdenas García, 306–27. Zamora: El Colegio de Michoacán, Gobierno del Estado de Michoacán, 2004.

Fresán Jiménez, Mariana. *Nierika: Una ventana al mundo de los antepasados*. Mexico: CONACULTA-FONCA, 2002.

Furst, Peter. "Shaft Tombs, Shell Trumpets and Shamanism: A Culture-Historical Approach to Problems in West Mexican Archaeology." Ph.D. diss., University of California, Los Angeles, 1966.

Galván, Javier. *Las tumbas de tiro del valle de Atemajac, Jalisco*. Mexico, INAH (Colección Científica, 239), 1991.

Gómez Chávez, Sergio. "Presencia del occidente de México en Teotihuacan: Aproximaciones a la política exterior del Estado teotihuacano." In *Ideología y política a través de materiales, imágenes y símbolos: Memoria de la Primera Mesa Redonda de Teotihuacan*, edited by María Elena Ruiz Gallut, 563–625. Mexico: UNAM, Instituto de Investigaciones Antropológicas, Instituto de Investigaciones Estéticas, INAH, 2002.

Gómez Gastelum, Luis. *Cacicazgos prehispánicos en el valle de Atemajac, Jalisco*. Mexico: Gobierno de Jalisco, Instituto Jalisciense de Antropología e Historia, Universidad de Guadalajara, n.d.

Hernández Díaz, Verónica. *Acercarse y mirar: Homenaje a Beatriz de la Fuente*. Edited by María Teresa Uriarte and Leticia Staines Cicero, 329–56. Mexico: UNAM, 2004.

———. *El arte de los muertos y el espacio de los vivos: La cultura de tumbas de tiro del antiguo occidente de México*. Ph.D. diss. in art history, Universidad Nacional Autónoma de México, Facultad de Filosofía y Letras, manuscript.

———. "Los estudios de las regiones mesoamericanas de Occidente y Guerrero." In *El México antiguo: Primera parte*, edited by Pablo Escalante. México: Centro de Investigación y Docencia (CIDE), Fondo de Cultura Económica (FCE), forthcoming a.

———. "Los janamus grabados de Tzintzuntzan." *Anales del Instituto de Investigaciones Estéticas* (México, UNAM, Instituto de Investigaciones Estéticas) no. 89 (Fall 2006a): 197–212.

———. *Los janamus grabados en la arquitectura prehispánica y virreinal de Tzintzuntzan, Michoacán*. Master's thesis in art history, Universidad Nacional Autónoma de México, Facultad de Filosofía y Letras, 2006b.

———. "Muerte y vida en la cultura de tumbas de tiro." In *Miradas renovadas al occidente de México*. Mexico: UNAM, Instituto de Investigaciones Estéticas, forthcoming b.

Hers, Marie-Areti. "Las salas de las columnas en La Quemada." In *Arqueología del Norte y del Occidente de México: Homenaje al doctor J. Charles Kelley*, edited by Barbro Dahlgren and María de los Dolores Soto de Arechavaleta, 93–113. Mexico: Universidad Nacional Autónoma de México, 1995.

———. *Los toltecas en tierras chichimecas*. Mexico: Universidad Nacional Autónoma de México, Instituto de Investigaciones Estéticas, 1989.

Hrdlicka, Ales. "The Region of the Ancient 'Chichimecs' with Notes on the Tepecanos and the Ruin of La Quemada, Mexico." In *American Anthropologist*, Vol. 3 (July-September, no. 3, 1903): 380–440. Mill Wood, New York: American Anthropological Association, Krauss Reprint.

Jaramillo Luque, Ricardo. "Consideraciones sobre la arqueología del valle de Valparaíso, Zacatecas, Occidente y Norte de México." In *Arqueología del norte y del occidente de México: Homenaje al doctor J. Charles Kelley*, edited by Barbro Dahlgren and María de los Dolores Soto, 173–79. Mexico: UNAM, 1995.

Kelley, Charles. "Speculations on the Culture History of Northwestern Mesoamerica." In *The Archaeology of West Mexico*, edited by Betty Bell, 19–39. Ajijic, Jalisco: Sociedad de Estudios Avanzados del Occidente de México, West Mexican Society for Advanced Study, 1974.

Kindl, Olivia. *La jícara huichola: Un microcosmos mesoamericano*. Mexico, D.F.: INAH, Universidad de Guadalajara, 2003.

Long, Stanley V. *Archaeology of the Municipio of Etzatlan, Jalisco*. Ph.D. diss., University of California, Los Angeles, 1966.

———. "Formas y distribución de tumbas de pozo con cámara lateral." In *Razón y Fábula* (Bogota: Universidad de los Andes) No. 1 (May, 1967): 73–87.

Macías Goytia, Angelina. *Huandacareo: Lugar de juicios, tribunal*. Mexico, D.F.: INAH (Colección Científica, 222), 1990.

Martínez Donjuán, Guadalupe. "Los olmecas en el estado de Guerrero." In *Los olmecas en Mesoamérica*, edited by John E. Clark, 143–63. Mexico, D.F.: Citibank, 1994.

Matadamas Díaz, Raúl. "Pictografías de San Pedro Jaltepetongo, Cuicatlán." In *Historia del arte de Oaxaca*, Vol. 1, *Arte prehispánico*, edited by Margarita Dalton and Verónica Loera, 201–9. Oaxaca: Instituto Oaxaqueño de las Culturas, 1997.

Meighan, Clement W., ed. *The Archaeology of Amapa, Nayarit*. Los Angeles: University of California-Los Angeles, The Institute of Archaeology (Monumenta Archaelogica, vol. 2), 1976.

Mountjoy, Joseph. "La cultura indígena en la costa de Jalisco, el municipio de Puerto Vallarta." In *Introducción a la arqueología del Occidente de México*, edited by Beatriz Braniff Cornejo, 339–69. Mexico: Universidad de Colima, INAH, 2004b.

———. "Excavaciones de dos panteones del Formativo Medio en el valle de Mascota, Jalisco, México." Report presented to FAMSI (Fundación para el Avance de los Estudios Mesoamericanos), at http://www.famsi.org/reports/03009es/index.html, 2004a.

Mountjoy, Joseph, and Mary K. Sandford. "Burial Practices During the Late Formative/Early Classic in the Banderas Valley Area of Coastal West Mexico." In *Ancient Mesoamerica*, 313–27. New York: Cambridge University Press (no. 17), 2006.

Muller, Florencia. *La cerámica de Cuicuilco B: Un rescate arqueológico*. Mexico, D.F.: INAH (Colección Científica, 186), 1990.

Oliveros, Arturo. *Hacedores de tumbas en El Opeño, Jacona, Michoacán*. Zamora: El Colegio de Michoacán, H. Ayuntamiento de Jacona, 2004.

Oliveros, Arturo, and Magdalena de los Ríos Paredes. "La cronología de El Opeño, Michoacán: Nuevos fechamientos pro radio-carbono." In *Arqueología* (Mexico: INAH) No. 9–10 (December 1993): 45–48.

Olsen Bruhns, Karen. *Ancient South America*. Cambridge and New York: Cambridge University Press, 1994.

Pajares Ayuela, Paloma. *Cosmatesque Ornament: Flat Polychrome Geometric Patterns in Architecture*. Translated by María Fleming Alvarez. New York: Norton, 2001.

Pereira, Grégory, Gerald Migeon, and Dominique Michelet. "Transformaciones demográficas y culturales en el centro-norte de México en vísperas del Posclásico: los sitios del Cerro Barajas (suroeste de Guanajuato)." In *Reacomodos demográficos del Clásico al Posclásico en el centro de México*, edited by Linda Manzanilla, 123–36. Mexico, D.F.: UNAM, Instituto de Investigaciones Antropológicas, 2005.

Pollard, Helen P. *Taríacuri's Legacy: The Prehispanic Tarascan State*. Norman: University of Oklahoma Press, 1993.

Roth, Leland M. *Entender la arquitectura: Sus elementos, historia y significado*. Barcelona: Gustavo Gili, 2003.

Sánchez Correa, Sergio, and Emma G. Marmolejo Morales. "Algunas apreciaciones sobre el 'Clásico en el Bajío central', Guanajuato." In *La época Clásica: Nuevos hallazgos, nuevas ideas: seminario de arquelogía*, edited by Amalia Cardós de Méndes, 267–78. Mexico: INAH-Museo Nacional de Antropología e Historia, 1990.

Serna, Rosalío. "Perspectivas de invesigación a través del Catálogo de sitios arqueológicos de Colima." *Barro Nuevo* (Colima: Ayuntamiento de Colima, INAH) no. 6 (July-September 1991): 16–21.

Smith, Michael E. "A model for the diffusion of the shaft tomb complex from South America to West Mexico." In *Journal of the Steward Anthropological Society* (University of Illinois) 9, nos. 1 and 2, (Fall 1977, Spring 1978): 177–204.

Taladoire, Eric. "The Architectural Background of the Pre-Hispanic Ballgame: An Evolutionary Perspective." In *The Sport of Life and Death: The Mesoamerican Ballgame*, edited by E. Michael Whittington, 97–115. New York: Thames and Hudson, 2001.

———. "El juego de pelota precolombino." *Arqueología Mexicana* (Mexico: INAH, Raíces) no. 9 (August-September 1994): 6–15.

Uriarte, María Teresa, ed. *El juego de pelota en Mesoamérica: Raíces y supervivencia*. Mexico: Siglo Veintiuno Editores, 1992.

Valdez, Francisco. "The Sayula Basin. Ancient Settlements and Resources." In *Ancient West Mexico: Art and Archaeology of the Unknown Past*, edited by Richard F. Townsend, 216–31. New York: Thames and Hudson; Chicago: Art Institute of Chicago, 1998.

Von Winning, Hasso. *Arte prehispánico del Occidente de México*. Edited by Phil C. Weigand and Eduardo Williams, translated by Eduardo Williams and Brigitte Boehm de Lameiras. Zamora: El Colegio de Michoacán; Guadalajara: Secretaría de Cultura de Jalisco, 1996.

Von Winning, Hasso, and Olga Hammer. *Anecdotal Sculpture of Ancient West Mexico*. Los Angeles: The Ethnics Arts Council of Los Angeles, 1972.

Weigand, Phil C. *Evolución de una civilización prehispánica: Arqueología de Jalisco, Nayarit y Zacatecas.* Zamora: El Colegio de Michoacán, 1993.

———. *La evolución y ocaso de un núcleo de civilización: La tradición Teuchitlán y la arqueología de Jalisco.* Guadalajara: Secretaría de Cultura del Gobierno de Jalisco (Serie Antropología en Jalisco. Una visión actual, 1–2), 1996.

———. "La tradición Teuchitlán del Occidente de México." In *Tradiciones arqueológicas*, edited by Efraín Cárdenas García, 216–41. Zamora: El Colegio de Michoacán, Gobierno del Estado de Michoacán, 2004.

Weigand, Phil C., and Christopher Beekman. "The Teuchitlan Tradition Rise of a Statelike Society." In *Ancient West Mexico: Art and Archaeology of the Unknown Past*, edited by Richard F. Townsend, 34–51. Chicago: Art Institute of Chicago, 1998.

Weigand, Phil C., and Acelia García de Weigand. "La arquitectura prehispánica y la secuencia cultural en la cuenca de Chapala, Jalisco: observaciones preliminares." In *Las cuencas del occidente de México: Época prehispánica*, edited by Eduardo Williams and Phil C. Weigand, 293–323. Zamora: El Colegio de Michoacán; Mexico, D.F.: Centro de Estudios Mexicanos y Centroamericanos, Instituto de Investigación Científica para el Desarrollo en Cooperación, 1996.

———. "La tradición Teuchitlán. Las temporadas de excavación 1999–2000 en los Guachimontones." In *Estudio histórico y cultural sobre los huicholes*, edited by Phil C. Weigand, 129–47. Colotlán, Jalisco: Universidad de Guadalajara, Campus Universitario del Norte, 2002.

Zepeda García-Moreno, Gabriela. "Cañada de la Virgen, Allende, Guanajuato," *Arqueología Mexicana* (Mexico: INAH, Raíces) vol. XIII, no. 73 (May-June 2005): 56–59.

———. *Ixtlán: Ciudad del viento.* Tepic, Nayarit: INAH, Grupo ICA, 1994.

Chapter 7
Northern Mexico

Aboites Aguilar, Luis. "Resumen chihuahuense: breviario de indios, españoles, trabajadores y cholos." In *Papeles norteños*, edited by Beatriz Braniff, 107–20. Mexico, D.F.: INAH, 1997.

Braniff, Beatriz. "Arqueología del norte de México." In *La Sierra Gorda: Documentos para su historia*, edited by Margarita Velasco Mireles, 359–97. Mexico, D.F.: INAH, Vol. II, 1996–97ᵃ [1975].

———. "Paquimé: pequeña historia de las Casas Grandes." In *Papeles norteños*, edited by Beatriz Braniff, 71–106. Mexico, D.F.: INAH, 1997b.

Crespo, Ana María, and Rosa Brambila, eds. *Querétaro prehispánico.* Mexico, D.F.: INAH, 1991.

Guevara Sánchez, Arturo. "Oasisamérica en el Posclásico: la zona de Chihuahua." In *Historia antigua de México*, Vol. III, *El horizonte Postclásico y algunos aspectos intelectuales de las culturas mesoamericanas*, edited by Linda Manzanilla and Leonardo López Luján, 329–51. Mexico City: CONACULTA; UNAM, M.A. Porrúa, 1994–95.

Hers, Marie-Areti. "Las salas de las columnas en La Quemada." In *Arqueología del norte y del occidente de México: Homenaje al doctor J. Charles Kelley*, edited by Barbro Dahlgren and María de los Dolores Soto de Arechavaleta, 93–113. Mexico: UNAM, Instituto de Investigaciones Antropológicas, 1995.

———. "La sombra de los desconocidos: los no mesoamericanos en los confines tolteca-chichimecas." In *La gran chichimeca: El lugar de las rocas secas*, edited by Beatriz Braniff, 65–70. Milan: Jaca Book; Mexico: CONACULTA, 2001a.

———. *Los toltecas en tierras chichimecas.* Mexico: UNAM, Instituto de Investigaciones Estéticas, 1989.

———. "Zacatecas y Durango. Los confines toltecas-chichimecas." In *La gran chichimeca: El lugar de las rocas secas*, edited by Beatriz Braniff, 113–54. Milan: Jaca Book; Mexico: CONACULTA, 2001b.

Jiménez Betts, Peter. "La Quemada, Zacatecas." *Arqueología Mexicana* (Mexico: INAH, Raíces) vol. XII , no. 67 (May-June 2004): 80–87.

Kelley J., Charles. "Archaeology of the Northern Frontier: Zacatecas and Durango." In *Handbook of Middle American Indians*, vol. 11, part 2, edited by Robert Wauchope, 768–801. Austin: University of Texas Press, 1971.

López Austin, Alfredo, and Leonardo López Luján. *El pasado indígena.* México: Colegio de México, Fideicomiso Historia de las Américas, Fondo de Cultura Económica, 1996.

Mejía Pérez Campos, Elizabeth. "Ranas y Toluquilla, Querétaro." *Arqueología Mexicana* (Mexico: INAH, Raíces) vol. IX, no. 50 (July-August 2001): 68–71.

———. *Toluquilla, una cultura serrana.* Querétaro: Gobierno del Estado de Querétaro, 2002.

Mejía Pérez Campos, Elizabeth, and Alberto Herrera Muñoz. "El sur de la Sierra Gorda: Ranas y Toluquilla." *Arqueología Mexicana* (Mexico: INAH, Raíces) vol. XIII, no. 77 (January-February 2006): 38–41.

Michelet, Dominique. *Río Verde, San Luis Potosí.* Mexico: Centre d'études mexicaines et centraméricaines, 1984 [Spanish translation 1996].

Nárez, Jesús. *Materiales arqueológicos de Balcón de Montezuma, Tamaulipas.* Mexico, D.F.: INAH, 1992.

Plog, Stephen. *Ancient Peoples of the American Southwest.* New York: Thames and Hudson, 1997.

Schaafsma, Curtis F., and Carroll L. Riley, eds. *The Casas Grandes World.* Salt Lake City: University of Utah Press, 1999.

Velasco Mireles, Margarita. "Escaleras semicirculares en la Sierra Gorda." In *Querétaro prehispánico*, edited by Ana María Crespo and Rosa Brambila, 253–68. Mexico, D.F.: INAH (Colección Científica, 238), 1991.

———. "El mundo de la Sierra Gorda." *Arqueología Mexicana* (México: INAH, Raíces) vol. XIII, no. 77 (January-February 2006): 28–37.

———. "El Norte de Mesoamérica: la Sierra Gorda." In *Mesoamérica y Norte de México, siglo IX–XII*, Seminario de Arqueología "Wigberto Jiménez Moreno," Federica Sodi Miranda, coord., 459–66. Mexico, Museo Nacional de Antropología, INAH, 1990.

———, ed. *La Sierra Gorda: documentos para su historia.* Mexico: INAH, vol. II, 1997.

Villalpando C., Elisa. "Los pobladores en Sonora." In *La gran chichimeca: El lugar de las rocas secas*, edited by Beatriz Braniff, 211–35. Milan: Jaca Book; Mexico: CONACULTA, 2001.

Chapter 8
Central Veracruz

Andrade Guerrero, Martín Alberto. "Sitio arqueológico Las Puertas: Excavación en arquitectura de tierra: Un edificio construido de terracotta." Bachelor's thesis, Escuela Nacional de Antropología e Historia, Mexico City, 2002.

Arellanos Melgarejo, Ramón. *La arquitectura monumental postclásica de Quiahuiztlan: Estudio monográfico.* Xalapa: Universidad Veracruzana, 1997.

Arellanos, Ramón, and Lourdes Beauregard. "Dos palmas totonacas." *La palabra y el hombre, nueva época* (Universidad Veracruzana, Xalapa, Veracruz) No. 38–39 (April-September 1981): 144–60.

Braniff, Beatriz. "La colonización mesoamericana de la Gran Chichimeca." In *La gran chichimeca: El lugar de las rocas secas*, edited by Beatriz Braniff, 211–35. Milan: Jaca Book; Mexico: CONACULTA, 2001.

Brüggemann, Jürgen Kurt. "Análisis urbano del sitio arqueológico del Tajín." In *El Proyecto Tajín, Tomo II*, edited by Jürgen Kurt Brüggemann, 81–125 Mexico, D.F.: Dirección de Arqueología, INAH (Cuaderno de Trabajo No. 9), 1991.

———. "La ciudad y la sociedad." In *Tajín*, by Jürgen Kurt Brüggemann, Álvaro Brizuela Absalón, Sara Ladrón de Guevara, Patricia Castillo, Mario Navarrete, and René Ortega, 47–78. Mexico City: Gobierno del Estado de Veracruz, 1992a.

———. *Guía oficial Tajín.* Mexico City: Gobierno el Estado de Veracruz, INAH, Salvat, 1992b.

———. "El medio geográfico-cultural." In *Tajín*, by Jürgen K. Brüggemann, Sara Ladrón de Guevara, and Juan Sánchez Bonilla, 15–38. Mexico City: El Equilibrista; Madrid: Turner Libros, 1992c.

———. *Mozomboa, Veracruz: Un sitio arqueológico del postclásico veracruzano: Análisis de los materiales cerámicos y arquitectónicos.* Mexico City: INAH (Colección Científica, No. 308, Serie Arqueología), 1996.

———. "El problema cronológico del Tajín." *Arqueología. Revista de la Coordinación Nacional de Arqueología del Instituto Nacional de Antropología e Historia/Segunda época*, No. 9–10 (January-December 1993): 61–72.

———. "Reconocimiento de superficie en el área aledaña a Tajín." In *Antropología e historia en Veracruz*, by various authors, 451–54. Xalapa: Gobierno del Estado de Veracruz-Llave, Instituto de Antropología e Historia de la Universidad Veracruzana, 1999.

———. "La zona del Golfo en el Clásico." In *Historia antigua de México, Volumen II: El horizonte clásico*, edited by Linda Manzanilla and Leonardo López Luján, 13–46. Second edition (revised and expanded). Mexico City: CONACULTA/INAH, UNAM-Coordinación de Humanidades/Instituto de Investigaciones Antropológicas, Grupo Editorial Miguel Ángel Porrúa, 2001.

Brüggemann, Jürgen Kurt, et al. *Zempoala: El estudio de una ciudad prehispánica.* Mexico City: INAH (Colección Científica, No. 232, Serie Arqueología), 1991.

Brüggemann, Jürgen Kurt, Álvaro Brizuela Absalón, Sara Ladrón de Guevara, Patricia Castillo, Mario Navarrete, and René Ortega. *Tajín.* Mexico City: Gobierno del Estado de Veracruz, 1992.

Cortés Hernández, Jaime. *Filobobos.* Mexico City: Guía. Salvat/INAH, 1994.

Cuevas Fernández, Héctor, Juan Sánchez Bonilla, Alfonso García y García, Yamile Lira López, and René Ortega Guevara. *El Tajín. Estudios Monográficos.* Xalapa: Universidad Veracruzana, 1995.

Daneels, Annick. "Algunos problemas en la cronología del Golfo veracruzano." In *Quinto Coloquio Pedro Bosch Gimpera: Cronología y periodización en Mesoamérica y el Norte de México*, edited by Annick Daneels, 263–82. Mexico City: Instituto de Investigaciones Antropológicas de UNAM, 2009.

———. "Ballcourts and Politics in the Lower Cotaxtla Valley: A Model to Understand Classic Central Veracruz?" In *Classic Veracruz: Cultural Currents in the Ancient Gulf Lowlands*, edited by Philip Arnold III and Christopher A. Pool. Washington D.C.: Dumbarton Oaks, 2008.

———. *El patrón de asentamiento del periodo Clásico en la cuenca baja del río Cotaxtla, Centro de Veracruz. Un estudio de caso de desarrollo de sociedades complejas en tierras bajas tropicales.* Doctoral thesis, UNAM, Mexico City, 2002.

———. "El Protoclásico en el centro de Veracruz. Una perspectiva desde la cuenca baja del Cotaxtla." In *Arqueología Mexicana. IV Coloquio Pedro Bosch Gimpera, Vol. 2: Veracruz, Oaxaca y mayas*, edited by Ernesto Vargas Pacheco, 453–88. Mexico City: Instituto de Investigaciones Antropológicas de UNAM, 2005.

———. *Proyecto Tajín: Temporada 1991–1992. Edificio 22: Primera parte. Investigación arqueológica.* Mexico City: Archivo Técnico del INAH. Exp. 311.42 (D)/5-11, Legajo 2. 1992.

Daneels, Annick, and Fernando A. Miranda Flores. "Cerro del Toro Prieto. Un centro ceremonial en el Valle de Córdoba." In *Contribuciones a la historia prehispánica de la región Orizaba-Córdoba*, edited by Carlos Serrano Sánchez, 73–86. Mexico City: UNAM/IIA (Cuadernos de divulgación 2) and H. Ayuntamiento de Orizaba, 1998.

Dirección de Medios de Comunicación, INAH. "El edificio principal de Las Puertas en Jamapa, Veracruz." *Arqueología Mexicana* Vol. XI, No. 63 (2003): 10.

Drucker, Philip. *Ceramic Stratigraphy at Cerro de las Mesas, Veracruz, Mexico.* Bulletin 141, Bureau of American Ethnology. Washington D.C.: Smithsonian Institution, 1943.

Dupaix, Guillaume. *Antiquités Mexicaines: Relation des trois expéditions du Capitaine Dupaix, ordonnées en 1805, 1806 et 1807, par le roi Charles IV.* Paris: Bureau des Antiquités Mexicaines; Imprimerie Jules Didot l'Aîné. 1834.

Fahmel Beyer, Bernd. *La arquitectura de Monte Albán.* Mexico City: Instituto de Investigaciones Antropológicas, UNAM, 1991.

García Cook, Ángel. "The Historical Importance of Tlaxcala in the Cultural Development of the Central Highlands." In *Handbook of Middle American Indians, Supplement 1 (Archaeology)*, edited by V. Bricker, 244–76. Austin: University of Texas Press, 1981.

García Márquez, Agustín. *Los Aztecas en el Centro de Veracruz.* Mexico City: Instituto de Investigaciones Antropológicas, UNAM, 2005.

García Payón, José. "Archaeology of Central Veracruz." In *Handbook of Middle American Indians* (general editor Robert Wauchope), *Vol. 11: Archaeology of Northern Mesoamerica, Part 2*, edited by Gordon F. Ekholm and Ignacio Bernal, 505–42. Austin: University of Texas Press, 1971.

———. "Centro de Veracruz." In *Historia de México* (general editor Miguel León-Portilla), *Tomo II: Periodos Preclásico y Clásico*, edited by Ignacio Bernal and Miguel León-Portilla, 433–50. Barcelona: Salvat Editores S.A., 1974 [Salvat Mexicana de Ediciones, Mexico City, 1978].

———. *El Tajín: Official Guide.* Mexico City: INAH, 1976.

———. "Tumbas con mausoleo de la región central de Veracruz." *UniVer* Year II, vol. II, 13 (1950): 7–23.

Gyarmati, János. "Archaeological sites in the river valley of Río Necaxa, Veracruz, Mexico." *Artes Populares* (Budapest, Hungary: Yearbook of the Department of Folklore, Elte Eötvos Loránd University) 15 (1988): 64–103.

———. "Investigaciones arqueológicas en el Valle del Río Necaxa, Veracruz, México." *Mexicon* XVII (4) (1995): 67–70.

Hers, Marie-Areti. "Zacatecas y Durango: Los confines Tolteca-Chichimecas." In *La gran chichimeca: El lugar de las rocas secas*, edited by Beatriz Braniff, 211–35. Milan: Jaca Book; Mexico: CONACULTA, 2001.

Inomata, Takeshi, and Stephen Houston, eds. *Royal Courts of the Ancient Maya.* 2 vols. Boulder: Westview Press, 2001.

Izquierdo, Ana Luisa. "La arquitectura funeraria de Quiahuistlan." *Cuadernos de Arquitectura Mesoamericana: Arquitectura del Golfo* (Facultad de Arquitectura, UNAM, Mexico City) 1, no. 8 (September 1986).

Jiménez Lara, Pedro. "Reconocimiento de superficie dentro y fuera de la zona arqueológica del Tajín." In *Proyecto Tajín, Tomo II*, edited by Jürgen Kurt Brüggemann: 5–63. Mexico City: INAH (Cuaderno de Trabajo de la Dirección de Arqueología 9), 1991.

Kaufman, Terrence, and John Justeson. "Epi-Olmec Hieroglyphic Writing and Texts." In *Notebook for the Maya Hieroglyphic Forum at Texas.* Austin: University of Texas at Austin, 2001.

Ladrón de Guevara, Sara. *Imagen y pensamiento en El Tajín.* Xalapa: Universidad Veracruzana; Mexico City: INAH, 1999.

Laporte Molina, Juan Pedro. "Alternativas del Clásico Temprano en la relación Tikal-Teotihuacan: Grupo 6C-XVI, Tikal, Petén, Guatemala." Doctoral thesis, UNAM, Mexico City, 1989.

Lira López, Yamile. "Un estudio de la secuencia cerámica encontradsa en el sitio arqueológico de Chalahuite." In *Zempoala: el estudio de una ciudad prehispánica*, by Jür-

gen Brüggemann et al., 171–219. Mexico City: Colección Científica, Serie Arqueología 232, INAH.

Maldonado Vite, María Eugenia. "Astronomía Prehispánica en la Cuenca Baja del Río Papaloapan." Bachelor's thesis, faculty of anthropology, Universidad Veracruzana, Xalapa, Veracruz, 1996.

Márquez, Pedro José. *Due Antichi Monumento di Architectura Messicana Illustrati.* Rome, 1804.

Marquina, Ignacio. *Arquitectura Prehispánica.* Memorias 1. Mexico City: INAH, 1951.

Medellín Zenil, Alfonso. *Cerámicas del Totonacapan: Exploraciones en el Centro de Veracruz.* Xalapa: Universidad Veracruzana, Instituto de Antropología, 1960.

Mejía, Elisabeth. "Interpretación preliminar respecto a la temporalidad de Toluquilla, Querétaro." In *Quinto Coloquio Pedro Bosch Gimpera: Cronología y periodización de Mesoamérica y el Norte de México*, edited by Annick Daneels. Mexico City: Instituto de Investigaciones Antropológicas, UNAM, 2009.

Merino Carrión, Leonor, and Ángel García Cook. "Proyecto Arqueológico Huasteca." *Arqueología* 1 (1987): 31–88.

Michelet, Dominique. *Río Verde, San Luis Potosí.* Mexico: Centre d'études mexicaines et centraméricaines, 1984 [Spanish translation 1996].

Miller, Mary Ellen. "Rethinking the Classic Sculptures of Cerro de las Mesas, Veracruz." In *Settlement Archaeology of Cerro de las Mesas, Veracruz, Mexico*, edited by Barbara L. Stark, 26–38. Institute of Archaeology Monograph 34. Los Angeles: University of California, 1991.

Navarrete Hernández, Mario, and René Ortega Guevara. "Arquitectura." In *Tajín*, by Jürgen Kurt Brüggemann, Álvaro Brizuela Absalón, Sara Ladrón de Guevara, Patricia Castillo, Mario Navarrete Hernández, and René Ortega Guevara, 133–72. Xalapa: Gobierno de Estado de Veracruz: Veracruz en la Cultura. Encuentros y Ritmos, 1992.

Ortega Guevara, Jaime M. "El Zapotal. Un sitio funerario del Clásico Tardío." In *Identidad y testimonio de Veracruz: Estudios de antropología e historia de Veracruz*: 75–97. Xalapa: Gobierno del Estado de Veracruz, 2000.

Ortega Guevara, René. "Restauración de la gran plaza denominada Xicalcoliuhqui." In *El Tajín: Estudios monográficos*, by Héctor Cuevas Fernández, Juan Sánchez Bonilla, Alfonso García y García, Yamile Lira López, and René Ortega Guevara, 125–51. Xalapa: Universidad Veracruzana, 1995.

Ortega Guevara, René, and Alfonso García y García. "Informe de los trabajos de conservación y restauración de la pirámide de los Nichos en el Tajín, Veracruz. Temporada de 1985." In *Proyecto Tajín, Tomo III*, edited by Jürgen Kurt Brüggemann, 137–54. Mexico City: Instituto Nacional de Antropología e Historia (Cuaderno de Trabajo de la Dirección de Arqueología 10), 1991.

Pascual Soto, Arturo. *El Tajín: En busca de los orígenes de una civilización.* Mexico City: Instituto de Investigaciones Estéticas de la Universidad Nacional Autónoma de México, CONACULTA, INAH, 2006.

Pescador Cantón, Laura. "Las canchas de juego de pelota y su articulación a la estructura urbana en Tajín, Veracruz." Bachelor's thesis, ENAH, Mexico City, 1992.

Ruiz Gordillo, Omar. "Asentamientos prehispánicos en la región de Coyoxquihui." *Cuadernos de Trabajo de los Centros Regionales, Centro Regional Veracruz*, Vol. 5 (1985): 47–71.

———. *Oceloapan: Apuntes para la historia de un sitio arqueológico en Veracruz.* Cuadernos de Trabajo. Mexico City: INAH, 1989.

———. *Paxil: La conservación en una zona arqueológica en la región de Misantla, Veracruz.* Colección Textos Básicos y Manuales. Serie Conservación. Mexico City: INAH, 1999.

Stark, Barbara L. "Cerro de las Mesas: Social and Economic Perspectives on a Gulf Center." In *El urbanismo en Mesoamérica: Urbanism in Mesoamerica, Vol. 1*, edited by G. Mastache and W. Sanders, 391–422. Mexico City:

INAH; University Park: Pennsylvania State University, 2003.

———. "Formal Architectural Complexes in South-Central Veracruz, Mexico: A Capital Zone?" *Journal of Field Archaeology* 26 (2)(1999): 197–225.

———, ed. *Settlement Archaeology of Cerro de las Mesas, Veracruz, México.* Los Angeles: University of California (Monograph 34, Institute of Archaeology), 1991.

Torres Guzmán, Manuel. "Los entierros múltiples en El Zapotal." In *Prácticas funerarias en la costa del Golfo de México*, edited by Yamile Lira López and Carlos Serrano Sánchez, 203–12. Xalapa: Universidad Veracruzana; Mexico City: Instituto de Investigaciones Antropológicas, UNAM, Asociación Mexicana de Antropología Biológica, 2004.

———. "Hallazgos en el Zapotal, Ver. (Informe preliminar, segunda temporada)." *Boletín del INAH*, Segunda época, July-September (1972): 3–8.

Valenzuela, Juan. "Las exploraciones efecuadas en los Tuxtlas, Veracruz." *Anales del Museo Nacional de Arqueología, Historia y Etnología* 3 (1945): 83–107.

Vásquez Zárate, Sergio. "Investigaciones arqueológicas en Zacate Colorado y Corralillos, Ver." In *Memoria del V Foro Anual "Docencia, Investigación, Extensión y Difusión de la Facultad de Antropología,"* edited by Sergio Vásquez Zárate, 25–29. Xalapa: Fondo para el Fomento de las Actividades de la Universidad Veracruzana, 1997.

Villalobos Pérez, Alejandro. "Aproximaciones al desarrollo urbano por fechamiento de sistemas constructivos. Segunda parte: El Tajín, Veracruz." *Cuadernos de arquitectura mesoamericana* (División de Posgrado, Facultad de Arquitectura, UNAM, Mexico City, 1986) 8, 37–49.

Wilkerson, S. Jeffrey K. "The Garden City of El Pital: the Genesis of Classic Civilization in Eastern Mesoamerica." *National Geographic Research and Exploration* 10 (1) (1994): 56–71.

———. *El Tajín: Una guía para visitantes.* Veracruz: Museo de Antropología de Xalapa and H. Ayuntamiento de Papantla: Mexico City: Imprenta Madero, 1987.

Wyllie, Cherra. "Children of the Cultura Madre: Late Classic Southern Veracruz Art, Hieroglyphs, and Religion." In *Cultural Currents in the Ancient Gulf Lowlands*, edited by Philip Arnold III and Christopher A. Pool. Washington D.C.: Dumbarton Oaks, 2008.

Chapter 9
The Huastec Region

Ahuja Ormachea, Guillermo. "El Monumento 32 de Tamtoc." *Arqueología Mexicana* No. 79, INAH, Mexico, 2006.

Arias Melo Granados, Martha. "El Formativo en la Cuenca Baja del Pánuco." Bachelor's thesis, major in Archeology, Escuela Nacional de Antropología e Historia, INAH-SEP, Mexico, 1982.

Dávila Cabrera, Patricio, and Diana Zaragoza Ocaña. Informe Técnico Parcial, Tantoc Project, 1994 Season. Archivo Técnico, INAH, Mexico.

———. "Tantoc: una ciudad en la Huasteca." *Arqueología Mexicana* (INAH, Mexico) no. 54 (2002): 66–69.

Du Solier Massieu, Wilfredo. "Estudio arquitectónico de los edificios Huaxtecas." *Anales del INAH* (Mexico) vol. I (1945): 121–45.

Ekholm, Gordon F. *Excavations at Tampico and Panuco in the Huasteca, Mexico.* Anthropological Papers of the American Museum of Natural History, Vol. XXXVIII, part V. New York: American Museum of Natural History, 1944.

Fewkes, Jessie W. "Certain antiquities of eastern Mexico." *Twenty-fifth annual report of the Bureau of American Ethnology.* Washington, D.C.: Secretary of the Smithsonian Institution, 1903–4.

García Payón, José. "Centro de Veracruz." *Historia de México*, vol. 2, 2nd ed. Mexico: Salvat Mexicana de Ediciones, S.A. de C.V., 1978: 433–50.

———. "La Huasteca." *Historia de México*, vol. 2, 2nd ed. Mexico: Salvat Mexicana de Ediciones, S.A. de C.V., 1978: 407–32.

———."Impresiones de mi primer visita a la zona arqueológica de Castillo de Teayo, Ver." *Archivo Técnico* (Mexico: INAH) (1944).

Gutierrez Mendoza, Gerardo. "Patrón de asentamiento y cronología en el sur de la Huaxteca: sierra de Otontepec y Laguna de Tamiahua." Bachelor's thesis, Escuela Nacional de Antropología e Historia, INAH, Mexico, 1996.

Hernández Reyes, Carlos. "La tumba del Barrio Huey Taixco, Jaltocan Huasteca Hidalguense." *Huaxteca, el Hombre y su Pasado*, Revista de Ciencias Históricas y Antropológicas (Fundación Eduard Seler, San Luís Potosí) Year 1, no. 2 (July-December 1996): 65–80.

Hosler, D., and Guy Stresser Péan. "The Huastec region: a second locus for the production of bronze alloys in ancient Mesoamerica." *Science* 257 (1992): 1215–1220.

Littmann, Edwin R. "Ancient mortars, stuccos and plasters of Mesoamerica." *American Antiquity* (The Society for American Archaeology at the University of Utah Press, Salt Lake City) vol. 25, no. 1 (July 1959).

MacNeish, Richard S. *An early archaeological site near Panuco, Vera Cruz*. Philadelphia: Transactions of the American Philosophical Society (New Series, Vol. 44, part 5), 1954.

Marquina, Ignacio. *Arquitectura Prehispánica*. Mexico: Memorias del Instituto Nacional de Antropología e Historia, INAH-SEP, 1951.

Mayén Anguiano, José Antonio Álvarez, and Morrison Limón B. *Informe Técnico: labores de recorrido, topografía, excavación y registro arqueológico en el predio conocido como "Isla Pitaya" o "Isla Pitahaya". Municipio de Tampico, Tamaulipas, Mexico.* Ciudad Victoria: Archivo Técnico, Centro INAH Tamaulipas, 2006.

———. *Proyecto Cholula.* Mexico: Secretaría de Educación Pública, INAH (Serie Investigaciones No. 19), 1970.

Meade, Joaquín. *La Huasteca época antigua* Mexico City: Publicaciones Históricas, Editorial Cossio, 1942.

———. La Huasteca Poblana, Lecturas Históricas de Puebla 44, Gobierno del Estado de Puebla, Secretaría de Cultura, Comisión Puebla V Centenario, Puebla, 1991.

———. *La Huasteca Veracruzana*, Monografías Huastecas III, Vol. I. Mexico, Editorial Citlaltépetl, 1962–63.

Medellín Zenil, Alfonso. Recorrido por la Huasteca Meridional, technical report, Archivo Técnico, INAH, Mexico, 1956.

Merino Carrión, Leonor, and Ángel García Cook. "El formativo temprano en la cuenca baja del río Pánuco: fases Chajil y Pujal." *Arqueología* (INAH, Mexico) 28 (2002): 49–74.

———."Proyecto Arqueológico Huaxteca." *Arqueología* (INAH, Mexico) 1 (1987).

———. "Secuencia cultural para el formativo en la cuenca baja del río Pánuco." *Arqueología* (INAH, Mexico) 32 (2004): 5–27.

Müelleried, Frederick K. G. "Algunas observaciones sobre los 'cues' en la Huasteca." *El México Antiguo* 2 (1924): 20–29.

Muir, Jhon M. "Data on the Structure of Pre-Columbian Huastec Mounds in the Tampico Region, Mexico." *Journal of the Royal Anthropological Institute of Great Britain and Ireland*, vol. 56 (1926): 231–38.

Ochoa Sálas, Lorenzo. *Frente al espejo de la memoria: la costa del Golfo al momento del contacto.* San Luis Potosí, Mexico: Editorial Ponciano Arriaga, CONACULTA, and Instituto de Cultura, 1999.

———. *Huaxtecos y totonacos.* Mexico: CONACULTA, 1990.

———. *Historia Prehispánica de la Huaxteca.* Mexico: UNAM, 2nd ed., 1984.

Orellana Tapia, Rafael. *Informe de los trabajos de reconstrucción y consolidación de Castillo de Teayo, Ver.,*

durante la primera temporada de 1948. Archivo Técnico, INAH, Mexico, 1948.

Pérez Silva, Carlos, and Diana P. Radillo Rolón. Technical Report, Rescate Arqueológico del Altar-Estela, at the Celaya-El Triunfo II site, El Mante, Tamaulipas, Archivo Técnico, Centro INAH Tamaulipas, Mexico, 2007.

Prieto, Alejandro. *Historia, geografía y estadística del Estado de Tamaulipas*. Ciudad Victoria: Gobierno del Estado de Tamaulipas, 1873.

Ramírez Castilla, Gustavo A. *Las Flores: historia de un sitio arqueológico de la Huasteca Tamaulipeca*. Ciudad Victoria: Instituto Tamaulipeco para la Cultura y las Artes, 2000.

———. *Panorama Arqueológico de Tamaulipas*, Ciudad Victoria: Programa de Estímulo a la Creación y al Desarrollo Artístico de Tamaulipas, Gobierno del Estado de Tamaulipas, Instituto Tamaulipeco para la Cultura y las Artes 2007.

———. "Reporte de la visita a los sitios arqueológicos de la Región de Huejutla, Hidalgo." Archivo Técnico, Centro INAH, Tamaulipas, 2007b.

Ramírez Castilla, Gustavo A., Pamela Reza, Román Chávez, Carlos V. Pérez Silva, and Victor H. Valdovinos. *Informe técnico parcial del Salvamento Arqueológico L.T. Champayán-Anahuác-Potencia*. Unpublished manuscript, Archivo Técnico, Centro INAH Tamaulipas, Ciudad Victoria, 2001.

Sanders, William T. "Cultural Ecology and Settlement Patterns of the Gulf Coast." In *Handbook of Middle American Indians*, vol. 11. Austin: University of Texas Press, 1971: 543–57.

Stresser Péan, Guy and Claude. *Tamtok, sitio arqueológico huasteco, su historia, sus edificios*, vol. I. Mexico: Instituto de Cultura de San Luis Potosí, El Colegio de San Luis A.C., CONACULTA-INAH, Centro Francés de Estudios Centroamericanos, 2001.

———. *Tamtok, sitio arqueológico huasteco, su historia, su vida cotidiana*, vol. II. Mexico: Instituto de Cultura de San Luis Potosí, CONACULTA-INAH, Centro Francés de Estudios Centroamericanos, Fomento Cultural Banamex, 2005.

Walz Caviezel, Claudia. "Un sitio postclásico en la Huasteca: Agua Nueva." Bachelor's thesis, Escuela Nacional de Antropología e Historia, INAH, Mexico, 1991.

Zaragoza Ocaña, Diana M. "La Huasteca siglos XV y XVI, propuesta de subáreas culturales, Tamohi como estudio de caso." Ph.D. diss., Instituto de Investigaciones Antropológicas, UNAM, Mexico, 2003.

Zaragoza Ocaña, Diana M., and Patricio Dávila Cabrera. *Proyecto para la determinación geográfica del área cultural Huasteca*, Season 2004 Report, Archivo Técnico INAH, Mexico, 2004.

———. *Proyecto para la determinación geográfica del área cultural Huasteca*, 2005 Preliminary report. Mexico: Archivo Técnico INAH, 2005.

———. "Una torre maya en la Huasteca," presentation at the XIV Encuentro de Investigadores de la Huasteca, Ciudad Valles, S.L.P, 2007.

Chapter 10
Oaxaca

Bernal, Ignacio. "The Mixtecs in the Valley Archaeology." In *Ancient Oaxaca*, edited by John Paddock, 345–66. Stanford, Cal.: Stanford University Press, 1966–70.

Bernal, Ignacio, and Lorenzo Gamio. *Yagul: El Palacio de los Seis Patios*. Mexico: UNAM, Instituto de Investigaciones Antropológicas, 1974.

Blanton, Richard E. *Monte Albán: Settlement Patterns at the Ancient Zapotec Capital*. New York: Academic Press, 1978.

Chadwick, Robert. "The Tombs of Monte Albán I Style at Yagul." In *Ancient Oaxaca*, edited by John Paddock, 245–55. Stanford, Cal.: Stanford University Press, 1966–70.

Lind, Michael. "Monte Albán y el Valle de Oaxaca durante la fase Xoo." In *Monte Albán: Estudios recientes*.

Oaxaca: Proyecto Especial Monte Albán 1992–1994, 1994.

Magaloni, Diana. Personal communication, Mexico City, August 2007.

Marcus, Joyce, and Kent Flannery. *Zapotec Civilization: How Urban Society Evolved in Mexico's Oaxaca Valley*. New York: Thames & Hudson, 1996.

Marquina, Ignacio. *La Arquitectura Prehispánica*. Mexico: INAH-SEP, 1951.

Miller, Arthur G. *The Painted Tombs of Oaxaca, Mexico: Living with the Dead*. New York: Cambridge University Press, 1995.

Urcid, Javier. "Monte Albán y la Escritura Zapoteca." In *Monte Albán: Estudios recientes*, 77–97. Oaxaca: Proyecto Especial Monte Albán 1992–1994, 1994.

Winter, Marcus. *Oaxaca: The Archaeological Record*. Mexico, D.F.: Minutiae Mexicana, 1989.

———. "El proyecto Especial Monte Albán 1992–1994. Antecedentes, intervenciones y perspectivas." In *Monte Albán: Estudios recientes*. Oaxaca: Proyecto Especial Monte Albán 1992–1994, 1994.

Chapter 11
The Maya Region

Abrams, Elliot. *How the Maya Built their World: Energetics and Ancient Architecture*. Austin: University of Texas Press, 1994.

Agurcia Fasquelle, Ricardo. "Copán: arte, ciencia y dinastía." In *Los Mayas*, edited by Peter Schmidt, Mercedes de la Garza, and Enrique Nalda, 337–355. Milan: Rizzoli; Mexico: CONACULTA, 1999.

———. "Rosalila, Temple of the Sun-King." In *Understanding Early Classic Copan*, edited by Ellen Bell, Marcello Canuto, and Robert Sharer, 101–12. Philadelphia: University of Pennsylvania Museum of Archaeology and Anthropology, 2004.

Aveni, Anthony F., Anne S. Dowd, and Benjamin Vining. "Maya Calendar Reform? Evidence from Orientations of Specialized Architectural Assemblages." *Latin American Antiquity* 14(2) (2003):158–78.

Aveni, Anthony F., Sharon Gibbs, and Horst Hartung. "The Caracol Tower at Chichén Itzá: An Ancient Astronomical Observatory?" *Science* 188 (1975): 977–85.

Aveni, Anthony F., and Horst Hartung. "Uaxactun, Guatemala, Group E and Similar Assemblages: An Archaeoastronomical Reconsideration." In *World Archaeoastronomy*, edited by A. F. Aveni, 441–61. Cambridge: Cambridge University Press, 1989.

Aveni, Anthony F., Susan Milbrath, and Carlos Peraza Lope. "Chichén Itzá's legacy in the astronomically oriented architecture of Mayapán." *Res* 45 (2004): 123–43.

Chase, Arlen F., and Diane Z. Chase. "El paisaje urbano maya: la integración de los espacios construidos y la estructura social en Caracol, Belice." In *Reconstruyendo la ciudad maya: el urbanismo en las sociedades antiguas*, edited by Andrés Ciudad Ruiz, María Josefa Iglesias Ponce de León, and María del Carmen Martínez Martínez, 92–122. Madrid: Sociedad Española de Estudios Mayas, 2001.

Chase, Diane Z., and Arlen F. Chase. "Yucatec Influence in Terminal Classic Northern Belize." *American Antiquity* 47(3) (1982): 596–614.

Cobos, Rafael, and Terance L. Winemiller. "The Late and Terminal Classic-Period Causeway Systems of Chichen Itza, Yucatan, Mexico." *Ancient Mesoamerica* 12(2) (2001): 283–91.

Dahlin, Bruce H. "The Barricade and Abandonment of Chunchucmil: Implications for Northern Maya Warfare." *Latin American Antiquity* 11(3) (2000): 283–98.

García Moll, Roberto. "Shield Jaguar and Structure 23 at Yaxchilan." In *Courtly Art of the Ancient Maya*, edited by Mary E. Miller and Simon Martin, 264–67. San Francisco: Fine Arts Museums of San Francisco; New York: Thames & Hudson Inc., 2004.

Guderjan, Thomas H. "E-Groups, Pseudo-E-Groups, and the Development of the Classic Maya Identity in the Eastern Peten." *Ancient Mesoamerica* 17 (2006): 97–104.

Hansen, Richard D. "Continuity and Disjunction: The Pre-Classic Antecedents of Classic Maya Architecture." In *Function and Meaning in Classic Maya Architecture*, edited by Stephen D. Houston, 49–122. Washington, D.C.: Dumbarton Oaks Research Library and Collection, 1998.

Hohmann, Hasso, and Annegrete Vogrin. *Die Architektur von Copán, Honduras*. Graz: Akademische Druck-und Verlagsanstalt, 1982.

Inomata, Takeshi. "Plazas, Performers, and Spectators: Political Theaters of the Classic Maya." *Current Anthropology* 47(5) (2006): 805–42.

Jones, Christopher. "Twin-Pyramid Group Pattern: A Classic Maya Architectural Assemblage at Tikal, Guatemala." Ph.D. thesis, University of Pennsylvania, 1969.

Laporte, Juan Pedro, and Vilma Fialko. "New Perspectives on Old Problems: Dynastic References for the Early Classic at Tikal." In *Vision and Revision in Maya Studies*, edited by Flora Clancy and Peter D. Harrison, 33–66. Albuquerque: University of New Mexico Press, 1990.

Littmann, Edwin R. "Ancient Mesoamerican Mortars, Plasters, and Stuccos: Comalcalco, Part II." *American Antiquity* 23(3) (1948): 292–96.

Palacios, Enrique. *En los confines de la selva lacadona; exploraciones en el estado de Chiapas*. Mexico: Secretaría de Educación Publica, 1928.

Pijoan, José. *Arte precolombiano, mexicano y maya*. Madrid: Espasa Calpe (Summa Artis: Historia General del Arte X), 1991.

Piña Chan, Román. *Cultura y ciudades mayas de Campeche: Calakmul, Edzná, Becán, Xpuhil, Jaina, Hochob, Chicanná, Dzibilnocac, Hormiguero, Río Bec, El Tigre*. Mexico: Editora del Sureste, 1985.

Ruiz Lhuillier, Alberto. *Palenque: el Templo de las Inscripciones*. Mexico: UNAH (Collección científica), 1973.

Shaw, Justine. "Maya *Sacbeob*: Form and Function." *Ancient Mesoamerica* 12(2) (2001): 261–72.

Stuart, David. "'The Fire Enters His House': Architecture and Ritual in Classic Maya Texts." In *Function and Meaning in Classic Maya Architecture*, edited by Stephen D. Houston, 373–425. Washington, D.C.: Dumbarton Oaks Research Library and Collection, 1998.

———. "Kings of Stone: A consideration of stelae in ancient Maya ritual and representation." *Res* 29/30 (1996): 148–71.

Taube, Karl. "The Jade Hearth: Centrality, Rulership, and the Classic Maya Temple." In *Function and Meaning in Classic Maya Architecture*, edited by Stephen D. Houston, 427–78. Washington, D.C.: Dumbarton Oaks Research Library and Collection, 1998.

Toscano, Salvador. *Arte precolumbino de México y de la América central*. 2nd ed. Mexico: UNAM, Instituto de Investigaciones Estéticas, 1952.

Wauchope, Robert. "House Mounds of Uaxactún, Guatemala." *Contributions to American Archaeology* (Carnegie Institution of Washington Publication 436) 2(7) (1934): 107–71.

Webster, David, and Stephen D. Houston. "Piedras Negras: The Growth and Decline of a Classic Maya Court Center/Piedras Negras: El Desarollo y decadencia de una corte maya del Clásico." In *Urbanism in Mesoamerica/El Urbanismo en Mesoamérica*, vol. 1, edited by W. T. Sanders, A. G. Mastache, and R. H. Cobean, 427–49. Mexcio: INAH; University Park: Pennsylvania State University, PA, 2003.

Chapter 12
Architectural Terminology in Maya and Nahua Texts

Anders, Ferdinand, Maarten Jansen, and Luis Reyes García. *Códice Borbónico. El libro del cihuacoatl homenaje para el año del fuego nuevo: libro explicativo del llamado Códice Borbónico*. Mexico: Fondo de Cultura Económica, 1991.

Arzápalo Marín, Ramón, ed. *Calepino de Motul. Diccionario maya-español*. Mexico: UNAM, Dirección General de Asuntos del Personal Académico, Instituto de Investigaciones Antropológicas. Vol. I, 1995.

Aubin, Joseph Marius Alexis. *Memorias sobre la pintura didáctica y la escritura figurativa de los antiguos mexicanos*. Edition and introduction by Patrice Giasson. Mexico: UNAM, Instituto de Investigaciones Histórica (Serie Cultura Náhuatl, Monografías 26), 2002.

Balfet, Hélène, Marie-France Fauvet-Berthelot, and Susana Monzón. *Normas para la descripción de vasijas cerámicas*. Mexico: Centre D'Études Mexicaines et Centroamericaines (CEMCA), 1992.

Barrera Vásquez, Alfredo and Silvia Rendón. *El libro de los libros de Chilam Balam*. Mexico: Fondo de Cultura Económica (Lecturas Mexicanas, 38), 1984.

Berdan, Frances F., and Patricia Rieff Anawalt. *The Codex Mendoza*. Berkeley: University of California Press, 4 vols., 1992.

Biro, Peter. "The Inscriptions of Two Lintels of Ikil and the Realm of Ek' B'ahlam," at *Mesoweb*: www.mesoweb.com/features/biro/Ikil.pdf, 2003.

Boot, Erik. *Continuity and Change in Text and Image at Chichén Itzá, Yucatán, Mexico: A Study of the Inscriptions, Iconography, and Architecture at a Late Classic to Early Postclassic Maya Site*. Leiden: CNWS Publications, 2005.

———. "More on the GRASS/REED Logograph as Jal" (manuscript), 2006.

———. "The Updated Preliminary. Classic Maya-English, English-Classic Maya Vocabulary of Hieroglyphic Readings." Document to be published at *Mesoweb Resources*: www.mesoweb.com, 2007.

Carrasco Vargas, Ramón, and Marinés Colón González. "El reino de Kaan y la antigua ciudad maya de Calakmul," *Arqueología Mexicana* (Mexico, Editorial Raíces) vol. XIII, no. 75 (2005); 40–47.

Christenson, Allen J. *Popol Vuh. The Sacred Book of the Maya*. New York: Winchester Books, 2003.

Chuchiak, John F. "The Indian Inquisition and the Extirpation of Idolatry: The Process of Punishment in the Provisorato de Indios of the Diocese of Yucatán, 1563–1812." Ph.D. thesis, Tulane University, New Orleans, 2000.

Coe, Michael D. *El desciframiento de los glifos mayas*. Mexico, Fondo de Cultura Económica (Sección de Obras de Antropología), 1995.

———. *The Maya Scribe and His World*. New York: Grolier Club, 1973.

Colas, Pierre L., and Alexander W. Voss. "Un juego de vida o muerte: el juego de pelota maya." In *Los mayas: una civilización milenaria*, edited by Nikolai Grube, 186–91. Colonia: Editorial Könemann, 2001.

Coto, Fray Thomas de. *[Thesavrvs verborū] Vocabulario de la lengua cakchiquel v[el] guatemalteca, nueuamente hecho y recopilado con summo estudio, trauajo y erudición*. Edited by René Acuña. Mexico: UNAM, Instituto de Investigaciones Filológicas, 1983.

Culbert, T. Patrick. *Tikal Report No. 25. Part A. The Ceramics of Tikal: Vessels from the Burials, Caches and Problematical Deposits*. Philadelphia: University of Pennsylvania Museum, 1993.

DeFrancis, John. *Visible Speech: The Diverse Oneness of Writing Systems*. Honolulu: University of Hawaii Press, 1989.

Dibble, Charles E. *Codex en Cruz*. Salt Lake City: University of Utah Press, 1981.

———. "Writing in Central Mexico." In *Handbook of Middle American Indians* (general editor, Robert Wauchope), *vol. 10. Archaeology of Northern Mesoamerica, Part 1*, edited by Gordon F. Ekholm and Ignacio Bernal, 322–32. Austin: University of Texas Press, 1971.

Domínguez, Marilyn. "Murales con temas acuáticos en Calakmul." In *Arqueología Mexicana* (Mexico, Editorial Raíces) vol. XII, no. 71 (2005): 14.

Durán, Fray Diego. *Historia de las Indias de Nueva España e Islas de la tierra firma*. Edited by Ángel María Garibay K. Mexico: Porrúa (Biblioteca Porrúa, 37), 2 vols., 1967.

Eberl, Markus. *Muerte, entierro y ascensión: ritos funerarios entre los antiguos mayas*. Mérida: Ediciones de la Universidad Autónoma de Yucatán (Tratados 21), 2005.

Eberl, Markus, and Victoria R. Bricker. "Unwinding the Rubber Ball: The Glyphic Expression nahb' as a Numeral Classifier for 'Handspan'." *Research Reports on Ancient Maya Writing* (Washington, Center for Maya Research). 55 (2004): 19–56.

Edmonson, Munro S. *Heaven Born Merida and its Destiny: The Book of Chilam Balam of Chumayel*. Austin: University of Texas Press, 1986.

Garza, Mercedes de la. *Sueño y alucinación en el mundo náhuatly maya*. Mexico: Instituto de Investigaciones Filológicas, Centro de Estudios Mayas, UNAM, 1990.

Graham, Ian. *Archaeological Explorations in El Peten, Guatemala*. New Orleans: Tulane University (Middle American Research Institute, Publication 33), 1967.

———. *Corpus of Maya Hieroglyphic Inscriptions, vol. 3, part 2. Yaxchilán*. Cambridge: Peabody Museum of Archaeology and Ethnology, Harvard University, 1979.

———. *Corpus of Maya Hieroglyphic Inscriptions, vol. 3, part 3. Yaxchilán*. Cambridge: Peabody Museum of Archaeology and Ethnology, Harvard University, 1982.

———. *Corpus of Maya Hieroglyphic Inscriptions, vol. 4, part 2. Uxmal*. Cambridge: Peabody Museum of Archaeology and Ethnology, Harvard University, 1992.

———. *Corpus of Maya Hieroglyphic Inscriptions, vol. 7, part 1. Seibal*. Cambridge: Peabody Museum of Archaeology and Ethnology, Harvard University, 1996.

Graham, Ian, and Eric von Euw. *Corpus of Maya Hieroglyphic Inscriptions, vol. 3, part 1. Yaxchilán*. Cambridge: Peabody Museum of Archaeology and Ethnology, Harvard University, 1977.

———. *Corpus of Maya Hieroglyphic Inscriptions, vol. 4, part 3. Uxmal, Xcalumkin*. Cambridge: Harvard University, Peabody Museum of Archaeology and Ethnology, 1992.

Graham, Ian, and Peter L. Mathews. *Corpus of Maya Hieroglyphic Inscriptions, vol. 6, part 2. Toniná*. Cambridge: Harvard University, Peabody Museum of Archaeology and Ethnology, 1996.

———. *Corpus of Maya Hieroglyphic Inscriptions, vol. 6, part 3. Toniná*. Cambridge: Peabody Museum of Archaeology and Ethnology, Harvard University, 1999.

Graulich, Michel. *Códice Azcatitlan*. Translated into Spanish by Leonardo López Luján. Paris: Socíete des Americanistes, 1995.

Grube, Nikolai. "Hieroglyphic Inscriptions from Northwest Yucatán. An Update of Recent Research." In *Escondido en la selva: Arqueología en el norte de Yucatán. Segundo Simposio Teoberto Maler, Bonn 2000*, edited by Hanns J. Prem, 339–66. Mexico: Universidad de Bonn, INAH, 2003.

———. "La historia dinástica de Naranjo, Petén," in *Beiträge zur Allgemeinen und Vergleichenden Archäologie* (Mainz am Rhein: Verlag Philipp von Zabern) 24 (2004): 195–213.

———. "An Investigation of the Primary Standard Sequence on Classic Maya Ceramics." In *Sixth Palenque Round Table, 1986*, edited by Merle G. Robertson and Virginia M. Fields, 223–32. Norman: University of Oklahoma Press, 1991.

———. "The Primary Standard Sequence in Chocholá Style Ceramics." In *The Maya Vase Book: A Corpus of Rollout Photographs of Maya Vases*, vol. 2, edited by J. Kerr, 320–30. New York: Kerr Associates, 1990.

Grube, Nikolai, and Maria Gaida. *Die Maya: Schrift und Kunst im Ethnologischen Museum Berlin*. Berlin: SMB DuMont, 2006.

Grube, Nikolai, and Simon Martin. "Patronage, Betrayal, and Revenge: Diplomacy and Politics in the Eastern Maya Lowlands." In *Notebook for the XXVIIIth Maya Hieroglyphic Forum at Texas, March, 2004*, pp. II-1–II-95. Austin: Maya Workshop Foundation, 2004.

Grube, Nikolai, Simon Martin, and Marc U. Zender. "Palenque and its Neighbors." In *Notebook for the XXVIth Maya Hieroglyphic Forum at Texas, March 2002*. Austin: University of Texas at Austin, 2002.

Guenter, Stanley. "La Corona Find Sheds Light on Site Q Mystery." *The PARI Journal* (San Francisco, The Pre-Columbian Art Research Institute) vol. VI, no. 2 (Fall 2005): 14–16.

———. "A Reading of the Cancuen Looted Panel," at *Mesoweb*:
, 2002.

Haeserijin, V., Esteban. *Diccionario K'ekchi' Español.* Guatemala: Editorial "Piedra Santa," 1979.

Hill, Archibald A. "The Typology of Writing Systems." In *Papers in Linguistics in Honor of Leon Dostert*, edited by William M. Austin, 92–99. The Hague: Mouton, 1967.

Houston, Stephen D. "Archaeology and Maya Writing" *Journal of World Prehistory* (New York and London, Plenum Press) 3, no. 1. (1989): 1–32.

———. "Classic Maya Depictions of the Built Environment." In *Function and Meaning in Classic Maya Architecture*, edited by S. D. Houston, 333–72. Washington, D.C.: Dumbarton Oaks Research Library and Collection, 1998.

———. *Hieroglyphs and History at Dos Pilas: Dynastic Politics of the Classic Maya.* Austin: University of Texas Press, 1993.

———. "Into the Minds of Ancients: Advances in Maya Glyph Studies." *Journal of World Prehistory* 14, no. 2 (2000); 121–201.

Houston, Stephen D., John Robertson, and David Stuart. "The Language of Classic Maya Inscriptions." *Current Anthropology* 41, no. 3 (2000): 321–56.

———. *Quality and Quantity in Glyphic Nouns and Adjectives.* Washington: Center for Maya Research (Research Reports on Ancient Maya Writing, 47) , 2001.

Houston, Stephen D., David S. Stuart, and Karl A. Taube. "Folk Classification of Classic Maya Pottery." *American Anthropologist* (Washington) 91, no. 3 (1989): 720–26.

———. *The Memory of Bones: Body, Being, and Experience among the Classic Maya.* Austin: University of Texas Press, 2006.

Houston, Stephen D., and Karl A. Taube. "Name-Tagging in Classic Mayan Script." *Mexicon: Aktuelle Informationen und Studien zu Mesoamerika/News and Studies on Mesoamerica/Noticias y contribuciones sobre Mesoamérica* IX, no. 2 (1987): 38–41.

Hruby, Zachary X., and Mark B. Child. "Chontal Linguistic Influence in Ancient Maya Writing: Intransitive Positional Verbal Affixation." In *The Linguistics of Maya Writing*, edited by Søren Wichmann, 13–26. Salt Lake City: University of Utah Press, 2004.

Hull, Kerry M. "Verbal Art and Performance in Ch'orti' and Maya Hieroglyphic Writing." Ph.D. thesis, University of Texas at Austin, faculty of the graduate school, 2003.

Jones, Christopher, and Linton Satterthwaite. *Tikal Report, No. 33, Part A, The Monuments and Inscriptions of Tikal: The Carved Monument.* Philadelphia: University of Pennsylvania Museum, 1983.

Karttunen, Frances. *An Analytical Dictionary of Nahuatl.* Norman: University of Oklahoma Press, 1992.

Kaufman, Terrence S., and William M. Norman. "An Outline of Proto-Cholan Phonology, Morphology and Vocabulary." In *Phoneticism in Mayan Hieroglyphic Writing*, edited by John S. Justeson and Lyle Campbell, 77–166. Albany: Institute for Mesoamerican Studies State University of New York at Albany (Publicación, 9), 1984.

Klein, Cecilia. "Woven Heaven, Tangled Earth: A Weaver's Paradigm of the Mesoamerican Cosmos." In *Ethnoastronomy and Archaeoastronomy in the American Tropics*, edited by Anthony F. Aveni and Gary Urton. New York: Academy of Sciences (Annals of the New York Academy of Sciences, 385), 1982.

Krochock, Ruth. "Hieroglyphic Inscriptions at Chichen Itzá, Yucatán, México: The Temples of the Initial Series, the One Lintel, the Three Lintels, and the Four Lintels." *Research Reports on Ancient Maya Writing* (Washington, Center for Maya Research) 23–25 (1989): 7–14.

Lacadena, Alfonso. "El anillo jeroglífico del Juego de Pelota de Oxkintok." In *Oxkintok 4. Misión Arqueológica de España en México*, 177–84. Madrid: Ministerio de Cultura, Dirección General de Bellas Artes y Archivos, Instituto de Conservación y Restauración de Bienes Culturales, 1992.

———. "Apuntes para un estudio sobre literatura maya antigua." To be published in *Texto y contexto: perspectivas interculturales en el análisis de la literatura maya yucateca*, edited by Antje Gunsenheimer, Tsubasa Okoshi Harada, and John F. Chuchiak. Bonn: BAS (Estudios Americanistas de la Universidad de Bonn), 2002.

———. "El corpus glífico de Ek' Balam, Yucatán, México." Report to FAMSI: http://www.famsi.org/cgi-bin/ print_friendly.pl?file=01057es, 2003a.

———. "La escritura de tradición náhuatl: comentarios, reflexiones y propuestas." *Revista Española de Antropología Americana* (forthcoming), n.d.[a].

———. "Los jeroglíficos de Ek' Balam." *Arqueología Mexicana* (Mexico, Editorial Raíces) vol. XIII, no. 76 (2005): 64–69.

———. "On the Reading of Two Glyphic Appellatives of the Rain God." In *Continuity and Change: Maya Religious Practices in Temporal Perspective. Acta Mesoamericana, vol. 14*, edited by Daniel Graña-Beherens, Nikolai Grube, Christian M. Prager, Frauke Sasche, Stefanie Teufel, and Elisabeth Wagner, 87–98. Markt Schwaben: Verlag Anton Saurwein, 2004.

———. *Reference Book for the Maya Hieroglyphic Workshop—The European Maya Conference Series.* London: Wayeb, 2001.

———. "Los signos fonéticos wa$_1$ y wa$_2$ y el logograma WA en la escritura náhuatl" (manuscript), n.d.[b].

———. "El sufijo verbalizador -Vj (-aj / -iij) en la escritura jeroglífica maya." In *De la tablilla a la inteligencia artificial*, 843–65. Zaragoza: Instituto de Estudios Islámicos y del Oriente Próximo, 2003b.

———. "Tradiciones regionales de escribas: implicaciones metodológicas para el desciframiento de la escritura náhuatl" (manuscript), 2003c.

Lacadena, Alfonso, and Søren Wichmann. "The Distribution of the Lowland Maya Languages in the Classic Period." In *La organización social entre los mayas prehispánicos, coloniales y modernos: Memoria de la Tercera Mesa Redonda de Palenque*, edited by Vera Tiesler Blos, Rafael Cobos, and Merle Greene Robert, 277–319. Mexico: CONACULTA, INAH, Universidad Autónoma de Yucatán, 2002.

———. "The Dynamics of Language in the Western Lowland Maya Region." Presentation at *The 2000 Chacmool Conference*. Calgary, November 9–11, 2000.

———. "Harmony Rules and the Suffix Domain: A Study of Maya Scribal Conventions." At http://email.eva .mpg.de/%7Ewichmann/harm-rul-suf-dom7.pdf, n.d.

———. "Longitud vocálica y globalización en la escritura náhuatl." Presentation at the *Primer Simposio Europeo sobre Códices del Centro de México*, Universidad Complutense de Madrid, October 28 to 30, 2004a (manuscript).

———. "On the Representation of the Glottal Stop in Maya Writing." In *The Linguistics of Maya Writing*, edited by Søren Wichmann, 103–62. Salt Lake City: University of Utah Press, 2004b.

Landa, Fray Diego de. *Relación de las cosas de Yucatán.* Preliminary study, chronology, and revision of text by María del Carmen León Cázares. Mexico: CONACULTA (Cien de México), 1994.

Lee, Thomas A. *Los códices mayas.* Tuxtla Gutiérrez: Universidad Autónoma de Chiapas, 1985.

León-Portilla, Miguel. *La Matrícula de Tributos. Edición especial de Arqueología Mexicana, 14.* México: Editorial Raíces (Serie Códices), 2003.

Lockhart, James. *Los nahuas después de la Conquista: Historia social y cultural de la población indígena del México central, siglos XVI–XVIII.* Mexico: Fondo de Cultura Económica, 1996.

López Austin, Alfredo. *Cuerpo humano e ideología: Las concepciones de los antiguos nahuas.* 3rd ed. Mexico: UNAM, Instituto de Investigaciones Antropológicas (Serie Antropológica, 39). 2 vols., 1989.

López de Cogolludo, Fray Diego. *Historia de Yucatán.* Campeche: Gobierno del Estado de Campeche. 3 vols., 1996.

Macazaga Ordoño, César. *Nombres geográficos de México.* Photographs by Antonio Toussaint. Mexico: Editorial Cosmos, 1979.

MacLeod, Barbara. "Deciphering the Primary Standard Sequence." Ph.D. dissertation, University of Texas at Austin, 1990.

Manrique Casañeda, Leonardo. "Ubicación de los documentos pictográficos de tradición náhuatl en una tipología de sistemas de registro de escritura." In *Primer Coloquio de Documentos Pictográficos Náhuatl*, 159–70. Mexico, UNAM, 1989.

Martin, Simon. "A Broken Sky: The Ancient Name of Yaxchilán as Pa' Chan." *The PARI Journal* (San Francisco, The Pre-Columbian Art Research Institute) vol. V, no. 1 (2004a): 1–7.

———. "Preguntas epigráficas acerca de los escalones de Dzibanché." In *Los cautivos de Dzibanché*, edited by Enrique Nalda, 105–15. Mexico: INAH, 2004b.

Martin, Simon, and Nikolai Grube. *Crónica de los reyes y reinas mayas: la primera historia de las dinastías mayas.* Mexico: Editorial Planeta, 2002.

McLung de Tapia, Emily. *Ecología y cultura en Mesoamérica.* 2nd ed. Mexico: UNAM, Instituto de Investigaciones Antropológicas (Cuadernos, Serie Antropológica, 30), 1984.

Mediz Bolio, Antonio. *Libro de Chilam Balam de Chumayel.* Prologue, introduction, and notes by Mercedes de la Garza. Mexico: Secretaría de Educación Pública (Cien de México), 1988.

Miller, Mary E., and Simon Martin. *Courtly Art of the Ancient Maya.* San Francisco: Fine Arts Museums of San Francisco/Thames and Hudson, 2004.

Mohar Betancourt, Luz María. *Mapa de Coatlinchan. Líneas y colores en el Acolhuacan.* Mexico: INAH, Benemérita Universidad Autónoma de Puebla (Códices Mesoamericanos, II), 1994.

Molina, Fray Alonso de. *Vocabulario en lengua castellana y mexicana y mexicana y castellana.* Preliminary study by Miguel León-Portilla. 3rd ed. Mexico: Editorial Porrua (Biblioteca Porrua, 44), 1992.

Montgomery, John. *The Monuments of Piedras Negras, Guatemala.* Albuquerque: University of New Mexico, Department of Art and Art History, 1998.

Moore, Oliver. *Reading the Past: Chinese.* London: British Museum Press, 2000.

Mora-Marín, David. "A Logographic Value HU7 (~ 7U7) 'to Blow' or 'Sacred, Moral, Power' for the God.N Verbal Glyph of the Primary Standard Sequence." At *Wayeb Notes, No. 27*, 2007: http://www.wayeb.org/notes/ wayeb_notes0027.pdf.

Morán, Fray Pedro. *Arte de la lengua cholti que quiere decir lengua de milperos.* Compuesto en este pueblo de lacandones llamado de la Señora de los Dolores, el 24 de junio de 1695 (manuscript).

Nalda, Enrique. "Dzibanché. El contexto de los cautivos." In *Los cautivos de Dzibanché*, edited by Enrique Nalda, 13–55. Mexico: INAH, 2004.

Nicholson, Henry B. "Phoneticism in the Late Pre-Hispanic Central Mexican Writing System." In *Meso-*

american Writing Systems, edited by Elizabeth P. Benson, 1–46. Washington, D.C., Dumbarton Oaks Research Library and Collections, 1973.

Niederberger, Christine. "Paisajes, economía de subsistencia y agrosistemas." In Temas mesoamericanos, edited by Sonia Lombardo and Enrique Nalda, 11–50. Mexico: INAH, Dirección General de Publicaciones del Consejo Nacional para la Cultura y las Artes (Colección Obra Diversa), 1996.

Peñafiel, Antonio. Nombres geográficos de México. With interpretations by Dr. Cecilio A. Robelo, edition by César Macazaga Ordoño. Mexico: Editorial Cosmos, 1977.

Pérez Suárez, Tomás. "Acróbatas y contorsionistas en la plástica olmeca." In Los investigadores de la cultura maya, 13, tomo II, 537–44. Campeche: Universidad Autónoma de Campeche, 2005.

Pope, Maurice. The Story of Decipherment: From Egyptian Hieroglyphs to Maya Script. New York: Thames and Hudson, 1999.

Quiñones Keber, Eloise. Codex Telleriano-Remensis: Ritual, Divination, and History in a Pictorial Aztec Manuscript. Foreword by Emmanuel Le Roy Ladurie; illustrations by Michel Besson. Austin: University of Texas Press, 1995.

Ramírez, José Fernando. Códice Boturini. México: Vargas Rea, 1952.

Reents-Budet, Dorie J., Joseph W. Ball, Ronald L. Bishop, Virginia M. Fields, and Barbara MacLeod. Painting the Maya Universe: Royal Ceramics of the Classic Period. Durham and London: Duke University Press, 1994.

Robertson, John. "The Possibility and Actuality of Writing," in The First Writing: Script Invention as History and Process, edited by Stephen Houston, 16–38. Cambridge: Cambridge University Press, 2004.

Robertson, Merle Green. The Sculpture of Palenque, Vol. III: The Late Buildings of the Palace. Princeton: Princeton University Press, 1985.

Robicsek, Francis, and Donald M. Hales. The Maya Book of the Dead: The Ceramic Codex. The Corpus of Codex Style Ceramics of the Late Classic Period. Charlottesville: University of Virginia Art Museum, 1981.

Roys, Ralph L. The Book of Chilam Balam of Chumayel. 2nd. ed. Norman: University of Oklahoma Press, 1967.

Sampson, Geoffrey. Writing Systems: A Linguistic Introduction. Stanford: Stanford University Press, 1985.

Savkic, Sanja. "El color en el Códice de Dresde (según la información de las fuentes escritas y de las lingüísticas)." Master's thesis in Mesoamerican Studies, Universidad Nacional Autónoma de México, Facultad de Filosofía y Letras, Mexico, 2007.

Schele, Linda, and David Freidel. A Forest of Kings: The Untold Story of Ancient Maya. New York: William Morrow and Company, Inc., 1990.

Schele, Linda, and Nikolai Grube. "Copán Note 86. The Glyph for Plaza or Court." In The Copán Notes. Antigua: Copán Mosaics Project, 1990.

Schele, Linda, and Peter L. Mathews. The Bodega of Palenque, Chiapas, Mexico. Washington, D.C.: Dumbarton Oaks, Trustees for Harvard University, 1979.

———. The Code of Kings: The Language of Seven Sacred Maya Temples and Tombs. New York, Charles Scribner, 1998.

Schele, Linda, and Mary E. Miller. The Blood of Kings: Dynasty and Ritual in Maya Art. New York: George Braziller, Inc.; Fort Worth: Kimbell Art Museum, 1986.

Sedat S., Guillermo. Nuevo diccionario de las lenguas k'ekchi' y española. Chamelco: Instituto Lingüístico de Verano, 1955.

Seler, Eduard. "Mexican Picture Writings of Alexander von Humbolt." In Bureau of American Ethnology, Bulletin 28, 177–229. Washington, D.C.: Smithsonian Institute, 1904.

Siméon, Rémi. Diccionario de la lengua náhuatl o mexicana. Translated by Josefina Oliva de Coll. 9th ed. in Spanish. Mexico: Siglo XXI Editores (Colección América Nuestra, 1), 1992.

Smith, Robert E. Ceramic Sequence at Uaxactun, Guatemala. New Orleans: Tulane University, Middle American Research Institute, Carnegie Institution of Washington (Publication, 20), 2 vols., 1955.

Staines Cicero, Leticia. "Las tapas de bóveda pintadas y su lugar en el cosmos." In Acercarse y mirar: Homenaje a Beatriz de la Fuente, edited by María Teresa Uriarte and Leticia Staines Cicero, 239–53. Mexico: UNAM, Instituto de Investigaciones Estéticas, 2004.

Stuart, David S. "'The Fire Enters his House': Architecture and Ritual in Classic Maya Texts." In Function and Meaning in Classic Maya Architecture, edited by Stephen D. Houston, 373–425. Washington, D.C.: Dumbarton Oaks Research Library and Collection, 1998.

———. "Hieroglyphs on Maya Vessels." In The Maya Vase Book: A Corpus of Rollout Photographs of Maya Vessels, Vol. I, edited by Justin Kerr, 149–60. New York, Kerr Associates, 1989.

———. "La ideología del sacrificio entre los mayas." Arqueología Mexicana (México, Editorial Raíces) vol. XI, no. 63 (2003): 24–29.

———. "The Inscribed Markers of the Coba-Yaxuna Causeway and the Glyph for Sakbih." At Mesoweb: www .mesoweb.com/stuart/notes/Sacbe.pdf, 2006a.

———. The Inscriptions from Temple XIX at Palenque. A Commentary. Photographs by Jorge Pérez de Lara. San Francisco: The Pre-Columbian Art Research Institute, 2005.

———. "Lectura y escritura en la corte maya." Arqueología Mexicana (Mexico, Editorial Raíces) vol. VIII, no. 48 (2001): 48–53.

———. "The lu-Bat Glyph and its Bearing on the Primary Standard Sequence." Manuscript presented at the Primer Simposio Mundial sobre Epigrafía Maya, August 1986, Guatemala.

———. "Las nuevas inscripciones del Templo XIX, Palenque." Arqueología Mexicana (Mexico, Editorial Raíces) vol. VIII, no. 45 (2000a): 28–33.

———. "The Palenque Mythology." In Sourcebook for the 30th Maya Meetings. March 14–19, 2006, 85–194. Austin: The University of Texas at Austin, Department of Art and Art History, The Mesoamerican Center, 2006b.

———. "Ritual and History in the Stucco Inscription from Temple XIX at Palenque." The PARI Journal (San Francisco, The Pre-Columbian Art Research Institute) vol. I, no. 1 (2000b): 13–19.

———. "A Study of Maya Inscriptions." Doctoral dissertation in anthropology, Vanderbilt University, Faculty of the Graduate School, Nashville, 1995.

Stuart, David S., and Stephen D. Houston. Classic Maya Place Names. Washington, D.C.: Dumbarton Oaks Research Library and Collection (Studies in Pre-Columbian Art and Archaeology, No. 33), 1994.

Stuart, David S., Barbara MacLeod, Yuriy Polyukhovich, Stephen D. Houston, and Simon Martin. "Glyphs on Pots. Decoding Classic Maya Ceramics." In Sourcebook for the 29th Maya Hieroglyphic Forum, 110–97. Austin: The University of Texas at Austin, Department of Art and Art History, Maya Workshop Foundation, 2005.

Tate, Carolyn E. Yaxchilán: The Design of a Maya Ceremonial City. Austin: University of Texas Press, 1992.

Taube, Karl A. The Major Gods of Ancient Yucatan. Washington, D.C.: Dumbarton Oaks Research Library and Collection (Studies in Pre-Columbian Art and Archaeology, 32), 1992.

———. "A Prehispanic Maya Katun Wheel." Journal of Anthropological Research (Santa Fe, University of New Mexico) 44, no. 2 (1988): 183–203.

Thompson, J. Eric S. A Catalog of Maya Glyphs. Norman: University of Oklahoma Press, 1962.

———. Un comentario al Códice de Dresde: Libro de jeroglifos mayas. Translated by Jorge Ferreiro Santana. Mexico: Fondo de Cultura Económica, 1988.

———. Historia y religión de los mayas. Translated by Félix Blanco. Mexico: Siglo XXI Editores (Colección América Nuestra, 7), 1975.

Tokovinine, Alexander. "Divine Patrons of the Maya Ballgame." At Mesoweb: www.mesoweb.com/features/tokovinine/Ballgame.pdf, 2002.

———. "People from a Place: Re-Interpreting Classic Maya 'Emblem Glyphs.'" Presentation given at the 11th European Maya Conference: Ecology, Power, and Religion in Maya Landscapes. Malmö, Sweden (manuscript), 2006.

Torre, Mario de la, ed. Lienzo de Tlaxcala. Texts by Josefina García Quintana and Carlos Martínez Marín. Mexico: Cartón y Papel de México, S.A. de C.V., 1983.

Vail, Gabrielle. "The Gods in the Madrid Codex: An Iconographic and Glyphic Analysis." Ph.D. dissertation, Tulane University, New Orleans, 1996.

Valero de García Lascuráin, Ana Rita. Códice Cozcatzin. Paleographic versión and transliteration of Nahuatl by Rafael Tena. Mexico: INAH, Benemérita Universidad Autónoma de Puebla, 1994.

Valle, Perla. Códice de Tepetlaoztoc (Códice Kingsborough) Estado de México. Toluca: El Colegio Mexiquense, 1994a.

———. Códice de Tlatelolco. Mexico: INAH, Universidad Autónoma de Puebla, 1994b.

———. "Un pueblo entre las cuevas. Los topónimos de Tepetlaoztoc en el Códice Kingsborough," originally published in Amerindia, no. 23. Taken from http://celia.cnrs.fr/FichExt/Am/A_23_04.htm, 1998.

Velásquez García, Erik. "Los escalones jeroglíficos de Dzibanché." In Los cautivos de Dzibanché, edited by Enrique Nalda, 79–103. Mexico: INAH, 2004b.

———. "The Maya Flood Myth and the Decapitation of Cosmic Caiman." The PARI Journal (San Francisco, Pre-Columbian Art Research Institute) vol. VII, no. 1 (2006): 1–10.

———. "La vida cotidiana de los mayas durante el Periodo Clásico." In Historia de la vida cotidiana en México I: Mesoamérica y los ámbitos indígenas de la Nueva España. edited by Pilar Gonzalbo Aizpuru, 99–136. Mexico: Fondo de Cultura Económica, El Colegio de México, 2004a.

Vogt, Evon Z. Ofrendas para los dioses: Análisis simbólico de rituales zinacantecos. Mexico: Fondo de Cultura Económica (Sección de Obras de Antropología) , 1979.

Wald, Robert F. "The Languages of the Dresden Codex: Legacy of the Classic Maya." In The Linguistics of Maya Writing, edited by Søren Wichmann, 27–58. Salt Lake City: University of Utah Press, 2004.

Wichmann, Søren. "Hieroglyphic Evidence for the Historical Configuration of Eastern Ch'olan," 2001, to be published in Research Reports on Ancient Maya Writing.

Williams, Barbara J., and H. R. Harvey. The Códice de Santa María Asunción. Households and Lands in Sixteenth-Century Tepetlaoztoc. Salt Lake City: University of Utah Press, 1997.

Woodard, Roger D. "Introduction." In The Cambridge Encyclopedia of the World's Ancient Languages, edited by R. D. Woodard, 1–18. Cambridge: Cambridge University Press, 2004.

Woodard, Roger D. "Introduction." In The Cambridge Encyclopedia of the World's Ancient Languages, edited by R. D. Woodard, 1–18. Cambridge: Cambridge University Press, 2004.

Zavala, Lauro José, ed. Códice Osuna. Prologue by Luis Chávez Orozco. Mexico: Instituto Indigenista Interamericano, 1947.

Zender, Marc U. "Glyphs for 'Handspan' and 'Strike' in Classic Maya Ballgame Texts." The PARI Journal (San Francisco, The Pre-Columbian Art Research Institute) vol. IV, no. 4 (Spring 2004): 1–9.

———. "Teasing the Turtle from its Shell: AHK and MAHK in Maya Writing." The PARI Journal (San Francisco, The Pre-Columbian Art Research Institute) vol. VI, no. 3 (2006): 1–14.

INDEX OF NAMES

PHOTOGRAPHY CREDITS